Intercreditor Equity in Sovereign
Debt Restructuring

Intercreditor Equity in Sovereign Debt Restructuring

ASTRID IVERSEN

Great Clarendon Street, Oxford, OX2 6DP,
United Kingdom

Oxford University Press is a department of the University of Oxford.
It furthers the University's objective of excellence in research, scholarship,
and education by publishing worldwide. Oxford is a registered trade mark of
Oxford University Press in the UK and in certain other countries

© Astrid Iversen 2023

The moral rights of the author have been asserted

First Edition published in 2023

All rights reserved. No part of this publication may be reproduced, stored in
a retrieval system, or transmitted, in any form or by any means, without the
prior permission in writing of Oxford University Press, or as expressly permitted
by law, by licence or under terms agreed with the appropriate reprographics
rights organization. Enquiries concerning reproduction outside the scope of the
above should be sent to the Rights Department, Oxford University Press, at the
address above

You must not circulate this work in any other form
and you must impose this same condition on any acquirer

Public sector information reproduced under Open Government Licence v3.0
(http://www.nationalarchives.gov.uk/doc/open-government-licence/open-government-licence.htm)

Published in the United States of America by Oxford University Press
198 Madison Avenue, New York, NY 10016, United States of America

British Library Cataloguing in Publication Data

Data available

Library of Congress Control Number is on file at the Library of Congress

ISBN 978–0–19–286690–5

DOI: 10.1093/oso/9780192866905.001.0001

Printed and bound in the UK by
TJ Books Limited

Links to third party websites are provided by Oxford in good faith and
for information only. Oxford disclaims any responsibility for the materials
contained in any third party website referenced in this work.

Foreword
Awn Shawkat Al-Khasawneh[1]

'A house of debt is a house in whose interior no light shines.' Sumerian proverb

It gives me great pleasure to write a foreword to this timely book on the topical and challenging subject of intercreditor equity in sovereign debt restructuring. The genesis of Dr Astrid Iversen's book is her dissertation, submitted for the degree of Philosophiae Doctor (PhD) at the University of Oslo Faculty of Law in April 2020. I had the distinct privilege of acting on the adjudication committee of Dr Iversen's dissertation. Thus, I can claim some familiarity with the development and growth of her work, culminating in this book.

It is said that a good book stands on its own merits and Dr Iversen's certainly does. At the outset, the book is invariably well written, closely argued, and comprehensive in a way that effectively tackles a complex topic.

In national jurisdictions, the problem that arises when a debtor is unable to meet his or her obligations to several creditors are normally resolved through domestic legislation and judicial decisions, thus ensuring a high degree of legal certainty. By contrast, no such mechanisms or institutions exist in the context of sovereign debt, except at a rudimentary level. The author of this book, very bravely, seeks to standardize the problem of sovereign debt restructuring and she does so from the point of view of creditors, utilizing the concept of equity. Moreover, the book aims not to effect total forgiveness of debt but rather forgiveness for reducing debt to a sustainable level. To my mind, a problem arises. In the first place, equity is, by definition, a moral concept and any review of its developments in all major legal systems would confirm this. An example may be taken from Roman law, where the formalistic hard and fast rules were attenuated by notions akin to equity. The work of the Roman jurist Papinian is often credited with introducing such concepts of morality and fairness in what had been hitherto a formalistic body of law.[2] Similarly, the development of equity in the common law, historically through the Exchequer of Pleas or Court of Exchequer, was unmistakably motivated by considerations of fairness and natural law.

It can also be easily discerned that these moral considerations relating to the relief or attenuation of debt were present in the major monotheistic religions. For example,

---

[1] Former Vice President of the International Court of Justice, 2006–2009; Former Judge of the International Court of Justice, 2000–2011; Former Prime Minister of the Hashemite Kingdom of Jordan, 2011–2012.
As Edvard Hambro put it, 'a good book needs no introduction'.

[2] Papinian, a highly esteemed Syrian-Roman jurist originating from Homs, Syria, was attested to have integrated his moral considerations into the development of law and governance. To Papinian, the function of equity was 'to aid, supplement or correct the civil law'.

the notion of *shemitat kesafim* was developed in Jewish law with the aim of relieving all debtors from their debts every seven years, which in itself attests to the considerable importance of the problem of debt in biblical times.[3] Strikingly, the Lord's Prayer also states, 'forgive us our debts, as we also have forgiven our debtors'.[4] The idea of total forgiveness of debts was prominent within the Jewish and Christian tradition. In the same vein, Islamic law strictly prohibits usury, which it considers to be a major sin.

The aversion to indebtedness is, however, not confined to the monotheistic religions. The relinquishment of debts as an equitable solution has a long history. Bronze Age communities in Mesopotamia developed prohibitions with the aim of preventing creditors from taking advantage of their debtors and enacted periodic general debt forgiveness in order to restore a semblance of equality in society by wiping the slate of debts clean. The problem was plainly widespread: this is attested to in the old Sumerian proverb that 'I have carried salt rocks on my shoulders, but no burden is heavier than debt'.

Alas, the relinquishment of debts has never worked completely. Classical times are replete with examples of indebted sovereigns whose subjects had to bear the onerous burden of their foreign wars or royal extravagances. For example, one of the earliest cases of sovereign debt default is noted to have taken place in the fourth century BC when Dionysius I of Syracuse defaulted on his debts to his subjects that he had borrowed against promissory note-like instruments. In order to 'restructure' his governmental debt, Dionysius issued a decree that demanded all silver coins be given to the government on pain of death. Having collected the coins, Dionysius re-minted them. Dionysius' resolution of his debt problem through the expropriation of subjects earned him the moniker 'the father of currency devaluation'.[5] Another early example is the debt of the Greek city of Miletus, which defaulted on its loan from Lysimachus in the third century BC and appealed to another Greek city, Cnidus, to satisfy the debt. Cnidus initially refused to provide the loan. Instead, a public bond offering was posed as the solution and Cnidus encouraged its citizens to subscribe. Years later, Miletus fell into further debt and, once again, unable to secure a loan, was prompted to request its citizens to subscribe to bond issue amounts. The European Middle Ages are equally replete with indebted sovereigns borrowing from a range of creditors, often with high interest rates.

There is no paucity of recent cases either, all of which have become significantly more complex than what was faced by Greek despots or Medieval princes centuries ago. One thinks immediately of the debt crises of Argentina, Peru, and Greece over recent decades, which necessitated political and legal action that have become characteristics of the treatment of sovereign debt and preferential creditors. Sovereign debts are definitely not a new phenomenon; yet modern cases are bedevilled by increasing

---

[3] Also, in biblical texts, Deuteronomy 15.1 provides: 'At the end of every seven years you must cancel debts. This is the manner of remission: Every creditor shall cancel what he has loaned to his neighbour. He is not to collect anything from his neighbour or brother, because the Lord's time of release has been proclaimed.'

[4] Matthew 6:12.

[5] M Winkler, *Foreign Bonds: An Autopsy—A Study of Defaults and Repudiations of Government Obligations* (Roland Swain Company 1933).

complexity and ambiguous legal rules. There being no uniform legal framework, the one aspect that can be said to be consistent is the very existence of debtors and creditors. As Max Winkler ominously spoke of sovereign defaults in 1933, 'Tomorrow they may be swept out of office. Today they can live only by yielding to the multiple undertaking of expenditures ... In order to enjoy the present, they cheerfully mortgage the future.'[6]

In the present book, Dr Iversen does not claim to solve the problem of debt at the national or the international level, a task that all these moral considerations, buttressed sometimes with divine commandments, have failed to achieve. Instead, the book is concerned with the management of sovereign debt and its restructuring in the international context. The idea that has been advanced supports, to a degree, a standard practice whereby sovereign debt is resolved with respect to multiple creditors on the basis that an indebted sovereign will reach a stage where it is in a position to discharge its obligations towards creditors, rather than through total relief of debt.

The world being what it is, and in light of the preceding historical examples, what comes to mind is an often quoted saying by the prominent fifteenth-century Egyptian jurist, Al-Sha'rani, who stated that 'the wisest of people are those who can best interpret the rules of their times'. It is appropriate to recall those imperishable words as we attempt to trace the rules on intercreditor equity and how sovereign debt have been and ought to be resolved. Seen from this angle, Dr Iversen's book fulfils a useful function in increasing certitude of the law in a world so structured that there will always be debtors and creditors, the latter often backed by military and/or economic force.

An example can be taken from the Anglo-German naval blockade imposed against Venezuela in 1902–03 in response to amassing foreign debts owed by Venezuela, which gave the blockading nations an advantage over other creditors. So much for the *pari passu* principle. Another blatant example is the Ottoman Public Debt Arbitration of 1924–25, wherein a single arbitrator, appointed under the Lausanne Peace Treaty of 1923, effectively placed the majority of the Ottoman Empire's public debts on Turkey, thereby departing from international law principles on State succession.[7] The arbitrator also declined any changes to the apportionment of debts according to the territorial revenue rule, as can be seen in his refusal of any exceptions regarding tax revenues for the passage on the Tigris and Euphrates Rivers as well as the Hejaz Railway. Moreover, the arbitrator applied the treaty provisions to Bulgaria's liability, despite the fact that Bulgaria was not a signatory to the Lausanne Peace Treaty.[8] These examples, permeated by abuse, raise significant questions and concerns as to how sovereign debt ought to be treated under international law.

It is also noteworthy that, in national societies, governments often take measures to mitigate the burden of debt on their citizens. In the 2008 recession in the United States, the government, while not effecting a total debt relief, took positive and concrete measures to lighten the burden of the debt crisis on its citizens. An example is

---

[6] ibid.
[7] *Affaire de le dette publique ottoman (Bulgarie, Irak, Palestine, Transjordanie, Grèce, Italie et Turquie)* (1925) 1 RIAA 529 (sole arbitrator Eugène Borel).
[8] See further, Moritz Holm-Hadulla, 'Ottoman Debt Arbitration' in *Max Planck Encyclopaedia of International Law* (Oxford University Press 2007).

seen in the government's introduction of alternative measures to prevent foreclosures on homes and the establishment of small banks at reduced interest rates. The government also introduced new lending programs to provide liquidity in support of various financial institutions. The hope is expressed that such measures, taken in one of the largest economies in the world, could be transplanted into the international plane. Weak economies admittedly cannot replicate the same, which only confirms the proposition that a greater degree of international cooperation is needed if the international economic and financial system is to have any moral attributes.

Whilst the above is somewhat critical of the fundamental assumptions on which the present book is based, this in no way detracts from its importance as an attempt to bring some cohesion into a phenomenon so prevalent in modern international relations and, at that, a multifaceted phenomenon with wide ramifications for states and their populations, touching political, economic, and social spheres. Dr Iversen's book takes note of and carefully reviews nebulous modern developments in the area of sovereign debts, albeit from the point of view of creditors, with the aim of solidifying cohesion, clarity, and certitude in this most important area of international law and relations. I hold out the hope that the lessons gained from Dr Iversen's work will prevent abuses akin to the ones from the early twentieth century.

In our interdependent world and the uncertain climate of our global economy, this book raises questions that we can no longer avoid answering. The breadth of the subject, both in significance and scope, cannot be overstated; yet Dr Iversen's book has successfully offered a concise outlook for systemic reform. Having read and reread the book in its latest version, I unhesitatingly recommend this serious work to the interested reader and, with any luck, to decision-makers. In a feat of irony, it must be said that the international community owes Dr Iversen a large debt for her commendable contribution to the legal literature in this field.

Preface

Throughout history, sovereign debt default and restructuring have been associated with disputes between creditors concerning distribution of economic losses. Such intercreditor conflicts are disrupting debt crisis resolution efforts and are likely also to occur in the future. This does not mean that there is no room for improvement of the current financial system in the area of sovereign debt. To reduce the risk of sovereign defaults, debt management practices and systems for reducing the risk of overborrowing should constantly be scrutinized and sought to be improved. Mechanisms for decreasing conflicts between creditors and incentivizing them to constructively partake in debt crisis resolution with the sovereign debtors and co-creditors are of key importance. Efforts to reduce intercreditor conflicts are often discussed from a political or an economic viewpoint. However, legal mechanisms cannot be overlooked as they create incentives for creditor and debtor behaviour. Active creditors have used the law to enhance their legal position vis-à-vis its co-creditors in negotiation and in lawsuits following a settled debt restructuring agreement. This book seeks to go beyond the common claim that the intercreditor equity is essential to ensure a successful debt restructuring and establish the actual legal content of rules providing creditors with a right to equal or preferential treatment in a debt restructuring. Only by establishing these legal starting points is it possible to improve the existing system for sovereign debt crisis resolution. The book seeks to fill gaps in the legal literature on intercreditor equity conflicts as well as to contribute to the literature on reform of the legal framework governing sovereign debt.

The book is an extension of my PhD thesis which I submitted to the Faculty of Law at the University of Oslo in April 2020. I have finalized this substantially revised and expanded version while working as an Associate Professor at the Inland Norway University of Applied Sciences and as a Postdoc in the 'Central Banks' Expanding Role in Financial Markets' joint project between the Inland Norway University and the University of Oslo. The project is funded by the Finance Market Fund and managed by the Norwegian Research Council.

The writing of this book has benefited from the help, direct and indirect, of a significant number of people and institutions, to whom I want to express my gratitude. First and foremost, I wish to thank my supervisors, Mads Andenas and Michael Waibel, for invaluable input. I also want to thank Mads for his generous and hospitable nature and for always keeping the door open, and Michael for facilitating an instructive and inspiring term at the Lauterpacht Centre for International Law in Cambridge, when he was Deputy Director.

I further wish to express my gratitude to the examiners of my thesis: Professor Freya Baetens, Judge Awn Shawkat Al-Khasawneh, and Dr Mamadou Hébié. They kindly accepted to assess my work and provided valuable feedback both in writing and during the engaging three-hour defence, that enabled me to transform the PhD thesis into a monograph. I also wish to thank Professor Stephan Schill who assessed an early draft of my thesis and provided feedback in my midway assessment.

Discussions and input received at conferences have also contributed to shaping the monograph into its final form. In particular, I want to thank participants and discussants at the Postgraduate and Early Professionals/Academics Network of the Society of International Economic Law (PEPA/SIEL) Conference in Nicosia in 2018 and London in 2019, the Interdisciplinary Sovereign Debt Research and Management Conference (DebtCon) in Washington DC in 2019 and Florence in 2022, as well as the European Society for International Law (ESIL) Research Forum in Glasgow in 2022.

I am also indebted to Oxford University Press for their faith in my book project. In particular, I want to thank Rachel Mullaly, Matthew Williams, and Amy Marchant for their professionalism and patience, and for always responding promptly to all my editorial questions along the way. Thanks are also due to the four anonymous reviewers of my monograph. James G Devaney and Katherine Llorca patiently assisted in language vetting and in revising the manuscript at different stages.

The list of other people who helped with my research in one way or another is long and include those with whom I have discussed the ideas presented in this monograph as well as those who have supported me in other ways. In particular, I wish to thank Alexander Næss Skjønberg, Domenico Zippoli, Erlend E Gjein, Giuseppe Bianco, Hayk Kupelyants, Johan V Wibye, Johann R Leiss, Johannes H Meyer, Ludovica Chiussi, Marianne Brekken, Markus Jerkø, Piotr Garbacz, Sebastian Grund, Sjur S Ellingsæter, Tuva Jin Hauge, and Trude Myklebust.

Changemaker Norge, SLUG—Debt Justice Norway, and all the people working for these two NGOs have been a major source of inspiration concerning sovereign debt issues over the past decades. These organizations are the reason I got interested in sovereign debt issues and it has been an honour to sit on the boards of both organizations.

Finally, I am grateful to my parents and my brother who have taught me that mountain hikes and saltwater swims are essential for enduring all life's challenges, including academic ones; and to Bjørn for his patience and for laughing at me when I take myself too seriously.

The book reflects developments up to May 2022.

Astrid Iversen
Oslo
May 2022

Overview of Contents

Table of Cases	xvii
Table of Legislation	xxiii
List of Abbreviations	xxvii
Introduction	1
1. The Role of Intercreditor Equity in Sovereign Debt Restructuring	10
2. Sovereign Powers in Crisis Resolution	22
3. Intercreditor Equity Rules Applicable to Debt Instruments Governed by International Law	57
4. Intercreditor Equity Rules Applicable to Debt Instruments Governed by Domestic Law	77
5. International Law Protection of Creditors Holding Debt Instruments Governed by Domestic Law	128
6. Interconnected and Conflicting Rights	163
7. Systemic Challenges and the Future of Intercreditor Equity Disputes	175
8. The Outlook for Broader Systemic Reform	203
Bibliography	211
Index	223

Contents

Table of Cases	xvii
Table of Legislation	xxiii
List of Abbreviations	xxvii
Introduction	1
Intercreditor Equity—Challenges of a Non-Uniform Standard	1
Approach of the Book	3
Terminology	6
Priority	7
Ranking	7
Subordinated debt	7
Preferred creditors/preferential debts	7
Equal treatment	8
Ladder of priority	8
Debt restructuring	8
1. The Role of Intercreditor Equity in Sovereign Debt Restructuring	10
1.1 Introduction	10
1.2 Equal Treatment	10
1.3 Differential Treatment	11
1.4 Intercreditor Equity and Sustainable Debt Restructurings	13
1.4.1 Introduction	13
1.4.2 Sustainable debt restructurings	14
1.4.3 Debtor–creditor conflicts	18
1.4.4 Intercreditor conflicts	20
2. Sovereign Powers in Crisis Resolution	22
2.1 Introduction	22
2.2 Governing Law and the Local Law Advantage	23
2.2.1 Introduction	23
2.2.2 Governing law of sovereign debt instruments	24
2.2.3 Doctrines concerning internationalization of state contracts	25
2.2.4 The local law advantage	30
2.3 The Jurisdiction of Courts in Private International Law	32
2.3.1 Introduction	32
2.3.2 Recast Brussels Regulation—the jurisdiction of courts in the EU	33
2.3.3 US law	37
2.3.4 English law	39
2.3.5 Preliminary conclusion	40

2.4 Sovereign Immunity   41
       2.4.1 Introduction   41
       2.4.2 The concept of sovereign immunity   41
       2.4.3 The sources of law   44
       2.4.4 Debt restructuring—immunity and mixed activities   45
       2.4.5 Preliminary conclusion   53

3. Intercreditor Equity Rules Applicable to Debt Instruments Governed by
   International Law   57
   3.1 Introduction   57
   3.2 The Equality Rule   58
   3.3 Subordination   60
   3.4 Secured Creditors   61
   3.5 Preferred Creditor Status   63
        3.5.1 Introduction   63
        3.5.2 Justification for providing multilateral financial institutions
               with preferred status   64
        3.5.3 Preferred creditor status under customary international
               law—the case of the IMF   65
        3.5.4 Means of acquiring the status of preferred creditor—particular
               international law   68
   3.6 The Compatibility of Preferential Treatment with the Equality Rule   74

4. Intercreditor Equity Rules Applicable to Debt Instruments Governed by
   Domestic Law   77
   4.1 Introduction: Legal Status of the Creditor and Governing Law   77
   4.2 *Pari Passu* Clause   80
        4.2.1 Introduction   80
        4.2.2 The origin of the clause   82
        4.2.3 Recent case law   86
        4.2.4 Contractual reform: Governmental and market reactions to the
               rateable payment interpretation in *NML v Argentina*   94
        4.2.5 Prevalence of variations of the *pari passu* clause—practical issues 95
        4.2.6 Preliminary conclusions   96
   4.3 Collective Action Clauses and Exit Consent—Intercreditor Equity and
        Majority Decisions   98
        4.3.1 Introduction   98
        4.3.2 General features of exit consent and CACs   99
        4.3.3 Equal treatment requirements in *pari passu* and uniform
               applicability clauses   104
        4.3.4 CACs and the risk of abuse by minority creditors   105
        4.3.5 Relevance of case law from domestic law   109
        4.3.6 Judicial scrutiny of majority decisions   110
        4.3.7 Minority protection—good faith as a standard for majority decisions 112
        4.3.8 Discriminatory majority decisions   117
        4.3.9 Preliminary conclusion   118
   4.4 Vulture Fund Legislation   120

	4.4.1 Introduction	120
	4.4.2 Belgium	122
	4.4.3 The United Kingdom, the Isle of Man, and Jersey	124
	4.4.4 France	125
	4.4.5 Preliminary conclusions	126
5.	International Law Protection of Creditors Holding Debt Instruments Governed by Domestic Law	128
	5.1 Introduction	128
	5.2 The International Minimum Standard—Intercreditor Equity in Customary International Law	129
	5.2.1 Introduction	129
	5.2.2 Types of claims covered by diplomatic protection	130
	5.2.3 Substantive protection	133
	5.2.4 Preliminary conclusion	134
	5.3 International Investment Agreements (IIAs)	136
	5.3.1 Included protection and jurisdiction over sovereign debt claims	136
	5.3.2 Substantive protection	140
	5.3.3 Preliminary conclusion	148
	5.4 ECHR—Protection of Property and the Prohibition Against Discrimination	149
	5.4.1 Introduction	149
	5.4.2 Covered protection	150
	5.4.3 Protection of property	151
	5.4.4 Prohibition against discrimination	153
	5.4.5 Preliminary conclusion	161
6.	Interconnected and Conflicting Rights	163
	6.1 Introduction	163
	6.2 Domestic Law Interference with Creditor Rights in Debt Instruments Governed by International Law	164
	6.3 International Law Interference with Creditor Rights in Debt Instruments Governed by Domestic Law	167
	6.4 Conflicting Creditor Obligations—A Case Study of the ECB's Holdings of Domestic Law Governed Sovereign Bonds	169
	6.4.1 Introduction	169
	6.4.2 The ECB's obligations and the TFEU	170
	6.4.3 The ECB's participation in debt restructurings	173
7.	Systemic Challenges and the Future of Intercreditor Equity Disputes	175
	7.1 Introduction	175
	7.2 Systemic Challenges	176
	7.2.1 Fragmentation and diverging objectives	176
	7.2.2 Debtor states' room for manoeuvre	183
	7.2.3 Sovereign powers and privatized economic crisis resolution measures	186
	7.2.4 Preliminary conclusion	188

7.3	The Future of Intercreditor Equity Disputes	189
	7.3.1 The emerging general principle of good faith as a cohesion tool	189
8.	The Outlook for Broader Systemic Reform	203
8.1	A Case Study on the Need for Reform	203
8.2	COVID-19 and Exogenous Shocks	205
8.3	Reform and Political Will	207

Bibliography   211
Index   223

Table of Cases

INTERNATIONAL AND REGIONAL COURTS AND TRIBUNALS

Court of Justice of the European Union
Accorinti and others v European Central Bank (T-79/13)
  ECLI:EU:T:2015:756 .... 158–59, 173–74
Fahnenbrock and others v Greece (C-226/13, C-245/13, C-247/13,
  and C-578/13) ECLI:EU:C:2015:383 .... 34, 36–37
Gauweiler and others v Deutscher Bundestag (C-62/14)
  ECLI:EU:C:2015:400 .... 171–72, 173–74
Kuhn v Greece (C-308/17) ECLI:EU:C:2018:911 .... 35–36, 37
Lechouritou and others v Germany (C-292/05) ECLI:EU:C:2007:102 34
Pringle v Ireland and others (C-370/12) ECLI:EU:C:2012:756 .... 171–72, 174
Weiss and others v European Central Bank (C-493/17)
  ECLI:EU:2018:1000 .... 171–72, 173–74

European Court of Human Rights
Fredin v Sweden, App no 12033/86, unreported 18 February 1991 154–55
Gaygusuz and Turkey (intervening) v Austria, App no 17371/90,
  unreported 16 September 1996 .... 154, 155, 159
Inze v Austria, App no 8695/79, unreported 28 October 1987 154
Kopecký v Slovakia, App no 44912/98, unreported 7 January 2003 150–51
Lithgow and others v United Kingdom, App nos 9006/80, 9262/81,
  9263/81, 9265/81, 9266/81, 9313/81, and 9405/81, unreported
  8 July 1986 .... 154–55, 157, 159–60
Malysh and others v Russia, App no 30280/03, unreported 11 February 2010 .... 150–52, 153
Mamatas and others v Greece, App nos 63066/14, 64297/14, and 66106/14,
  unreported 21 July 2016 .... 2, 31, 32, 150–54, 155, 156–59, 183–86, 201
Thlimmenos v Greece, App no 34369/97, unreported 6 April 2000 153–54
Van der Mussele v Belgium, App no 8919/80, unreported 23 November 1983 154–55

International Arbitration Cases
Abaclat and others v Argentina, ICSID Case No ARB/07/5, Decision on
  Jurisdiction and Admissibility, 4 August 2011 .... 136–37, 138–39
Alemanni and others v Argentina, ICSID Case No ARB/07/8, Decision on
  Jurisdiction and Admissibility, 17 November 2014 138–39
Ambiente Ufficio SpA and others v Argentina, ICSID Case No ARB/08/9,
  Decision on Jurisdiction and Admissibility, 8 February 2013 138–39
Biwater Gauff (Tanzania) Ltd v Tanzania, ICSID Case No ARB/05/22,
  Award, 24 July 2008 138–39
Ceskoslovenska Obchodni Banka, AS v Slovakia, ICSID Case No ARB/97/4,
  Decision on Jurisdiction, 24 May 1999 138
CMS Gas Transmission Co v Argentina, ICSID Case No ARB/01/8, Award,
  12 May 2005 147–48

xviii TABLE OF CASES

Fedax NV v Venezuela, ICSID Case No ARB/96/3, Decision on Jurisdiction,
  11 July 1997 137–38
Feldmann v Mexico, ICSID Case No ARB(AF)/99/1, Award, 16 December 2002 141–42
Genin, Eastern Credit Ltd, Inc and AS Baltoil v Estonia, ICSID Case No
  ARB/99/2, Award, 25 June 2001 .... 147–48, 181–82
Global Trading Resource Corp and Globec International, Inc v Ukraine, ICSID
  Case No ARB/09/11, Award, 1 December 2010 137–38
Grand River Enterprises Six Nations Ltd and others v United States, UNCITRAL,
  Award, 12 January 2011 .... 147–48, 181
Lauder v Czech Republic, UNCITRAL, Final Award, 3 September 2001 147–48
Metalclad Corp v Mexico, ICSID Case No ARB(AF)/91/1, Award, 30 August 2000 144
Methanex Corp v United States, UNCITRAL, Final Award on Jurisdiction
  and Merits, 3 August 2005 .... 141–42, 147–48
Norwegian Shipowners' Claims (Norway v United States) (1922) I RIAA
  307 (PCA) 130–31, 143–44
Nykomb Synergetics Technology Holding AB v Latvia, SCC Arbitration
  Institute, Award, 16 December 2003 147–48
Ottoman Public Debt Case (Bulgaria, Iraq, Palestine, Transjordan, Greece,
  Italy, and Turkey) (1925) 1 RIAA 529 (PCA) vii
Parkerings-Compagniet AS v Lithuania, ICSID Case No ARB/05/08, Award,
  11 September 2007 147–48
Pope & Talbot Inc v Canada, UNCITRAL/NAFTA, Award on the Merits of
  Phase 2, 10 April 2001 .... 141, 143, 180
Poštová banka, as and Istrokapital SE v Greece, ICSID Case No ARB/13/8,
  Award on Jurisdiction, 9 April 2015 .... 28–29, 136–37, 140
Preferential Treatment of Claims of Blockading Powers against Venezuela
  (Germany, Great Britain, and Italy v Venezuela), PCA Case No 1903-01,
  Award, 22 February 1904 (Venezuelan Preferential Case) 27–63, 75, 76, 130–31
Salini Costruttori SpA v Morocco, ICSID Case No ARB/00/4, Decision on
  Jurisdiction, 23 July 2001 137–38
Saluka Investments BV v Czech Republic, UNCITRAL, Partial Award,
  17 March 2006 .... 147–48, 200
SD Myers, Inc v Canada, UNCITRAL/NAFTA, Partial Award,
  13 November 2001 .... 141–42, 143, 147–48
Técnicas Medioambientales Tecmed, SA v Mexico, ICSID
  Case No ARB(AF)/00/2, Award, 29 May 2003 200
Texaco Overseas Petroleum Co and California Asiatic Oil Co v Libya, 17 ILM 1,
  Award, 19 January 1977 26
Trail Smelter Arbitration (United States v Canada) (1941) III Rep Int Arbitr
  Awards 1905 194
Waste Management, Inc v Mexico, ICSID Case No ARB (AF)/9/00/3,
  Award, 30 April 2004 .... 145–46, 147–48, 181–82

International Court of Justice

Barcelona Traction, Light and Power Co, Ltd (Belgium v Spain)
  (New application 1964, Second phase) [1970] ICJ Rep 3 27–28
Diallo (Ahmadou Sadio) (Guinea v Democratic Republic of Congo)
  (Preliminary objections) [2007] ICJ Rep 582 27–28
International Status of South West Africa (Advisory Opinion) [1950] ICJ Rep 128 193,
                                                                                199–200
Jurisdictional Immunities of the State (Germany v Italy: Greece Intervening)
  [2012] ICJ Rep 99 .... 41–42, 44–45

TABLE OF CASES   xix

Nuclear Tests Case (New Zealand v France) [1974] ICJ Rep 457 194
Obligation to Negotiate Access to the Pacific Ocean (Bolivia v Chile)
    [2018] ICJ Rep 507 200
Pulp Mills on the River Uruguay (Argentina v Uruguay) [2010] ICJ Rep 14 194

Permanent Court of International Justice

Case concerning Certain German Interests in Polish Upper Silesia
    (Germany v Poland) (1926) PCIJ Series A no 7 .... 130–31, 143–44
Case concerning the Factory at Chorzów (Germany v Poland)
    (1927) PCIJ Series A No 17 194
Case concerning the Payment in Gold of Brazilian Federal Loans
    Contracted in France (France v Brazil) (1929) PCIJ Series A no 21 .... 25, 27–28, 79
Case concerning the Payment of Various Serbian Loans Issued in France
    (France v Kingdom of the Serbs, Croats, and Slovenes) (1929)
    PCIJ Series A no 20 .... 24–25, 27–28, 30, 77, 79, 133
Chinn (Oscar) (United Kingdom v Belgium) (1932) PCIJ Series A/B no 61 ..... 130–31, 143–44
Société commerciale de Belgique (Belgium v Greece) (1939) PCIJ Series A/B no 78 .... 59, 167
SS Lotus (France v Turkey) (1927) PCIJ Series A no 10 66

World Trade Organization

United States—Import Prohibition of Certain Shrimp and Shrimp Products
    (India and others v United States) (WT/DS58/AB/RW) 22 October 2001
    (App Body) 194

NATIONAL COURTS

Austria

Oberster Gerichtshof (4 Ob 227/13f) unreported 20 May 2014 55
Oberster Gerichtshof (8 Ob 67/15h) unreported 30 July 2015 55
Oberster Gerichtshof (8 Ob 125/15p) unreported 25 November 2015 55
Oberster Gerichtshof (4 Ob 163/15x) unreported 27 January 2016 55

Belgium

Decision no 61/2018, unreported 31 May 2018 (Const Ct) 121–22, 123–24
Elliot Associates, LP (No 2000/QR/92) unreported 26 September 2000
    (Brussels CA) 86–87
Nicaragua v LNC Investments and Euroclear Bank SA (RK 240/03) unreported
    11 September 2003 (Brussels Comm Ct) 87

France

Administration des chemins de fer du gouvernement iranien v Société Levant Express
    Transport, Bull civ I no 86, unreported 25 February 1969 (Cass 1 Civ Div) 44
Decision no 2016-741, unreported 8 December 2016 (Const Council) 126

Germany

Bundesgerichtshof (VI ZR 516/14) unreported 8 March 2016 50
Bundesgerichtshof (XI ZR 193/14) unreported 24 February 2015 51–52
Bundesgerichtshof (XI ZR 796/16) (Unidentified Holders of Greek Government
    Bonds v Greece) unreported 19 December 2017 50–52
Bundesverfassungsgericht (16 BVerfGE 27) (Empire of Iran Case) unreported 1963 .... 43, 49

xx   TABLE OF CASES

Bundesverfassungsgericht (2 BvM 1/03) (Argentine Necessity Case) unreported
    8 May 2007 .... 78, 192–93
Bundesverfassungsgericht (2 BvR 824/15) unreported 3 July 2019 ...... 192–93, 194, 199–200

Italy
Decision no 11225 (Borri v Argentina) 27 Maggio 2005 (Cass) 52–54

Portugal
Decision 399/2010 (Surtax on Personal Income Tax 2010) (Const Ct) 17

United Kingdom
Allen v Gold Reefs of West Africa [1900] 1 Ch 656 (CA) 110, 114
Assénagon Asset Management SA v Irish Bank Resolution Corp Ltd [2012]
    EWHC 2090 (Ch) 112, 114, 115–17, 119
British America Nickel Corp Ltd v MJ O'Brien Ltd [1927] AC 369 (PC) 114–15, 116, 119
Citco Banking Corp NV v Pusser's Ltd [2007] BCC 205 (PC) 111–12
Donegal International Ltd v Zambia [2007] EWHC 197 (Comm) 124
Ebrahimi v Westbourne Galleries Ltd [1973] AC 360 (HL) 114
Greenhalgh v Arderne Cinemas [1951] Ch 286 (CA) 119
Kensington International Ltd v Democratic Republic of the Congo [2003]
    EWCA Civ 709 87
Knighthead Master Fund LP & others v Bank of New York Mellon [2003]
    EWCA Civ 709 .... 93–94, 97
Knighthead Master Fund LP & others v Bank of New York Mellon [2014]
    EWHC 3662 (Ch) 89–90, 91–92
Knighthead Master Fund LP & others v Bank of New York Mellon [2015]
    EWHC 270 (Ch) 90, 91–92
Kuwait Airways Corp v Iraqi Airways Corp [1995] 1 WLR 1147 (HL) 48
Northern Assurance Co Ltd v Farnham United Breweries Ltd [1912]
    2 Ch 125 (Ch D) 110–11
O'Neill v Phillips [1999] 1 WLR 1092 (HL) 114
Owners of Cargo Lately Laden on Board the Marble Islands v Owners of the
    I Congreso del Partido [1983] 1 AC 244 (HL) 43, 47–50
Redwood Master Fund & others v TD Bank Europe Ltd and others [2002]
    EWHC 2703 (Ch) 104, 114–15, 116–18, 119
Trendtex Trading Corp v Central Bank of Nigeria [1977] QB 529
    (CA (Civ Div)) 40, 42, 44, 47

United States
Ajdler v Province of Mendoza, No 17-CV-1530 (VM) 2017 WL 3635122
    (SDNY 2017) 92–93, 96
Ajdler v Province of Mendoza, 890 F3d 95 (2d Cir 2018) 92
Aladdin Hotel Co v Bloom, 200 F 2d 627 (8th Cir 1953) 111
Alfred Dunhill of London, Inc v Cuba, 425 US 682 (1976) 44
Argentina v NML Capital, Ltd, 134 S Ct 2819 (2014) 88
Argentina v Weltover, Inc, 504 US 607 (1992) 37–38, 43, 46–47
Atlantica Holdings v Sovereign Wealth Fund, 813 F 3d 98 (2d Cir 2016) 38
Bolivarian Republic v Helmerich & Payne International Drilling Co. See Venezuela v
    Helmerich & Payne International Drilling Co
Callejo v Bancomer, SA, 764 F 2d 1101 (5th Cir 1985) 38
Crédit Français v Sociedad, 128 Misc 2d 564 (NY Sup Ct 1985) 113–14

De Sanchez v Banco Central de Nicaragua, 770 F 2d 1385 (5th Cir 1985) 38–39
Elliott Associates, LP v Banco De La Nacion, 194 FRD 116 (SDNY 1999) 86
Elliott Associates, LP v Banco De La Nacion, 194 F 3d 363 (2d Cir 1999) 86, 93–94
Elliott Associates, LP v Peru, 12 F Supp 2d 328 (SDNY 1998) 86
EM Ltd v Argentina, 473 F 3d 463 (2d Cir 2007) 165, 167–68
Export-Import Bank of China v Grenada, No 13 Civ 1450 (HB) (SDNY 19 August 2013) ... 89
Hackettstown National Bank v DG Yuengling Brewing Co, 74 F 110
  (2d Cir 1896) 110–11, 113–14
Katz v Oak Industries Inc, 508 A 2d 873 (Del Ch 1986) 110–11, 112–14
Kensington International, Ltd v BNP Paribas SA, No 03602569 (SC NY 2003) 87
Macrotecnic International Corp v Argentina, No 02 Civ 5932 (TPG) (SDNY 2004) 87
Marblegate Asset Management v Education Management Corp, 111
  F Supp 3d 542 (SDNY 2015) 117
Marblegate Asset Management v Education Management Finance, 846 F 3d 1
  (2d Cir 2017) 117
NML Capital, Ltd v Argentina, 699 F 3d 246 (2d Cir 2012) 18–19, 20–21
NML Capital, Ltd v Argentina, No 03 Civ 8845 (TPG) (SDNY 23 February 2012) 88
NML Capital, Ltd v Argentina, No 08-cv-6978 (TPG) (SDNY 7 December 2011) 88
NML Capital, Ltd v Argentina, No 08-cv-6978 (TPG) (SDNY
  21 November 2012) 88, 165–66, 199
NML Capital, Ltd v Argentina, No 08-cv-6978 (TPG) 727 F 3d 230 (2d Cir 2013) 88–89,
  91–92, 93–94, 95–97, 165–67, 168
NML Capital, Ltd v Argentina, No 08-cv-6978 (TPG) (SDNY 21 August 2014) 89–90
Red Mountain Finance, Inc v Democratic Republic of Congo (CD Cal 21 May 2001) 87
Si Group Consort Ltd v Ukraine, No 15 CV 3047-LTS 1 (SDNY 30 January 2017) 38–39
Venezuela v Helmerich & Payne International Drilling Co, 137 S Ct 1312 (2017) 38–39
White Hawthorne v Argentina, No 16-Civ-1042 (TPG) 2016 WL 7441699 (SDNY 2016) 93
Yucyco, Ltd v Slovenia, 984 F Supp 209 (SDNY 1997) 111

Table of Legislation

INTERNATIONAL INSTRUMENTS

Argentina-Italy Bilateral Investment Treaty
   1990 136–37
   Art 1(1)(c) 136–37
Articles of Agreement of the International
   Monetary Fund 1944 . . . . 68, 73
   Art IV 17
   Art V 68
      s 3(b)(iii) 68
      s 3(b)(iv) 68
      s 4 68
Canada-European Union Comprehensive
   Economic and Trade Agreement
   2016 (CETA) 136–37
   Art 8(1) 136–37
   Art 8(3) 136–37
   Art 8.10(2) 147–48, 181
   Annex 8-B 136–37
Charter of the United Nations 1945
   Ch VII 209
   Art 2(1) 41–42
Chile-United States Free Trade
   Agreement 2003 145
China-Peru Free Trade Agreement 2009
   Ch 10 Annex 8 139–40
Convention on Jurisdiction and the
   Enforcement of Judgments in Civil
   and Commercial Matters 1968 . . . 52–53
Convention on the Privileges and
   Immunities of the United
   Nations 1946
   Art 21 43–44
Convention on the Settlement of
   Investment Disputes between States
   and Nationals of Other States 1966
   (ICSID Convention) 137–39, 140
   Art 25 137–38
   Art 25(1) 137–38
European Convention on Human
   Rights and Fundamental
   Freedoms 1950 (ECHR) 32, 128,
            149–62, 168, 169, 179–86, 195, 200
   Art 6 123
   Art 13 123

   Art 14 . . . . 149, 150, 153–54,
          155, 156, 158, 159, 160, 161, 179
   Protocol 1 Art 1 . . . . 123, 149–52, 153,
          154, 156, 159, 160, 161, 179
   Protocol 12 153–54
European Convention on State
   Immunity 1972 44
   Annex 39
European Financial Stability Facility
   Framework Agreement as Amended
   with effect from the Effective
   Date of the Amendments 2011 . . . 70–71
   Preamble 70
   rec 1 70
   Art 16.1 70–71
Greece-Slovak Republic Bilateral
   Investment Treaty 1991 136–37
   Art 1(1) 136–37
India Model Bilateral Investment
   Treaty 2016 139–40
International Covenant on Economic,
   Social and Cultural Rights 1966 17
International Law Commission (ILC)
   Articles on the Responsibility of States for
   Internationally Wrongful Acts 2001
   Arts 35–37 76
International Law Commission (ILC) Draft
   Articles on Diplomatic Protection
   2006 130
   Art 1 . . . . 130, 133
International Law Commission (ILC)
   Draft Articles on Jurisdictional
   Immunities of States and Their
   Property 1991 44–45
North American Free Trade Agreement
   1992 (NAFTA) 144
   Art 1102(2) 141
   Art 1105 . . . . 147–48, 181
   Art 1105(1) 147–48
   Art 1110 145
Peru-Singapore Free Trade Agreement 2008
   Art 10.18 139–40
Statute of the International Court
   of Justice 1945 . . . . 57–58, 189, 190
   Art 38 . . . . 57–58, 189, 194

xxiv   TABLE OF LEGISLATION

Art 38(1)(a) 128
Art 38(1)(b) 66, 128
Art 38(1)(c) 57–58, 128, 176,
      189, 190–91, 192–93, 194
Trans-Pacific Partnership Agreement 2016
   Art 9.1 136
Treaty of Lausanne 1923 vii
United Nations Convention on
   Jurisdictional Immunities of States
   and Their Property 2004 .... 44–45, 125
   Art 18............................ 125
   Art 19............................ 125
   Art 21............................ 125
United Nations General Assembly
   Resolution 68/304 (2014), Towards
   the establishment of a multilateral
   legal framework for sovereign debt
   restructuring processes 197, 209
United Nations General Assembly Resolution
   69/313 (2015), Addis Ababa Action
   Agenda of the Third International
   Conference on Financing for
   Development 197
United Nations General Assembly Resolution
   69/319 (2015), Basic Principles on
   Sovereign Debt Restructuring
   Processes 198–99, 201–2,
                              207, 208–9
United Nations Security Council
   Resolution 1483 (2003), The situation
   between Iraq and Kuwait 209
United States Model Bilateral Investment
   Treaty 2012 136
United States-Uruguay Bilateral
   Investment Treaty 2005 145
   Annex G 139–40
Vienna Convention on the Law of
   Treaties 1969 .... 58–59, 194
   Art 26........................ 58–59
   Art 34........................ 58–59

EU LEGISLATION

Treaties

Agreement amending the Treaty establishing
   the European Stability Mechanism
   2021 103
Charter of Fundamental Rights of the
   European Union [2012]
   OJ C326/391 .... 17, 32, 158–59
   Art 16............................ 123
   Art 20............................ 158
   Art 21............................ 158

Art 52............................ 158
Protocol (No 4) to the Treaty on the
   Functioning of the European Union
   on the Statute of the European System
   of Central Banks and of the European
   Central Bank [2016] OJ C202/230
   Art 21......................... 173–74
Treaty establishing the European Stability
   Mechanism 2012 .... 71–72, 73, 103
   rec 10 71–72
   rec 13 71–72
Treaty on European Union (TEU)
   [2012] OJ C326/13
   Art 4(2) 172
Treaty on the Functioning of the
   European Union (TFEU)
   [2012] OJ C326/47 170–72
   Art 49........................... 123
   Art 56........................... 123
   Art 123 172–74
   Art 122(2) 69–70
   Art 123(1) 170, 171–73, 174
   Art 125 .... 171, 172
   Art 125(1) 170–71, 172, 174
   Art 127(1) 171–72
   Art 267 171–72
   Art 282(2) 171–72

Regulations

Regulation (EC) No 44/2001 of 22 December
   2000 on jurisdiction and the
   recognition and enforcement of
   judgments in civil and commercial
   matters (Brussels I Regulation)
   [2001] OJ L12/1 .... 33, 34, 55
Regulation (EC) No 1393/2007 of the
   European Parliament and of the
   Council of 13 November 2007 on the
   service in the Member States of judicial
   and extrajudicial documents in civil
   or commercial matters (service of
   documents) [2007] OJ L324/7 .... 36, 37
   Art 1(1) 36, 37
Regulation (EC) No 593/2008 of the
   European Parliament and of the
   Council of 17 June 2008 on the law
   applicable to contractual
   obligations (Rome I) [2008]
   OJ L177/6 123
Regulation (EU) No 407/2010 of
   11 May 2010 establishing a European
   financial stabilisation mechanism
   [2010] OJ L118/1 69–70

Regulation (EU) No 1215/2012 of the
   European Parliament and of the Council
   of 12 December 2012 on jurisdiction
   and the recognition and enforcement
   of judgments in civil and commercial
   matters (recast) (Brussels I Recast)
   [2012] OJ L351/1 .... 33–35, 36,
          37, 40–41, 50–51, 123, 124
   Art 1(1) 34, 36
   Art 1(1)(a) 35
   Art 5 34
   Art 6 34
   Art 7 34–35
   Art 7(1)(a) 34–35
   Art 18(1) 34
   Art 21(2) 34
   Art 24 34
   Art 25 34–35
   Art 25(1) 34–35

Decisions

Decision (EU) 2010/281 of the European
   Central Bank of 14 May 2010
   establishing a securities markets
   programme (ECB/2010/5) [2010]
   OJ L124/8 72–73
   rec 3 72–73
Decision (EU) 2015/774 of the European
   Central Bank of 4 March 2015 on a
   secondary markets public sector asset
   purchase programme (ECB/2015/10)
   [2015] OJ L121/20 73
   rec 8 73

NATIONAL LEGISLATION

Argentina

Law 26,017 of 2005 (Lock Law) 88, 89,
                                93, 160–61
   Art 2 160–61
Law 26,547 of 2009 88
Law 26,866 of 2013 88

Australia

Foreign State Immunities Act 1985 ... 45–46

Austria

Unemployment Insurance Act 159

Belgium

Civil Code
   Art 1134 123

Constitution of Belgium 123
   Art 10 123
   Art 11 123
   Art 16 123
   Art 23 123
Judicial Code
   Art 1412 122
Law of 6 April 2008 to prevent the seizure
   or transfer of public funds intended
   for international cooperation, in
   particular through the technique of
   vulture funds 122, 199
Law of 12 July 2015 on the fight against
   the activities of vulture funds 122,
               123–24, 126, 127, 199
   Art 2(2) 122
   Art 2(4) 122–23
Law of 23 August 2015 inserting into
   the Judicial Code an article 1412
   quinquies governing the seizure of
   property belonging to a foreign power
   or to a supranational or international
   organization under public law 122

France

Code of Civil Procedure of
   Enforcement 125
Declaration of the Rights of Man and
   of the Citizen 1789 126
Law No 2016-1691 of 9 December
   2016 on transparency, anti-corruption,
   and modernization of economic
   life 125,
                                126, 199
   Art 59 .... 125, 126
   Art 60 125–26

Germany

Act on Debt Security from Total
   Issues 2009
   s 12(3) 100–1
Basic Law
   Art 100(2) 192

Greece

Constitution of Greece 32
Law No 4050/2012 on the Rules of
   Amendment of Titles Issued or
   Guaranteed by the Hellenic
   Republic with the Bondholders'
   Agreement (Bondholder
   Act) 34, 36–37, 50–51, 55, 151–52

Ireland

Euro Area Loan Facility Act 2010 69–70

Isle of Man

Heavily Indebted Poor Countries (Limitation on Debt Recovery) Act 2012 ... 125, 199

Jersey

Debt Relief (Developing Countries) (Jersey) Law 2013 .... 125, 199

Luxembourg

Law of 10 August 1915 on commercial companies 70

Spain

Constitution of Spain
    s 135.3 177

United Kingdom

Civil Procedure Rules 1998
    (SI 1998/3132) 39, 40
    PD 6B 39–40
    para 3.1(6) 39
    para 3.1(7) 39
Debt Relief (Developing Countries) Act 2010 (c 22) 124–25, 126, 199
State Immunity Act 1978
    (c 33) 44, 45–46
    s 3(2) 45–46

United States

Bankruptcy Code (11 USC)
    s 1129(a)(10) 113–14
Foreign Sovereign Immunities Act 1976 (PL 94-583) 37–38, 42–43, 44, 46–47, 165
    s 1603(d) 43
    s 1604 37–38
    s 1605 37–38
    s 1605(a)(1) 37–38
    s 1605(a)(2) 37–38, 46–47
    s 1605(a)(3) 38–39
Trust Indenture Act 1939 (PL 76-253) 100–1, 113–14
    s 316 113–14
    s 316(b) 100–1

List of Abbreviations

BIS	Bank of International Settlements
BIT	Bilateral Investment Treaty
CAC	Collective Action Clause
CETA	Comprehensive Economic and Trade Agreement
CJEU	Court of Justice of the European Union
ECB	European Central Bank
ECHR	European Court of Human Rights
ECtHR	European Court of Human Rights
EFC	Economic and Financial Committee
EFSF	European Financial Stability Facility
EFSM	European Financial Stabilisation Mechanism
EIB	European Investment Bank
ESCB	European System of Central Banks
ESM	European Stability Mechanism
EU	European Union
FET	Fair and Equitable Treatment
FSIA	Foreign Sovereign Immunities Act
G10	Group of Ten
G20	Group of Twenty
GATT	General Agreement on Tariffs and Trade
GLF	Greek Loan Facility
HIPC	Heavily Indebted Poor Countries
IBRD	International Bank for Reconstruction and Development
ICJ	International Court of Justice
ICMA	International Capital Market Association
ICSID	International Centre for Settlement of Investment Disputes
IIA	International Investment Agreement
IIF	Institute of International Finance
ILA	International Law Association
ILC	International Law Commission
ILO	International Labor Organization
ILOR	International Lender of Last Resort
IMF	International Monetary Fund
MFN	Most Favoured Nation
NAFTA	North America Free Trade Agreement
NSWF	Norwegian Sovereign Wealth Fund
NT	National Treatment
OECD	Organisation for Economic Co-operation and Development
OMT	Outright Monetary Transactions

PCIJ	Permanent Court of International Justice
PSI	Private Sector Involvement
PSPP	Public Securities Purchase Programme
SME	Securities Market Programme
SMSF	Secondary Market Support Facility
TFEU	Treaty on the Functioning of the European Union
TIA	Trust Indenture Act
UK	United Kingdom
UN	United Nations
UNCITRAL	United Nation Commission on International Trade Law
UNCTAD	United Nations Conference on Trade and Development
US	United States of America
USA	United States of America
WTO	World Trade Organization

Introduction

Intercreditor Equity—Challenges of a Non-Uniform Standard

This book provides a comprehensive legal study of intercreditor equity—rules providing for equal and differential treatment of creditors—in sovereign debt restructurings.[1] The question of intercreditor equity is one of the most conflictual issues in debt restructuring, both historically and today. It is paramount to creditors in the unfortunate event of a debt restructuring and it is equally important to debtor states so that they can manage restructuring processes as efficiently as possible and ensure a sustainable debt crisis resolution. In other words, understanding the multifaceted issue of intercreditor equity rules is essential to the understanding of sovereign debt.

Sovereign borrowing can contribute to economic and social development and help achieve economic stability in any state.[2] All states borrow, for example, to promote development, invest in infrastructure, fund warfare, as a monetary policy tool, to ensure that the government has sufficient cash reserves, and to develop and maintain a well-functioning domestic financial market.[3] States can borrow money from other states and international finance institutions such as the International Monetary Fund (IMF). They can also borrow money in the commercial markets, from private banks, or by issuing bonds.

As is the case with private individuals and corporate debtors, states sometimes default on their payment obligations.[4] There are many reasons why states may default and end up in a debt crisis, including poor economic management, external economic shocks, civil wars, and natural disasters, to name just a few.[5] In contrast to corporations and private individuals, states facing solvency problems or defaulting on payment obligations are not protected by comprehensive domestic or international legal insolvency procedures or liquidation rules. Although common in ordinary domestic bankruptcy procedures, a state facing severe debt problems will not have its

---

[1] In this book, sovereign mainly refers to states' central governments.
[2] Yuefen Li and Ugo Panizza, 'The Economic Rationale for the Principles on Promoting Responsible Sovereign Lending and Borrowing' in Carlos Espósito and others (eds), *Sovereign Financing and International Law: The UNCTAD Principles on Responsible Sovereign Lending and Borrowing* (Oxford University Press 2013) 15.
[3] See, for example, Norges Bank, 'About Government Debt' (1 January 2022) <https://www.norges-bank.no/en/topics/Government-debt/About-government-debt/> accessed 14 March 2022.
[4] For an overview of sovereign debt restructurings (1950–2010), see Christoph Trebesch and others, 'Sovereign Debt Restructurings 1950–2010: Literature Survey, Data, and Stylized Facts' (IMF Working Paper, August 2012).
[5] See, for example, Jerome E Roos, *Why Not Default? The Political Economy of Sovereign Debt* (Princeton University Press 2019). On the relationship between sovereign default and economic activity in the defaulting country, see Michael Tomz and Mark LJ Wright, 'Do Countries Default in "Bad Times"?' (Working Paper, Federal Reserve Bank of San Francisco, 25 May 2007).

Intercreditor Equity in Sovereign Debt Restructuring. Astrid Iversen, Oxford University Press. © Astrid Iversen 2023.
DOI: 10.1093/oso/9780192866905.003.0001

assets seized and distributed amongst its creditors. In general, there is no comprehensive legal framework weighing various considerations—of the debtor state, society as a whole, creditors as a group, and intercreditor equity—against each other. One common crisis resolution tool for states is to restructure the debt, which implies making the debt burden manageable through a renegotiation of the outstanding debt agreements. Such restructurings are in principle dependent on voluntary acceptance by the creditors concerned.

Disagreements over intercreditor equity is one of the main sources of sovereign debt disputes. Indeed, they constitute a major obstacle to reaching sustainable debt restructuring agreements and thereby to solving debt crises. At the core of intercreditor equity disputes is the question of the distribution of cost between creditors: when sovereign debtors are faced with payment difficulties, and have limited resources available, they are forced to decide how much they are able to pay and which creditor they will prioritize. During restructuring negotiations and following agreement on a debt restructuring plan, different creditors frequently claim that they have not been treated equally compared to other creditors, or that they should have been treated preferentially and have not been.

A recent example is Greece's debt restructuring in 2012. This was the biggest restructuring plan to date and equal treatment concerns were raised by several creditors. For example, the Norwegian Sovereign Wealth Fund (NSWF), which had invested in Greek sovereign bonds, voted against the adoption of the restructuring agreement, arguing that it discriminated against investors. To elaborate, during the restructuring negotiations, the Director of the NSWF argued that it was discriminatory that the European Central Bank (ECB) and the European Investment Bank (EIB) had not participated in the restructuring process on the same terms as the other creditors holding similar sovereign bonds, but had instead received preferential treatment.[6] Also, after Greece had concluded its restructuring agreement, certain retail investors sought compensation before the European Court of Human Rights (ECtHR) claiming that they had been discriminated against when they were forced to accept a reduction in Greece's debt during the restructuring. They argued that since they were non-professional retail investors, they should not have been required to understand investment risk, nor take on the same economic losses in the restructuring process as professional institutional investors, such as investment banks and insurance companies.[7] As the example indicates, there is today great variation in the types of creditors holding sovereign debt with different aims and objectives spanning states, central banks, international organizations, and retail investors, to institutional investors such as insurance firms and commercial banks. The complexity of the creditor base typically corresponds with the complexity of a restructuring process.

---

[6] Karianne Steinsland and others, 'Oljefondet stemte nei til Hellas-avtalen', *Aftenposten* (Oslo, 16 March 2012) <https://www.aftenposten.no/okonomi/i/naPJQ/oljefondet-stemte-nei-til-hellas-avtalen> accessed 14 March 2022. See also Melissa Boudreau and G Mitu Gulati, 'The International Monetary Fund's Imperiled Priority' (2014) 10 Duke Journal of Constitutional Law & Public Policy 119.

[7] *Mamatas and Others v Greece*, App no 63066/14, 64297/14, and 66106/14, 21 July 2016 [ECtHR]. The Court did not agree with the claimants. See Section 4.4 for further discussion. See also Astrid Iversen, 'The Future of Involuntary Sovereign Debt Restructurings: *Mamatas and Others v Greece* and the Protection of Holdings of Sovereign Debt Instruments under the ECHR' (2019) 14 Capital Markets Law Journal 34.

Despite the common nature of intercreditor equity claims, the actual content of a right to equal or preferential treatment in sovereign debt restructuring seems to be poorly understood by both creditors and sovereign debtors. Intercreditor equity rules are challenging to establish because of the lack of a comprehensive legal framework for sovereign debt crisis resolution; there is no set of coordinated rules for distributing losses among creditors. Instead, a number of disparate rules in national and international law, both public and private, regulate various aspects of the restructuring process, influencing the outcome of a restructuring agreement. Among these rules are rules regulating issues of intercreditor equity in a debt restructuring, which are found in different areas of law such as contract law, human rights law, and international investment law. Sovereign debt crisis resolution and, in particular, intercreditor equity disputes in a sovereign debt restructuring are inherently politicized issues. Nevertheless, the law plays an important and often overlooked role in debt restructurings. The various intercreditor equity rules are decisive with regard to a debtor state's room for manoeuvre—their policy space—when implementing a sovereign debt restructuring.

The aim of the book is, first, to map and establish the content of these intercreditor equity rules and analyse how they influence the restructuring process. This research helps creditors improve the prediction of their legal rights and calculate the returns on their investments in sovereign debt obligations. It also improves a sovereign debtor's understanding of the boundaries within which its debt restructuring offer must be designed and is instructive when drafting future sovereign debt instruments. Secondly, and equally important, the book and the analyses of intercreditor equity rules seek to shed light on the functioning of the legal framework governing sovereign debt more broadly. It does so by analysing the extent to which intercreditor equity rules and the surrounding legal framework of sovereign debt restructuring are compatible with public policy considerations, defined as a debtor state's possibility to ensure monetary and financial stability and establish sustainable debt burdens.[8] A particular goal in this regard is to analyse debtor states' room for manoeuvre to implement sustainable debt restructurings, including the extent to which states can use their sovereign powers to solve economic crises. Together, these discussions will help us explore the risks involved when a state, whose role is to implement policies for public purposes (such as solving a debt crisis), operates on financial markets and is subject to rules tailored for actors with commercial intentions and objectives.

Approach of the Book

The subject of the book—intercreditor equity in sovereign debt restructuring—draws upon several legal disciplines and lies at the intersection of public international law,

---

[8] The term 'public policy' is used in a number of contexts with different, yet equally valid, definitions. Broadly speaking, public policy typically refers to the state or the government's implementation of measures to maintain order and address the needs of its citizens. In this book, the term specifically refers to a debtor state's need to ensure monetary and financial stability, and implement crisis resolution measures that ensure a sustainable debt burden in the long run.

domestic public and private law, as well as private international law. When analysing intercreditor equity rules, the spectrum of relevant sources of law is broad and it can be challenging to explore the intersection between the various relevant legal spheres. Moreover, intercreditor equity in sovereign debt restructurings is a specialist topic. Nevertheless, the book seeks to be accessible to a broad readership by explaining the general legal framework of sovereign debt and the underlying dilemmas of debt restructurings, in particular in Chapters 1 and 2. Chapter 1 places the topic of intercreditor equity in the broader debate on sovereign debt restructuring. Chapter 2 discusses rules concerning (i) the governing law of a sovereign debt instrument, (i) the jurisdiction of courts, and (iii) sovereign immunity in sovereign debt restructuring disputes. The three sets of rules form an important part of the legal framework of sovereign debt and influence the extent to which creditors may enforce their intercreditor equity rights. Knowledge of these rules is necessary to understand intercreditor equity disputes.

Because the title refers to 'intercreditor equity', one might assume that the book is mainly concerned with how creditors linked to a single debtor may hold each other accountable if an intercreditor equity rule is violated; that is, whether a creditor can enforce an intercreditor equity claim against another creditor. However, rights and obligations stemming from a loan instrument exist mainly between each creditor and the respective debtor. In contrast to the relationship between the owners of stock in a single company, for example, there are typically no general obligations between creditors to the same debtor. The question of intercreditor equity is therefore mainly decided by reference to the rules engaging the debtor state and the extent to which each of the creditors is able to enforce these rules against the debtor. Some exemptions exist, where a creditor may have an intercreditor equity claim against another creditor. In the book, this case is discussed in the context of the abuse of minority rights in majority voting procedures (such as collective action clauses) in Section 4.3.

The fact that the vast majority of intercreditor equity obligations are owed by the debtor state also explains the chosen structure of the book, in particular Chapters 3–5, which explore and seek to establish the content of core intercreditor equity rules, the majority of which are obligations of the state. A key objective behind the structure adopted in these chapters is to make it easy to understand which laws are applicable to different types of creditors holding specific debt instruments in various situations. To achieve this, it is necessary to distinguish between creditors who are subjects of international law and domestic law and debt instruments governed by international law or domestic law. A complicating factor is that some creditors and debtors may be subjects of both international and domestic law. Moreover, international law can be applicable to debt instruments governed by both domestic and international law. To make the analysis of the intercreditor equity rights as clear as possible, Chapter 3 discusses intercreditor equity rules in international law applicable to debt instruments governed by international law, Chapter 4 examines intercreditor equity rules in domestic law, and Chapter 5 concerns international law protection of creditors holding debt instruments governed by domestic law. Chapter 6 discusses how intercreditor equity rules in international and domestic law are interrelated *de jure* and *de facto*, including which rights may collide and how these collisions may be solved. This is important because debt instruments governed by international law and debt instruments governed by

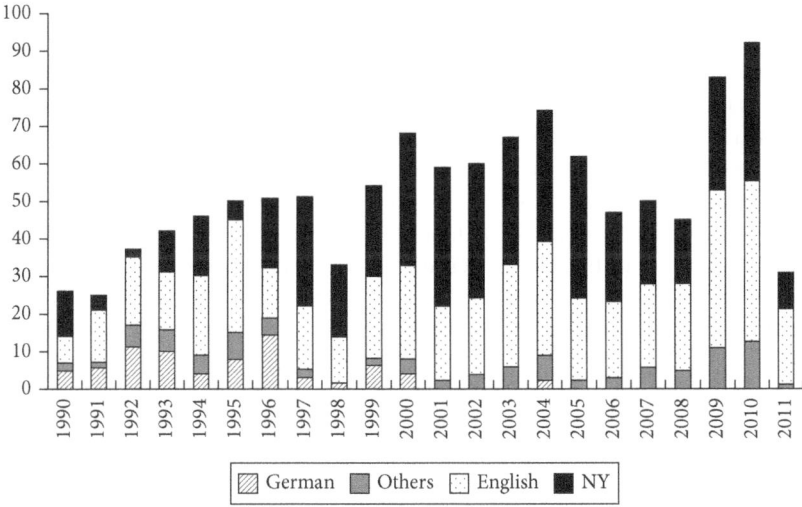

Figure 1 Total number of bond issues by governing law.
Figure from Bradley and Gulati, 'Collective Action Clauses for the Eurozone' (2013) 12.

domestic law can both be subject to restructuring by the same sovereign debtor at the same time.

Drawing on analyses from Chapters 3 to 6, Chapter 7 discusses intercreditor equity and systemic challenges. More specifically, it discusses whether intercreditor equity rules and the surrounding legal framework of sovereign debt restructuring are compatible with public policy considerations. This includes analyses of debtor states' room for manoeuvre to implement sustainable debt restructurings and the extent to which debtor states should be treated similarly to ordinary private law subjects and restricted from using sovereign powers to implement crisis resolution measures. Finally, Chapter 8 discusses potential systemic improvements to the legal framework governing debt crisis resolutions and the future of intercreditor equity disputes.

To a certain extent, the book attempts to remain detached from specific national jurisdictions and instead focuses on current international trends dominating the legal framework of sovereign debt restructuring. Nevertheless, debt instruments are subject to the laws of one or more specific jurisdictions, and a legal dispute takes place in a specific forum. In the field of sovereign debt, certain jurisdictions dominate. Throughout the book, there will be a special focus on, and an over-representation of examples from legislation and case law from New York and England and Wales.[9] The justification for this is that the laws of England and New York are those in which international sovereign bonds are most commonly issued (see Figure 1). In 2020, sovereign bonds issued in these jurisdictions were estimated to represent approximately 45%

---

[9] For the purposes of this book, references to the law of England and Wales will be simply referred to as English law.

and 52%, respectively, of the nominal amount of outstanding stock of international sovereign bonds.[10]

The selection of case law discussed in this book corresponds to (i) cases in which countries have implemented a debt restructuring and (ii) cases where issues related to a restructuring have ended up in court. In the past 30 years, Argentina and Greece are the two countries that have implemented the most significant restructurings both in terms of the amount of money involved and the number of court cases that have arisen in relation to a restructuring. These two countries will therefore dominate the examples in the book when discussing intercreditor equity rules in both international and domestic law. For the most part, the case law stemming from the Argentine and the Greek debt restructurings has taken place in European or US courts.

As a result of the European debt crisis that started in 2009, there have been many developments on the continent concerning sovereign debt management. Moreover, and to the best of my knowledge, so-called vulture fund legislation, which curbs the rights of certain aggressive creditors, only exists in European countries. For these reasons, the book also has a special focus on European jurisdictions.

The book is not exhaustive in its treatment of intercreditor equity rules. As described above, this book has a special focus on English and New York law, as well as on developments in European jurisdictions. Other provisions in debt instruments, in domestic law (such as constitutional law), and in international treaties may also influence the intercreditor equity rights of creditors more indirectly; these are not touched on in this book. Moreover, both treaty protection of creditors and creditor protection in debt instruments evolve and new intercreditor rules are likely to develop. The ambition of the book is to examine the *core* intercreditor equity rules that have played, or are likely to play, an important part in present day sovereign debt restructurings.

Terminology

Despite the fact that there are no coordinated insolvency procedures for sovereign debtors, the legal and economic literature often adopts terminology from domestic insolvency law when discussing sovereign debt and intercreditor equity issues. The transplant of terms and concepts is often imprecise, confusing, or misleading. Concepts familiar to domestic insolvency law do not necessarily have a clear meaning when applied to the sovereign debt context. In fact, some of the concepts are at the centre of legal disputes, such as the *pari passu* clause (see Section 4.2). Nevertheless, the domestic terminology can be a useful prop and to a certain extent will also be referred to in this book. Some key terms are presented below.

---

[10] IMF, 'The International Architecture for Resolving Sovereign Debt Involving Private-Sector Creditors—Recent Developments, Challenges, And Reform Options' (Policy paper, 23 September 2020) n 27.

Priority

In domestic law, in case of bankruptcy and liquidation, the debtor's assets are confiscated and turned into money for distribution between the creditors. Priority typically refers to the right of a creditor to get their claim fully satisfied out of a debtor's pool of assets *before* other creditors' claims. In the case of ordinary domestic restructuring, it typically refers to the situation in which claim x has priority over claim y, implying that claim x cannot be reduced unless claim y has been fully written off first.

Sovereign debtors do not go bankrupt and their property is not seized and distributed to creditors. However, a sovereign debtor may be unable to pay all claims that fall due. In this book and in the context of a debt restructuring, priority refers to the right of certain creditors or certain debt obligations to (re-)payment *before* other creditors and debt obligations. It can also refer to a right not to have one's claim written off unless non-priority claims have been fully written off first or, more generally, a right not to participate in a debt restructuring.

Ranking

The ranking of an obligation typically refers to debts that have higher or lower priority compared to other debt obligations. In the literature it is, however, often unclear whether the ranking of an obligation refers simply to legal ranking or also to a right to priority in payment. In this book, ranking is used interchangeably with priority—meaning priority in payment—unless otherwise specified.

Subordinated debt

Subordinated debt, or junior debt, means that a debt has a lower ranking compared to other debts. In domestic insolvency law, the effect of subordination is that in liquidation or other specified circumstances, debt will be paid in full before payments can be made on the subordinated debt. It is less clear what the consequences of subordination are in sovereign debt contexts. The answer depends on a subordination agreement. The consequence may be that other creditors have a right to be paid in full before subordinated creditors or that subordinated creditors must participate in debt restructuring while other creditors are exempted.

Preferred creditors/preferential debts

The term preferred creditor status is used in relation to creditors who have a claim to preferred treatment concerning the settlement of debts. Corresponding debts that enjoy such treatment will be called preferential debts.

A preference consists of a right to priority of payment for one's claim where a debtor lacks the resources to honour all incurred debts. It is also used in relation to creditors (or debts) that are provided with preferential terms or altogether exempted from a restructuring. Preferential treatment can also be used to describe a secured creditor's rights in collateral, which is a preference in fulfilment of contract. Whether a specific rule discussed in the book encompasses all or only some of these approaches may vary.

When discussing preferred creditors and preferential debts, it is important to remember that in most cases, accepting a restructuring agreement is voluntary. The term preferred creditor does not necessarily refer to a specific legal right.

Equal treatment

In this book, equal treatment normally refers to the principle that similarly situated creditors should be treated equally. The characteristics and circumstances that are sufficiently comparable to conclude that creditors are similarly situated may vary.

Ladder of priority

A central part of corporate bankruptcy regimes is the bankruptcy ladder of priorities. This ladder of priority determines the hierarchy of various creditors with regard to the debtor's assets in a final liquidation. There are no formal ladders of priority for sovereign debtors similar to that in domestic corporate bankruptcy law, nor is there an informal consensus on how such a ladder should be arranged.[11] In practice, priority in sovereign debt is typically determined by the order of payment in time. For example, a creditor who is paid in full on Monday will often, in practice, rank prior to a creditor whose debt is due on Tuesday because after the payment on Monday, there may be nothing left to pay the creditor on Tuesday.[12]

Debt restructuring

There is no universally accepted definition of sovereign debt restructuring. In this book, the term restructuring refers to an 'exchange of outstanding sovereign debt instruments, such as loans or bonds, for new debt instruments or cash through a legal process'.[13] Such restructurings are in principle dependent on voluntary acceptance by the creditors concerned. Compared to the outstanding debt instruments, the conditions of the new debt instrument usually imply either (i) extending the maturity dates on the principal or interest falling due under the affected debts and introducing grace periods; (ii) reducing the principal amount of the debt; (iii) reducing the interest rate

---

[11] Lee C Buchheit, 'Sovereign Debt in the Light of Eternity' in Rosa M Lastra and Lee C Buchheit (eds), *Sovereign Debt Management* (Oxford University Press 2014) 391.
[12] Philip R Wood, 'Corporate Bankruptcy Law and State Insolvencies' in Rosa M Lastra and Lee C Buchheit (eds), *Sovereign Debt Management* (Oxford University Press 2014) 391–92.
[13] Trebesch and others (n 4) 7.

(in the case of bond debt, often referred to as 'coupon adjustment'); or (iv) a combination of all three tools.

The aim of restructuring is to obtain a sustainable level of debt and thereby improve the sovereign debtor's capacity to repay over time.[14] The focus in this book is on distressed debt restructurings, where the restructuring terms are less favourable to the creditor than the original terms of the bond or loan.[15]

---

[14] ibid.
[15] This definition is in line with the one provided by Standard & Poor. ibid.

1
The Role of Intercreditor Equity in Sovereign Debt Restructuring

1.1 Introduction

Intercreditor equity rules, which are disparate in nature, have a number of different aims and objectives and affect the sovereign debt restructuring process in various ways.

National general insolvency law procedures—applicable to individuals, corporations, and, in some jurisdictions, subnational entities—contain rules that govern the distribution of losses caused by the insolvency of a debtor. It is common to ascribe *pari passu* distribution, where creditors suffer losses *pro rata*, as the main distributional principle guiding such rules. However, there are numerous exceptions to this principle. The power of individuals and corporations to grant security interests over their assets that remain effective in insolvency procedures prioritizes secured creditors over unsecured creditors. In addition, general insolvency law priority rules often contain some element of consumer protection, protection for unsophisticated investors, and other vulnerable creditors such as employees. Such domestic insolvency procedures also seek to prevent dissenting creditors within the different classes from 'exploiting the process for their own benefit'.[1] Such legislation tries to balance the interests of debtors, society, and creditors (among themselves) to obtain a fair distributive result.

In a situation where there is no general insolvency framework, which is the case for sovereign debtors, disparate rules govern the restructuring process. And, since this process is only binding on those creditors who voluntarily accept it, there are no clear answers as to what role equal and preferred treatment play in the restructuring. The effect of these rules can vary depending on the specific facts of a case, such as the type of creditors involved and the underlying factors of the economic crisis of the sovereign debtor. The following sections discuss the key roles that equal and differential treatment of creditors may have in sovereign debt restructuring.

1.2 Equal Treatment

It is costly and time-consuming for a creditor to commence legal proceedings against a defaulting sovereign debtor. Voluntary restructurings are therefore a common tool for sovereign debtors facing a debt crisis. If creditors are reluctant to begin proceedings in court to seek full payment in accordance with the debt instrument, equal (*pro*

---

[1] Lee C Buchheit, 'The Search for Intercreditor Parity' (2002) 8 Law & Business Review of the Americas 73, 73. See also Section 1.4 in this chapter discussing various challenges to reaching a sustainable sovereign debt restructuring agreement.

Intercreditor Equity in Sovereign Debt Restructuring. Astrid Iversen, Oxford University Press. © Astrid Iversen 2023.
DOI: 10.1093/oso/9780192866905.003.0002

rata) treatment of all creditors in a restructuring is preferable as it minimizes the costs involved for each individual creditor participating in the debt restructuring. In other words, if the restructuring is accepted by the broadest range of creditors possible, the financial burden for each of the individual participating creditors is reduced.[2] This way, parity of treatment of creditors is deemed to influence the willingness of creditors to participate in a restructuring process.

For many creditors, the issue of intercreditor equity in sovereign debt crisis resolution is not only a question of cost efficiency but also of personal incentives. No-one likes to lose money and creditors are no exception, yet this is normally the consequence of a debt restructuring. The dissatisfaction a creditor may experience when accepting losses is exacerbated by co-creditors who are able to escape restructuring and thereby avoid sharing in those losses on an equal basis.[3] To incentivize creditors to accept a restructuring offer, and so prevent them from jeopardizing the restructuring agreement through subsequent litigation, it is important that none of the creditors feel that other creditors have been treated preferentially without legitimate reason.[4] Thus, psychological factors also explain why equal treatment of creditors is deemed to improve the willingness of creditors to participate in a debt restructuring process.

1.3 Differential Treatment

Creditors may actively seek to hold out on a restructuring process to avoid economic losses. Creditors can also be kept out of the restructuring altogether or provided with more beneficial restructuring terms at the initiative of the debtor. There may be several reasons—economic, political, and ethical—for debtor states to treat creditors differently in a sovereign debt restructuring by excluding claims or providing terms that are more lenient for some creditors.

One reason is that differential treatment can contribute to improving a debtor state's economy, enabling the overall restructuring to be smaller than would otherwise be necessary in the short- or long term. One example in this regard is whether the sovereign debtor chooses to restructure debt governed by domestic or foreign law.[5] Several considerations influence a sovereign's choice. On the one hand, a sovereign can unilaterally change the terms of domestic law governing debt obligations by amending the law in question. From a legal perspective, it may therefore be easier to restructure debt governed by domestic law than debt governed by foreign law.[6]

---

[2] ibid. See also Lee C Buchheit and others, 'The Restructuring Process' in S Ali Abbas and others (eds), *Sovereign Debt: A Guide for Economists and Practitioners* (Oxford University Press 2020) 342–43.

[3] Buchheit (n 1) 73–74.

[4] It is also important that no-one feels that the other parties involved are free-riding on their losses with regards to the debtor state having to make structural economic changes (cuts to their national budget, increased taxes, etc).

[5] The economic argument in this example is dependent on the creditor holding debt issued in local currency. Lawyers typically refer to domestic debt as debt issued under domestic law, which may lead to some misunderstandings between economists and lawyers. See also Buchheit and others, 'The Restructuring Process' (n 2) 334.

[6] Lee C Buchheit and others, 'How to Restructure Sovereign Debt: Lessons from Four Decades' (PIIE Working Paper, 5 June 2019) 6.

Exclusively restructuring domestic debt may also help reduce reputational costs in the eyes of the international (capital) market, thus facilitating access to capital in international markets in the future. One example is Russia's default in 1997 and the subsequent restructuring which excluded foreign law bonds issued by the Russian Federation.[7] On the other hand, restructuring local debts may have collateral effects and undermine economic growth and recovery, because these debts may be held largely by local institutions such as domestic banks.[8] Moreover, the government in a debtor state may have political incentives to avoid the restructuring of domestically held debt. For example, a government that coercively restructures domestically owned debt may find it more difficult to get re-elected. Today, this latter point has less force than it once did. Traditionally, domestic debt was governed by domestic law, denominated in local currency, and locally held; external debt, in contrast, was typically governed by foreign law, held abroad, and denominated in a foreign currency. This is less often the case today, now that non-resident creditors may hold debt governed by domestic law (denominated in either local or foreign currency) and resident creditors may hold foreign law debt denominated in foreign currencies.[9]

Another reason for sovereign debtors to provide certain creditors with special treatment in a debt restructuring is related to the characteristics and investment objectives of specific creditors, which may vary considerably. One may distinguish between categories of multilateral official creditors, bilateral official creditors, and private creditors. Moreover, there are bondholders, trade creditors and contractors, and creditors who are banks and provide traditional bank loans. Creditors in the first category alone range from retail investors (non-professional investors), to institutional investors (investment funds, insurance companies, retirement funds, investment banks) who purchase sovereign bonds on the secondary market at or near par and hold them on a long-term basis, to distress debt funds who buy defaulted or near-defaulted debt on the secondary market at large discounts. For each of these categories there are arguments in favour of differential treatment, sometimes regardless of the fact that the creditors hold the same type of debt instrument. For example, and as mentioned above in relation to the 2012 restructuring in Greece, some may question whether non-professional retail investors with little knowledge of the financial risk of sovereign debt should be treated in the same way as professional investment banks in a restructuring if they hold the same type of sovereign bond.

To summarize, how intercreditor equity rules affect a sovereign debt restructuring process—whether the various rules pull in the same or different directions and therefore make the process easier or more difficult—is typically hard to answer *ex ante*.

---

[7] ibid.
[8] ibid.
[9] Anna Gelpern and Brad Setser, 'Domestic and External Debt: The Doomed Quest for Equal Treatment' (2003–04) 35 Georgetown Journal of International Law 795, 795.

1.4 Intercreditor Equity and Sustainable Debt Restructurings

1.4.1 Introduction

Sovereign debt restructurings are typically painful for all parties involved; the debtor state, its citizens, and its creditors. The goal of a debt restructuring is normally to make the debt burden sustainable and thereby also improve the sovereign debtor's capacity to repay over time.[10] This means that debt restructuring should be implemented only if it is strictly necessary and only to the extent that the debtor state reaches a sustainable level of debt. This will minimize the negative consequences associated with a restructuring. Under the current framework of sovereign debt, there are several obstacles to the implementation of 'optimal' debt restructuring.

As already mentioned, there is no comprehensive legal insolvency procedure in international or domestic law for sovereign debtors. Rather, debt restructuring is normally based on a voluntary agreement between the sovereign borrower and its creditors.[11] Only creditors who accept the restructuring agreement are bound by it. As a result, the system of sovereign debt restructuring is fragmented and based on a number of *ad hoc* arrangements between the debtor and creditors. In this system, sovereign debtors are in some ways more vulnerable than private debtors and in other ways, less so. On the one hand, if a sovereign is unable to service its debt, it cannot seek the protection of bankruptcy laws to restructure or delay payments, as private debtors can. On the other hand, creditors will find it difficult to seize non-commercial public assets in lieu of payment for a defaulted sovereign debt, due to the rules on sovereign immunity.[12] This *ad hoc* system and reliance on voluntary renegotiations to implement a sovereign debt restructuring can make it challenging for the state to reach a sustainable level of debt and thus solve a debt crisis.

The consequence of a poorly implemented or unsuccessful debt restructuring can be that a crisis is prolonged for several years or even decades. To cite Buchheit and others, the consequences may be that '[a] return to normal economic activity may be delayed, credit market access frozen, trade finance unavailable, capital flight endemic, financial sector instability chronic and foreign direct investment withered'.[13] The International Monetary Fund (IMF) has also pointed out that sovereign debt restructurings often suffer from the problem of 'too little, too late' and hence fail to achieve lasting debt sustainability.[14]

---

[10] Christoph Trebesch and others, 'Sovereign Debt Restructurings 1950–2010: Literature Survey, Data, and Stylized Facts' (IMF Working Paper, August 2012) 7. A rescheduling that defers contractual payments may be referred to as an indirect debt reduction, while a reduction in the face (nominal) value of the old instruments is referred to as a direct debt relief. When this book refers to restructuring, both these concepts are included.

[11] Sovereign debt restructuring can also include involuntary or coercive elements, typically laid down by law or in the contract itself. Sometimes the restructuring is forced through the use of retrospective legislation, which may cause more conflict, as in the Greek restructuring in 2012.

[12] See discussion in Section 2.4.

[13] Buchheit and others, 'The Restructuring Process' (n 2) 328.

[14] IMF, 'Sovereign Debt Restructuring—Recent Developments and Implications for the Fund's Legal and Policy Framework' (Policy paper, 26 April 2013) 15.

This Section 1.4 will elaborate further on key factors that pose a challenge to successful debt restructuring. Section 1.4.3 explains how the diverging interests of creditors and debtors affect a sovereign debt restructuring. Conflicting interests between various types of creditors is thereafter discussed in Section 1.4.4. Before examining the issues just described, Section 1.4.2 first discusses what constitutes a sustainable level of debt and shows that sustainable debt restructuring is hotly debated and can be difficult to establish.

1.4.2 Sustainable debt restructurings

Sovereign debt restructuring is, as mentioned, a contract-based tool to resolve debt crises. A debt crisis is assumed to be resolved if the resulting debt levels are sustainable. It can, however, be difficult to establish what constitutes a sustainable level of debt and thus a sustainable debt restructuring.

Not all restructurings are desirable from a societal point of view. For example, state debtors can misuse the restructuring regime and the goodwill of creditors to reduce their debt burdens to an extent that goes beyond what is actually needed to resolve a debt crisis. Moreover, restructurings are not always able to solve a debt crisis, particularly when the amount of debt to be restructured is limited. The goal is to implement debt restructuring only if it is strictly necessary and, then, only to the extent necessary to ensure that the level of debt is sustainable for the debtor state. Questions of necessity and debt sustainability are closely related, since debt restructuring is only necessary if and to the extent that a state's debt levels are unsustainable. Whether restructuring is necessary and how comprehensive restructuring should be for the debt burden to become sustainable must be considered in conjunction with alternative crisis management tools states can use to deal with economic crises and payment difficulties. The following sections first discuss alternative crisis resolution measures and why these may not be sufficient to solve a crisis before discussing how one decides what is a sustainable debt level.

Debt restructuring is deemed necessary when debt levels are unsustainable and alternative crisis resolution tools are ill-adapted to redress the economic crisis of the state. As an alternative to restructuring, a sovereign debtor may choose to raise taxes from its citizens, implement structural reforms and cut government spending,[15] lend more money to pay existing obligations[16] and/or implement expansive fiscal policies. If the debt is denominated in local currency, a sovereign debtor may also seek to inflate the currency to reduce the debt burden.[17] However, despite the existence of these

---

[15] Economic reforms are often necessary for the debtor state to improve its crisis-stricken economy. When implementing a sovereign debt restructuring, creditors, international lenders of last resort such as the IMF, and other countries typically expose the debtor country to considerable pressure for it to reform its economy by cutting public spending. In its Article IV Consultations, in which IMF assesses its Member States' economies, the institution may also recommend policy reform and austerity measures affecting public spending on public goods. Though not obliging the debtor state to implement such measures, they are often made a condition for crisis lending and acceptance of a restructuring offer.

[16] The IMF is a global lender of last resort, while the European Stability Mechanism (ESM) has a similar role at the regional level.

[17] With varying success, states have sought to escape the real burden of indebtedness through monetary policies seeking to strengthen the currency (making it less burdensome to repay debt denominated

tools, a state can be *de facto* unable to pay its obligations as they fall due.[18] There is a limit to how heavily a state can tax its citizens and its corporations before the economy deteriorates significantly. Furthermore, structural reforms may not be sufficient to turn the economy around and it may take some time for the effects to set in depending on how grave the financial crisis is. The state may lack access to fresh credit due to political or market considerations.[19] It is for these reasons that sovereign debt restructuring may be necessary to resolve a debt crisis.

Moreover, if a debtor defaults on its payment obligations or other conflicts related to the terms and conditions of a loan arise, a creditor will normally want to bring the debtor to court to establish and enforce their rights under the contract, such as the right to payment. However, legal proceedings in cases of sovereign debt are challenging, as sovereign states are protected by rules on sovereign immunity.[20] While a creditor can typically obtain a judgment confirming its claim, the court does not have the authority to manage the different claims *ex post* and creditors will thus encounter difficulties in enforcing the payment judgment. Consequently, sovereign debt issues have historically been addressed through direct and voluntary renegotiation of the terms of the loan contract between sovereign debtors and their creditors.

The process of establishing a sustainable level of debt for a particular state in a particular situation is difficult in practice. In addition, this process is heavily politicized and debated at length in the economic literature.[21] It can be difficult to obtain reliable information about a state's economic and social situation. Moreover, predicting the effects of structural reforms and future economic developments is subject to great uncertainty. Both these factors make it challenging to calculate and agree upon the correct level of sustainable debt in specific circumstances.[22] It is typically the role of the IMF, or other regional finance-related institutions, to confirm implicitly that the amount of debt relief requested by the debtor country is sufficient to achieve sustainability, but also that the debtor country is not requesting more than strictly needed.[23]

---

in foreign currency) or by implementing inflationary policies (to increase the money in circulation by lowering the interest rate or 'printing money' to increase the relative debt burden if it is issued in domestic currency). Each of these tools may have adverse effects on the economy and a state's desire to implement the different mechanisms may depend on the type of crisis it is experiencing, how the economy is constructed, etc. See, for example, Buchheit and others, 'How to Restructure Sovereign Debt: Lessons from Four Decades' (n 6) 6.

[18] In principle, a state cannot go bankrupt. With regards to external debt, a sovereign state may be unable to buy foreign currency to repay its foreign currency obligations. Nevertheless, there is a limit to how much a state can increase taxes. Furthermore, there are certain limits on the portion of resources a state can channel towards debt service (at the expense of expenditures, such as security, health, and education) while still ensuring basic human rights and maintaining the operations of the state.

[19] See, for example, discussion in R Gaston Gelos and others, 'Sovereign Borrowing by Developing Countries: What Determines Market Access?' (IMF Working Paper, 11 January 2004).

[20] On state immunity, see, in general, Hazel Fox and Philippa Webb, *The Law of State Immunity* (Oxford International Law Library, 3rd edn, Oxford University Press 2015). Immunity from jurisdiction is less problematic these days as it is commonly acknowledged that states issuing bonds as commercial actors are generally not protected by immunity rules. States do, however, enjoy immunity from enforcement measures, meaning that creditors will have difficulties seizing state property. Questions of sovereign immunity and enforcement of sovereign debt claims are discussed in Section 2.4.

[21] Buchheit and others, 'How to Restructure Sovereign Debt: Lessons from Four Decades' (n 6) 3.

[22] ibid.

[23] The IMF conducts debt sustainability analysis (DSA), which assesses the feasibility of policy adjustment and the availability of financing from different sources. The DSA plays an important role in discussions

However, the IMF does not have a formal say in negotiations over when to initiate a debt restructuring or how much debt should be restructured.[24]

One key element in the general debate about debt sustainability assessments (which also determines when it is necessary to restructure) is whether the assessment simply considers how much a state is able to pay in 'pure' economic terms or whether it also includes social factors. The former is typically calculated on the basis of debt and debt service in relation to GDP, exports, and revenue, while the latter includes measures of the social and economic development of the state, such as a state's need for public spending on social goods, that is, to fulfil certain human rights (such as health, education, labour rights, and social security).[25]

Comprehensive cuts in public spending during a crisis may have negative effects on the economy.[26] Since the 1950s and the time of Keynes, many economists have argued that the economy is demand-driven, meaning (in simplified terms) that growth in supply is a response to growth in demand, such that economic growth can only be induced by increasing demand. Pro-cyclical policies have the potential to worsen an economy in crisis. Therefore, austerity measures—such as comprehensive cuts in social security benefits, increases in health and education costs for citizens, and weaker labour rights—may decrease demand and weaken the economy. In the wake of the Greek debt crisis, a number of economists criticized the harsh austerity measures adopted and the IMF has since admitted that they 'failed to realise the damage austerity would do to Greece'.[27] An assessment of whether restructuring is necessary and how much of the debt needs to be restructured to make the debt burden sustainable can be inaccurate and flawed if the social consequences of austerity measures and their impact on the rest of the economy are not taken into account.

about whether a country requires debt restructuring. The IMF's DSA hence plays a role in the decision on whether debt restructuring will take place, regardless of whether it is an IMF- or outside-supported adjustment programme. See ibid 4.

[24] Buchheit and others, 'The Restructuring Process' (n 2) 343. See also Buchheit and others, 'How to Restructure Sovereign Debt: Lessons from Four Decades' (n 6) 3–4.

[25] The IMF and the World Bank have a joint Debt Sustainability Framework (DSF), which is designed to guide the borrowing decisions of low-income countries in a way that matches their financing needs with their current and prospective ability to repay debt. A key part of the framework is Debt Sustainability Analysis (DSA), a structured examination of a country's debt that debt experts from the IMF and World Bank conduct regularly in low-income and middle-income countries. See IMF, 'The Debt Sustainability Framework for Low-Income Countries' (*International Monetary Fund*, 13 July 2018) <https://www.imf.org/external/pubs/ft/dsa/lic.htm> accessed 13 March 2022. The DSA is currently undergoing a review, see World Bank, 'New Reforms to DSF to Provide a Simpler and More Comprehensive Way to Assess Risks to Debt Sustainability' (*World Bank*, 10 February 2017) <https://www.worldbank.org/en/news/feature/2017/10/02/new-reforms-to-dsf-to-provide-a-simpler-and-more-comprehensive-way-to-assess-risks-to-debt-sustainability> accessed 29 February 2020. Civil society organizations continue to criticize the framework even after the suggested changes, see, for example, Mark Perera and Tim Jones, 'Debt Sustainability Review: Tinkering around the Edges While Crises Loom' (*Bretton Woods Project*, 12 June 2017) <https://www.brettonwoodsproject.org/2017/12/debt-sustainability-review-tinkering-around-edges-crises-loom/> accessed 14 March 2022.

[26] See, for example, Jonathan D Ostry and others, 'Neoliberalism: Oversold?—Instead of Delivering Growth, Some Neoliberal Policies Have Increased Inequality, in Turn Jeopardizing Durable Expansion' (2016) 53 Finance & Development 38, discussing an IMF study concluding that austerity policies can do more harm than good.

[27] Larry Elliott and others, 'IMF Admits: We Failed to Realise the Damage Austerity Would Do to Greece', *The Guardian* (6 May 2013) <http://www.theguardian.com/business/2013/jun/05/imf-underestimated-damage-austerity-would-do-to-greece> accessed 11 March 2022.

This debate on sustainable debt levels is dominated by economists. But there is also a legal side to questions of social costs, debt sustainability and debt restructurings. Cuts in public spending can have an enormous effect on social, cultural, and economic rights, such as labour rights and rights to education and health.[28] Several national courts have reviewed certain fiscal consolidation policy reforms related to social protection and found them unconstitutional. In 2013, the Portuguese Constitutional Court ruled that four fiscal consolidation measures in the budget were both unlawful and unconstitutional. The cuts mainly affected civil servants and pensioners.[29] In Latvia, the 2010 budget proposed new spending cuts and tax increases, including a 10% cut in pensions and a 70% decrease for so-called working pensioners. The Latvian Constitutional Court held that these pension cuts were in breach of the constitution, as they violated the right to social security, and the cuts were reversed.[30] In Romania, the 15% pension cut that was proposed in May 2010 was also declared unconstitutional.[31]

UN Independent Experts and Special Rapporteurs, in particular the Independent Expert on foreign debt and human rights, have also expressed concern about the legal rights of citizens in connection to economic reform policies. In particular, they have shown concern regarding the 'general approach of the IMF to social security reforms that has sometimes put fiscal objectives above the objective of ensuring respect for the right to social security as a human right as set out in international human rights law'.[32] The Independent Expert on foreign debt and human rights has also argued that:

> the European Commission has a legal obligation to ensure that any memorandum of understanding it signs must be consistent with the Charter of Fundamental Rights of the European Union (the 'EU Charter') and international human rights law binding its Member States. This includes the International Covenant on Economic, Social and Cultural Rights ratified by all states of the EU.[33]

It is likely to be an uphill battle for affected citizens in a debtor country to argue that the international institutions and creditors are breaching their social and economic rights when a state implements sovereign debt restructuring and related fiscal policy reforms. This is because international institutions' push for cuts in public spending are typically only fronted indirectly as a condition for the state to receive crisis loans or

---

[28] See, for example, Juan Pablo Bohoslavsky, 'Report of the Independent Expert on the Effects of Foreign Debt and Other Related International Financial Obligations of States on the Full Enjoyment of All Human Rights, Particularly Economic, Social and Cultural Rights' (20 December 2017).
[29] Constitutional Court Decision 399/2010 (*Surtax on Personal Income Tax 2010*) (Portugal).
[30] Letter from UN Human Rights Special Procedures (Special Rapporteurs, Independent Experts & Working Groups), 'Open Letter to the IMF' (21 December 2017) 4.
[31] ibid.
[32] ibid. They pointed out several governments with IMF programmes or who, under IMF advice (Art IV Consultations), had pursued fiscal consolidation measures that cut social expenditures to such a degree that national legislation and human rights standards as contained in internationally agreed conventions and recommendations of the International Labour Organization (ILO) were sidelined. They further propose that 'the Fund could play a crucial role in assisting States in strengthening their social protection systems in collaboration with other international organizations such as the ILO and other UN agencies that have worked on these issues for a long time'.
[33] Juan Pablo Bohoslavsky, 'Has the EU Sacrificed Human Rights on the Altar of Austerity?' (*Equal Times*, n.d.) <https://www.equaltimes.org/even-in-the-face-of-austerity-and> accessed 8 May 2018.

debt sustainability assessments. The decision to cut public spending or alternatively seek to resolve a debt crisis through other means is made by the relevant government. The UN expert argues that there is a need for guiding principles for assessing the human rights impact of economic reform policies.[34] The question is whether or not a particular level of debt can be labelled sustainable if social, cultural, and economic rights are sidelined as a result.

In sum, there are interesting and important legal questions related to how austerity measures affect the legal rights of the citizens and how they can uphold these rights. These constitute legal arguments in favour of including social factors when analysing when restructuring is necessary and whether a debt burden is sustainable. For example, one could argue on a legal basis that a minimum level of social and economic rights must be ensured for debt to be considered sustainable.

There are many interesting economic discussions on austerity measures and how fiscal consolidation measures (such as cuts in public goods) may affect the economy, but these fall outside the scope of this book which focuses instead on the legal aspects. Nor will the book engage any further in the discussion regarding the correct way to assess debt sustainability. Instead, the book takes as its starting point the idea that there are situations in which debt restructuring is necessary, but that disagreement over what constitutes a sustainable level of debt is an obstacle for both initiating and concluding a debt restructuring.

1.4.3 Debtor–creditor conflicts

A restructuring inherently entails a conflict between the debtor, on the one hand, and the creditors on the other ('debtor–creditor conflict').[35] The debtor state seeks to ease the contract terms by prolonging its maturity, lowering the interest rate, or even cutting its nominal value. At the same time, a restructuring implies 'haircuts' for creditors.[36] In the context of sovereign debt restructuring, 'haircuts' typically refer to the percentage difference between the present value of creditors' debt instruments and the value of new debt instruments received during restructuring (discounted at market rates prevailing immediately after the debt restructuring).[37] The conflicting interests need to be overcome for the relevant parties to reach agreement. A sovereign debt restructuring can be the best, or even the only, solution to a sovereign's financial crisis and can thus also be the best solution for the creditors as a group, as this gives the

---

[34] ibid.

[35] In a sovereign debt restructuring, the interests of the state and its citizens are not always the same. For the sake of simplicity, in this book, the interests of citizens are assumed to be safeguarded by and equated to the interests of the debtor state.

[36] Astrid Iversen, 'Solvency II and Sovereign Bonds' in Mads Andenas and others (eds), *Solvency II: A Dynamic Challenge for the Insurance Market* (Il Mulino 2017) 9. Their interests are not always contradictory; however, the debtor is likely to be punished by the market (through more expensive credit) if it misuses its power and requires bigger haircuts from the creditors than what is strictly necessary.

[37] Juan J Cruces and Christoph Trebesch, 'Sovereign Defaults: The Price of Haircuts' (CESifo Working Paper Series, CESifo 2011).

sovereign time to 'change policies and turn around its economy, eventually allowing greater payments to the group of all creditors than if the sovereign simply defaulted'.[38]

Several factors may prevent the debtor and the creditors as a group from reaching a sustainable debt restructuring agreement. First, as mentioned in previous sections, creditors and debtors may disagree on the need for debt restructuring based on available information. Second, a sovereign debtor may abuse the restructuring institution and ask for more comprehensive debt restructuring than is strictly necessary to reach a sustainable debt burden, so that most creditors find the restructuring excessive and/or confiscatory.[39] Such a situation constitutes a moral hazard leading to inefficient restructurings, inflicting unnecessary losses on the creditors.[40] Rules incentivizing or allowing potential misuse of the restructuring regime by debtors will drive up the cost of borrowing for the sovereign, as the creditors will have to price in this risk.[41] Additionally, creditors may find the implementation unnecessarily coercive and consequently become prejudiced against the sovereign debtor, which also can affect future market access for the country.[42] Third, since creditors must accept economic losses in a debt restructuring, they may be tempted to deny that the state is facing a debt crisis. Creditors may argue that the state should do more internally to improve its economy, by passing structural reforms or raising taxes, before making a case for restructuring. Creditors may also drag out the restructuring process in the hope that official sector creditors, such as international lenders of last resort or cooperating states, will bail out the sovereign debtor and thereby shield the creditors from losses. The IMF is a global lender of last resort, while the European Stability Mechanism (ESM) has a similar role at the European level. If debt restructuring negotiations are postponed or protracted, this may lead to a deteriorating economy requiring even more comprehensive restructuring further down the line. Fourth, and for the same reasons, creditors may refuse to accept any restructuring agreement or, alternatively, may only accept a restructuring agreement that is less comprehensive than is actually necessary to achieve a sustainable debt level. Fifth, a sovereign debtor may be reluctant to recognize solvency

---

[38] Stephen Choi, 'Supplemental Declaration of Stephen Choi', Dkt # 483, filed to the court in *NML Capital, Ltd v Republic of Argentina* 699 F.3d 246 (2d Cir 2012). There is a vast literature on the economic effects of debt relief and debt restructurings. See, among others, Gong Cheng and others, 'The Macroeconomic Effects of Official Debt Restructuring: Evidence from the Paris Club' (2019) 71 Oxford Economic Papers 344.

[39] Buchheit and others, 'The Restructuring Process' (n 2) 328.

[40] Moral hazard typically occurs when someone takes more risks than they otherwise would because the cost of these risks is borne by someone else. For example, moral hazard occurs when someone increases their exposure to risk when insured. See 'Moral Hazard', *Wikipedia* (2022) <https://en.wikipedia.org/wiki/Moral_hazard> accessed 20 December 2022.

[41] Many academics have discussed this moral hazard. Here is just one example of the general line of argument: 'Much of the debate surrounding possible changes to (or reform of) the institutions governing sovereign debt restructuring has been aimed at reducing the costs (in terms of both time and other resources) associated with reaching agreement as to the terms of that restructuring. While this appears to be in the best interests of a sovereign country that is already in default, it is important to note that reductions in the costs of default will also affect the incentives of the country to borrow appropriately and avoid default in the future. In turn, this will affect the terms on which creditors will lend to the sovereign. That is, it is entirely possible that the country in default may be made worse off through the introduction of a relatively costless debt restructuring process if this process significantly limits their ability to borrow in the future.' See Mark LJ Wright, 'Sovereign Debt Restructuring: Problems and Prospects' (2012) 2 Harvard Business Law Review 153, 159–60.

[42] Buchheit and others, 'The Restructuring Process' (n 2) 329.

problems for fear of triggering capital outflows, increased borrowing costs, or reduced access to the credit market altogether, thus amplifying the economic crisis. In such cases, the restructuring process may be postponed or entirely excluded, with the possible result that the economic crisis deteriorates and creditors suffer even bigger losses.

1.4.4 Intercreditor conflicts

Several factors related to intercreditor relations make it challenging to reach a sovereign debt restructuring agreement. First, there has been a rapid rise in bond financing both in external and domestic sovereign debt markets. There are often several thousand (if not hundreds of thousands) creditors holding the same type of bond and residing in different jurisdictions. The sheer number of creditors who need to communicate and coordinate their interests and actions may make it challenging to reach a restructuring agreement.

Second, there are numerous types of creditors potentially involved in a sovereign debt restructuring, with different interests: states; international lenders of last resort; small retail investors; and both big and small institutional investors, such as banks and pension funds. Furthermore, some may be holding debt denominated in external currencies, while others hold debt in local currency. When bargaining in a debt restructuring process, and considering whether or not to hold out, creditors obviously take into account their own interests and economic situation so as not to end up with economic problems themselves, whether in the short- or long term. The fact that creditors have different roles, interests, and concerns increases the chances of them having different approaches to what is an acceptable restructuring offer. A retail investor may be more hurt (brought closer to bankruptcy) by accepting a restructuring and the associated economic losses compared to a large investment bank. Alternatively, a creditor who is a domestic bank may have a vested interest in supporting restructuring (compared to a bank based in a foreign country) in order to ensure improvements in the local economy. Such differences can drag out the negotiation process and make it difficult to reach a comprehensive restructuring agreement. Moreover, and as mentioned above, the fact that that there is no agreed methodology for establishing a threshold for when it is necessary to restructure makes it challenging to reach a restructuring agreement within a reasonable period of time.

Third, a sovereign debt restructuring is to a certain extent a zero-sum game. A simplified and stylized picture of a restructuring situation looks like this: a sovereign debtor is unable to pay its creditors the full amount due to them on the scheduled maturity dates and hence seeks to renegotiate its debts. Each creditor seeks to maximize their profits and all co-creditors are therefore potential competitors. As mentioned, a restructuring can be described as a voluntary renegotiation of loan terms. It is possible for a creditor to seek preferential treatment or to choose not to participate in a restructuring (to hold out) because of the lack of binding insolvency procedures for states. Although an offer to restructure may be beneficial to the group of creditors as a whole, individual (less risk averse) creditors may benefit from 'demanding a disproportionately greater payment than the amount received by the rest of the creditors in a restructuring'.[43] This way, creditors who seek not to participate in the restructuring

---

[43] Stephen Choi, 'Supplemental Declaration of Stephen Choi', Dkt # 483, filed to the court in *NML Capital, Ltd v Republic of Argentina* 699 F.3d 246 (2d Cir 2012), 8.

in hope of recovering full payment on the contractual claim (holdout creditors) take advantage of the financial concessions granted by fellow creditors to the debtor state in the restructuring process.[44] In other words, they free-ride on their co-creditors by letting them take the loss of the haircut. If the holdout risk is perceived to be significant, creditors who otherwise would be willing to participate in a restructuring may be reluctant to do so, as the non-holdout creditors will have to make additional contributions to the shortfall to enable the debtor to reach a sustainable debt level.[45] This makes it challenging to reach a sustainable restructuring agreement on a voluntary basis.

Disputes over intercreditor equity—both those that are purely legal and those that are more politically based—will continue to play an important role in debt restructuring negotiations. The book does not aim to recommend a single approach or one intercreditor equity rule that will fit all types of debt restructuring scenarios. There is no one-size-fits-all when it comes to economic crisis management and debt restructurings. Moreover, a rule that weighs the interests of different actors and distributes the economic burden between creditors is impossible without reforming the legal framework and establishing a comprehensive debt restructuring procedure.

Without claiming then that there is some uniform understanding of what intercreditor equity should look like, this book seeks to examine developing legal trends. For example, lawsuits against Greece in the wake of the global financial crisis starting in 2007/2008 and lawsuits against Argentina the past two decades have brought about change and so significantly influenced the development of the legal framework governing sovereign debt and our understanding of intercreditor equity. Because no comprehensive monographs on intercreditor equity rules currently exist, there is not merely a need to documenting trends but there is also a need to examine the basic intercreditor equity rules relevant to sovereign debt restructurings. This will be covered in Chapters 3–5.

---

[44] Ordinary creditors will normally accept that a solution be sought through debt restructuring; they will not have the resources to litigate for full payment, as the search for attachable property is expensive and time-consuming, often entailing multiple court cases around the world. Some specialized creditors have the resources to pursue litigation and use this as a business strategy: to hold out from restructuring and claim full payment under the original contracts. See Iversen (n 36) 9.

[45] Buchheit and others, 'The Restructuring Process' (n 2) 342.

2
Sovereign Powers in Crisis Resolution

2.1 Introduction

Chapters 3–5 of this book map and establish the core content intercreditor equity rules. A number of other rules, belonging to the broader legal framework governing sovereign debt, also affect the question of intercreditor equity. Rules concerning: (i) the governing law of a sovereign debt instrument, (ii) the jurisdiction of courts, and (iii) sovereign immunity are three such essential sets of rules that influence intercreditor equity issues. More specifically, they influence whether foreign courts will accept jurisdiction over a sovereign debt restructuring dispute.

The three sets of rules influence intercreditor equity issues in two mains ways. First, they affect the ability of creditors to enforce their intercreditor equity rights in the context of a restructuring. States are sovereign under international law and therefore free to implement legislation within their own jurisdiction. By adopting legislation, a sovereign debtor can unilaterally amend the terms of a debt instrument. This is sometimes referred to as 'the local law advantage'.[1] If a debt instrument is governed by the laws of a state other than that of the sovereign debtor, the sovereign debtor will not be able to use the local law advantage. The choice of governing law influences the rights and obligations under a debt instrument and the sovereign debtor's power to choose how to treat its creditors vis-à-vis each other. Private international law on the jurisdiction of courts and sovereign immunity may, on a procedural basis, preclude foreign courts from assessing the lawfulness of certain acts of a debtor state.[2] This way, both sets of rules reserve disputes arising under a debt instrument for courts of the debtor state. The assumption is that local courts (courts of the sovereign debtor) will be more deferential to the sovereign debtor in cases of unilateral modification of creditors' rights under a debt contract, including when intercreditor equity is at issue. This assumption is often difficult to verify, but it does underpin, for example, the modern international investment law regime.[3] It is necessary to examine the rules concerning

---

[1] Yannis Manuelides, 'Using the Local Law Advantage in Today's Eurozone (with Some References to the Republic of Arcadia and the *Mamatas* Judgment)' (2019) 14 Capital Markets Law Journal 469. See also Mitu Gulati and Lee C Buchheit, 'Use of the Local Law Advantage in the Restructuring of European Sovereign Bonds' (2018) 3 University of Bologna Law Review 2, 172.

[2] Sometimes these two sets of rules are also interconnected. See, for example, Sections 2.3.3 and 2.4.4.1 on US rules on jurisdiction and sovereign immunity. See also Hayk Kupelyants, *Sovereign Defaults Before Domestic Courts* (Oxford Private International Law Series, Oxford University Press 2018) 279.

[3] Several other reasons may also explain why some creditors may wish to litigate bond disputes in a court other than that of the sovereign debtor and, in particular, in the bigger financial centres. First, in choosing a big financial centre, many creditors believe that judges are more specialized in dealing with financial matters. Second, though this is not necessarily the case, the choice of jurisdiction often coincides with choice of law. As discussed in the previous section, choosing a governing law other than that of the sovereign debtor immunizes the terms of the sovereign debt instruments from unilateral modification through legislation. Moreover, the law of financial centres, such as New York and England, is often well known and thus more

governing law, the jurisdiction of courts, and sovereign immunity in conjunction with the substantive intercreditor equity rules (Chapters 3–5) to establish a more realistic picture of creditors' ability to *enforce* their rights to preferred or equal treatment in the context of a restructuring.

The second way in which the three sets of rules influence intercreditor equity issues is that, seen from the sovereign debtor's perspective, they map the outer boundaries within which the state must design a restructuring offer. Together, the substantive rules and the rules concerning governing law, the jurisdiction of courts, and sovereign immunity shed light on how much room for manoeuvre the sovereign debtor has to implement a sovereign debt restructuring, choose how to treat its creditors, and obtain a sustainable level of debt. The challenges related to debtor states' policy space or room for manoeuvre to implement debt crisis resolution measures are further discussed in Chapter 7.

Chapter 2 is structured as follows. Section 2.2 discusses private international law concerning governing law and how the choice between domestic and foreign law is decisive for a sovereign debtor's ability to unilaterally amend the terms of a debt instrument because of the so-called local law advantage. Sections 2.3 and 2.4 examine rules and case law concerning courts' jurisdiction under private international law and sovereign immunity, respectively, to map how they affect creditors' ability to enforce their intercreditor equity rights.

2.2 Governing Law and the Local Law Advantage

2.2.1 Introduction

Choice of governing law influences the rights and obligations under a debt instrument, including the extent to which a sovereign debtor may choose how to treat its creditors vis-à-vis each other. This influence transpires in two main ways. First, the laws applicable to sovereign debt instruments vary across jurisdictions. This means that the rules that regulate creditor rights will vary depending on which law governs the debt instrument.[4] Second, states are sovereign under international law and therefore free to implement legislation within their own jurisdictions. As far as the sovereign debtor is concerned, this includes the ability to unilaterally amend the terms of a debt instrument by means of legislation (the 'local law advantage'). If a debt instrument is governed by the laws of a state other than that of the sovereign debtor, the sovereign debtor will not be able to use the local law advantage. This 'local law advantage' will be the main focus of Section 2.2. Before exploring this topic, however, Section 2.2.2 will discuss more generally how to establish which laws govern various types of sovereign debt instruments.

---

familiar to creditors than the law of the sovereign debtor. If governing law is non-domestic, it is common to seek a court in a jurisdiction of the governing law. See also ibid 61.

[4] For example, some rules explicitly seek to hinder certain holdout creditors from enforcing their claims, such as the vulture fund legislation discussed in Section 4.4.

2.2.2 Governing law of sovereign debt instruments

An uncontroversial starting point is that loan agreements between two (or more) states and between a state and an international finance institution can be entered into by the parties in their capacity as subjects of public international law. Such loan agreements can therefore be governed by international law.[5] Chapter 3 of the book discusses intercreditor equity rules found in international law that are applicable when debt instruments are governed by international law.

More controversial is the situation in which a state borrows from private law subjects. The question of the applicable law in this situation has been extensively discussed in legal theory and opposite views have been put forward and continue to coexist. Several prominent authors have examined the issue and reached their conclusions from different angles.[6] Some writers argue that the state contract is directly subject to the international rule of *pacta sunt servanda*, while others argue that state 'contracts cannot be the subject of international disputes since international law contains no rules respecting their forms and effect'.[7] Jennings described this question as one of the hardest questions of international law, '[f]or, it cannot be considered apart from the relationship of international law and municipal law; the relationship of public international law and private international law; the question of the subjects of international law; and the limits of domestic jurisdiction and the reserved domain'.[8]

The basic starting point is, however, that contracts between a state and a private legal person under domestic law (a non-state legal personality or capacity) are not contracts concluded by states in their capacity as subjects of public international law. The contracting of sovereign debt is made by virtue of the country's private autonomy.[9] In the 1929 Case concerning the Payment of Various Serbian Loans Issued in France (hereafter *Serbian Loans Case*), the Permanent Court of International Justice (PCIJ) stated that '[a]ny contract which is not a contract between States in their capacity as subjects of international law is based on the municipal law of some country'.[10]

---

[5] States have the capacity to enter into international agreements with each other and to decide that these obligations will be governed by international law. An organization may enter into legal relations both on the international plane and with persons of private law within particular systems of municipal law. In principle, the relations of an international organization with other persons of international law will be governed by international law. When an issue arises in relations with persons of private law, the question may be regulated by a choice of law provision in a treaty, which refers to a system of municipal law or possibly to 'general principles of law'. Otherwise, everything will depend on the forum before which the issue is brought and on the applicable conflict of law rules. See James Crawford, *Brownlie's Principles of Public International Law* (8th edn, Oxford University Press 2012) 190.

[6] See Hop Dang, 'The Applicability of International Law as Governing Law of State Contracts' (2010) 17 Australian International Law Journal 133, 133. See also less recent discussion in Edwin M Borchard, 'Contractual Claims in International Law' (1913) 13 Columbia Law Review 457; Robert Y Jennings, 'State Contracts in International Law' (1961) 37 Yearbook of International Law 156.

[7] Samy Friedman, *Expropriation in International Law* (Stevens 1953), as cited by Jennings (n 6) n 1.

[8] Jennings (n 6) 156.

[9] Edwin M Borchard, *State Insolvency and Foreign Bondholders*, vol 1 (Yale University Press 1951) 231; Irmgard Marboe and August Reinisch, 'Contracts between States and Foreign Private Law Persons' in Rüdiger Wolfrum (ed), *Max Planck Encyclopedia of Public International Law* (Oxford University Press 2019) s A.2.

[10] Case concerning the Payment of Various Serbian Loans Issued in France (*France v Kingdom of the Serbs, Croats and Slovenes*) (Judgment) (1929) PCIJ Series A no 20, para 86 (hereafter *Serbian Loans Case*).

If states' loan agreements with private parties in principle are subject to some municipal law—also referred to as domestic or national law—the next question to arise is *which* state's law is applicable to the contract. The answer is found in private international law, more specifically, in the choice of law rules that seek to identify the laws governing international relationships.[11] Which law governs the contract must be identified by the conflict rules of the 'state where the court where the action is brought has its venue' (*lex fori*).[12] Each state has its own conflict of law rules.[13] In contractual matters, private international law is generally dominated by the principle of party autonomy, recognized as a conflict of law rule in the vast majority of states participating in international trade and business.[14] It follows that the parties to a contract are free to choose the law governing their relationship or to choose, in other words, which law(s) the court or tribunal shall apply to each aspect of the dispute.[15]

The principle of party autonomy under private international law implies that parties to a state contract can expressly choose not only a particular system of domestic law but also public international law.[16]

2.2.3 Doctrines concerning internationalization of state contracts

Some writers assume that if the parties to a state contract choose international law as the governing law, this places the contract on the international plane (it is 'internationalized'). It is very uncommon that a loan agreement between a state and a private legal

---

[11] Giuditta Cordero-Moss, *International Commercial Contracts: Applicable Sources and Enforceability* (Cambridge University Press 2014) 134. In the *Serbian Loans Case* (n 10) para 86, the court stated that '[t]he question as to which this law is forms the subject of that branch of law which is at the present day usually described as private international law or the doctrine of the conflict of laws. The rules thereof may be common to several States and may even be established by international conventions or customs, and in the latter case may possess the character of true international law governing the relations between States. But apart from this, it has to be considered that these rules form part of municipal law.'

[12] ibid.

[13] In Case concerning the Payment in Gold of Brazilian Federal Loans Contracted in France (*France v Brazil*) (Judgment) (1929) PCIJ Series A no 21 (hereafter *Brazilian Loans Case*), the court held that there was a presumption that the law of the contract was that of the contracting state. This approach was later rejected in favour of the more general formula of private international law such that agreements between states and foreign private law persons should be governed, like any other international contract, by the law of the country with which the contract has the closest link. See also Marboe and Reinisch (n 9) s A.2. It is another issue that the general principle of private international law would in many cases lead to the law of the State party to the contract being applied, especially if there is no choice of law provision in the loan agreement.

[14] See Cordero-Moss (n 11) 135.

[15] If a law is not explicitly chosen in the contract, and there is nothing in the bond or other circumstances binding the bondholder that substantiates a conclusion that the contract is subject to another law, there is some authority in favour of assuming that the governing law is that of the sovereign debtor. In the *Serbian Loans Case* (n 10), the court stated that '[o]nly the individuality of the borrower is fixed; in this case it is a sovereign State which cannot be presumed to have made the substance of its debt and the validity if the obligations accepted by it in respect thereof, subject to any law other than its own' (para 91). Kupelyants argues that this view is somewhat outdated and should be modified. For more details on the governing law of sovereign debt instruments, see, in general, Kupelyants (n 2).

[16] Crawford (n 5) 631. Jennings has also argued that there are no basic objections to the existence of an international law of contract. He points out that in the field of nationality, for example, rights created in municipal law may be evaluated according to international law standards. See, in general, Jennings (n 6).

person under domestic law (a non-state legal personality or capacity) would explicitly provide for international law to apply as the governing law in a choice of law clause, so this problem seldom arises in the area of sovereign debt. Nevertheless, discussions on the 'internationalization' of state contracts—that is, the lifting of the contract into the international plane, are still present in this field of law, at least at the theoretical level. Several authors have argued that factors other than choice of law clauses pointing explicitly to international law may result in a state contract being internationalized. In general, this school of thought supports the view that the breach of a state contract by the contracting government of itself creates international responsibility.[17] The internationalization of the contract not only means that the contract is governed by international legal principles instead of being based on a state's domestic law; it also means that the private contracting partner is elevated to the same plane as the state and becomes a subject of international law.

An early theoretical attempt to decouple state contracts from domestic law argued that state contracts are governed by certain legal standards.[18] In creating these theories, scholars borrowed from public international law and French administrative law, arguing that there is a distinction between the law applicable to the contract and another set of rules, which provides a legal basis for the contract.[19] This legal basis, which precedes the law applicable to the contract, is in some theories found in 'general principles' of domestic law, but according to the majority of theories it is found directly in international law.[20]

A slightly different approach to detaching state contracts from domestic law is the concept of 'internationalization'. This concept suggests that certain state contracts are governed by international law, typically when (i) the contract itself refers to principles of international law and (ii) the *nature* of the agreement is subject to international law.[21] Writers arguing for the international law character of state contracts also point to the doctrine of acquired rights and the principle of *pacta sunt servanda*, along with certain decisions of international tribunals, in support of their view. However, Crawford claims that there is little evidence that the 'internationalized contract' idea corresponds to existing law.[22]

The various doctrines concerning 'internationalization' of state contracts seem to have some common denominators. First, they seek to align the two legal regimes that otherwise regulate the parties to a state contract: international law and domestic law. Second, they all attempt to neutralize the state contract from the political risk posed

---

[17] The issue of breaches of state contracts is also relevant to investment treaty arbitration, of which state loans may be a part. Under a bilateral investment treaty (BIT), investment contracts are invoked by reference to treaty standards of investment protection. However, there is a distinction between treaty and contract claims in investor state arbitration. (Crawford (n 5) 628–29).

[18] Patrick Wautelet, 'International Public Contracts: Applicable Law and Dispute Resolution' in Mathias Audit and Stephan W Schill (eds), *The Internationalization of Public Contracts* (Bruylant 2013) n 17.

[19] See discussion in ibid 4.

[20] ibid 5.

[21] *Texaco Overseas Petroleum Company, California Asiatic Oil Company v The Government of the Libyan Arab Republic*, 17 ILM 1, Award (19 January 1977) adopted such an approach. It has also been suggested that—depending on the explicit or implicit intention of the parties or the nature of the contract—the basis for this legally binding obligation was public international law. See also Marboe and Reinisch (n 9) s B.

[22] Crawford (n 5) 628.

by the contracting states—the risk that a state may change its laws and thereby modify the content of the contract in its favour—by detaching the state contract from domestic law and bringing the contract into the international arena. As mentioned, the sovereign contract party may act in breach of a contract, legislate in a way that makes the contract worthless (eg currency restrictions), use its powers under domestic law to annul the contract, or repudiate the contract in conflict with its own law.[23] In other words, if the state, through the exercise of its sovereignty, alters the local law and thereby escapes its contractual obligations to the detriment of the creditor, and contrary to the original intention of the contract, it would not necessarily breach the contract as understood under domestic law.[24] As Wautelet has so aptly stated, a state 'comes into the contractual relationship with its exorbitant powers and sometimes bad manners',[25] implying that contracting with sovereign states often involves a political risk.

One way of protecting private contracting parties from the sovereign's powers is to disconnect contracts concluded by states from the application of domestic law and bring them into the domain of international law. It can be argued that the theorized 'internationalization' of contracts is motivated by the aim of minimizing the political risks associated with entering into contracts with a state.

This is clearer when examining doctrines of state contract in international law in the specific historical context in which they came about. Historically, if a state breached a contract with a national of a foreign country, diplomatic protection was often invoked. In short, (legal) diplomatic protection means that the state of the private investors takes on a claim for their nationals and against the state owing an obligation. This can be said to elevate the contract claim to the international law level.[26] Rules in international law decide the extent to which a state is able to take on a claim on behalf of domestic law subjects.[27] There are many examples of states assuming debt claims against other states on behalf of their citizens,[28] indicating that there is 'nothing inherent in the structure of international law and in the relationship between international law and municipal law that inhibits the sanctioning of contractual obligations by international

---

[23] ibid 156.
[24] Jennings (n 6) 157.
[25] Wautelet (n 18) 2.
[26] Accepted in several mixed claims commissions and in cases before the Permanent Court of Justice (PCJ). For example, both the *Brazilian Loans Case* (n 13) and *Serbian Loans Case* (n 10) dealt with the contractual fulfilment of sovereign loan agreements subject to national law, between a French bondholder and the Brazilian State and the Serbian State respectively. In the two cases, the PCJ determined its jurisdiction by accepting that the French state had the right to represent and protect its nationals before the court, even in civil law matters. See, in general, Michael Waibel, *Sovereign Defaults before International Courts and Tribunals* (Cambridge University Press 2011).
[27] Diplomatic protection still exists as a concept under international law. More recently, Barcelona Traction, Light and Power Company, Limited (*Belgium v Spain*) (New application 1964, Second phase) [1970] ICJ Rep 3 (hereafter *Barcelona Traction Case*) and Ahmadou Sadio Diallo (*Republic of Guinea v Democratic Republic of Congo*) (Preliminary objections) [2007] ICJ Rep 582 (hereafter *Diallo Case*), in particular, have contributed to clarifying the legal requirements for states to be able to take on a claim in the international sphere on behalf of domestic law subjects. The use of diplomatic protection in commercial cases has decreased.
[28] See, for example, *Preferential Treatment of Claims of Blockading Powers against Venezuela (Germany, Great Britain and Italy v Venezuela)*, PCA Case No 1903-01, Award (22 February 1904) (hereafter *Venezuelan Preferential Case*); *Serbian Loans Case* (n 10); *Brazilian Loans Case* (n 13).

law'.[29] However, whether or not a state chooses to take on a claim on behalf of its nationals who have contracted with a foreign state has varied a lot, both between governments of different states but also between governments of the same state.[30] Moreover, the question of whether or not a government should actually intervene in such disputes has often been less legal and more policy-driven.[31] Often, states were reluctant to take on debt claims on behalf of their nationals. At a time where modern international investment law based on treaty protection was not yet developed, a private creditor holding sovereign debt claims on foreign states was left without much legal protection. This may contribute to explaining 'why scholars attempted to build a legal framework protecting private contracting parties'.[32]

Today, attempts to create a legal doctrine with regard to state contracts have to a large extent been abandoned.[33] There are several factors that may explain this development.[34] First, documentation regarding state contracts is often confidential and hence only disclosed during disputes. Second, some tribunals followed the reasoning of the various internationalization doctrines, while many did not. As a result, it was difficult to see a coherent pattern with regards to whether and how international law regulates state contracts. Third, there are a wide variety of agreements concluded by the state with private individuals and corporations and it does not always make sense to compare one practice to another. Fourth, the demise of the doctrines may be related to theoretical flaws in the doctrines themselves: (i) the theories on state contracts only encompassed some of the contracts concluded by a state and a foreign company or individual, and it proved difficult to decide with precision which contracts should be subject to the special regime and why; (ii) the theory sometimes rested their case on objective factors, such as factors defining an international contract, while in other instances the theory looked to the intention of the parties when considering whether international law could regulate the contract; and (iii) some doctrines attempt to consider private companies and individuals as subjects of international law. Although it is generally accepted that private individuals and corporations can derive rights from international law, the idea that they are subjects of international law is generally disavowed.[35]

Finally, there is a fifth overarching reason that may explain why the attempts to create a doctrine on 'internationalizing' state contracts have faltered. In the last decades, an alternative legal framework has emerged which may be more fit for the protection of foreign investment and foreign creditors.[36] There has been a rapid growth both in bilateral and multilateral treaties protecting foreign investments and in the use of arbitration as a means of resolving disputes arising out of such investment contracts. The development of the investment regime seems to have decreased the need to elaborate a specific doctrine for contracts between private parties and the state in general.

---

[29] Jennings (n 6) 161.
[30] Borchard (n 6) 1.
[31] Jennings (n 6) 158.
[32] Wautelet (n 18) 4.
[33] ibid 6.
[34] ibid 2–3, 8.
[35] ibid 8.
[36] ibid 9.

It is still a subject of debate whether sovereign loan agreements—or more specifically sovereign bonds—are covered by the protection offered in international investment treaties. In a few cases, sovereign bonds have been involved in legal disputes in investment cases.[37] But, compared to ordinary investment contracts and concession agreements, sovereign debt contracts have typically been protected from unilateral changes by the sovereign state by other means. As previously mentioned, the vast majority of sovereign debt agreements are governed by the laws of a jurisdiction other than that of the debtor state.[38] Sovereign debt contracts have often been further insulated from the influence of the sovereign debtor by choosing a forum other than the courts and arbitral tribunals available within the debtor state.[39] For sovereign debt contracts, the governing law and forum chosen are normally the law and domestic courts of the jurisdiction of major financial centres.[40] It can be argued that as the law has developed and found alternative tools to protect those who contract with the state and so decrease political risk, the need for doctrines covering state contracts has lessened.

In sum, whether or not international law is applicable to a loan agreement between a private party and a sovereign debtor is primarily a result of the choices made by the parties to the contract and private international law. Choice of law rules may refer to common or general principles of law and thereby remove the contract from the law of any particular state (so reducing political risk), but this does not transform the contractual relationship into a public international law obligation, nor does it change the legal capacity of the contracting parties as such.[41] More generally, there seems to be widespread agreement with Crawford's view that a state contract cannot just be placed on the international plane as 'a state contract is not a treaty and cannot involve state responsibility as an international obligation'.[42] This is also the approach followed in this book. Consequently, Chapter 4 discusses intercreditor equity rights in domestic laws applicable to debt instruments governed by some domestic law. Subjects of international law, such as states and international organizations, can also hold debt instruments that are governed by domestic law. As a starting point, these international law creditors are subject to the same rules as private legal subjects. The extent to which these creditors are bound by ordinary domestic private law regulation varies across jurisdictions. Creditors holding debt instruments governed by domestic law may

---

[37] See for example *Poštová banka, a.s. and Istrokapital SE v Hellenic Republic*, ICSID Case No ARB/13/8, Award on Jurisdiction (9 April 2015) (hereafter *Postova Banka v Hellenic Republic*). See also Waibel (n 26). For further discussion on investment law protection, see Section 5.3.
[38] Ursula Kriebaum and August Reinisch, 'Property, Right to, International Protection' in Rüdiger Wolfrum (ed), *Max Planck Encyclopedia of Public International Law* (Oxford University Press 2019) para 11.
[39] In principle, this would be an arbitration tribunal or the court of a foreign jurisdiction. As long as absolute sovereign immunity closed national courts to sovereign creditors, arbitration rudimentarily filled the resulting gap in creditor protection. In the second half of the nineteenth century and prior to the Second World War, arbitration clauses in sovereign debt instruments were quite common. Once national courts started hearing sovereign debt cases, the need for such arbitration clauses declined. After the Second World War, this type of arbitration became extremely rare. Waibel (n 26) 157.
[40] Marboe and Reinisch (n 9) s C.3. See also 'Approach of the Book' section of the Introduction.
[41] ibid s C.1. It is not common to choose international law as the governing law of domestic law debt instruments, because international law rules are often more abstract and less fit to deal with general questions of commercial obligations and breaches of contract. IMF, 'Strengthening the Contractual Framework to Address Collective Action Problems in Sovereign Debt Restructuring' (Staff report, 9 February 2014) 6; Marboe and Reinisch (n 9) s C.3.
[42] Crawford (n 5) 631. See also Marboe and Reinisch (n 9) s D.2.

enjoy protection under international law through rights established by states.[43] These international law rules regulating the intercreditor equity rights of creditors holding domestic law governed debt are discussed in Chapter 5.

2.2.4 The local law advantage

In accordance with the two previous sections, contracts between a sovereign state and a private legal person are not contracts concluded by states in their capacity as subjects of public international law. These contracts are therefore governed by the domestic law of a state.[44] It is debated whether sovereign bonds and other sovereign debt contracts in capital markets regulated by the domestic law of the sovereign debtor country are public or private contracts. Whether a state contract is regulated by special public contract rules must be decided on the basis of the law governing the contract.[45] The characterization of the contractual relationship in debt instruments subject to the laws of a third country is less debated.[46] For debt issued in and under the laws of a major financial jurisdiction, it is settled that these generally constitute commercial relationships. With the rise of the sovereign bond as the most important source of loan capital for states, it is fair to assume that the majority of sovereign loans today are subject to domestic law. The rest of this section discusses only these types of state loans (not debt contracts subject to international law) with the assumption that they constitute transactions of a private nature and are therefore, in principle, subject to the rules governing commercial loans.[47]

Despite the commercial nature of these loans, contracts between a state and a private individual are distinct from ordinary contracts between private parties because one of the contracting parties has 'other rights and obligations with regards to its internal legal order than a private individual'.[48] In the context of sovereign lending, the most important feature is that under international law, a state is a sovereign which is free to adopt laws within its own jurisdiction. Some, ascribing a positive connotation to the practice, refer to the possibility of amending the local law and thereby altering the terms of a debt contract as the 'local law advantage'.[49] In other words, when a debt is regulated by the laws of the sovereign debtor, the debtor can change local law to facilitate debt restructuring, including terms concerning intercreditor equity. This is a risk that investors take when they buy local law debt instruments.[50] By selecting the

---

[43] Kriebaum and Reinisch (n 38) para 1.
[44] *Serbian Loans Case* (n 10) para 86.
[45] See Section 3.1 for a discussion on the applicable law and public versus private law state contracts.
[46] One of the reasons is that if a state contract is subject to the laws of a foreign jurisdiction, it is, as will be shown in the following section, unable to change the terms and conditions of the loan agreement by adopting laws and regulations. The fact that a significant amount of sovereign debt is regulated by the laws of the big financial centres confirms the view that sovereign loan agreements—at least those issued under foreign law—should be perceived as commercial instruments. See further discussion in Section 3.1.
[47] See, in general, Marboe and Reinisch (n 9)s A.3 and C.3.27. See also discussion in Section 1.3 of this book.
[48] ibid s A.3.
[49] Manuelides (n 1); Lee C Buchheit and others, 'How to Restructure Sovereign Debt: Lessons from Four Decades' (PIIE Working Paper, 5 June 2019) 20; Gulati and Buchheit (n 1).
[50] Buchheit and others (n 49) 20; Gulati and Buchheit (n 1).

law of a foreign country to govern a debt instrument, a sovereign debtor is normally prohibited from amending that contract through legislation. The legal argument underlying this view is not controversial. FA Mann has written:

> If one asks in what circumstances an international wrong committed by a foreign State may involve a breach of contract made by the same State with an alien, the field, properly analysed, is very limited, for the question makes sense only where three conditions coincide.
>
> In the first place the contract must be governed by the law of the State which is a party to the contract and has committed the wrong. If the contract is governed by any other legal system, the breach is most unlikely to be in any sense legally relevant. Thus a contract of concession granted, but wrongfully repudiated or modified, by a given State in law necessarily continues to exist unaffected if it is governed by the law of another State or by international law (assuming the latter alternative to be possible). Discharge or variation of a contract is subject to its proper law. This will not recognize interference by another legal system except as a fact creating impossibility of performance. Even so, it is hard to imagine any legal system which would allow a party to a contract to rely on self-induced impossibility to get rid of its legal obligations or to bring a contract to an end against the will of the other party to it.[51]

Emerging market bonds targeted at foreign investors have typically been issued under, and governed by, foreign law.[52] Euro area governments have generally been able to issue sovereign instruments under their own laws.[53] This also seems to be the case for other developed economies. One explanation for this is that investors trust the government not to exploit the possibility to unilaterally amend the loan terms.[54]

The use of the local law advantage played an important role in the 2012 Greek restructuring. In Greece, the local law advantage was not directly used to change the payment terms of the bonds that were about to be restructured, but it retroactively implemented a majority voting mechanism equivalent to a so-called collective action clause (CAC),[55] which made it easier to implement a successful restructuring and avoid potential holdout creditors.[56] In principle, the same procedure could be used in other Euro area countries and in debtor countries whose debts are governed by local law, to implement an advantageous debt restructuring plan, including deciding issues of intercreditor equity.

---

[51] Frederick A Mann, *Further Studies in International Law* (Oxford University Press 1990) 188–89.
[52] Branimir Gruić and Philip Wooldridge, 'Enhancements to the BIS Debt Securities Statistics' [2012] BIS Quarterly Review 63, 64–65. See also Gulati and Buchheit (n 1) 173.
[53] Marcos Chamon and others, 'Foreign-Law Bonds: Can They Reduce Sovereign Borrowing Costs?' (ECB Working Paper Series, June 2018).
[54] At the same time, some argue that the explanation may be related to the currency of the debt. Euro area sovereign debt is foreign currency denominated, in the sense that the issuing country has no unilateral control over their own state's monetary policy. If a debt is issued in domestic currency, it is easier to expropriate foreign creditors through means such as devaluation, inflation, or capital control. See Gulati and Buchheit (n 1).
[55] For further discussions on CACs and retroactive implementation of CACs, see Section 4.3.
[56] This is further discussed in Section 4.3 in relation to *Mamatas and Others v Greece*, App nos 63066/14, 64297/14, and 66106/14, 21 July 2016 (ECtHR). See also Gulati and Buchheit (n 1).

The state is not, however, completely free to make use of this local law advantage. Several elements influence and limit the extent to which a state may unilaterally make changes to the terms of the debt instrument and affect established rights concerning intercreditor equity. The success of a unilateral restructuring based on amendment of local law relies on the implementation being in accordance with the debtor state's constitution and applicable international agreements signed by the debtor state. In particular, constitutional protection as well as human rights and investment law treaties concerning the protection of property rights are relevant, such as the Charter of Fundamental Rights of the European Union (CFR) or the European Convention on Human Rights (ECHR). It cannot automatically be assumed that all constitutions are as flexible as the Greek Constitution, which allowed legislation to retroactively interfere with private property rights (in the bonds).[57]

An assessment of whether a restructuring based on unilateral amendment of the local law is in line with the constitution and international human rights obligations concerning the protection of property is likely to be stricter if the debt instrument is subject to a majority voting procedure. This can be implemented either by legislation[58] or as a contract clause in the sovereign bonds (eg CACs). Moreover, the stronger the restructuring incentive created by the tool (eg CACs), the more difficult it is to convince a court that retroactive legislation interfering with property rights is justified. This is particularly so when rules contain proportionality requirements. In the *Mamatas* case, the European Court of Human Rights (ECtHR) accepted retroactive legislation implementing a majority voting procedure, concluding that the interference with creditors' property rights was proportionate.[59] To justify this, the court referred to the fact that CACs were a widely used tool in the market[60] and had already been made mandatory in bonds issued by Euro area governments.[61]

2.3 The Jurisdiction of Courts in Private International Law

2.3.1 Introduction

Under what circumstances will foreign courts accept jurisdiction over a dispute related to a debt restructuring of a foreign sovereign debtor? Private international law rules on the jurisdiction of courts decide whether courts from jurisdictions other than those of the sovereign debtor can assume jurisdiction in cases related to sovereign debt restructuring. If foreign courts are barred from assuming jurisdiction, creditors are left with the option of enforcing their contractual rights in the courts of the

---

[57] Gulati and Buchheit (n 61) 5. A discussion on constitutional protection across jurisdictions is potentially very time consuming and is outside the scope of this book. For constitutional requirements concerning retrofit restructuring in the United States, see Melissa A Boudreau, 'Restructuring Sovereign Debt under Local Law: Are Retrofit Collective Action Clauses Expropriatory' (2011) 2 Harvard Business Law Review Online 164.
[58] Such as in the Euro area.
[59] See Section 4.4 for further discussion of the case.
[60] See discussion in Section 4.3.
[61] See discussion in Section 4.3.

sovereign debtor or in no court at all. The underlying assumption in this section is that local courts are more likely to defer to a sovereign debtor in cases of unilateral modification of creditors' rights under a debt contract.

The original approach to the question of court jurisdiction in sovereign debt cases was that any '[c]ourt other than those of the debtor state are likely to consider themselves incompetent; and suits in the courts of the debtor are not likely to be fruitful'.[62] This view is clearly outdated, as has been demonstrated by the many domestic law cases concerning sovereign debt disputes discussed in this book. Nevertheless, a foreign court does not necessarily have jurisdiction over all types of sovereign debt disputes. Whether a specific court has jurisdiction over a specific sovereign debt dispute has to be decided in accordance with the laws of the forum of the court seized. As will be seen in this section, party autonomy is recognized in most key commercial jurisdictions. This implies that jurisdiction clauses (choice of court clauses) are typically decisive for whether a court accepts jurisdiction in a case. Further, there is normally some additional requirement that there be a certain connection between the contract and the chosen forum for courts to accept jurisdiction (nexus requirement).

In the EU, Regulation (EC) No 1215/2012 (hereafter Recast Brussels Regulation) governs the question.[63] The various EU countries may have a coexisting jurisdictional regime in addition to the Recast Brussels Regulation. Section 2.3.2 starts by discussing the Recast Brussels Regulation. Sections 2.3.3 and 2.4.4 discuss US and English rules, respectively. The aim is to consider whether the different rules on a procedural basis preclude foreign courts from assessing the lawfulness of acts of debtor states related to a restructuring.

2.3.2 Recast Brussels Regulation—the jurisdiction of courts in the EU

2.3.2.1 Jurisdiction in commercial matters

The Recast Brussels Regulation regulates questions of jurisdiction in the EU in commercial cases.[64] The Regulation takes precedence over domestic rules on jurisdiction, which only apply in areas not covered by EU law (residual jurisdiction). As will be seen in the following discussion, if a sovereign debt related dispute is considered a commercial matter, the EU regulation provides, subject to certain requirements, that foreign courts can assume jurisdiction over the dispute. If the subject matter of the claim falls outside the scope of the Regulation, domestic rules apply.

---

[62] Borchard (n 9) 37.
[63] Regulation (EU) No 1215/2012 of the European Parliament and of the Council of 12 December 2012 on jurisdiction and the recognition and enforcement of judgments in civil and commercial matters [2012] OJ L 341 (European Union) (hereafter Brussels I Recast). The Recast Brussels Regulation regulates jurisdiction and the recognition and enforcement of judgments between EU Member States. It applies to legal proceedings instituted on or after 10 January 2015 and judgments given in proceedings instituted on or after 10 January 2015. The Recast Brussels Regulation repeals Council Regulation (EC) No 44/2001 of 22 December 2000 on jurisdiction and the recognition and enforcement of judgments in civil and commercial matters [2001] OJ L12/1 (European Union) (heareafter Brussels I Regulation).
[64] Recast Brussels Regulation (n 63).

According to Article 5 of the Recast Brussels Regulation, the Brussels regime applies if the defendant is domiciled in an EU Member State. If not, Article 6 provides that the national laws of the jurisdiction of the seized court apply, subject to Articles 18(1) (consumer contracts), 21(2) (employment contracts), 24 (exclusive jurisdiction), and 25 (jurisdiction agreements). There seems to be agreement that the Recast Brussels Regulation's reference to the domicile of the 'defendant' also includes EU Member States, or an EU subnational authority or central bank.[65] A sovereign debtor that is an EU Member State therefore falls under the scope of the Recast Brussels Regulation. If a defendant debtor state is not a Member State of the EU, the jurisdiction must be decided in accordance with national law. However, according to Article 6, the Recast Brussels Regulation is applicable if the sovereign debt instrument contains an agreement on the choice of court in favour of a court of an EU Member State.

As briefly mentioned above, the Recast Brussels Regulation may apply, according to Article 1(1), to actions against states but only to 'civil and commercial matters'. 'Civil and commercial matters' is an autonomous concept under the Regulation. Whether a dispute related to sovereign debt is of such a character must be determined according to the objective of the Regulation itself and based on the general principles that stem from the corpus of the national legal systems.[66]

According to the case law of the Court of Justice of the European Union (CJEU), contracts entered into by a state in the exercise of their governmental powers—an *acta iure imperii*—fall outside the scope of the Regulation. It can be challenging to establish which state acts fall outside the scope of the regulation and which fall within as commercial acts (*acta iure gestionis*).

The issuance of bonds or other contracting of debt in capital markets is generally categorized as *acta iure gestionis* under the Recast Brussels Regulation.[67] It is more challenging to categorize subsequent state action which interferes with the rights established under the initial commercial activity, such as a sovereign debt restructuring. The rest of Section 2.3.2 will discuss the case law stemming from the 2012 Greek restructuring dealing with this exact topic: whether a restructuring is an *acta iure imperii* and therefore precluded from being assessed by foreign courts under the Recast Brussels Regulation. The most important feature of the restructuring in the context of the discussion in this section is that it was enabled by the adoption of the Greek Bondholder Act, which retroactively implemented a majority voting procedure in all debt instruments governed by Greek law. Greece was then able to implement a debt restructuring with the support of a majority of bondholders and at the same time bind holdout creditors.[68]

Before looking into the issue of the categorization of state acts in the lead up to a restructuring, it must be noted that, if it is established that the Recast Brussels Regulation is applicable, there are several grounds of jurisdiction that can be invoked in the

---

[65] *Lechouritou v Germany* [2007] ECLI:EU:C:2007:102. The case concerns an action against Germany where the Court of Justice assumed that the Brussels I Regulation (n 63) was applicable. See also Kupelyants (n 2) 63.

[66] Kupelyants (n 2) 64.

[67] See, for example, *Stefan Fahnenbrock and Others v Hellenische Republik* [2015] ECLI:EU:C:2015:383 (hereafter *Fahnenbrock*).

[68] The Greek restructuring is further discussed in Section 4.3.

context of a dispute arising in the context of a sovereign debt contract. According to Article 25 of the Recast Brussels Regulation, Member State courts can accept jurisdiction based on an agreement on choice of forum between the parties to a contract regardless of their domicile. This is a common basis for jurisdiction in sovereign debt related disputes. Article 25(1) provides that the substantive validity of such a jurisdiction agreement is governed by the law of the Member State of the seized court. In the absence of choice of forum agreements, creditors can seek to establish special jurisdiction under Article 7 of the Recast Brussels Regulation. Of relevance to a dispute concerning sovereign debt, the Article provides that a sovereign debtor who is a Member State may be sued in another Member State 'in matters relating to a contract, in the courts for the place of performance of the obligation in question' (Article 7(1) (a)). Alternatively, in matters relating to tort, delict or quasi-delict, a sovereign debtor can be sued in the courts for the place where the harmful event occurred or may occur. The applicable forum in a sovereign debt dispute will depend on the facts of the underlying case.[69]

2.3.2.2 Categorization of the restructuring act—*acta iure imperii* vs *acta iure gestionis*

The question of categorization—whether disputes arising from state acts related to sovereign debt restructuring should be considered as 'civil and commercial matters' or as *acta iure imperii* and therefore precluded from being assessed by foreign courts under the Recast Brussels Regulation—arose in several cases stemming from the 2012 Greek restructuring.

Kuhn v Hellenische Republik (hereafter *Kuhn*) is a 2018 case from the CJEU, which concerns a request for a preliminary ruling on the interpretation of Article (1)(a) of the Recast Brussels Regulation.[70] The underlying case concerned proceedings between the Greek Republic and Mr Leo Kuhn in Austrian courts, in the aftermath of the 2012 Greek restructuring. Mr Kuhn claimed fulfilment of the original borrowing terms of bonds issued by Greece or compensation for the non-fulfilment of those terms as a result of the restructuring. The factual situation was that prior to 2011, Mr Kuhn, residing in Austria, had acquired Greek sovereign bonds through a custodian bank established in Austria. The bonds were subject to Greek law and traded on the Athens stock exchange as 'uncertificated' securities (book-entry securities). The question posed by the Austrian courts to the CJEU was whether Austrian courts had jurisdiction in this case. The relevant Article (7)(1)(a) provides that a 'person' may be sued in the courts of another Member State if that is 'the place of performance of the obligation in question'. The question was whether the interpretation of this provision is determined by the borrowing terms established at the time that the bonds were issued or by the place of effective fulfilment of those terms, such as the payment of interest (Austria).[71]

---

[69] For a more thorough discussion of the possibility of establishing special jurisdiction in cases related to sovereign debt, see Kupelyants (n 2) 68–72.
[70] *Leo Kuhn v Hellenische Republik* [2018] ECLI:EU:C:2018:911 (hereafter *Kuhn*).
[71] The securities were registered in the Greek Central Bank's securities settlement system. Mr Kuhn's sovereign bonds, which matured on 20 February 2020, conferred entitlement to repayment of the capital on maturity and to the payment of interest. The payment was to be made to Mr Kuhn's account in the custodian bank. (ibid [15]–[16]).

Before answering this question, the CJEU would have to consider whether the Recast Brussels Regulation was applicable. The court concluded that the situation in the main proceedings did not fall within the meaning of 'civil and commercial matters' under Article 1(1) of the Recast Brussels Regulation, insofar as the dispute concerned the sovereign right of a Member State to legislate in order to restructure its public debt.[72] The court only identified the legislation—the Greek Bondholder Act—as the relevant act, when considering whether the Recast Brussels Regulation was applicable. They did not deem it relevant that the initial issuance of bonds was commercial.

This conclusion may seem to contradict a previous judgment of the same court in *Fahnenbrock v Hellenic Republic* (hereafter *Fahnenbrock*) from 2015. The case concerned German bondholders' claim for compensation for interference with property rights and breach of contractual obligations in the aftermath of the 2012 Greek restructuring.[73] In *Fahnenbrock*, the German Regional Court (Landesgeriecht Kiel) requested that the CJEU settle the interpretation of Article 1(1) of Regulation (EC) No 1393/2007 concerning the transmission of documents between authorities in EU Member States in judicial and extrajudicial matters (Service Regulation).[74] More specifically, the referring court asked whether the concept of 'civil or commercial matters' within that provision covered judicial proceedings for compensation for disturbance of ownership and property rights, contractual performance and damages, such as those at issue in the main proceedings, brought by private persons who are holders of state bonds against the issuing state.[75] In its judgment, the CJEU first described Greece's issuance of sovereign bonds as having the characteristics of a commercial activity.[76] It continued by stating that the restructuring was enabled by the retroactive implementation of the CACs by law (the Greek Bondholder Act). The court stated that this Act

---

[72] ibid [43] of the judgment states that 'Article 1(1) of Regulation No 1215/2012 is to be interpreted as meaning that a dispute, such as that at issue in the main proceedings, relating to an action brought by a natural person having acquired bonds issued by a Member State, against that State and seeking to contest the exchange of those bonds with bonds of a lower value, imposed on that natural person by the effect of a law adopted in exceptional circumstances by the national legislator, according to which those terms were unilaterally and retroactively amended by the introduction of a CAC allowing a majority of holders of the relevant bonds to impose that exchange on the minority, does not fall within 'civil and commercial matters' within the meaning of that article.'

[73] *Fahnenbrock* (n 67).

[74] Regulation (EC) No 1393/2007 of the European Parliament and of the Council of 13 November 2007 on the service in the Member States of judicial and extrajudicial documents in civil or commercial matters (service of documents), and repealing Council Regulation (EC) No 1348/2000 [2007] OJ L324/79 (European Union) (hereafter Service Regulation).

[75] ibid Art 1(1) states that '[t]his Regulation shall apply in civil and commercial matters where a judicial or extrajudicial document has to be transmitted from one Member State to another for service there. It shall not extend in particular to revenue, customs or administrative matters or to liability of the State for actions or omissions in the exercise of State authority (*acta iure imperii*)'. The CJEU insisted that 'civil and commercial matters' within the meaning of Art 1(1) of the Service Regulation should be regarded as an independent concept and interpreted by referring, in particular, to the objectives and scheme of that Regulation. See *Fahnenbrock* (n 67) [39].

[76] Among other things, the CJEU stated that 'the issue of bonds does not necessarily presuppose the exercise of powers falling outside the scope of the ordinary legal rules applicable to relationships between individuals'. (*Fahnenbrock* (n 67) [53]).

falls within the framework of the management of public finances and, more specifically, the restructuring of the public debt, in order to deal with a severe financial crisis, and it is for those purposes that it introduced the possibility of exchanging the securities in the contracts concerned.[77]

However, the fact that the possibility to restructure was introduced by a law was not in itself decisive—according to the CJEU—in order to conclude that the state acted in the exercise of state authority. Rather, the court concluded that it was not clear that the legislation directly led to the restructuring, which interfered with the claimant's property (contractual right).[78] Consequently, it was not evident that the facts of the underlying case fell outside what might be characterized as 'civil and commercial'.

In the *Kuhn* case, on the other hand, the court was not open to the possibility that Greece could have acted as a private or commercial actor when implementing the debt restructuring based on the CACs. It indirectly suggested that the legislative act had caused the debt restructuring and that the act which gave rise to the dispute was the restructuring itself.

When comparing the *Kuhn* and *Fahnenbroch* cases, it must be noted that the interpretation of 'civil and commercial matters' under Article 1(1) of the Service Regulation is a concept independent from the Recast Brussels Regulation. In the *Kuhn* case, the CJEU underlined that the conclusion in *Fahnenbroch* was corroborated by a specific objective related to the scheme of the Service Regulation. A particularly important factor, which may explain the different reasoning and interpretation of the concept of 'civil and commercial' in the two regulations, is the fact that the Service Regulation only serves as a preliminary step in summoning a defendant before the court of an EU Member State.[79] The conclusion is that the approach taken in the *Kuhn* case—that the legislative act was the relevant act enabling the restructuring—does not contradict the *Fahnenbroch* case and should be applied when assessing courts' jurisdiction under the Recast Brussels Regulation.

2.3.3 US law

In the United States, questions of jurisdiction are closely related to and intertwined with questions of sovereign immunity, which are more thoroughly discussed in Section 2.4. What should be mentioned here is that the grounds for providing exceptions to sovereign immunity are the same as those providing courts with jurisdiction. It follows from §1604 of the Foreign Sovereign Immunities Act of 1976 (hereafter FSIA) that a sovereign state enjoys immunity, in respect of itself and its property, from the jurisdiction of the courts of another state. Under FSIA, a court may accept jurisdiction in a case concerning a foreign state if the dispute falls under one of the exceptions

---

[77] ibid [55].
[78] By stating that the implementation of the Greek Bondholder Act did not necessarily lead to the restructuring, the CJEU points to the fact that a restructuring is an option also available to private legal persons. It was the bondholder vote (under the CAC that was implemented by the Act) which interfered with the property/contractual rights of certain bondholders and not the Greek Bondholder Act itself.
[79] See also Kupelyants (n 2) 65.

to sovereign immunity. In short, according to §1605 FSIA, exceptions to sovereign immunity from jurisdiction can be based on state consent. US courts accept jurisdiction if the foreign state has conferred jurisdiction upon a US court in an agreement. According to §1605(a)(1) FSIA, such an agreement counts as a waiver of immunity. Together with the choice of US governing law, choice of court or forum agreements in favour of US courts are common in sovereign debt instruments. The FSIA also accepts jurisdiction over foreign states when the action concerns different commercial activities carried out by the foreign state (§1605(a)(2)). It is clear that the issuance of sovereign bonds and other contracting of debt in the market fall under the commerciality exception in FSIA.[80]

Section 1605(a)(2) FSIA also requires that the commercial activity has a specific nexus with the United States. More specifically, the FSIA provides jurisdiction if the action is based upon:

- a commercial activity carried on *in* the United States by the foreign state,
- an act performed *in* the United States in connection with a commercial activity of the foreign state elsewhere, or
- an act *outside* the territory of the United States in connection with a commercial activity of the foreign state elsewhere and which has a direct effect in the United States.

Despite the nexus requirement, sovereign debt does not have to be issued and sold in the United States to fall within the commercial exception from immunity. In *Argentina v Weltover*, the Supreme Court held that the residence of bondholder is not relevant and that the first alternative is applicable if the designated place of payment is in the United States.[81] US courts have also found that securities issued in a foreign jurisdiction but held by US parties may be exempted from immunity. For example, non-payment to US residents constituted a 'sufficient connection' even when the place of payment was not in the United States.[82]

In the United States, an interference with a debt contract for the sake of crisis management does not seem to affect the question of jurisdiction. As will be further discussed in Section 2.4 on immunity, in *Argentina v Weltover* the Supreme Court held that that the issuance of bonds was a 'commercial activity' under the FSIA, and the rescheduling of the maturity dates on those instruments was taken 'in connection with' that activity within the meaning of §1605(a)(2). Consequently, a court would generally not be barred from assuming jurisdiction in cases concerning restructurings.

Under certain circumstances, a sovereign debt restructuring can constitute an expropriation. §1605(a)(3) FSIA provides an exception from immunity and therefore allow courts to assume jurisdiction in certain cases concerning expropriation. This

---

[80] See, for example, *Republic of Argentina v Weltover, Inc* 504 US 607 (1992). See, in general, Kupelyants (n 2) 76–78, discussing the jurisdiction of US courts under the FSIA in sovereign debt related disputes.

[81] *Argentina v Weltover* (n 80) 619.

[82] See *Atlantica Holdings v Sovereign Wealth Fund* 813 F 3d 98 (2d Cir 2016); *Callejo v Bancomer, SA* 764 F 2d 1101 (5th Cir 1985).

exception covers rights in property taken in violation of international law, if that property or any property exchanged for such property is (i) present in the United States in connection with a commercial activity carried on in the United States by the foreign state, or (ii) is owned or operated by an agency or instrumentality of the foreign state and that agency or instrumentality is engaged in a commercial activity in the United States. It should be mentioned that the creditor may need to exhaust local remedies in the courts of the sovereign debtors before it commences proceedings before US courts under this provision. Moreover, the Supreme Court has made it clear that this expropriation exception is applicable when the facts 'do show (and not just arguably show) a taking of property in violation of international law'.[83] A failure to pay does not amount to expropriation. In accordance with international law,[84] US case law requires that the state 'nullified or otherwise prevented collection of a valid judgment, effectively confiscating the right to payment'.[85] The expropriation may not, however, apply to the sovereign debtor's own nationals.[86]

2.3.4 English law

The Civil Procedure Rules (CPR) set out the various grounds of jurisdiction of English courts. It is clear that sovereign bonds and other sovereign debt instruments traded on the market fall within the term 'contract' in the CPR.[87] In short, an English court may accept jurisdiction over disputes relating to the sovereign debts of another state on the following grounds:

- Claims made in respect of a breach of (a sovereign debt) contract committed within the jurisdiction (CPR PD6B 3.1(7));
- The (sovereign debt) contract is connected with England ('serviced out of the jurisdiction') in any of the following ways (CPR PD6B 3.1(6)):
  - the contract was made within the jurisdiction;
  - the contract was made by or through an agent trading or residing within the jurisdiction;
  - the contract is governed by English law.

Because England is an important financial centre, the place of missed payments under debt instruments governed by domestic law will often be England. In addition, sovereign debt instruments may have been made and issued in England. Moreover, if a debt instrument contains a choice of English law but makes no mention of a choice of

---

[83] *Bolivarian Republic v Helmerich & Payne* 137 S Ct 1312, pt IV (2017).
[84] See discussion in Section 4.2.
[85] *Si Group Consort Ltd v Ukraine* No 15 CV 3047-LTS 1 (SDNY 30 January 2017).
[86] *De Sanchez v Banco Central de Nicaragua* 770 F 2d 1385 (5th Cir 1985). For questions of standing and whether buyers of bonds on the secondary market have a contractual relationship with the issuer that forms a basis for an action, see Kupelyants (n 2) 78ff.
[87] The Annex to the European Convention on State Immunity of 1972, that England is still bound by, lists unacceptable grounds for accepting jurisdiction.

forum, an English governing law clause will be a grounds for jurisdiction as it qualifies as a service out of the jurisdiction (CPR PD6B).[88]

Similar to the United States, UK courts do not seem to put any emphasis on state acts later interfering with or repudiating an initial commercial contract falling under the scope of the CPR, even where the state intervention is done for public purposes such as crisis management. Courts do not seem to investigate whether a later interference is of a governmental nature and deem this as a reason for the court not to assume jurisdiction.[89]

2.3.5 Preliminary conclusion

Both in English and US law, courts will easily assume jurisdiction over a dispute arising from a sovereign debt contract that has a certain connection to the jurisdiction. Two common bases for assuming jurisdiction in sovereign debt cases are choice of law and choice of forum clauses, but these are not necessarily the only grounds for jurisdiction. In the United States, the fact that a later state activity interferes with a debt contract to obtain a stated public purpose (such as a restructuring in times of economic crisis) does not seem to affect the question of courts' jurisdiction. The same is true of English law. The initial activity of issuing bonds is the decisive act when considering jurisdiction, even where connected activities such as debt restructurings are involved.

The situation under the Recast Brussels Regulation and the assessment of what constitutes civil and commercial matters is more complex. In general, it can be argued that, in the context of the Recast Brussels Regulation, whether legal proceedings concerning sovereign acts related to a sovereign debt restructuring should be treated as a civil and commercial matter depends on the way a claim is advanced.[90] First, in many cases, debt instruments are explicitly governed by foreign law, which protects the contract from legislative changes made by the sovereign debtor. In such situations, a creditor does not have to challenge the legislation because these laws are irrelevant and inapplicable to contractual intercreditor equity rights. The creditor's claim will be treated as a contractual claim and the inapplicable governmental acts of the sovereign debtor (such as legislation) will only be regarded as factual background to the dispute.[91] Second, a sovereign debtor can try to alter the terms of a debt instrument unilaterally. This will most typically occur in situations where the contract is subject to domestic law, but theoretically it may also possible where the contract is governed by foreign law. In such a situation, creditors may need to challenge the governmental acts directly. The matter at hand may then (be categorized as *acta iure imperii* and consequently) fall outside the ambit of the Recast Brussels Regulation. The Regulation does not oblige foreign courts to accept jurisdiction and assess the dispute. Rather, in such situations, potential jurisdiction will have to be established based on national law.

---

[88] For a more thorough treatment of potential grounds for assuming jurisdiction, see Kupelyants (n 2) 72ff.
[89] See, for example, *Trendtex Trading Corporation v Central Bank of Nigeria* [1977] QB 529 (EWCA Civ).
[90] Kupelyants (n 2) 65.
[91] ibid.

On the basis of the foregoing, it can be argued that courts in EU Member States, in the United States, and in England all accept jurisdiction for disputes arising from a sovereign debt instrument that explicitly states it will be governed by the laws of one of these jurisdictions. Nevertheless, creditors who have been subject to a coercive restructuring have lower chances of litigating a claim arising from a debt contract in foreign courts under the Recast Brussels Regulation than under English or US law.

2.4 Sovereign Immunity

2.4.1 Introduction

Sovereign immunity is a key principle in national and public international law.[92] The rules constitute a procedural bar as to whether national courts of one state may exercise jurisdiction over another state and attach its assets.

The main question in this section is to what extent sovereign debtors enjoy immunity so that foreign courts cannot accept disputes arising from the issuance of sovereign bonds or subsequent restructurings. If a sovereign debtor is immune, creditors are left with fewer options to pursue their potential intercreditor equity claims. As in the previous section, this view rests on the assumption that national courts are more likely to be supportive of their own government's attempt to implement crisis resolution measures which interfere with creditors' rights than foreign courts.

Section 2.4.2 presents the concept of state immunity and the doctrine of restrictive immunity, which provides an exception from immunity for states engaging in certain commercial activity. Section 2.4.3 presents the relevant sources of law, before Section 2.4.4 discusses sovereign immunity exceptions in relation to sovereign debt restructurings in the United States, England, Germany, and Italy—jurisdictions where the relevant questions have arisen in more recent court cases.

2.4.2 The concept of sovereign immunity

In short, there are two categories of sovereign immunity protection for states in foreign jurisdictions: first, immunity from jurisdiction (or adjudication) and, second, immunity from enforcement measures (also referred to as immunity from execution). Immunity from jurisdiction limits the adjudicatory power of national courts and immunity from execution restricts the enforcement powers of national courts (and other state organs). In other words, the concept of state immunity covers both the state as such and its property.[93]

The immunity which one sovereign grants another in its own courts has traditionally been justified under the principle of state sovereignty. According to the principle

---

[92] For a discussion of the rules on sovereign immunity, see, in general, Hazel Fox and Philippa Webb, *The Law of State Immunity* (Oxford International Law Library, 3rd edn, Oxford University Press 2015).

[93] August Reinisch, 'European Court Practice Concerning State Immunity from Enforcement Measures' (2006) 17 European Journal of International Law 803, 803.

of sovereignty in international law, no state is to be subject to the will of another state. This is connected to the principle of equality, under which all states are considered to enjoy the same rank.[94] Sovereign immunity can be seen as a manifestation of these two principles and they may explain why it is deemed inappropriate for a sovereign state to be sued in the national courts of another sovereign state. A more functional explanation of sovereign immunity is that states are equal subjects of governance with exclusive power over a defined territory and the courts of one state should not be able to test the validity or legitimacy of another state's exercise of authority within its own territory.[95] Some legal scholars have also noted that state immunity in practice was probably based on 'the expedient of gaining reciprocity and because judicial actions caused diplomatic antagonism'.[96] While these justifications mainly concern immunity from jurisdiction, immunity from execution provisions are said to stem more directly from concerns about the disruption and political ramifications that can result from the seizure of a foreign state's property.[97]

The international rules on sovereign immunity have significant evolved from a doctrine of absolute immunity to a doctrine of relative or restrictive immunity. Before the twentieth century, most countries in the world had absolute immunity from the jurisdiction of foreign states. It was simply prohibited for private citizens to bring claims against foreign sovereigns in domestic courts. Consequently, enforcement measures were irrelevant.[98]

As the state has become more involved in commercial activities, the doctrine of sovereign immunity has—though to varying degrees—become more restrictive, meaning that it has become more difficult for states to invoke immunity as a protection. Today, most commercially significant jurisdictions subscribe to the 'restrictive' theory of sovereign immunity. The argument for a more restrictive approach is that absolute immunity is perceived to be unjust with regard to private contractors; when a 'sovereign descends to the market place, they must accept the sanctions of the market place'.[99] The essence of the restrictive doctrine is that states may only invoke immunity where the act concerned is governmental in nature (*acta iure imperii*) rather than commercial (*acta iure gestionis*).

---

[94] In Jurisdictional Immunities of the State (*Germany v Italy: Greece Intervening*) (Judgment) [2012] ICJ Rep 99 (hereafter *Jurisdictional Immunities*), the ICJ addressed the subject of sovereign immunity (and the legal basis for such immunity) for the first time. It stated that '[t]he Court considers that the rule of State immunity occupies an important place in international law and international relations. It derives from the principle of sovereign equality of States, which, as Art. 2, paragraph 1, of the Charter of the United Nations makes clear, is one of the fundamental principles of the international legal order' (*Jurisdictional Immunities*, para 57).

[95] Ivar Alvik, 'Statsimmunitet etter norsk rett og folkeretten' in Ole Kristian Fauchald and others (eds), *Festskrift til Carl August Fleischer, dog fred er ej det bedste* (Universitetsforlaget 2006) 16.

[96] Philip R Wood, *Conflict of Laws and International Finance*, vol 6 (The Law and Practice of International Finance Series, 1st edn, Sweet & Maxwell 2007) 557.

[97] Jonathan I Blackman and Rahul Mukhi, 'The Evolution of Modern Sovereign Debt Litigation: Vultures, Alter Egos, and Other Legal Fauna' (2010) 73 Law and Contemporary Problems 47, 48.

[98] Wood (n 96) 557.

[99] ibid 557, 560–70; Fox and Webb (n 92) 399ff. See, for example, Lord Denning's formulation in *Trendtex Trading Corporation v Central Bank of Nigeria* (n 89) [132]: 'If a government department goes into the market place of the world and buys boots or cement—as a commercial transaction—that government department should be subject to all the rules of the market place'. The principle of restrictive immunity is codified in national law in some jurisdictions, such as the FSIA in the United States.

Although the objective behind the immunity rules remains the same, jurisdictions distinguish between governmental and commercial acts in different ways.[100] A common approach is to consider an act commercial if the 'nature' of the activity is commercial, irrespective of whether the act may have a public 'purpose'.[101] As will be clear from the following sections, despite increasing agreement on the fact that international law today provides for a doctrine of restrictive immunity, it is still difficult to establish a clear consensus as to which state acts should be categorized as *iure imperii* on the one hand and which should be categorized as *iure gestionis* on the other.[102]

In addition to the commercial exception to immunity, a state can also waive its immunity voluntarily. This approach is consistent with the doctrine of absolute immunity and in some states, this is still the only way of obtaining an exception from immunity. Waivers of adjudication are, in some form or another, commonly found in sovereign debt instruments.[103]

In some jurisdictions, the courts accept various forms of implied waivers, as well as express waivers. Indeed, more bold acceptance of implied waivers has been seen in areas where states voluntarily undertake business of similar nature to that undertaken by private persons. What it takes for a court to accept a waiver from immunity differs across jurisdictions. Fox and Webb have identified three general legal techniques for obtaining such an implied waiver: (i) the state is deemed to consent to the local jurisdiction by engaging in a transaction on this basis; (ii) the state engages in commercial conduct clearly distinguishable its more usual state activity for a public benefit; and (iii) the state engages in such activities with and in the manner of a private person. The private law nature of the transaction engaged in provides additional evidence that the state voluntarily intended to subject itself to the foreign court.[104]

The rules and practices in different jurisdictions also vary when it comes to sovereign immunity from execution (enforcement measures). In general, the doctrine on sovereign immunity from execution tends to be more restrictive than the rules on sovereign immunity from jurisdiction. It is more difficult to establish whether something constitutes a 'commercial activity' (which would not be immune) in relation to the execution of a judgment over certain property, than in relation to establishing

---

[100] The Continental European view is different from that of England due to historical developments. See Fox and Webb (n 92) 402.

[101] By the 1960s, German courts had adopted the nature of the acts test: BVerfGE 16, 27 (1963) (hereafter *Empire of Iran* case). The US FSIA §1603(d) expressly provides that 'the commercial character of an activity shall be determined by reference to the nature of the course of conduct of particular transaction, or act, rather than by reference to its purpose'. This is also evident in the ruling in *Republic of Argentina v Weltover, Inc* 504 US 607 (1992). The UK State Immunities Act (SIA) avoids any express reference to the purpose or nature of the transaction, but it follows from case law that the nature test is decisive. See, for example, *Owners of Cargo Lately Laden on Board The Marble Islands v Owners of The I Congreso del Partido* [1983] 1 AC 244. See, in general, Fox and Webb (n 92) 411–12; Wood (n 96) 560–61.

[102] Fox and Webb (n 92) 399.

[103] Despite the fact that most countries today have a restrictive doctrine of sovereign immunity and hence state loan agreements are not immune from jurisdiction, waivers of sovereign immunity have become a very frequent feature in international loan agreements and bond issuances. See Patrick Wautelet, 'Vulture Funds, Creditors and Sovereign Debtors: How to Find a Balance?' in Mathias Audit (ed), *L'insolvabilité souveraine* (Science Po 2011) n 263.

[104] Fox and Webb (n 92) 407. Fox and Webb argue that a similar approach—based on these three listed factors—can also be useful when identifying whether acts are of a private law character and hence deprive a state of its immunity.

jurisdiction.[105] Today, sovereign immunity from execution still poses a great challenge for private parties to a state contract seeking a remedy for breach of contract. How big a restriction the rule on sovereign immunity from execution actually imposes will in the end depend on the rules of the jurisdiction where the private party is seeking to enforce the claim against the state and its property.[106] Issues related to immunity from enforcement measures of debt-related judgments will not be discussed further, as they have relatively few peculiarities that distinguish them from other enforcement measures against states. It is first and foremost the question of immunity from jurisdiction that is particular to sovereign debt issues.

2.4.3 The sources of law

Rules on sovereign immunity are based on both national and public international law.[107] At the national level, the transition to the restrictive doctrine of sovereign immunity happened in the French Cour de Cassation in 1969, in the US Supreme Court in 1976 and in the English Court of Appeal in 1977.[108] The doctrine of restrictive state immunity was the basis of the European Convention on State Immunity adopted by the Council of Europe in 1972 and was laid down in US and UK law in the Foreign Sovereign Immunities Act (FSIA) 1976 and the State Immunities Act (SIA) 1978, respectively.

The absence of a multilateral instrument setting out the rules of state immunity has remained a longstanding obstacle to any uniform law. At the international level, there was no authoritative text for the doctrine of restrictive immunity prior to 2004, so the rules had to be derived from international custom as evidence in treaties, national legislation, court decisions and other state practice.[109] In 1991, the ILC finalized its study of the law of state immunity based on all these sources resulting in the Draft Articles on Jurisdictional Immunities of States and their Property. The ILC concluded that there was a 'steady trend, with the exception of the People's Republic of China, towards all States accepting a restrictive doctrine and framed its draft Articles on that

---

[105] To establish that something constitutes a 'commercial activity' in relation to sovereign immunity from execution, a commercial purpose and not a commercial nature-test is often applied. In addition, many jurisdictions apply a nexus requirement between property seized and the relevant commercial activity. See, for example, Astrid Iversen, 'Holdout Creditor Litigation: An Assessment of Legislative Initiatives to Counter Aggressive Sovereign Debt Creditor Litigators' (University of Oslo Faculty of Law Research Paper, 6 February 2015) s 4.4.4.

[106] There seems to be broad agreement in most jurisdictions that attachment of property within the jurisdiction of the sovereign debtor itself is excluded. Furthermore, enforcement against military property, property related to the diplomatic services and property belonging to central banks is also in general excluded from attachment. See, for example, Art 21 of the UN Convention on Privileges and Immunities. See Fox and Webb (n 92) chs 16, 17.

[107] See, in general, ibid 2–3.

[108] Alvik (n 95) 19. The changes happened in the cases: *Administration des chemins de fer du gouvernement iranien v Société Levant Express Transport*, Cass Civ 1ère, 25 February 1969, Bull civ I no 86 (France); *Alfred Dunhill of London, Inc v Republic of Cuba* 425 US 682 (1976) (US); *Trendtex Trading Corporation v Central Bank of Nigeria* [1977] QB 529 (EWCA Civ) (UK). See Hazel Fox and Philippa Webb, *The Law of State Immunity* (Oxford International Law Library, 2nd edn, Oxford University Press 2008) 3. See also Wood (n 96) 560, operating with slightly different years.

[109] Fox and Webb, *The Law of State Immunity* (2008) 3.

basis'.[110] In 2004, the UN General Assembly adopted the Convention on Jurisdictional Immunities of States and their Property, based on the 1991 ILC Draft Articles. The Convention has not yet entered into force, but it is largely considered to express current customary international law.[111] Moreover, in its 2012 *Jurisdictional Immunities* judgment, the ICJ for the first time treated the question of restrictive immunity and indirectly recognized the commercial exemption from sovereign immunity.[112] The judgment was based on customary international law because there was no treaty concerning sovereign immunity between the two parties, Germany and Italy. In the *Jurisdictional Immunities* judgment, the ICJ recognized a category of state acts for which immunity may not bar proceedings against foreign states. The court refers to a distinction between state acts that can be categorized as being of a private law or commercial nature (*acta iure gestionis*) and acts that are of a governmental or authoritative nature (*acta iure imperii*).[113] It explicitly refrained from discussing the subject of *acta iure gestionis* any further, because it was asked to consider whether the acts of the German armed forces and other state organs—which were clearly *acta iure imperii*—constituted 'serious violations of international human right law or the international law of armed conflict' and whether these acts were exempted from immunity. Consequently, the ICJ provides little guidance as to the criteria to distinguish acts of commercial or private law nature from acts performed in the exercise of sovereign or governmental authority. International law is therefore still heavily reliant on state practice, including legislation and case law, in the area of sovereign immunity in order to distinguish *acta iure imperii* and *acta iure gestionis*.[114]

2.4.4 Debt restructuring—immunity and mixed activities

The section above established that, in addition to immunity waivers, states adhering to the doctrine of restrictive immunity are also exempted from sovereign immunity when engaging in commercial acts (*acta iure gestionis*). The criteria used to distinguish between state acts categorized as *iure imperii* and those categorized as *iure gestionis* are difficult to establish. As yet, there is no clear consensus across jurisdictions.[115] Nevertheless, there seems to be agreement that the doctrine of restrictive immunity classifies the *issuance* of sovereign bonds and other state borrowing on international markets as commercial in nature. These acts are not subject to immunity,

---

[110] ibid.
[111] See Alvik, 'Statsimmunitet etter norsk rett og folkeretten' (2006) 19.
[112] *Jurisdictional Immunities* (n 94).
[113] ibid para 60: 'The Court notes that Italy, in response to a question posed by a Member of the Court, recognized that those acts had to be characterized as *acta jure imperii*, notwithstanding that they were unlawful. The Court considers that the terms "*jure imperii*" and "*jure gestionis*" do not imply that the acts in question are lawful but refer rather to whether the acts in question fall to be assessed by reference to the law governing the exercise of sovereign power (*jus imperii*) or the law concerning non-sovereign activities of a State, especially private and commercial activities (*jus gestionis*). To the extent that this distinction is significant for determining whether or not a State is entitled to immunity from the jurisdiction of another State's courts in respect of a particular act, it has to be applied before that jurisdiction can be exercised'.
[114] International courts would also, necessarily, continue to rely upon domestic law in their rulings concerning sovereign immunity. See, in general, Fox and Webb (n 92) 402.
[115] ibid 399.

even if the proceeds are to be used for governmental purposes. The evidence for such a consensus is found both in national legislation and case law concerning disputes over sovereign lending agreements.[116] Moreover, in the report of the Working Group on Jurisdictional Immunities of States and their Property, the ILC lists a number of non-controversial commercial activities, among which the issuance of sovereign bonds.[117] It is more complicated to categorize a state's act as either *acta iure gestionis* or *acta iure imperii* when states implement economic crisis resolution measures, such as sovereign debt restructurings, which interfere with previously established creditor rights. This may be referred to as the issue of categorizing states' mixed activities or continuous transactions. The challenge of categorizing mixed activities can also arise when states have waived their immunity in, or in relation to, a debt instrument. In such cases, both the waiver and subsequent interference with creditors' rights in a debt instrument must be interpreted to establish whether a claim by a creditor in relation to a restructuring is immune from adjudication.

The following sections examine how key financial jurisdictions adhering to the doctrine of restrictive immunity characterize the activity of issuing debt instruments and subsequent restructuring, and consequently whether sovereign debtors are offered immunity in these cases. This will shed light on the extent to which creditors will be prevented from bringing a claim on intercreditor equity related to a debt restructuring before foreign courts and enforcing their actual right to equal or preferred treatment.

The following sections examine case law related to the question of commercial exceptions from immunity in sovereign debt restructurings in English, US, Austrian, German, and Italian courts. The background for most of the cases discussed can be found in the Argentine and Greek restructurings treated in Sections 3.2.3 and 4.4, respectively.

2.4.4.1 US law

In the United States, the *Argentina v Weltover* was the first case overturning earlier doctrine of absolute immunity.[118] The case concerned Argentine bonds issued in the 1980s, which were payable in in US dollars in one of several locations, including New York City. Due to a severe economic crisis, Argentina concluded it lacked sufficient foreign exchange to make repayment on the bonds when they matured and unilaterally extended the time for repayment and made bondholders a debt restructuring offer. When Argentina refused to pay the creditors who rejected the restructuring offer, the holdout creditors brought an action for breach of contract in the New York

---

[116] For example, borrowing and loan guarantees, including bond issues, are expressly commercial under the State Immunity Act (SIA) 1978; and Foreign State Immunities Act of 1985 (Australia), and have been held to be so in French (1974) and Italian (1984) case law. The same jurisdictions all apply the nature test. See Wood (n 96) 560–61. It should be noted that the UK SIA preserved immunity for loans made by international agreement; immunity was preserved too where states are parties to the dispute or have otherwise agreed (s 3(2)). The former practice of treating public loans as sovereign acts that hence were immune became less important as loans have increasingly been raised by states using commercial markets, private law methods and documentation. Such loans are generally held to be commercial transactions and not immune. See Fox and Webb (n 92) 405–06.

[117] ILC *Report of the Working Group on Jurisdictional Immunities of States and Their Property* UN Doc A/CN4/L576, para 54 (United Nations 1999).

[118] *Argentina v Weltover* (n 80).

District Court. Argentina argued that it was immune from adjudication, a question which in the end came before the US Supreme Court. In its judgment, the Supreme court held that that the issuance of the bonds was a 'commercial activity' under the FSIA and that the rescheduling of maturity dates on those instruments was taken 'in connection with' that activity within the meaning of §1605(a)(2).[119] It explained that when a foreign government acts, not as a regulator of a market, but in the manner of a private actor within that market, its actions are 'commercial' within the meaning of the FSIA.[120] That the rescheduling was due to a shortage of foreign reserves did not turn the activity into a governmental act (*acta iure imperii*). Rather, looking at both activities as a whole (ie the issuance and subsequent restructuring), the court characterized both as commercial activities and hence they were found not to be immune.

This case contributed to changing the boundaries of what constitutes an *acta iure gestionis*. Before *Argentina v Weltover*, internal, administrative, and legislative acts of a state, such as national legislation, were clearly treated as matters *iure imperii*.[121] More recent case law has taken the same approach as *Argentina v Weltover*. On numerous occasions, US courts have dealt with bondholder claims in relation to a restructuring—in particular stemming from Argentina's sovereign debt restructurings in 2005 and 2010—and accepted jurisdiction. In many of these cases, the sovereign debtor had included immunity waivers in the debt instruments[122] and consented to jurisdiction in specific jurisdictions or courts within the United States.[123]

2.4.4.2 English law
The restrictive theory of sovereign immunity and the commercial exception is applicable under English law. *Trendtext v Central Bank of Nigeria*—a Court of Appeal decision from 1977—established that if a state act is commercial in nature, the fact that it was done for governmental or political reasons does not result in sovereign immunity.[124]

Concerning the question of mixed activities or continuous transactions, some argue that English courts, similarly to those in the United States, follow the principle of 'once a trader always a trader'.[125] Case law suggests that the English approach is somewhat more complex. *I Congreso del Partido* deals with such continuous transactions.[126] This case concerns a contract for the sale of sugar between a company owned by the Republic of Cuba and a Chilean company. The claimants were the owners of cargo on board two vessels—*Playa Larga* and *Marble Island*—which were to ship the sugar to Chile. During the lifespan of the contract, the Chilean government was overthrown.

---

[119] ibid at 620.
[120] ibid at 607.
[121] Fox and Webb (n 92) 404.
[122] For example, s 22 of the Fiscal Agency Agreement of 19 October 1994 (Argentina).
[123] The act of state doctrine could have been a procedural bar for a court hindering it from assessing the substance of a case arising from a restructuring. However, the doctrine does not apply to sovereign defaults as in principle it does not extend to commercial transactions. Kupelyants (n 2) 16 and ch 6.
[124] *Trendtex Trading Corporation v Central Bank of Nigeria* (n 108); confirmed in *Owners of Cargo Lately Laden on Board The Marble Islands v Owners of The I Congreso del Partido* [1983] 1 AC 244 (see especially Lord Wilberforce's judgment at 262).
[125] Kupelyants (n 2) 283.
[126] *I Congreso del Partido* (n 124).

Cuba was unwilling to interact with the new Chilean government. It therefore ordered the two vessels that were on their way to deliver sugar in Chile to return. The Cuban government's decision was politically motivated. The claimants sued for breach of contract due to non-delivery and in tort for breach of duty. The sole question before the court was, however, whether Cuba should enjoy immunity.[127]

The court majority denied the Republic of Cuba sovereign immunity for both vessels, *Playa Larga* and *Marble Island*, while Lord Wilberforce (minority) accepted Cuba's claim for immunity in the case of *Marble Island*.[128] The main divide between the majority and the minority seems to have centred on the interpretation of the evidence and the significance of the particular facts and whether these constituted commercial or governmental acts.[129] What is more important for our purposes is Lord Wilberforce's authoritative statement of the law, which also touches upon questions of mixed activities or continuous transactions.[130] When giving an account for the immunity rules under English law, Lord Wilberforce criticized the principle of 'once a trader always a trader' and called it an over-simplification:

> If a trader is always a trader, a state remains a state and is capable at any time of acts of sovereignty. The question arises, therefore, what is the position where the act upon which the claim is founded is quite outside the commercial, or private law, activity in which the state has engaged, and has the character of an act done iure imperii. The 'restrictive' theory does not and could not deny capability of a state to resort to sovereign or governmental action: it merely asserts that acts done within the trading or commercial activity are not immune. The inquiry still has to be made whether they were within or outside that activity.[131]

---

[127] The cases ended up before English courts because a third vessel, I Congreso del Partido, was constructed, found, and arrested in England. The vessel was to be used for normal trading purposes. The owner of I Congreso del Partido was the Republic of Cuba and claimants in the case against both Playa Larga and Marble Island sought satisfaction of their claims against I Congreso.

[128] With regard to Playa Larga, the court unanimously held that the Republic of Cuba had acted as the owner of the ship, rather than in the exercise of sovereign powers. The claim to sovereign immunity was therefore denied. The decision to order the vessels to leave Chile and not deliver the cargo was politically motivated and had no commercial reason but this fact did not make it an *acta iure imperii*. The acts of Cuba in relation to the vessel Marble Island were also characterized as *iure gestionis* by the majority and consequently sovereign immunity was rejected. The majority argued that this claim was not based upon the initial refusal to deliver the sugar, but on the discharge of the sugar in North Vietnam. The majority found that this disposal was a private or commercial act, and not a sovereign act.

[129] *I Congreso del Partido* (n 124) 279. The exception was Lord Bridge of Harwich, who also pointed out with regret that the various opinions were divided on the interpretation of the evidence and the significance of the particular facts rather than on any question of legal principle. Lord Bridge of Harwich was the only judge who more or less openly disagreed with Lord Wilberforce's view on mixed activities when stating: 'having assumed a purely private law obligation, a sovereign state cannot justify a breach of the obligation on the ground that the reason for the breach was of a sovereign or governmental character. Example: State A, having ordered uniforms for its army from a supplier in State B, repudiates the contract; when sued in the courts of State B for damages, State A cannot claim immunity on the ground that, since the placing of the contract, a government of a new political complexion has made a sovereign decision, pursuant to a policy of total disarmament, to disband its army.' ibid.

[130] The authority of Lord Wilberforce is underlined by Lord Goff in in *Kuwait Airways Corporation v Iraqi Airways Corporation* [1995] 1 WLR 1147, 1158.

[131] *I Congreso del Partido* (n 124) 263.

Moreover, referring to the German *Empire of Iran* case,[132] Lord Wilberforce accepted

> that the existence of a governmental purpose or motive will not convert what would otherwise be an act jure gestionis, or an act of private law, into one done jure imperii, but beyond this proposition (which is not decisive here) they do not give direct guidance upon the questions we have to consider.[133]

The conclusion which emerged according to Lord Wilberforce and which seems to be supported by the majority[134] is that

> in considering, under the 'restrictive' theory whether state immunity should be granted or not, the court must consider the whole context in which the claim against the state is made, with a view to deciding whether the relevant act(s) upon which the claim is based, should, in that context, be considered as fairly within an area of activity, trading or commercial, or otherwise of a private law character, in which the state has chosen to engage, or whether the relevant act(s) should be considered as having been done outside that area, and within the sphere of governmental or sovereign activity.[135]

In sum, Wilberforce underlined that the key question when assessing sovereign immunity and mixed activities is what is the relevant act?[136] This could be the issuance of the debt or the restructuring. The latter can be enabled by either a legislative (governmental) act or a more ordinary commercial act initiated by the creditors, such as a bondholder vote to accept a restructuring under a CAC. Moreover, once a court has identified the relevant transaction and characterized it as commercial, it is the state itself who must show that a particular act performed in the context of that transaction was sovereign or governmental in nature. In the context of a sovereign debt restructuring then, while it is clear that the contracting of sovereign debt on the market is commercial in nature, it is not clear *ex ante* whether claims related to a subsequent restructuring will continue to be commercial and hence immune from adjudication. The answer depends on an examination of the facts of the particular situation, such as the means by which the restructuring is implemented. That being said, in many cases before English (and US) courts, creditor claims related to repayment under a debt instrument are typically governed by some foreign law (English or New York law). Governmental acts of the sovereign debtor, such as moratoriums or restructuring of certain debts by means of legislative acts, are inapplicable, because they cannot alter rights under foreign law. In practice, foreign courts will therefore not assess the

---

[132] *Empire of Iran* case (n 101).
[133] *I Congreso del Partido* (n 124) 267.
[134] That main divide is based on the interpretation of the evidence and the significance of the particular facts, and whether these are sufficient to constitute a commercial or a governmental act. While the other judges concur with Lord Wilberforce's description/establishment of sovereign immunity under English law, Lord Bridge Harwich disagrees with Lord Wilberforce's description of existing legal principles. See ibid at 279.
[135] ibid at 267.
[136] ibid at 263.

governmental acts of the sovereign debtor. This factor contributes to putting less pressure on courts as it also allows them to avoid assessing the substance of a claim.[137]

2.4.4.3 German law

In a judgment from 2016, the Bundesgerichtshof (the German Federal Court of Justice) treated a claim concerning the rights of holders of Greek bonds that had been restructured in 2012.[138] The court started by noting that sovereign states only enjoy immunity from adjudication under German law for acts *iure imperii* and not for acts *iure gestionis*.[139] Thereafter, the court found that the issuance of government bonds was generally considered a non-public legal act (*acta iure gestionis*) under customary international law.[140] It insisted that the legal nature of the general underlying relationship (*Grundverhältnis*) was not the decisive factor. Rather, whether immunity is granted to a state depends on the legal nature of the act or measure, on which the claim is based.[141] In the case at hand, the claimants challenged the involuntary debt restructuring by the Greek government that had exchanged their bonds for new bonds. These claims, the court held, were based on a violation of property rights in sovereign debt obligations. The restructuring interfering with the property rights constituted an *acta iure imperii* and was therefore immune from the jurisdiction of German courts.[142]

The fact that the restructuring itself was decided by a majority of bondholders, which is also common in restructurings of commercial companies, and not directly decided by the Greek state did not make the act *iure gestionis*.[143] The reason was that the restructuring, particularly of those bonds held by holdout creditors, was enabled by a change in the legal background regulation (the Greek Bondholder Act).

In *obiter dictum*, which only added to the confusion, the court stated that the application of the principle of state immunity in the current case did not conflict with the principle that state immunity is sometimes denied when a state disturbs the execution of a contract concluded under private law. The court argued that the question in the case at hand concerned whether the Greek legislator, as master of the contract, was entitled to introduce new rules into its legal system.[144]

Another case related to the Greek restructuring came before the Bundesgerichtshof in 2017 and helped to clarify the situation in German law.[145] The court confirmed that it followed from customary international law that states enjoy immunity with respect

---

[137] Mann (n 51) 188–89. See also Section 2.2.2.
[138] BGH, Urteil v 08.03.2016, VI ZR 516/14 (Germany).
[139] ibid para 12.
[140] ibid para 17.
[141] ibid.
[142] ibid para 18.
[143] ibid para 22.
[144] ibid para 25.
[145] BGH, Urteil v 19.12.2017, XI ZR 796/16 (Germany). For a case commentary, see Sebastian Grund, '*Unidentified Holders of Greek Government Bonds v Greece*, Appeal to Federal Court of Justice, XI ZR 796/16, ILDC 2881 (DE 2017) 19th December 2017, Germany' in André Nollkaemper and August Reinisch (eds), *Oxford Reports on International Law in Domestic Courts* (Oxford University Press 2006). The lower court dismissed the German bondholders' action, holding that Greece enjoyed sovereign immunity from proceedings with regard to the debt restructuring measures. The claims by the German bondholders were inadmissible and could not be brought in German courts because the Recast Brussels Regulation did not provide a legal basis for German courts' jurisdiction.

to governmental activities (*acta iure imperii*) but not commercial activities (*acta iure gestionis*). It further insisted that the distinction between sovereign and non-sovereign activities is not based on the motive or purpose of the state act, but rather on its nature or the resulting legal relationship. Moreover, this characterization of state acts must be made in accordance with the laws applicable in the jurisdiction where the action was brought.[146] Applied to the case at hand, the court distinguished between the nature of the original contractual agreement between Greece and its creditors, and the nature of the act with which the state implemented the restructuring. The court found that only the nature of the latter state act ought to be considered when deciding whether Greece should be immune from adjudication.[147] The Greek Bondholder Act implementing CACs retroactively was based on a legislative act, which the court categorized as a governmental act (*acta iure imperii*). Consequently, the act was immune and could not be reviewed by German courts. That the issuance of sovereign bonds was a commercial activity (*acta iure gestionis*) was not decisive.

Moreover, the type of legal claim brought against a sovereign was not relevant, according to the court, when determining whether Greece had a right to immunity from adjudication. Greece would remain immune with regard to debt restructuring measures based on (or enabled by) the Greek Bondholder Act regardless of whether the bondholders invoked their right to contractual performance, claimed damages, or demanded compensation for expropriation. This broad approach was necessary, because affirming any of the bondholders' claims would require the court to assess the legality (or illegality) of Greek legislation. To assess the lawfulness of a foreign state's legislation would not be reconcilable with the principle of equality of nations under international law and the principle that equals do not have authority over one another (*par in parem non habet imperium*).[148]

This interpretation of the sovereign immunity doctrine—where the court only relied on the latter act, which it characterized as an act *iure imperii*, and disregarded the fact that the issuance of bonds constituted an act *iure gestionis*—appears to diverge from an earlier decision by the Bundesgerichtshof.[149] In the earlier case from 2015, which concerned German bondholder claims against Argentina in relation to the Republic's debt restructuring in 2001 and 2005, the court accepted jurisdiction. In doing so, it did not, however, rely on a commercial exception from immunity, but on a waiver contained in the respective Argentine bonds.[150] Although the earlier question

---

[146] BGH, Urteil v 19.12.2017, XI ZR 796/16, paras 16–18 (Germany).

[147] This seems to contradict Fox and Webb's view of the situation under German law. See Fox and Webb (n 92) 414. They write: 'There seems to be no single method to solve these difficulties of characterization [in mixed activities]. To some extent they can be avoided by treating the whole issue as one of individuation. Once the events are characterized precisely and as narrowly as is reasonably possible, having regard to the factual and legal issues, as either a commercial transaction or a sovereign act, that characterization is to be treated as final. That approach seems to be borne out in the German cases which apply a presumption that once a State has entered the market a characterization of that act as commercial continues, regardless of the nature of the act constituting its subsequent breach.'

[148] BGH, Urteil v 19.12.2017, XI ZR 796/16, paras 21–26 (Germany).

[149] BGH, Urteil v 24.02.2015, XI ZR 193/14 (Germany).

[150] On the merits, the court concluded that Argentina was obliged to repay the bondholders as international law did not allow for the unilateral suspension of debt repayments by virtue of domestic legislation. It is important to underline here that the bonds were governed by German and not by domestic Argentine law.

was decided on the basis of a waiver, the Bundesgerichtshof could have minimized legal uncertainty in the 2017 case by comparing the Argentine and Greek cases. In particular, it would have been enlightening if the court had explained whether Greece would have been non-immune with regard to the government bonds had the bond contract included a waiver. This is crucial, because the new bonds that were exchanged for the old Greek bonds did include such a sovereign immunity waiver.[151]

Based on these decisions, the rules on sovereign immunity concerning sovereign debt and debt restructuring in Germany can be summarized as follows. First, German law relies on the 'nature' test when characterizing whether a state act is *iure gestionis* or *iure imperii*, and consequently whether it is immune or not. The issuance of government bonds on capital markets is found to be an activity of a commercial or private law nature that is not immune. Second, as the previous point highlights, German courts seek to identify individual acts when assessing whether immunity should be afforded to continuous or mixed activities. It thereby deviates from a strict interpretation of the earlier mentioned principle, 'once a trader always a trader'. Third, the type of legal claim brought against a sovereign debtor is not relevant when determining whether another state has a right to immunity from adjudication. Once the relevant state act is identified, the state remains immune with regard to this act regardless of whether the claimants invoke a contractual right, claim for damages, or demand compensation (eg for expropriation).[152] Fourth, the 2015 Bundesgerichtshof case concerning Argentine bonds indicates that an immunity waiver is sufficient for German courts to accept jurisdiction, even for legal questions concerning mixed activities, such as a restructuring. However, in that case, the court held that Argentine governmental acts did not have the capacity to alter obligations under German law and consequently the German courts did not need to assess the lawfulness of Argentina's acts. Although this is a question assessed only once the court has accepted jurisdiction and determined questions of immunity, one may speculate whether German courts would have assessed the immunity question differently if the governing law had been that of the issuer state (as it was in the Greek cases). In such a case, German courts would not have been able to circumvent an assessment of the lawfulness of governmental acts by the debtor state.

2.4.4.4 Italian law

A case stemming from the Argentine restructuring came before the Italian Corte di Cassazione in 2005.[153] The case concerned an Italian citizen who had bought global bonds issued by Argentina on the secondary market in New York.[154] As a response

---

[151] Grund (n 145).
[152] This was discussed in lower courts after the first Federal Court of Justice case dealing with the Greek restructuring from 2015. Some of the lower courts argued that bondholders could still invoke their contractual rights to repayment under the old government bonds, regardless of a restructuring. See Sebastian Grund, 'Enforcing Sovereign Debt in Court—A Comparative Analysis of Litigation and Arbitration Following the Greek Debt Restructuring of 2012' (2017) 1 University of Vienna Law Review 34.
[153] Cass, 27 Maggio 2005, n 11225 (hereafter *Borri v Argentina*) (Italy).
[154] In reality, the Italian claimants were not bondholders but investors. Technically, they were owners of 'beneficial interests in bonds'. Argentina issues bonds to a depository. The depository then issues 'participations' to brokers who thereafter sell them as 'beneficial interests' to purchasers. In the case of Argentina, the global bonds are governed by a Fiscal Agency Agreement of 19 October 1994 (Argentina). See also Beatrice I Bonafè, 'State Immunity and the Protection of Private Investors: The *Argentine Bonds* Case Before Italian Courts' (2006) 16 The Italian Yearbook of International Law Online 165, n 1.

to its severe economic crisis in the early 2000s, Argentina passed laws aimed at extending the term of interest payment (payment moratorium).[155] The claimant had requested an injunction from a lower court requiring Argentina to pay a sum of money due under the terms of the bonds. He argued that Italian courts had jurisdiction over the case under the Brussels I Convention because the issuance of bonds and sale on the secondary market was of a private or commercial character (*acta iure gestionis*), and because the case related to a contract under which Italy was the place of performance. Argentina opposed the injunction by claiming immunity from adjudication and argued that according to the agreement regulating the bonds, only Argentine and New York courts had jurisdiction. The court decided the case based on immunity rules. It held that Argentina's implementation of a payment moratorium was an *acta iure imperii* and therefore enjoyed immunity under international law, regardless of the fact that the initial issuance of the bonds was a commercial or private act.

2.4.5 Preliminary conclusion

Whether or not a sovereign debtor is immune from adjudication in foreign courts in cases concerning sovereign debt restructurings will severely limit a creditor's chances of enforcing their intercreditor equity rights.

In all the jurisdictions discussed, the activity of issuing bonds or contracting other debt instruments in the markets has been categorized as commercial (*acta iure gestionis*), and thus not normally immune from adjudication. This Section 2.4 on immunity has argued that in situations of mixed activity and continuous transactions, determining whether a sovereign debtor should be afforded immunity requires individuation of the act giving rise to a claim.[156] It is therefore necessary to establish whether a subsequent state act that in one way or another interferes with the rights of a creditor—including debt restructurings in their various forms—should be categorized as a governmental or commercial act. Moreover, it is necessary to establish whether the act of issuing the debt or the interference with the creditor right is decisive when assessing questions of immunity, or whether they should be considered in conjunction. The answers to these questions will determine whether a sovereign debtor state is immune (or not) from adjudication in foreign courts.

Some scholars have argued that it is the nature of the initial act of issuing sovereign bonds that is decisive when courts consider whether a sovereign debtor enjoys immunity under customary international law.[157] Although it is far from exhaustive,

---

[155] See Carlo Focarelli, '*Borri v. Argentina*, Request for a Ruling on Jurisdiction, Case No 11225, (2005) 88 Rivista di diritto internazionale 856, ILDC 296 (IT 2005), 27th May 2005, Italy; Supreme Court of Cassation' in André Nollkaemper and August Reinisch (eds), *Oxford Reports on International Law in Domestic Courts* (Oxford University Press 2006).

[156] Fox and Webb (n 92) 413.

[157] Bonafè (n 154) 169–71. Bonafè criticizes the Italian Supreme Court case discussed above arguing that '[t]he nature of the original legal relationship between Argentina and the private investors—the activity which formed the basis of the investor's suit before the Italian courts. The only activity which should have been taken into account in order to recognise or deny Argentina's immunity was the issuance of the bonds.' According to Bonafè, Argentina's later governmental act—the moratorium adopted by law—cannot influence the characterization of the act of issuing bonds as a commercial act and consequently Argentina should not have enjoyed immunity from adjudication.

the above discussion of case law from selected jurisdictions indicates that there is no uniform classification system for the commerciality exception in relation to a mixed activity such as a debt restructuring.[158] National legal systems classify governmental and commercial acts differently, particularly when subsequent acts interfere with an initial commercial activity in situations of mixed activities, such as sovereign debt restructuring. Different jurisdictions also seem to differ in the way they identify which act is *decisive* when characterizing a dispute arising from an activity as *iure imperii* or *iure gestionis*, and thereby deciding whether immunity should be afforded.

Under US law, sovereign debtors who have restructured debt unilaterally, for example by means of legislation, will typically not be immune from adjudication. The reason is that the initial issuance is deemed to be commercial or contain a waiver, and subsequent acts such as a restructuring are seen in connection with the initial commercial act.

UK courts have a more open approach to the question of immunity in the case of mixed activities. It is clear that the contracting of sovereign debt on markets is commercial in nature. However, it is not certain whether claims related to a subsequent restructuring will continue to be characterized as commercial and hence as immune from adjudication. Lord Wilberforce argued in favour of a holistic and context-based approach where, if a court has first characterized a transaction of the state as commercial (as issuance of sovereign debt clearly is), it is up to the state to show that a particular act that is performed in context of that transaction had a sovereign or governmental nature.

In the cases discussed, the German courts sought to identify individual acts when assessing whether immunity should be afforded to continuous or mixed activities. It thereby deviated from a strict interpretation of the principle 'once a trader always a trader'. More importantly, the type of legal claim brought against a sovereign debtor was not considered relevant when determining whether or not another state had a right to immunity from adjudication. Once the relevant state act is identified, the state remains immune with regard to this act regardless of whether the claimants invoke a contractual right, claim for damages, or demand compensation (eg for expropriation). Lastly, there is case law indicating that an immunity waiver is sufficient for German courts to accept jurisdiction for legal questions concerning mixed activities. However, it is unclear whether this is the case in situations where the governing law is that of the issuing country and not foreign law. In such situations, German courts cannot circumvent an assessment of the lawfulness of governmental acts of a state, because the debtor country's unilateral change to bond terms through national legislation is possible.

Finally, Italian law provides sovereign debtors with immunity when they unilaterally alter the contractual terms of sovereign debt instruments as a crisis resolution measure. The Italian Corte di Cassazione held that implementation of a payment moratorium was an *acta iure imperii* and that the sovereign debtor therefore enjoyed immunity under international law, regardless of the fact that the initial issuance of the bonds was a commercial or private act.

---

[158] Fox and Webb (n 92) 399, 414.

Regardless of differences across jurisdictions concerning the categorization of acts when determining whether a debt restructuring is immune from jurisdiction, some patterns have emerged. For the sake of systematization, two approaches to determining which act is relevant in cases of mixed activities can be identified.[159] According to the first approach, sovereign debt contracted on the market is identified as a commercial act (*acta iure gestionis*). A subsequent debt restructuring of that debt is identified as a related, yet separate, act and characterized as governmental (*acta iure imperii*). According to this approach, the later state act interfering with a creditor's right must be considered in isolation. Although the contracting of debt is commercial in nature, a creditor's claim related to a state act, such as legislation, which interferes with a creditor's right in a debt contract, is considered a governmental act. The Italian and German case law on sovereign immunity seem to take this approach. More specifically, in the two jurisdictions, the later state act, related to the debt restructuring, is considered the decisive act. Another way of understanding this is to consider the first commercial transaction—the issuance or contracting of debt—as changed into a governmental act through the later act. The Italian–German approach should not be interpreted as an EU position.[160]

A second approach consists in identifying an event or an act as narrowly as is reasonably possible, based on the factual and legal issues, and then characterizing it as a commercial or governmental act. Once this is done, the determination is treated as final. The assumption is that once a state has entered the market a characterization of that act as commercial continues, regardless of the nature of subsequent acts.[161] This approach is often referred to as 'once a trader always a trader'.[162] The US approach to

---

[159] National systems classify public and private acts differently. Establishing a legal formulation for the exception from immunity for commercial activity—where the *gestionis* versus *imperii* distinction is most at issue—has proved more difficult to the extent that the existence of such a classification in international law is questionable. See ibid 399.

[160] One example of an alternative route taken in the EU is Austria. In several cases related to the 2012 Greek restructuring, the Oberste Gerichtshof relied on the Brussels I Regulation when rejecting cases related to sovereign debt restructurings. However, through several *obiter dicta*, the courts noted that sovereign immunity rules barred Austrian courts from assessing the Greek Bondholder Act, even if it had altered contractual rights, because it constituted an *acta iure imperii*. At the same time, it indicated that the Greek government's issuance of sovereign bonds constituted a commercial act and that Greece cannot invoke sovereign immunity in relation to a contractual claim. It was not explained how one might assess the question of contractual breach without assessing the legality of the amended legislation affecting the contract. One possibility might be to treat the background law as facts and assess non-fulfilment as if the state were a private actor forced to follow domestic laws. See OBH 20.05.2014, 4 Ob 227/13f (Austria). (Later the same parties were also allowed to include the question concerning jurisdiction in OBH 27.01.2016, 4 Ob 163/15x (Austria); OBH 30.07.2015, 8 Ob 67/15h (Austria); OBH 25.11.2015, 8 Ob 125/15p (Austria)). For a discussion of the cases, see also Grund (n 152).

[161] Fox and Webb (n 92) 414. Fox and Webb state that German law takes this approach. However, this does not seem to be consistent with the two decisions from the Bundesgerichthof (BGH) discussed in this section.

[162] It is normally used to describe the alleged non-applicability of sovereign immunity to state activities of a commercial nature (*acta iure gestionis*) regardless of whether a commenced lawsuit stems from a subsequent state act that may be categorized as a governmental act (*iure imperii*). According to this principle, a sovereign debtor should not be allowed to unilaterally change the terms of the debt or otherwise interfere with the contractual rights of the creditors, including through the use of acts characterized as governmental that enable an involuntary restructuring, and so be shielded by rules of sovereign immunity from adjudication.

immunity would seem to fit this second category. The English approach is flexible and may be placed somewhere between the first and second approaches.

Whether or not the two different approaches necessarily lead to different results is debatable. If a foreign court accepts jurisdiction under the second approach and assesses the substance of a claim related to a debt restructuring, it should treat the sovereign debtor as any other private actor. An assessment of whether the sovereign debtor is liable for non-fulfilment of a contractual obligation or damages could take into consideration the background legal context, which the sovereign debtor (as any commercial actor) is obliged to respect. In this way, the foreign court would avoid having to assess the governmental act itself.

Regardless of variations in the categorization of state acts, the conclusion seems to be that the legality of sovereign debtors' implementation of crisis resolution measures is more likely to be shielded from assessment under German and Italian immunity laws as they provide for a narrower commerciality exception. This is especially so compared to US immunity rules in cases concerning debt restructurings. English laws seem to fall somewhere in between.

3
Intercreditor Equity Rules Applicable to Debt Instruments Governed by International Law

3.1 Introduction

Loan agreements between two (or more) states, as well as those between a state and an international finance institution that is a subject under international law, can be entered into by the parties in their capacity as subjects of public international law. Such loan agreements can therefore be governed by international law.[1] This chapter discusses intercreditor equity rules in international law that are applicable to, and among, creditors who are subjects of international law and who hold debt instruments governed by international law.

The so-called equality rules and their implications for intercreditor equity are examined in Section 3.2. Section 3.3 treats questions of how debt can be subordinated and Section 3.4 examines secured debts. Section 3.5 then discusses whether certain creditors have preferred creditor status under international law, while Section 3.6 considers the compatibility of preferential treatment and the equality rule. These sections all relate to rules that follow from treaty or custom.

Intercreditor equity rules in international law can also follow from general principles in accordance with Article 38(1)(c) of the International Court of Justice (ICJ) Statute. When identifying general principles, it is said that the ICJ must choose, edit, and adapt elements from other developed systems.[2] To examine whether intercreditor equity rules exist or are emerging as general principles of international law, it is therefore necessary to look to intercreditor equity rules stemming both from domestic and international law.[3] Since this requires analysis of the intercreditor equity rules examined in Chapters 3–5, the question of intercreditor equity rules as general principles

---

[1] James Crawford, *Brownlie's Principles of Public International Law* (8th edn, Oxford University Press 2012) 190; Rutsel Silvestre J Martha, *The Financial Obligation in International Law* (Oxford University Press 2015) 479.

[2] Their views are referred to in James Crawford, *Brownlie's Principles of Public International Law* (9th edn, Oxford University Press 2019)32.

[3] General principles of international law are formed within both domestic and international legal systems. See ibid 32, 35. Crawford refers to the views of Root and Phillimore, who were both members of the Committee of Jurists drafting the ICJ Statutes, from the United States and the United Kingdom respectively. They both regarded general principles as rules accepted in the domestic law of all civilized states. That general principles of international law are also formed within the international legal system follows from Marcelo Vázquez-Bermúdez *First Report on General Principles of Law (for International Law Commission, Seventy-first Session)* UN Doc A/CN4/732, s 257 (United Nations 2019). Whether these are two separate sources is still debated. For example, Crawford has suggested that general principles of law are 'a body of international law the content of which has been influenced by domestic law but which is still its own creation'. He also suggests that an international tribunal chooses, edits, and adapts elements from other developed systems. See Crawford (n 1) 35.

Intercreditor Equity in Sovereign Debt Restructuring. Astrid Iversen, Oxford University Press. © Astrid Iversen 2023.
DOI: 10.1093/oso/9780192866905.003.0004

of law will not be further discussed in this chapter. I will note here that the discussion in Chapters 3–5 makes it clear that the design of such rules varies substantially from one forum to another. Moreover, Chapter 6 shows that the underlying objectives of the various intercreditor equity rules are not uniform and do necessarily pull in the same direction. This suggests that no general principle of international law, in accordance with Article 38(1)(c) of the ICJ Statute, can be inferred from the sum of these existing intercreditor equity rules.[4] Nevertheless, Section 7.3.1 discusses the potential for single rules or groups of more similar intercreditor equity rules to develop into general principles of law in the future.

This chapter does not discuss intercreditor issues related to debt instruments held by international law subjects but governed by domestic law, nor does it discuss international law applicable to domestic law governed debt instruments. These questions are discussed in Chapters 4 and 5 respectively.

International law rules also play an important role in domestic legal systems. How international law affects debt instruments governed by domestic law depends on the governing law of the debt instrument and the laws potentially applicable in the jurisdiction of the seized court. The relation between intercreditor equity rights in debt instruments governed by domestic law and the international law rules discussed in this chapter will be considered in Chapter 6.

3.2 The Equality Rule

There are no legal insolvency procedures for sovereign states in international law. The question here is how debt instruments governed by international law and held by international law subjects rank relative to each other, in particular when a sovereign debtor faces payment difficulties.

The *pacta sunt servanda* rule, which is part of the general principles of international law, implies that a treaty in force binds the parties and must be executed in good faith.[5] It follows from this rule that agreements concerning sovereign borrowing between international law subjects, at least from a formal legal point of view, are independent and self-sufficient entities.[6] Further, the maxim *pacta tertiis nec nocent nec prosunt* expresses the fundamental principle that a treaty applies only between the parties to it. Crawford describes the *pacta tertiis* rule as being a corollary of the principle of consent and of the sovereignty and independence of states.[7] The Vienna Convention on

---

[4] Though the ICJ Statute addresses the law applicable to the Court, general practice has led Article 38 to be considered an authoritative statement of the sources of international law. See Robert Y Jennings, 'General Course on Principles of International Law' (1967) 121 Collected Courses of the Hague Academy of International Law 331; Alain Pellet, 'Article 38' in Andreas Zimmerman and others (eds), *The Statute of the International Court of Justice: A Commentary* (Oxford Commentaries on International Law, 2nd edn, Oxford University Press 2012) 731–870; Gleider I Hernández, *The International Court of Justice and the Judicial Function* (Oxford University Press 2014) 31.

[5] The principle is contained in Art 26 of the Vienna Convention on the Law of Treaties (opened for signature 23 May 1969, entered into force 27 January 1980) 1155 UNTS 331 (hereafter VCLT). See also Crawford (n 2) 363.

[6] Paul Reuter, *Introduction to the Law of Treaties* (A Publication of the Graduate Institute of International Studies, Geneva, José Mico and Peter Haggenmacher trs, 2nd edn, Paul Kegan International 1995) 100.

[7] Crawford (n 2) 384.

the Law of Treaties (VCLT) refers to this maxim in Article 34, which provides that a treaty does not create either obligations or rights for a third state without its consent. The customary rule, Crawford holds, also encompasses the idea that treaties cannot *infringe* the rights of third parties without their consent.[8] Consequently, no international agreement has absolute precedent over another.[9] In sum, the implication of *pacta sunt servanda* and *pacta tertiis* in the context of sovereign borrowing is that debt agreements between a state debtor and creditors that are states and international organizations (ie subjects of international law) constitute 'independent obligations that relate to each other as *res inter alios acta* and thus rank equal to each other'.[10] This can be referred to as the 'equality rule'.[11]

A case between Belgium and Greece before the Permanent Court of International Justice (PCIJ)—*Société commerciale de Belgique*—is a good example of this equality rule in action.[12] In this case, Belgium challenged Greece's attempt to unilaterally subordinate payment of pecuniary obligations contained in certain arbitral awards to restructured external debts. More specifically, it concerned (among other things) Greece's 1930 external debt settlement and the related issue of whether its terms breached Belgium's rights to payment according to the arbitral award rendered in favour of a Belgian company. A clause in the debt settlement agreement provided that if more favourable terms were given by Greece to other external loans or guarantees, equally favourable treatment should be given to loans covered by the agreement.[13] Greece sought to avoid the application of this provision, claiming instead that it had the right to subordinate the payment of the arbitral award. In its judgment, the PCIJ rejected Greece's claims, finding that if an international financial obligation is due and definitive, obligatory, and not subordinated, the debtor is bound to execute it. Greece as a sovereign debtor could not claim to subordinate payment of a financial obligation that had been imposed upon it only after it had settled its external public debt. This case demonstrates that a state's different pecuniary obligations are equally important and prioritizing the fulfilment of one obligation cannot justify the breach of another.

To say that there is a rule that international financial obligations in principle rank equally is not the same as saying that the principle of *par condicio creditorium* applies in international law. Under the latter, creditors have an equal right to have their outstanding claims covered out of the debtor's assets in domestic law. Under international law, however, states enjoy territorial sovereignty. Therefore, when sovereign debtors become insolvent, they cannot be wound up or their territory and assets liquidated and distributed to creditors as is typically the case with insolvent or bankrupt corporations.[14]

---

[8] ibid.
[9] Martha (n 1) 479–80.
[10] ibid.
[11] ibid.
[12] Société commerciale de Belgique (*Belgium v Greece*) (Judgment) (1939) PCIJ Series A/B no 78 (hereafter *Société commerciale de Belgique*). See also ibid 480.
[13] 'Under these agreements a percentage only of the sums due for interest is to be paid, nothing is to be paid in respect of sinking fund, and a clause is inserted that, if more favourable terms are given by the Greek Government to other external loans of or guaranteed by the Greek State, equally favourable treatment should be given to the loans covered by the agreements.' *Société commerciale de Belgique* (n 12) 13.
[14] Martha (n 1) 480.

3.3 Subordination

While the equality rule discussed above is the starting point in deciding how various debt agreements under international law relate to one another, it can be derogated from in various ways.[15] Specific creditors or classes of creditors can consent to a subordinated (junior) position with respect to a particular lender or to all other creditors. Subordination can therefore be defined as the act of yielding priority. A creditor can actively consent to such subordination by an express act of will (*de jure* subordination) or passively by inference from its behaviour (*de facto* subordination).[16] An active expression of consent to a subordinated position can be given: (i) by agreement between the state and the creditor(s) agreeing to be subordinated; (ii) by agreement with a third creditor(s); or (iii) through a unilateral, yet legally binding declaration made by the relevant creditor.

It may still be somewhat unclear what the *effect* of a subordinated creditor position is in the context of sovereign debt and a debt restructuring. In domestic insolvency law, the effect of subordination is that, in case of liquidation, subordinated creditors are only paid after the debts of non-subordinated creditors have been paid and only to the extent that the debtor still has assets left. As mentioned above, in the sovereign debt context, subordination (or preferred creditor status) relates first and foremost to the time of payment. Subordinated creditors must accept prioritization by the debtor of certain other creditors in case of payment difficulties. One could argue that a subordinated creditor may also have to accept that non-subordinated creditors be exempted from a debt restructuring. This implies that a non-subordinated creditor may have a claim against the debtor if the debtor exempts another equal ranking (non-subordinated) creditor from a restructuring (or offers preferential terms to this creditor). If this is not explicitly written into the terms of the debt instrument, such a solution is unlikely, because no creditor is obliged to agree to a restructuring. As long as the debt instrument does not specify otherwise, participation in a restructuring is voluntary and binds only those who accept the restructuring agreement. A creditor is typically free to choose not to participate in a restructuring provided there is no collective active clause (ie a majority voting provision that binds minority creditors to the will of the majority).[17]

Subordination clauses or other forms of *de jure* subordination are not common in debt instruments governed by international law. As stated above, instead of subordinating certain debts using express provisions, subordination can also be effected through conduct (*de facto* subordination). This form of subordination seems to be more common in public international finance. Although this does not constitute *de jure* subordination, the effect is similar from the debtor's point of view.[18]

---

[15] See also Rutsel Silvestre J Martha, 'Preferred Creditor Status under International Law: The Case of the International Monetary Fund' (1990) 39 International & Comparative Law Quarterly 801, 809–10.

[16] Martha (n 1) 484.

[17] See, in general, Section 4.3 on majority voting and collective action clauses (CACs).

[18] Martha (n 1) 485–86.

De facto subordination differs from express *de jure* subordination in several ways. First, *de facto* subordination does not follow from public international law, as is the case with *de jure* subordination. Second, *de facto* subordination is not predetermined but takes place *ex post*, whereas *de jure* subordination of debts takes place *ex ante*. Third, in a *de facto* subordination the creditor is still in possession of a claim, in line with the equality rule discussed above, but voluntarily chooses to relinquish it.

Since the second half of the twentieth century, it has been common practice for sovereign debtors to pay debts owed to multilateral financial institutions even if they are not servicing their other external debts. One example of such *de facto* subordination is the established practice of the Paris Club, where Member States restructure their claims but exclude debt owed to multilateral financial institutions.[19] The Paris Club is an informal group of official creditor states who seek to coordinate their approach to debtor states facing payment difficulties and provide debt rescheduling. It was originally formed in 1956 under French chairmanship to deal with Argentine payment difficulties. Since then, the Paris Club has reached 433 agreements with 90 different debtor countries. Since 1956, the debt treated in the framework of Paris Club agreements amounts to USD 583 billion.[20] In the Paris Club, the terms and conditions of restructuring agreements leading to *de facto* subordination are agreed between the creditors. The debtor is not a formal party to the restructuring agreement. In the absence of agreement between the relevant creditor and the debtor, it should be noted that the sovereign debtor may still, legally speaking, make regular payments to the subordinated creditor.[21]

3.4 Secured Creditors

It is rare for sovereign debtors to offer security when concluding loan agreements under public international law.[22] There are, however, exceptions to this rule and the question of collateralized public international debt is not a completely new phenomenon. One relatively modern example is a 1950 loan agreement between the World Bank and the state of Iraq which was secured by an assignment of royalties due to the

---

[19] ibid 486.
[20] Paris Club, 'Key Figures' (*Paris Club*, no date) <https://clubdeparis.org/en/communications/page/key-numbers> accessed 8 November 2019.
[21] Martha (n 1) 486. *De facto* subordination is not a complete or an inchoate subordination. According to Martha, a complete payment or claim subordination provision stipulates that the senior creditor will be paid prior to the junior creditor and requires the junior creditor to turn over any payment received from a debtor, until the senior's debt is paid in full. In cases of inchoate or default subordination, the subordination does not become enforceable until the debtor becomes the subject of a bankruptcy case or defaults on its obligations under senior loan documents. However, to obtain these effects, there is a need for an agreement.
[22] ibid 488. See also G Mitu Gulati and others, 'When Governments Promise to Prioritize Public Debt: Do Markets Care?' (2020) 6 Journal of Financial Regulation 41. In this chapter, secured creditors refers not only to creditors who have secured their debts in rights in property (*in re* rights) but also quasi-secured creditors. The latter type of creditors have been promised satisfaction from a particular fund or specified property or have been promised a security interest in the fund or property but are not 'separatist' as creditors secured by *ius in re*. Creditors who hold a *ius in re* as a security normally have an absolute right under domestic law which entitles them to realize their security separately from any settlement ('separatist right'). See Martha (n 15) 806.

country from three British oil companies. Similarly, in a 1957 loan provided by the World Bank, Iran secured the agreement by setting aside oil revenues.[23] A more recent example is the Euro area sovereign debt crisis in which Finland demanded security for its participation in the bailout arrangement for Greece and Spain.[24]

Collateralization of specified future revenues to secure public international debt restricts the autonomous powers of the sovereign debtor. Such practices raise several questions of intercreditor equity. First, how do secured creditors' claims relate to those of an unsecured creditor in such circumstances? The equality rule discussed above answers this question: in short, a sovereign debtor's obligation to a creditor exists independently of other obligations and all obligations are of equal rank.

The *Venezuelan Preferential Case* before the Permanent Court of Arbitration discusses the relationship between the claims of a secured creditor and those of an unsecured creditor and sheds light on the consequences of the equality rule. The case concerns a controversy over pecuniary claims in the form of Venezuelan sovereign bonds. Bondholders from Great Britain, Germany, and Italy sought unsuccessfully to settle the dispute with Venezuela through diplomatic negotiations. In 1902, Great Britain, Germany, and Italy declared a blockade of Venezuelan ports, which included the use of force. Belgium, France, Mexico, the Netherlands, Norway, Spain, Sweden, and the United States (the 'neutral states') also held claims against Venezuela but did not apply any forcible measures to secure their claims. As a result of the blockade, Venezuela agreed to set aside 30% of customs revenue from two ports for the payment of the claims of all nations. The proposal was accepted by the claimant nations but Great Britain, Germany, and Italy (the 'blockading states') held that their claims should not rank equally with the claims of the neutral states that had not participated in the blockade. Instead, they claimed they should be given priority of payment. Venezuela declined to accept this view and the question was submitted to arbitration by agreement.[25] The tribunal held that Germany, Italy, and the United Kingdom did have a right to preferential treatment for the payment of their claims. According to the tribunal, Venezuela had acknowledged a distinction between the blockading states and the other neutral creditors in the negotiations held before the case was brought to the arbitral tribunal. Moreover, the neutral states had not objected to the blockading states' claim to preferential treatment during the diplomatic negotiations, nor had they acquired any rights from the war-like operations or the ensuing treaty, since they had not taken part. Lastly, the treaty in question did not contain any stipulations in their favour that could indicate a right to equal ranking in payment.[26] While concluding that the blockading powers had obtained security and the right to priority in payment, the tribunal also insisted—in line with the equality rule—that 'the rights acquired by

---

[23] Aron Broches, 'International Legal Aspects of the Operations of the World Bank' in *Selected Essays: World Bank, ICSID, and Other Subjects of Public and Private International Law* (Martinus Nijhoff 1995) 357–59. See also Martha (n 1) 488.
[24] Kati Pohjanpalo, 'Finland's Collateral Demand Fueled by Greek Bailout Fatigue', *Bloomberg.com* (30 August 2011) <https://www.bloomberg.com/news/articles/2011-08-29/finland-collateral-demand-fueled-by-bailout-fatigue> accessed 14 March 2022.
[25] Preferential Treatment of Claims of Blockading Powers against Venezuela (*Germany, Great Britain and Italy v Venezuela*), PCA Case No 1903-01, Award (22 February 1904), 103 (hereafter *Venezuelan Preferential Case*).
[26] ibid 109–10.

the neutral or pacific Powers with regard to Venezuela remain in the future absolutely intact and guaranteed by respective international arrangements'.[27]

This starting point does not provide much reassurance to the unsecured creditor in practice, as secured creditors have a prior claim to resources that the sovereign debtor could otherwise have used to pay the claims of the former. Secured debt hence effectively subordinates both existing and future unsecured creditors.[28]

Martha argues that it is important to moderate this statement because the creation of a security over specified receivables is a legally binding promise at the same level as the other unsecured debts, both deriving their obligatory force from the same principle of *pacta sunt servanda*.[29] In this context, he questions whether one can speak of secured debts in public international law at all, 'because a conventional undertaking to earmark revenues or allocation of certain of the debtor's assets to only specified creditors will have no effect on the debtor's legal ability to pay another creditor with those resources, even if it is then in default to the secured creditor(s)'.[30]

The second question related to secured debt claims is how they are ranked *inter se*, where two or more creditors claim a security interest in the same collateral. As long as no relative priority among the creditors has been agreed upon by the parties in the relevant legal instrument, the same equality rule applies between those creditors. This means that both claims are valid and the state must choose which obligation to default on.[31]

3.5 Preferred Creditor Status

3.5.1 Introduction

As discussed in Section 3.2, the equality rule regulates the relationship between international law creditors and debt claims governed by international law. The question in this section is whether, under international law, there exist any exceptions to the equality rule, which would give certain creditors a right to preferential treatment in the context of a debt restructuring.

Section 3.5.3 examines preferred creditor status under customary international law and considers whether the International Monetary Fund (IMF), in particular, has such a status. Section 3.5.4 discusses how one might acquire the status of preferred creditor (through various acts of will) under international law. The IMF and certain European multilateral creditors will be analysed. The extent to which preferential treatment under international law is compatible with the principle of sovereign equality is discussed in Section 3.6. First though, Section 3.5.2 presents the main arguments in favour of providing certain public international law actors with preferred creditor status.

---

[27] ibid 110.
[28] Martha (n 1) 490.
[29] ibid.
[30] ibid.
[31] ibid 489.

3.5.2 Justification for providing multilateral financial institutions with preferred status

The discussion of preferred creditor status under international law in the context of sovereign debt restructuring mainly concerns intergovernmental organizations and their debt claims. The relevant intergovernmental organizations are typically those providing loans to states or otherwise contributing to states' monetary and financial stability, such as the International Bank for Reconstruction and Development, regional development banks, the Bank for International Settlements (BIS), the IMF, and the European Stability Mechanism (ESM).[32]

A preference in this context typically entails priority in payment (in the temporal sense) if there are not sufficient resources to cover all debt obligations as they fall due. In other words, the debtor country would prioritize not defaulting on obligations owed to multilateral financial institutions, instead of fulfilling its obligations to other creditors. In the case of a restructuring, a preferred creditor status can also refer to a right to be exempted from a debt restructuring or to receive a preferential restructuring agreement. It also entails a corresponding obligation for a sovereign debtor to provide preferential treatment. Debts that enjoy such treatment are called preferential debts.

A combination of factors favours providing multilateral financial institutions with preferred creditor status in case of a restructuring. Some arguments may, however, vary according to the objectives of the specific organization. When discussing various justifications for providing such multinational financial institutions with preferred status, this section will mainly focus on the IMF. The IMF is the intergovernmental organization most often and most strongly assumed to have preferred creditor status under international law.[33] The subsequent section examining whether any creditors have preferred status under customary international law will also focus on the IMF for the same reasons.

A first factor in favour of providing certain international financial institutions with preferred status is that it is in the interests of Member States—both the current debtor state and potential future debtor states—that their resources not be adversely affected in a situation where the borrowing Member State is unable to meet all of its loan obligations. For example, the IMF's role as lender of last resort provides a strong incentive for borrowers to prioritize meeting loan obligations with regard to multilateral creditors.[34] If the institution was not given preferential treatment, it would limit the ability

---

[32] Giuseppe Bianco, 'Restructuring Sovereign Debt Owed to Private Creditors. The Appropriate Role for International Law' (PhD, University of Oslo 2017) 65–66.

[33] See also Melissa Boudreau and G Mitu Gulati, 'The International Monetary Fund's Imperiled Priority' (2014) 10 Duke Journal of Constitutional Law & Public Policy 119, 147. Boudreau and Gulati also write that loans granted by the ECB, the World Bank, the European Investment Bank, and so on, are deserving of similar status to the IMF, but they are not quite so clearly 'lenders of last resort' and thus the argument for priority is less clear. Moreover, unlike the IMF priority, Boudreau and Gulati note that the norm of granting priority to these institutions is not as well-established. For a policy discussion on the IMF's preferred creditor status, see Susan Schadler, 'The IMF's Preferred Creditor Status: Does It Still Make Sense After the Euro Crisis?' (CIGI Policy Brief, 20 March 2014).

[34] Martha (n 1) 494.

of Member States to obtain crisis funding from the IMF in the future. (Indeed, it could possibly endanger the very existence of the institution.) Relatedly, multilateral financial institutions often justify their priority ranking on the grounds that they are not commercial organizations seeking profitable lending opportunities. On the contrary, institutions such as the IMF lend to members at a time when other creditors are reluctant to do so and at interest rates that are below what would be charged by commercial creditors. By operating as an international lender of last resort (ILOR), the IMF helps states catalyse private financing, and so avoid adjustment and policies that could be harmful to themselves, private creditors, and other states. Treating the IMF's funds equally with other commercial claims in a restructuring would fundamentally undermine the IMF's capacity to continue as an ILOR in the future.[35] This would negatively affect the Member State's chances of gaining access to ordinary capital markets and restoring its economic and financial position.[36]

Second, there are also more systemic reasons for providing multilateral finance institutions with preferred status. For example, recognition of preferred status for the IMF is in the common interest of the international financial community because the IMF's financial activities are essential for financial stability and the general functioning the international monetary system.[37]

A third reason also relates to systemic risk. Gaining access to these institutions' resources is typically conditional—whether directly or indirectly—on an obligation for the Member State to undertake certain programmes to adjust its balance of payments. One may argue that these financial policies contribute to ensuring a sustainable debt burden and improving the economic situation of the country.[38] The point is that these adjustment programmes rely on the sustainable operation of the institution, which again depends on debtor countries prioritizing repayment of their outstanding claims.

Fourth, the resources needed to fund the operations of multilateral financial institutions are obtained through contributions from Member States.[39] The shareholder cooperative nature of these institutions can also be seen as an argument in favour of providing international organizations preferred status in a debt restructuring.[40]

3.5.3 Preferred creditor status under customary international law—the case of the IMF

The question discussed in the following is whether there is an obligation imposed mainly by customary international law to give priority to the repayment of debts owed

---

[35] Rosa M Lastra, 'The Role of the International Monetary Fund' in Rosa M Lastra and Lee C Buchheit (eds), *Sovereign Debt Management* (Oxford University Press 2014) 62.
[36] Martha (n 15) 803. Moreover, according to current Paris Club practices, a sovereign debtor will not qualify for sovereign debt restructuring in the Paris Club if it is not in a programme supported by the IMF. This factor decreases the chances that a debtor will recover economically if it is in arrears to the IMF and underlines the Member States' interest in actually prioritizing payments to the IMF.
[37] ibid 805.
[38] ibid.
[39] Martha (n 1) 494.
[40] ibid. See also Philip R Wood, 'Debt Priorities in Sovereign Insolvency' (1982) 1 International Financial Law Review 4, 8, n 14.

to the IMF and a right for the IMF to be provided with preferential treatment in a sovereign debt restructuring.

For a norm to have developed into customary international law there must be evidence that there exists (i) a relatively uniform and consistent state practice concerning a particular matter, and (ii) a belief among states that they are under an obligation to follow the norm—that it is accepted as law (*opinio juris*).[41]

Various factors could indicate that the IMF does in fact have a *de jure* right to preferred treatment under customary international law. First, in 1988, the IMF Interim Committee's Berlin Communiqué discussed overdue financial obligations owed to the IMF.[42] The Committee underlined 'the adverse impact of overdue obligations on the effectiveness of the Fund as a cooperative monetary institution'.[43] The Committee moreover 'urged all members, within the limits of their laws, to treat the Fund as a preferred creditor and to lend their active and tangible support to this cooperative endeavour, so as to bring countries with overdue obligations back into the mainstream of international economic relations'.[44] The Committee repeated its message in its Washington Communiqué of 4 April 1989, stating that 'the Fund, whose preferred creditor status was reaffirmed by the Interim Committee meeting in Berlin (West), must permanently enjoy the full support of the entire membership'.[45] These statements by the Fund's Interim Committee may be read as expressions of the IMF's legal right to preferential treatment in a debt restructuring. The more likely interpretation is that it called for its Member States to provide the IMF with preferential treatment in domestic law and that the committee's arguments should be read as providing an economic rationale for granting the IMF preferred creditor status.[46]

Second, the fact that the IMF is often exempted from restructuring processes may constitute a practice, which gives it a right to preferential treatment under general international law. However, it is doubtful whether consistent practice and *opinio juris* exist, both of which are required for a customary rule to emerge. The only consistent practice exempting IMF loans from restructuring processes is that of the Paris Club.[47]

---

[41] Art 38(1)(b) of the Statute of the International Court of Justice 3 Bevans 1179, 59 Stat 1055, TS No 993, 3 Bevans 1179, 59 Stat 1055, TS No 993 (United Nations 1945). See, for example, SS Lotus (*France v Turkey*) (Judgment) (1927) PCIJ Series A no 10, 28 (hereafter *SS Lotus*). See, in general, Crawford (n 2) 21–29. There are substantial difficulties in implementing this textbook definition of what constitutes customary law in practice. When considering international courts and tribunals, it is challenging to establish how much broad support a practice must have and how long it must have existed. Moreover, it is often hard to distinguish when a state is acting in a specific manner because it believes it is at liberty to do so and when it is acting under an obligation. See Boudreau and Gulati (n 33) 121–27.

[42] IMF—Interim Committee of the Board of Governors on the International Monetary System, 'Press Communiqué from Thirty-Second Meeting, Washington, April 3–4, 1989' (Appendix V to IMF's 1989 Annual Report, *International Monetary Fund*, 4 April 1989) 96 (item 5) <https://www.imf.org/external/pubs/ft/ar/archive/pdf/ar1989.pdf> accessed 11 November 2019.

[43] IMF—Interim Committee of the Board of Governors on the International Monetary System, 'Press Communiqué from Thirty-First Meeting, Berlin (West), September 25–26, 1988' (Appendix V to IMF's 1989 Annual Report, *International Monetary Fund*, 26 October 1988) 96 (item 5) <https://www.imf.org/external/pubs/ft/ar/archive/pdf/ar1989.pdf> accessed 11 November 2019.

[44] ibid.

[45] IMF—Interim Committee of the Board of Governors on the International Monetary System (n 42) 98 (item 4).

[46] Martha (n 15) 802, 825.

[47] ibid 809, n 30. See also Wood (n 40) 8.

Moreover, it is rather unclear whether *opinio juris* from the Paris Club Member States exists: neither the Paris Club as such nor its Member States have stated whether they perceive this to be a legal right or whether it is done for practical or pragmatic reasons.[48]

Against the existence of a customary rule on preference, it can also be argued, as Martha does, that the legal obligation to repay a loan and pay interest according to the contract terms is not of a comparable nature to that owed under an obligation to perform an act (repurchase of currency). In other words, such obligations to the IMF are not of a comparable nature to other loan obligations under international law.[49]

Scholars, such as Carreau, have argued in support of the view that the IMF has a preferred creditor right under customary international law.[50] Somewhat less assertive, Boudreau and Gulati have also suggested that customary international law may possibly provide the IMF with preferred status. They say that a thorough analysis of how courts actually decide questions of customary international law would be forward-looking and more complex than the state practice and *opinio juris* paradigm that dominates legal textbooks at present. They argue that, in reality, international courts appear to transform the inquiry from considering whether a customary rule has emerged to considering whether states might want a particular norm to be law. Under such a conception of international custom, a court may legitimately find that the IMF's *de facto* preferred creditor status has now evolved into a *de jure* preferred creditor status.[51]

Despite all this, the vast majority of legal scholars still reject the idea that customary international law currently provides a *de jure* preferred creditor status for the IMF or for any other intergovernmental financial institution. Rather, preferential treatment of the IMF in restructuring is the result of practical solutions constructed to meet the immediate necessities of a particular situation.[52] More generally, there seems to be broad agreement that there is no basis to support the priority claim of *any* individual creditor or class of creditors in general international law.[53] The objectives or justification for providing the IMF (or other international creditors with a similar role) with preferred status continues to exist and is followed as a *de facto* norm, but it is generally accepted by scholars that this is a *de facto* right.

---

[48] Martha (n 15) 825.
[49] ibid 809.
[50] Dominique Carreau, 'Le rééchelonnement de la dette extérieure des États' (1985) 112 Journal du droit international 5, 15.
[51] Boudreau and Gulati (n 33) 146–47.
[52] The following have all rejected the existence of a general rule in international law providing for relative priorities among the different classes of creditors in customary international law: Bianco (n 32) 66; Edwin M Borchard, 'International Loans and International Law' (1932) 26 Proceedings of the American Society of International Law at its Annual Meeting (1921–1969) 135, 155ff; Lee C Buchheit and others, 'The Restructuring Process' in S Ali Abbas and others (eds), *Sovereign Debt: A Guide for Economists and Practitioners* (Oxford University Press 2020) 331; Ernst H Feilchenfeld and others, 'Priority Problems in Public Debt Settlements' (1930) 30 Columbia Law Review 1115, 1115; Lastra (n 35) 61; Martha (n 1) 507; Wood (n 40) 5–6.
[53] Martha (n 15) 810.

3.5.4 Means of acquiring the status of preferred creditor—particular international law

As concluded above, there is no rule in customary international law providing particular creditors or particular classes of creditors with preferred status and hence no basis to support a priority claim based on custom. The question considered in this section is how a creditor can *acquire* the status of preferred creditor under international law.

Despite the fact that no customary rule to this effect exists, preferred creditor status can nonetheless be achieved through acts of will.[54] First, an international creditor may enter into an agreement with a sovereign debtor concerning preferred creditor status. Second, preferred creditor status can be established based on an act of will expressed between creditors who thereby create a right for a third party ('stipulation *pour autrui*').[55] In this situation, the third-party creditor cannot object to the termination of a treaty providing for such a right if the parties to the treaty (the other creditors) wish to terminate it. Third, preferred creditor status can be established by means of a unilateral act in which the debtor grants a creditor preferred status.[56] In these circumstances, the state or states in whose favour the right is declared cannot object to its withdrawal or modification, if the declarant debtor state so chooses.

3.5.4.1 The IMF

Under Article V of the Articles of Agreement of the International Monetary Fund (IMF Articles of Agreement) dealing with the 'Operations and Transactions of the Fund', the IMF has the power to become a preferred creditor by requiring security from Member States drawing on their Special Drawing Rights (SDRs).[57] Article V, section 4, of the IMF Articles of Agreement states that the IMF may, at its discretion, waive any of the conditions prescribed in section 3(b)(iii) and (iv) of Article V when a Member State wishes to purchase the currencies of other Member States from the IMF. According to the same section, the IMF must in this context take into consideration a member's willingness to pledge collateral security and may require as a condition of waiver the pledge of such collateral security. In so doing, Article V allows the IMF to become a secured creditor. In practice, the IMF has accepted offers of collateral from Member States who have wished to use its sovereign debt restructuring mechanism (SDRM), but it has never exercised the power to require such security.[58]

---

[54] ibid 811.
[55] See also ILC *Fifth Report by Sir Gerald Fitzmaurice, Special Rapporteur* UN Doc A/CN4/130, at 81 (United Nations 1960) (hereafter *Fifth Report*).
[56] ibid.
[57] Martha (n 15) 813–14. Martha also notes that before the second amendment, the IMF Articles of Agreement contained a provision suggesting that others would have a preference over the IMF. After the second amendment, this was no longer a question.
[58] ibid 814.

3.5.4.2 European multilateral financial institutions

The question of preferred creditors is also relevant within the European Union. The discussion centres on whether certain multilateral financial institutions, or certain creditors with a special public interest function, should have preferred creditor status or preferential treatment of their in debt restructurings. The discussion has become more pertinent in the course of the Euro crisis. The reason is that a number of crisis resolution measures were implemented, including: (i) various EU crisis packages from the ESM and its predecessors providing for loans, including the purchase of Member States' bonds; and (ii) the European Central Bank (ECB) implementing various unconventional monetary policy measures, including purchasing the sovereign bonds of Member States.

In line with the conclusion in Section 3.5.3, none of these institutions claim to have preferred creditor status under customary international law. The basis for their claimed status is, and has been, based on other legal grounds: whether it is acquired through an act of will under international law or based on statutes or contracts under domestic law. The following sections examine the legal basis for a potential claim of preferred creditor status by the ESM and its predecessors, as well as by the ECB.

3.5.4.2.1 The Greek loan facility and the European Financial Stability Mechanism

The first loan facility in the context of the European financial crisis was the Greek loan facility, from 2010, which was a bilateral loan regulated by international law from other Euro area countries to Greece. In this context, lenders were considered to have 'at least' *pari passu* status.[59] However, in a later loan facility granted to Ireland, the text of the agreement added that the borrower undertook 'not to grant to any other creditor or holder of its sovereign debt any priority to the Lenders'.[60] At this time, the IMF had already committed a substantial amount—EUR 30 billion—under a standby arrangement.[61] The fact that this loan had already been granted leaves some room for interpretation. Similar wording was also used in the agreement on bilateral loans between Ireland and the United Kingdom.[62] On 11 May 2010, the European Financial Stabilisation Mechanism (EFSM) was created by council regulation with the aim of providing financial assistance to any EU country that was experiencing, or was threatened by, severe financial difficulties.[63] When the EFSM was activated for the first time, in the case of Ireland, the agreement contained an even stronger clause stating that, '[t]he support from the EFSM needs to be supplied on terms and conditions similar to

---

[59] The Greek Loan Facility was the first financial support programme agreed for Greece in May 2010. It consisted of bilateral loans from Euro area countries, amounting to EUR 52.9 billion and a EUR 20.1 billion loan from the IMF. The EFSF, which was only established in June 2010, did not take part in this programme. See the section on Greece in ESM, 'Explainers' (*European Stability Mechanism*, no date) <https://www.esm.europa.eu/explainers> accessed 11 March 2022.

[60] See Euro Area Loan Facility Act 2010 (Ireland).

[61] Sven Steinkamp and Frank Westermann, 'The Role of Creditor Seniority in Europe's Sovereign Debt Crisis' (2014) 29 Economic Policy 495, 502.

[62] ibid.

[63] Council Regulation (EU) No 407/2010 of 11 May 2010 establishing a European Financial Stabilization Mechanism [2010] OJ L118/1 (European Union) established the European Financial Stabilisation Mechanism based on Article 122(2) of the Consolidated versions of the Treaty on European Union and the Treaty on the Functioning of the European Union [2016] OJ C202/1 (European Union) (hereafter TFEU).

those of the IMF'.[64] The statement is somewhat vague. The reference to the IMF could signal that the loans should be considered to have *de facto* priority under international law or that the agreement sought to establish *de jure* priority in an international agreement. Today, Euro states in need of financial assistance turn to the European Stability Mechanism (an issue to which we will return below). However, the EFSM remains in place for specific tasks, such as the lengthening of maturities for loans to Ireland and Portugal and providing so-called bridge loans.[65]

3.5.4.2.2 The European Financial Stability Facility
In June 2010, the Euro area Member States created the European Financial Stability Facility (EFSF), which was a temporary crisis resolution mechanism.[66] By means of a notarial deed, it was established as a public limited liability company in Luxembourg, governed by the laws of Luxembourg and in particular the Luxembourg Law of 10 August 1915.[67] The preamble of the EFSF Framework Agreement states that

> financial support to euro-area Member States shall be provided by EFSF in conjunction with the IMF and shall be on comparable terms to the stability support loans advanced by euro-area Member States to the Hellenic Republic on 8 May 2010 or on such other terms as may be agreed.[68]

The ambiguity regarding the status of the EFSM bilateral loans was accordingly shifted onto EFSF lending. However, in public statements, the EFSF and other policymakers have made it clear that they do not claim a preferred status for EFSF lending.[69]

That being said, it is important to note that the question of whether preferred creditor status has been acquired is somewhat different for the EFSF as compared to first loan facilities and the EFSM (and the IMF and the ESM) which have held (and continue to hold) debt instruments governed by international law. The EFSF also distinguishes itself from the IMF and the ESM in that it is not a subject of international law. As mentioned, the EFSF was established as a private company under the domestic law of Luxembourg, of which the 17 Euro states are the only shareholders. A Framework Agreement was thereafter entered into between the EFSF and its 17 shareholders to set out the decision-making rules of the EFSF and substantive guidance on its operation.[70] The Framework Agreement is not a formal treaty under international law,

---

[64] Steinkamp and Westermann (n 61) 502.
[65] See European Commission, 'European Financial Stabilisation Mechanism (EFSM)' (*europa.eu*, no date) <https://ec.europa.eu/info/business-economy-euro/economic-and-fiscal-policy-coordination/financial-assistance-eu/funding-mechanisms-and-facilities/european-financial-stabilisation-mechanism-efsm_en> accessed 11 March 2022.
[66] European Financial Stability Facility Framework Agreement as Amended with effect from the Effective Date of the Amendments (26 August 2011) <https://www.esm.europa.eu/sites/default/files/20111019_efsf_framework_agreement_en.pdf> accessed 12 March 2019 (hereafter EFSF Framework Agreement 2011).
[67] Ralf Jansen, 'The European Stability Facility (EFSF) and the European Stability Mechanism (ESM)—A Legal Overview' (no date) 2011 EUREDIA 417, 418.
[68] See EFSF Framework Agreement 2011 (n 66), rec 1 of the preamble.
[69] See, for example, ESM, 'Explainers' (n 59). Under the section 'How are the EFSF and ESM different', the ESM states that '[t]he ESM itself claims that the EFSF is a creditor rank equal (*pari passu*) among other creditors'.
[70] EFSF Framework Agreement 2011 (n 66).

because it was concluded between states and a private company. This is also clear from Article 16.1 of the Framework Agreement, which makes EFSF loans subject to the law of England and Wales.[71]

Today, the EFSF does not provide any further financial assistance, as this task is now performed by the European Stability Mechanism (ESM).[72]

3.5.4.2.3 *European Stability Mechanism—the permanent rescue fund*

In February 2012, all 17 Euro area Member States signed the Treaty Establishing the ESM (ESM Treaty).[73] The ESM is a permanent intergovernmental organization under international law based in Luxembourg. It assumes the tasks previously fulfilled by the EFSF and the EFSM in providing financial assistance to Euro area Member States. ESM offers financial assistance only in situations where regular access to market financing is impaired.[74] Lending is therefore restricted to circumstances in which no commercial lender would be willing to lend. This means that the ESM acts as an international lender of last resort, similar to the IMF.

The ESM relies on several instruments to fulfil its role. For instance, it provides ordinary loans within a macroeconomic adjustments programme and purchases bonds on the primary and secondary markets (the Secondary Market Support Facility).[75] The ESM has also created Pandemic Crisis Support, a credit line available to ESM members to support domestic financing of healthcare, cure, and prevention-related costs due to the COVID-19 crisis.[76] The bonds purchased are typically issued under, and governed by, domestic law, while the loans are governed by international law.[77]

The intended status of the ESM was clearly expressed in a press statement by the Euro group: 'an ESM loan will enjoy preferred creditor status, junior only to the IMF loan'.[78] This was justified by the ESM's role as a lender of last resort.[79] A first version

---

[71] Article 16.1 of the EFSF Framework Agreement 2011 (n 66) states that '[t]his Agreement and any non-contractual obligations arising out of or in connection with it shall be governed by and shall be construed in accordance with English law'. See also Bruno De Witte, 'Using International Law in the Euro Crisis: Causes and Consequences' (ARENA Working Paper, ARENA 2013) 4–5.
[72] ESM, 'Before the ESM' (*European Stability Mechanism*, no date) <https://www.esm.europa.eu/efsf-overview> accessed 11 March 2022.
[73] Treaty establishing the European Stability Mechanism (European Union) (hereafter ESM Treaty). Two versions of the treaty were signed: a first version, signed in July 2011, was not opened for ratification because the signatories had second thoughts about some of its content. A renegotiated version was signed in February 2012 and came into force in October 2012. For a discussion of why the ESM was established as an international organization, see De Witte (n 71) 6–7.
[74] ESM Treaty, rec 13.
[75] ESM, 'Lending Toolkit' (*European Stability Mechanism*, no date) <https://www.esm.europa.eu/assistance/lending-toolkit> accessed 11 March 2022.
[76] See Eurogroup, 'Eurogroup Statement on the Pandemic Crisis Support' (Press release, 5 August 2020) <https://www.consilium.europa.eu/en/press/press-releases/2020/05/08/eurogroup-statement-on-the-pandemic-crisis-support/> accessed 29 April 2022. In April 2020, the Euro area finance ministers (Eurogroup) decided on a comprehensive economic policy response to the COVID-19 crisis. On 23 April, the EU heads of state or government (European Council) endorsed this agreement. On 8 May, the Eurogroup agreed on the details attached to this credit line.
[77] Section 16.1 of the General Terms for ESM Financial Assistance Facility Agreements states that '[t]he Agreement and any non-contractual obligations arising out of or in connection with the Agreement shall be governed by and shall be construed in accordance with public international law'.
[78] Eurogroup, 'Statement by the Eurogroup' (Press release, 28 November 2010) 2 <https://www.consilium.europa.eu/uedocs/cms_data/docs/pressdata/en/ecofin/118050.pdf> accessed 14 March 2019.
[79] Steinkamp and Westermann (n 61) 504.

of the treaty was signed on 11 July 2011 and stated that, '[t]he ESM loans will enjoy preferred creditor status'.[80] In the final version of the ESM Treaty, priority was downplayed as it stated that 'the ESM loans will enjoy preferred creditor status in a similar fashion to those of the IMF, while accepting preferred creditor status of the IMF over the ESM'.[81] This means that in relation to programmes where the ESM purchases bonds on the primary and secondary market, it does not enjoy priority.[82]

It must be mentioned that, on various occasions since 2011, the maturities of EFSF and ESM loans have been extended.[83] This can be interpreted as a softening of the strong priority position previously expressed.

As with the EFSF debt instruments, the sovereign bonds purchased on the market are typically commercial instruments governed by domestic law and bought by private law subjects and public international law subjects alike. Establishing a right for the ESM under international law to be treated preferentially in the context of domestic law governed debt instruments may lead to some particular challenges that will be discussed in Chapter 6.

3.5.4.2.4 *The European Central Bank and unconventional monetary policy programmes*

Since the advent of the European financial crisis, the European System of Central Banks (ESCB) has also become an important creditor for Euro countries. In particular, the ESCB has become a key actor in the Euro area's sovereign bonds market through its various exceptional monetary policy programmes.[84]

On 14 May 2010, the ECB established the Securities Market Programme (SME),[85] which forms part of the Euro area's single monetary policy but which would only apply temporarily. The objective of the programme was to 'address the malfunctioning of securities markets and restore an appropriate monetary policy transmission mechanism'.[86] On 6 September 2012, the programme was discontinued and, on the same day, a new programme was announced: Outright Monetary Transactions (OMTs).[87]

---

[80] ESM Treaty, rec 10.
[81] ibid, rec 13.
[82] As noted by Steinkamp and Westermann, '[i]t is interesting to note that the seniority status of the ESM is only governed in its preamble—as a mutual understanding'. Furthermore, the authors noted that '[a]ccording to ESM chief, Klaus Regling, this is, however, legally binding as any "repeal or amendment of their earlier statement would therefore also require a decision by the Heads of State or Government. In several Member States it would require support by the national parliament."' (Steinkamp and Westermann (n 61) 505).
[83] On 21 July 2011, the heads of state extended the maximum maturity for the first time for Greece. See Herman Van Rompuy, 'The European Council in 2011' (Publications Office of the European Union January 2012) 54. Another example is EFSF's extension of loan maturities for Ireland and Portugal in 2013. See ESM, 'EFSF Extends Loan Maturities for Ireland and Portugal' (Press release, *European Stability Mechanism*, 24 June 2013) <https://www.esm.europa.eu/press-releases/efsf-extends-loan-maturities-ireland-and-portugal> accessed 11 March 2022. See also Steinkamp and Westermann (n 61) 505.
[84] The ESCB comprises the European Central Bank (ECB) and the national central banks of all EU countries, while the Eurosystem comprises the ECB and national central banks of Euro area countries only.
[85] Decision 2010/281/EU of the European Central Bank of 14 May 2010 establishing a securities markets programme [2010] OJ L124/8 (European Union 20 May 2010).
[86] ibid rec 3.
[87] ECB, 'Technical Features of Outright Monetary Transactions' (*European Central Bank*, 9 June 2012) <https://www.ecb.europa.eu/press/pr/date/2012/html/pr120906_1.en.html> accessed 11 March 2022.

These transactions allow the ECB to purchase sovereign bonds on the secondary markets and so preserve market access for Euro area sovereign borrowers. At the time of writing, this programme has not been used.

The ECB has communicated that the

> Eurosystem intends to clarify in the legal act concerning Outright Monetary Transactions that it accepts the same (pari passu) treatment as private or other creditors with respect to bonds issued by euro area countries and purchased by the Eurosystem through Outright Monetary Transactions, in accordance with the terms of such bonds.[88]

As such, the ECB confirms that the bonds acquired through OMTs are not intended to have preferred status in a restructuring.

On 4 March 2015, the ECB adopted the Public Securities Purchase Programme (PSPP), which allows the ECB to purchase sovereign bonds on the secondary market.[89] The PSPP is part of the Expanded Asset Purchase Programme, an ECB framework programme for the purchase of financial assets. Since the commencement of the PSPP, the ECB has been buying, among other financial assets, sovereign bonds with the aim of stimulating inflation and growth in the Euro area (a strategy often referred to as 'quantitative easing').[90] In the decision establishing the PSPP, the ECB states that

> [w]ith a view to ensuring the effectiveness of the PSPP, the Eurosystem hereby clarifies that it accepts the same (pari passu) treatment as private investors as regards the marketable debt securities that the Eurosystem may purchase under the PSPP, in accordance with the terms of such instruments.[91]

Consequently, neither the OMTs nor the PSPP require the ECB to be treated with preference.

To sum up, Section 3.5 has shown that although no creditor has preferred status under customary international law, creditors who are subjects of international law may still acquire such status under international law through various acts of will, including: (i) through an explicit agreement between creditor and debtor; (ii) through an agreement among creditors; or (iii) by a unilateral commitment from the debtor. The IMF's Articles of Agreement enable the institution to require (and accept) collateral that has similar effects to preferred creditor status, but this is seldom used in practice. Moreover, according to the ESM Treaty, the institution's ordinary loans offered to crisis-stricken Euro states are governed by international law and enjoy preference.

---

[88] ibid.

[89] Decision 2015/774/EU of the European Central Bank of 4 March 2015 on a secondary markets public sector asset purchase program [2015] OJ L121/20 (European Union) (hereafter Decision 2015/774/EU). Securities purchased under PSPP have been made available for securities lending in a decentralized manner by Eurosystem central banks since 2 April 2015.

[90] For information about ECB's asset purchase programme, see, in general, ECB, 'Asset Purchase Programmes' (*European Central Bank*, 3 August 2022) <https://www.ecb.europa.eu/mopo/implement/app/html/index.en.html> accessed 11 March 2022.

[91] Decision 2015/774/EU, rec 8.

This section has mainly focused on intercreditor equity rules and ranking among subjects of international law holding debt instruments governed by international law. Sovereign bonds purchased on the market by the ESM and the ECB are commercial instruments governed by some domestic law. The bonds are multiparty instruments and can be purchased by private law subjects and public international law subjects alike. The ESM and the ECB do not claim to have preferred creditor status when holding such sovereign bonds. Nevertheless, there is legislation at the EU level that may prohibit the ECB from participating in certain sovereign debt restructuring processes. This could lead to particular challenges due to the fact both the ESM and the ECB may be expected to take on losses in a debt restructuring of debt governed by domestic law on the same basis as private sector creditors. These and other questions on how the rights and obligations of creditors and debtors under international law and domestic law interact (and potentially collide) are further discussed in Chapter 6.

3.6 The Compatibility of Preferential Treatment with the Equality Rule

The right to be paid with priority or to be exempted from a debt restructuring is challenged when third parties are not legally bound to respect this right.[92] At issue is the question whether particular treatment of one creditor is a tolerable form of discrimination against another creditor. In other words, is the preferred creditor right for some creditors is compatible with the equality rule (discussed in Section 3.2)?

When examining the question of whether third parties are legally bound to respect other creditors' preferred creditor status, it is necessary to distinguish between third parties who are subjects of international law and third parties who are domestic law subjects. This section, and the rest of this chapter, only discusses whether preferred creditor claims are compatible with third parties' claims relating to debt instruments governed by international law. It will not discuss whether claims stemming from debt instruments governed by international law are compatible with claims stemming from debt instruments governed by domestic law. Nevertheless, it can be briefly noted that, as a basic starting point, domestic law is incapable of interfering *de jure* with international law obligations. Moreover, how preferential international law obligations interfere with creditor rights under domestic law depends on the law of the forum seized and the governing law of the debt instrument. The way in which intercreditor equity rights related to debt instruments governed by domestic law and international law interact with each other is further discussed in Chapter 6.

As a starting point, the equality rule discussed in Section 3.2 provides that a loan agreement is between a specific debtor and its creditor(s), and the fulfilment of a contract is independent and valid regardless of parallel existing loan agreements between the debtor and other creditors. However, the equality rule can be derogated from and preferred creditor status can be acquired either by an agreement to that effect,

---

[92] Martha (n 1) 509.

creditors creating a right for a third party or through a unilateral decision made at the debtor's discretion.

The earlier discussed *Venezuelan Preferential Case* is a clear example where the arbitral tribunal accepted an agreement providing for preferential treatment of only some of Venezuela's creditors.[93] That debtors are free to grant preferential treatment to certain creditors without violating the equality rule is also reflected in the Fifth Report on the Law of Treaties to the International Law Commission (ILC) by Special Rapporteur Sir Gerald Fitzmaurice, where he discusses the potential consequences of one treaty right interfering with another. Fitzmaurice writes that incidentally unfavourable effects on a third party by the simple operation of a treaty must be accepted.[94] Moreover, Fitzmaurice writes that third parties 'will be called upon, or will find themselves obliged, to accept, or anyhow will accept, and in that sense be bound by, the situation of law or fact, or the settlement or status, created by the treaty'.[95] However, the incidental effect cannot rise to the level of a breach of a third party's enforceable international right.[96] The duty for a third party to accept the unfavourable effects does not of course, Fitzmaurice underlines, apply where a treaty impairs the actual legal rights, or purports to create legal liabilities or disabilities for the third state without its consent. In such cases, the third party is 'immediately entitled to intervene'.[97]

Martha has neatly summarized the issue of whether preference and the equality rule collide in the context of sovereign debt, stating that '[a]n act of will (unilateral or consensual) to grant a preferred creditor status is ... unobjectionable unless it amounts to a breach of treaty, a tortious interference with a treaty, or an impediment against due performance of a treaty'.[98] In this context, the term treaty covers all international debt agreements between two (or more) subjects of international law that is regulated by international law.

It is a separate question, which would need to be considered in context with the facts of a specific case, whether the effects of a treaty (or another act of will) providing a creditor with preferred status would amount to such an interference or an infringement of a legal right of a third party. It is unlikely that the mere granting of preferred creditor status to an international law subject would amount to an interference with

---

[93] Formally speaking, the preferential treatment agreement was between Venezuela and some of the creditor governments. See *Venezuelan Preferential Case* (n 25).

[94] *Fifth Report* (n 55) at 81. Art 17 2.1(a) states that 'the mere fact that a treaty operates to the disadvantage or detriment of a third State is not a ground on which its validity can be impugned, or on which the third State can refuse to recognize it'. See also ibid at 97, para 67. Moreover, Fitzmaurice discusses the duty of states to accept and tolerate the incidentally unfavourable effects of lawful and valid treaties. He states that '[p]rovided that no legal right of the third State is infringed ... the third State does not suffer any legal wrong, or possess any right of recourse against the parties, merely by reason of the fact that it is adversely affected by the operation of the treaty, or that the treaty is incidentally unfavourable to it'. See ibid at 80–81, in particular Art 19.

[95] *Fifth Report* (n 55) at 97, para 68.

[96] Martha (n 1) 509.

[97] *Fifth Report* (n 55) at 101, para 79.

[98] Martha (n 15) 822. The *Fifth Report* (n 55) at 101 para 79 describes the more general approach (citing Roxburgh): 'In practice, there seem to be three classes of cases in which such rights are liable to be violated: (a) when the treaty violates a universally accepted rule of International Law, (b) when it is inconsistent with the safety of the third state, and (c) when it violates rights previously acquired by the third state.' Although the Report insists that Roxburgh's three heads of exception would be formulated differently at the time of writing the ILC Report, Fitzmaurice suggests that 'the principles involved remain the same'.

the performance of an international obligation (a debt obligation governed by international law). However, a preferred creditor may be held liable by other creditors who are subjects of international law if the right to a preferred status is asserted and there is an unreasonable exercise of right or power causing loss or damage (to third parties).[99]

The next question arising relates to the *consequences* of a situation where a subsequent undertaking has been entered into in contradiction to a special agreement promising the equal treatment of certain creditors. Would such a special agreement promising equal treatment of creditors lead to any subsequent undertaking to the contrary being void? Or would it simply give rise to international responsibility? Fitzmaurice argued that, to the extent that treaties have an unlawful object, or purport to impair or ignore the rights of one or more third states, they would be invalid.[100] Martha is of the view that it would be more in conformity with the logic of the law of treaties if subsequent undertakings contradicting preferred creditor status simply gave rise to international responsibility.[101] Under the law of treaties, an existing international commitment (aside from peremptory norms) does not constitute one of the grounds for invalidity of treaties.[102] The ordinary consequences following the finding of a breach of international law—international responsibility—are restitution, compensation (damages) and satisfaction.[103] This is also reflected in the ILC Articles on the Responsibility of States for Internationally Wrongful Acts, Articles 35–37. This solution would also be in conformity with the equality rule discussed in Section 3.2 and the *Venezuelan Preferential Case*, which both held that, regardless of an established right to preferential payment, the rights of third parties and the debtor's obligations towards the other creditors remain binding and enforceable.

Whether or not creditors holding debt instruments governed by domestic law may object to creditors who are subjects of international law trying to establish a *de iure* preferred creditor status for their debt instruments governed by international law (or domestic law for that matter) is discussed in Chapter 6.

---

[99] Martha (n 15) 823–24.
[100] *Fifth Report* (n 55) at 100, para 79.
[101] Martha (n 15) 823.
[102] Martha (n 1) 509, n 84.
[103] Crawford (n 1) 569–80.

4
Intercreditor Equity Rules Applicable to Debt Instruments Governed by Domestic Law

4.1 Introduction: Legal Status of the Creditor and Governing Law

This chapter analyses those intercreditor equity rules found in domestic law sources which are applicable to creditors holding sovereign debt instruments governed by domestic law. Before analysing the substance of these rules, it is necessary to establish which sovereign debt instruments are governed by domestic laws and the types of creditors that can hold such debt instruments.

Sections 2.2.2 and 2.2.3 examined the issue of which law applies when a state borrows from private legal persons (a non-state legal personality or capacity): international or domestic law, or some combination of both.[1] The basic starting point is that contracts between a state and a private legal person under domestic law are not contracts concluded by states in their capacity as subjects of public international law. The contracting of sovereign debt results from the state's private autonomy[2] and is regulated by domestic law.[3] Today, it is commonly accepted that states can enter into contracts with private legal persons, as well as subjects of international law, by virtue of their own private autonomy. Essentially, creditors who are also subjects of international law (states and international organizations) are obliged to follow the same rules as ordinary commercial creditors.[4]

Regardless of core similarities, a sovereign debt agreement governed by domestic law is distinct from an ordinary contract between private parties. That is, sovereign debt agreements are concluded between entities, one of which is sovereign with specific rights and obligations with regard to the internal legal order, while the other is a private individual.[5] Many legal systems recognize this and contain specific rules for contracts entered into by a sovereign (often referred to as 'public contracts').[6] In

---

[1] Robert Y Jennings, 'State Contracts in International Law' (1961) 37 Yearbook of International Law 156, 156.

[2] Irmgard Marboe and August Reinisch, 'Contracts between States and Foreign Private Law Persons' in Rüdiger Wolfrum (ed), *Max Planck Encyclopedia of Public International Law* (Oxford University Press 2019) s A.2.

[3] Case concerning the Payment of Various Serbian Loans Issued in France (*France v Kingdom of the Serbs, Croats and Slovenes*) (Judgment) (1929) PCIJ Series A no 20, para 86 (hereafter *Serbian Loans Case*): '[a]ny contract which is not a contract between States in their capacity as subjects of international law is based on the municipal law of some country'. For a discussion of international law protection of domestic law contracts, see Chapter 5.

[4] Questions concerning potential conflicting obligations of an international law creditor under domestic and international law are discussed in Chapter 6.

[5] Marboe and Reinisch (n 2) s A.3.

[6] ibid.

Intercreditor Equity in Sovereign Debt Restructuring. Astrid Iversen, Oxford University Press. © Astrid Iversen 2023.
DOI: 10.1093/oso/9780192866905.003.0005

particular, the French legal system has developed the concept of an administrative contract that takes into account the sovereign powers of the state when contracting.[7] Whether a sovereign debt contract is regulated by special public contract rules must be decided based on the law governing the contract.

The prevalence of certain jurisdictions in choice of law provisions indicates that a wide range of sovereign debt instruments should be considered ordinary commercial private law instruments. To elaborate, while states have been reluctant to subject some of their contracts to foreign law (especially investment contracts regarding natural resources), states normally agree that foreign law may govern their financial contracts.[8] Today, most loan agreements concluded between banks and states are—by means of choice of law provisions—expressly governed by the law of one of the major financial centres.[9] With regards to sovereign bonds, which have emerged in the period post-1980 as the primary source of sovereign debt, practice varies. Some countries have been able to issue bonds governed by their own law, but the laws of New York and England still have prevalence, regulating approximately 52% and 45% respectively of the notional amount of outstanding stock of *international* sovereign bonds.[10] If a state contract is governed by the laws of a foreign jurisdiction, it is generally immune to changes to the terms and conditions which could otherwise be implemented by the sovereign debtor's adoption of laws and regulations. In such situations, the loan instrument would therefore be subject to the same legal conditions as ordinary commercial loans. The fact that a substantive amount of sovereign debt is regulated by the laws of the big financial centres confirms the view that sovereign loan agreements, at least those issued under foreign law, are in principle regarded as commercial private law contracts.[11] In sum, loans contracted by states, including financial operations involving the issuance of bonds, constitute transactions of a private nature and are in principle subject to the rules governing commercial loans.

While not all debt instruments are governed by foreign law, this does not imply that they are instead public law instruments. Traditionally, stable developed economies have been able to issue bonds governed by their own law.[12] There is a lack of easily accessible data concerning the governing law of sovereign debt instruments. However, in recent years, we have seen an increase in middle-income and developing countries issuing sovereign debt instruments in domestic currencies in their domestic market, which is likely to correlate with issuances under domestic law.[13] Whether these debt

---

[7] ibid.

[8] Patrick Wautelet, 'International Public Contracts: Applicable Law and Dispute Resolution' in Mathias Audit and Stephan W Schill (eds), *The Internationalization of Public Contracts* (Bruylant 2013) 32.

[9] ibid 32–33.

[10] IMF, 'Fourth Progress Report on Inclusion of Enhanced Contractual Provisions in International Sovereign Bond Contract' (Policy paper, International Monetary Fund 21 March 2019) 5, n 9.

[11] Marboe and Reinisch (n 2) s C.3.27. See also BVerfG, 08.05.2007, 2 BvM 1/03, Rn. 1-95 (Germany) (hereafter *Argentine Necessity Case*).

[12] Branimir Gruić and Philip Wooldridge, 'Enhancements to the BIS Debt Securities Statistics' [2012] Bank for International Settlements Quarterly Review 63, 64–65.

[13] In recent years, there has been an increase in the number of developing countries issuing sovereign bonds in domestic currency on the domestic market as well, which is likely to correlate with issuances under domestic law. It is claimed that the primary market is usually a reliable indicator of the currency of denomination and governing law and that in most countries bonds issued in the local market are typically issued in the local currency and under the local law. Exceptions normally apply to international financial centres and dollar or euro economies. See ibid.

instruments are based on a public or private law contract may vary and must be established individually according to the relevant governing law. In particular, sovereign bonds issued on commercial markets are likely to be regarded as private law instruments. Regardless of whether a debt instrument is governed by public or private law, this chapter assumes that the contract provisions and statutes discussed are applicable to all domestic law debt instruments.

Which law governs a debt instrument subject to domestic law must be identified by the conflict of law rules of the state in which the action is brought (the *lex fori*).[14] Each state has its own conflict of law rules.[15] In contractual matters, private international law is generally dominated by the principle of party autonomy, recognized as a conflict of law rule in the vast majority of states participating in international trade and business.[16] It follows that the parties to a contract are free to choose the law governing their relationship or, in other words, to choose what law(s) the court or tribunal shall apply to each aspect of the dispute.[17]

This chapter does not further problematize the choice of law regulating a sovereign debt related issue under private international law.[18] Rather, it discusses the interpretation of central contract clauses and other domestic law rules regulating intercreditor equity in sovereign debt restructuring in jurisdictions commonly chosen by the parties to a sovereign debt agreement. As mentioned above, today most loan agreements concluded between banks and states are expressly governed by the law of one of the major financial centres, and in particular New York and English law. For this reason, the discussion about the interpretation of standard contract provisions is primarily focused on these two jurisdictions.

It should be mentioned that, although relatively uncommon today, the parties to a sovereign debt instrument governed by domestic law can choose to let certain debt

---

[14] Giuditta Cordero-Moss, *International Commercial Contracts: Applicable Sources and Enforceability* (Cambridge University Press 2014) 134.
[15] In the Case concerning the Payment in Gold of Brazilian Federal Loans Contracted in France (*France v Brazil*) (Judgment) (1929) PCIJ Series A no 21 (hereafter *Brazilian Loans Case*), the Permanent Court of International Justice (PCIJ) held that there was a presumption that the law of the contract was that of the contracting state. This latter approach was later rejected in favour of the more general formula of private international law such that agreements between states and foreign private law persons are governed by the law of the country with which the contract had the closest link (see Marboe and Reinisch (n 2) s A.2). The general principle of private international law would, in many cases, lead to the law of the state party to the contract being applied. If a law is not explicitly chosen in the contract, and there is nothing in the bond or other circumstances which are binding on the bondholder that substantiate a conclusion that the contract is subject to another law, there is some authority in favour of assuming that the governing law is that of the sovereign debtor. In the *Serbian Loans Case* (n 3) para 42, the International Court of Justice (ICJ) stated that '[o]nly the individuality of the borrower is fixed; in this case it is a sovereign State which cannot be presumed to have made the substance of its debt and the validity if the obligations accepted by it in respect thereof, subject to any law other than its own'. Kupelyants argues that this view is outdated and should be modified. For more details on the governing law of sovereign debt instruments, see, in general, Hayk Kupelyants, *Sovereign Defaults Before Domestic Courts* (Oxford Private International Law Series, Oxford University Press 2018) ch 4.
[16] See Cordero-Moss (n 14) 135.
[17] For questions regarding limitations on party autonomy posed by national and international law, see, in general, Cordero-Moss (n 14).
[18] For a comprehensive discussion of private international law and the governing law of sovereign debt instruments, see Kupelyants (n 15). See also Chapter 2 of this book for a discussion of the jurisdiction of courts over disputes related to debt restructurings.

instruments be subordinated. They may create securities or other preferred positions by means of contract similar to the intercreditor equity rules under international law discussed in Chapter 3. Similarly, in domestic law, one creditor's preferred right to payment may interfere with that of another creditor (see Section 3.6). Generally, if a creditor does not receive payment in accordance with her contract, she has a claim against the debtor. The extent to which the creditor also has a claim against a creditor who does receive payment depends, generally speaking, on the law governing the debt instrument and the law of the court seized in a dispute. Traditional subordination, security, and priority clauses are less common in debt instruments governed by domestic law.

The rest of the chapter is structured as follows: Section 4.2 examines the content and effects of the so-called *pari passu* clause. Section 4.3 discusses collective action clauses (CACs) and exit consent. It also touches on potential minimum protection of minority creditors in debt restructurings implemented by majority voting procedures. Section 4.4 analyses special national legislation in Belgium, the United Kingdom, France, and in the Euro area, with the common aim of curbing certain rights of creditors who allegedly seek to free-ride on their co-creditors and thereby constitute an obstacle to debt crisis resolution (vulture fund legislation).

International law protection related to intercreditor issues arising from, or in relation to, debt instruments governed by domestic law is then treated in Chapter 5.

4.2 *Pari Passu* Clause

4.2.1 Introduction

A *pari passu* clause is a standard clause in public and private international unsecured debt obligations and can be found both in syndicated loan agreements and in bond issuances.[19] While such clauses grew in popularity in the nineteenth and twentieth centuries, they were only included in a minority of sovereign bonds during this period. Today, almost all modern sovereign debt contracts contain such a clause. Despite their increasing popularity, however, general understanding of such clauses and their operation has remained poor.[20]

The exact formulation of a *pari passu* clause varies. In simple terms, however, it can be said that the clause occurs in two main forms.[21] The first variation may be something akin to: 'The bonds will at all times rank pari passu with all other unsecured and unsubordinated External Indebtedness of the issuer.' Over the past decade or so, it has

---

[19] Rodrigo Olivares-Caminal, *Legal Aspects of Sovereign Debt Restructuring* (Sweet & Maxwell 2009) 84.
[20] Benjamin Chabot and G Mitu Gulati, 'Santa Anna and His Black Eagle: The Origins of *Pari Passu*?' (2014) 9 Capital Markets Law Journal 216, 1.
[21] Olivares-Caminal (n 19) 84–85. Chabot and Gulati (n 20) 4 also refer to the two main forms described below. Gelpern refers to four different types, but also focuses on the difference between clauses including the payment wording and those that do not. Anna Gelpern, 'The Importance of Being Standard' in (ECB January 2017) Legal Issues on Government Debt Restructuring 23, 30–32. Others operate with a distinction between three different types of *pari passu* clauses, such as W Mark C Weidemaier and others, 'Origin Myths, Contracts, and the Hunt for *Pari Passu*' (2011) 38 Law & Social Inquiry 84.

become increasingly popular to also include the word 'payment', which is the core of the second type of clause: 'The bonds will rank equally in right of payment with all of the issuer's other External Indebtedness.'

In the first type of clause, the focus is on the word 'rank', which refers to the formal legal ranking of the debt. In the second type, the word 'payment' opens up the interpretation to possibly also encompassing an obligation to pay equally ranking debtholders on an equal basis. It is the second type of clause, in particular, and variants thereof that have caused the most debate and been the basis for the most important legal claims.[22]

The notion of equal ranking comes from ordinary bankruptcy, where assets are liquidated and distributed to creditors when a company goes bankrupt. In unsecured, cross-border corporate bonds, the meaning of the *pari passu* clause is well established: '[I]n the event of liquidation, such a clause ensures that the debt in question will have the same priority as the debtor's other unsecured debt'[23]—a pro rata right to the debtors' pool of assets. Sovereign debtors can experience severe payment difficulties, but they cannot go bankrupt and be taken over or liquidated by their creditors.[24] Their citizens and land masses are not seized and then divided proportionally among creditors. The meaning of the *pari passu* clause in international sovereign bond contracts is therefore less clear and subject to disagreement.

Concerning the second type of *pari passu* clause, which includes the payment wording, there are two main interpretations which are debated. Most legal practitioners and academics agree that the clause only refers to the legal 'ranking' of the debt and aims to protect the creditor from the legal subordination of their claim in favour of others.[25] Others disagree with this narrow reading, arguing instead that the *pari passu* clause protects against *de facto* subordination and encompasses a payment obligation requiring the sovereign to pay its creditors on a pro rata or rateable basis. This interpretation is sometimes referred to as the broad reading of the *pari passu* clause.[26]

With respect to restructured sovereign debt, the broad reading of the clause may provide a legal basis for a creditor to seek specific performance, such as requiring that the debtor cannot pay other debts of equal rank without making a rateable payment to other creditors benefiting from the clause. This means that the debtor state will be

---

[22] A third variation on the clause includes 'and shall be paid as such' at the end of the standard stating 'ranks equally'. See Weidemaier and others (n 21) 84.

[23] IMF, 'Strengthening the Contractual Framework to Address Collective Action Problems in Sovereign Debt Restructuring' (Staff report, 9 February 2014) 9.

[24] Chabot and Gulati (n 20) 4.

[25] IMF, 'Strengthening the Contractual Framework' (n 23) 10. See, for example, Lachlan Burn, 'Pari Passu Clauses: English Law after *NML v Argentina*' (2014) 9 Capital Markets Law Journal 2, 5; Chabot and Gulati (n 20) 9; Lee C Buchheit and Jeremiah S Pam, 'The *Pari Passu* Clause in Sovereign Debt Instruments' (2004) 53 Emory Law Journal 869, 883–89.

[26] Olivares-Caminal (n 19) 84–85. The modern literature on the *pari passu* clause in sovereign debt instruments is too vast to allow citation of all the relevant articles. Some key articles include Buchheit and Pam (n 25); Anna Gelpern, 'Contract Hope and Sovereign Redemption' (2013) 8 Capital Markets Law Journal 132; W Mark C Weidemaier, 'Sovereign Debt after *NML v Argentina*' (2013) 8 Capital Markets Law Journal 123; Weidemaier and others (n 21); Chabot and Gulati (n 20); Anna Gelpern, 'Courts and Sovereigns in the *Pari Passu* Goldmines' (2016) 11 Capital Markets Law Journal 251. See also FMLC, 'Analysis of the Role, Use and Meaning of *Pari Passu* Clauses in Sovereign Debt Obligations as a Matter of English Law' (FMLC Paper, March 2005); FMLC, '*Pari Passu* Clauses: Analysis of the Role, Use and Meaning of *Pari Passu* Clauses in Sovereign Debt Obligations as a Matter of English Law' (April 2015).

prevented from making payments due to the holder of restructured bonds, unless it also makes rateable (pro rata) payments due to the bondholders of non-restructured bonds (holdout creditors). Buchheit and Pam have specified three further possible consequences of a pro rata payment interpretation:[27]

1. It provides a legal basis for a judicial order directed to a third-party creditor instructing that creditor not to accept a payment from the debtor unless the *pari passu* protected lender receives a rateable payment.
2. A court can direct a third-party financial intermediary to freeze any non-rateable payments received from the debtor and to turn over to the *pari passu*-protected creditor its rateable share of the funds.
3. It can make a third-party creditor that has knowingly received and accepted a non-rateable payment answerable to the *pari passu*-protected creditor for a rateable share of the funds.

These consequences show that the pro rata payment interpretation is a potentially powerful tool to force the debtor state to choose between paying all creditors or none, with the risk of being cut off from the credit market. Economic theory suggests that a borrower can be made better off by agreeing to harsh penalties in the event that it fails to perform. If enforceable, such penalties can alter the defaulting borrower's profitability and serve as a commitment mechanism pushing the borrower to fulfil its contract. For the debtor to agree to such harsh penalties in case of default, a borrower must pay, and the *pari passu* clause may be an example of such a bargain.[28] In other words, it is argued that a pro rata interpretation will discipline the sovereign borrower, which may lead to cheaper credit for the state.

A contrary view is that such an interpretation may significantly hamper the process of debt restructuring as it discourages creditors from taking part in voluntary debt restructuring, the failure of which may also result in more expensive credit for a sovereign borrower. Some legal scholars have even suggested that '[o]nly an insane issuer would agree to such a provision', where the debtor could only pay its restructured debt if it paid all other creditors at the same time on a pro rata basis.[29]

4.2.2 The origin of the clause

In search of the proper construction of the *pari passu* clause in sovereign debt instruments, a number of practising lawyers and legal scholars have sought to trace the origins of this clause.

Buchheit and Pam assert that the *pari passu* clause migrated from secured domestic debt instruments to unsecured cross-border debt instruments, undergoing gradual changes on its way.[30] In short, they found that the clause evolved in three phases in Anglo-American credit agreements. The original form occurred during the nineteenth

---

[27] Buchheit and Pam (n 25) 880. See also Olivares-Caminal (n 19) 85.
[28] Andrei Shleifer, 'Will the Sovereign Debt Market Survive?' (2003) 93 American Economic Review 85, 9.
[29] Burn (n 25) 5. See also Chabot and Gulati (n 20) 9; Buchheit and Pam (n 25) 883–89.
[30] Buchheit and Pam (n 25) 894ff.

and early twentieth centuries, which was the clause's first phase. During this period, the clause appeared in domestic secured debt instruments and confirmed the rateable interests of the debtholders in the collateral securing that specific instrument. In the second phase, around the mid-twentieth century, cross-border lending was largely unsecured. The reason for the decline in secured lending was that creditors had less trust in collateral security for emerging market bonds. In practice, collateral had proved to be of very little help in securing payment of bonds where the issuer defaulted, particularly a sovereign issuer. The consequence of the decline in secured lending was that the *pari passu* clause was no longer needed.[31] To secure themselves, lenders in this second period were protected by the so-called negative pledge clause. This clause generally precludes a borrower from creating liens over its assets or revenues in favour of certain creditors without equally and on a pro rata basis securing the other creditor benefiting from the clause. The purpose of the clause is to avoid erosion of credit positions and ensure that the assets of the borrower remain unencumbered and available to satisfy the claims of all unsecured creditors in case of a bankruptcy.[32] The third phase of the *pari passu* clause was the late twentieth century. Private capital had started flowing to emerging markets from a new type of lender, namely international commercial banks. These institutions included a negative pledge clause to safeguard their credit position as unsecured lenders. Buchheit and Pam argue that international commercial banks were also afraid of involuntary subordination of their claims and sought to solve this through contractual protection, by implementing a version of the *pari passu* clause that spoke of '*pari passu* in priority of payment'.[33]

Without going into further details about the development of the *pari passu* clause according Buchheit and Pam, it is important to emphasize that at no time did their findings suggest that the *pari passu* clause required a borrower to make a rateable payment to all of its equally ranking creditors.[34] It is true that lenders may be concerned about borrowers making differential payments to similarly situated creditors. Buchheit and Pam argue, however, that lenders who wish to address the question of payment distribution would do so explicitly through specific contract clauses on their right to rateable payments and related remedies to enforce such rights against the debtor and co-creditors. Sharing clauses have, for instance, been a standard feature of syndicated commercial bank loans and constitute an intercreditor agreement in the bank syndicate to share (on a rateable basis) any payments and recoveries amongst themselves.[35]

Further, trust indentures or trust deeds are a common feature of bonds issued under the jurisdiction of New York and England, respectively. Such trustees are normally obliged to distribute all payments and recoveries among the bondholders on a rateable

---

[31] The market's demand for secured sovereign bonds diminished, especially after the financial crisis of 1929, when it became clear that the security features had 'little effect in promoting monetary recoveries from defaulting sovereign issuers' (ibid 898).

[32] ibid 893–94; Philip R Wood, *International Loans, Bonds, Guarantees, Legal Opinions*, vol 3 (The Law and Practice of International Finance Series, 2nd edn, Sweet & Maxwell 2007) 72–81, in particular 77–78 concerning sovereign loans.

[33] Buchheit and Pam (n 25) 894.

[34] ibid 917.

[35] ibid 918.

basis. Enforcement actions against the borrower are normally also centralized in the trustee, to preserve the goal of actual rateable sharing. Another way of ensuring that payment is distributed in a certain way is intercreditor agreements, which can be found both in project finance transactions and in corporate debt workouts.

Lastly, subordination agreements are another instrument that can be applied when lenders to the same borrower want to establish legally enforceable priorities (which are sometimes also used outside the context of bankruptcy). The content of the subordination agreements varies, but all seek to establish payment priorities among creditors that would otherwise have an equal-ranking claim against the borrower.[36] These contractual tools all address the issue of the borrower making differential payments to similarly situated creditors. It does not make sense then that they would appear in the same contract as the *pari passu* clause, if they produce similar effects.[37] Consequently, the interaction of the *pari passu* clause jointly with these other clauses in sovereign debt instruments would seem to go against a pro rata payment interpretation of the *pari passu* clause.

Buchheit and Pam conclude that the pro rata payment interpretation in sovereign debt instruments has become possible because the wording of the clause is vague. When boilerplate clauses 'detach themselves from the market's memory of where they originated and what they were designed to achieve', it creates the possibility of misinterpretation and misuse.[38]

Both Buchheit and Olivares-Caminal suggest that the better explanation for how the *pari passu* clause ended up in sovereign debt instruments is that the clause migrated through the ignorance or inattention of contract drafters, from cross-border corporate syndicated loan agreements to sovereign bond issuances.[39] Buchheit has explained the process in the following words:

> [T]he permanent bedrock upon which rests the activity of the entire legal profession is plagiarism ... the mythical fellow who prepared the first loan agreement for a sovereign borrower marked up a loan agreement for a corporate borrower ... [t]he process was then repeated countless thousands of times until some lawyer somewhere was told to go off and draft the first sovereign debt restructuring agreement, and he or she just naturally fulfilled this commission by marking up the last sovereign loan agreement. And that, as they say, was that.[40]

Gulati and Chabot trace the *pari passu* clause in sovereign bonds back to a Spanish language bond issued in Mexico in 1843.[41] The bond was part of the consolidation and restructuring of a series of prior Mexican bonds that had been defaulted on during the prior two decades.[42] They argue that the reason for the inclusion of the *pari passu*

---

[36] ibid 919.
[37] ibid 920; Olivares-Caminal (n 19) 93.
[38] Buchheit and Pam (n 25) 917–18.
[39] Olivares-Caminal (n 19) 93.
[40] Lee C Buchheit, 'The Negative Pledge Clause: The Games People Play' (1990) 9 International Financial Law Review 10, 10.
[41] Chabot and Gulati (n 20).
[42] ibid 10.

clause in the Mexican 1843 bond was the fear that gunboats would be sent in to engage in an extrajudicial enforcement. It was not related to creditors' fears of future granting of preference and involuntary subordination via new legislation, or about the timing of the issuance and the like. The authors pose the question whether, under international law of the time, unequal treatment of creditors was considered adequate justification for gunboat diplomacy.[43] The authors also found that the *pari passu* clause in the Mexican bond included a payment wording. This may change the view that the payment wording gradually came about through amendments in the 1980s.[44]

Gulati and Chabot agree that modern lawyers may have simply copied the clause from the documents of predecessors without understanding its meaning, as others have suggested. However, they also argue that the people who first drafted the clause were likely to have known what it meant and this may contribute to shedding light on the proper construction of the clause.[45] The authors do not want to conclude what effect these findings may have on the interpretation of the current day *pari passu* clause and underline that courts may establish the content of the present-day clause regardless of history, theories about its origin, and the motivation of early drafters.

Weidemaier and others, however, are more explicitly sceptical of any suggestion that modern 'lawyers thoughtlessly imported the *pari passu* clause from cross-border corporate bonds and have been copying it in new bond deals ever since'.[46] In a thorough study, they examine both the origin and data on the development of the *pari passu* clause in sovereign bonds. Perhaps more importantly, they also check this data against the many different stories that professional lawyers come up with when explaining the origin of the clause in sovereign debt. Even though they find aspects of several origin stories reasonable, the authors suggest that

> sovereign debt lawyers behave collectively more like sophisticated market actors than the stories imply. Instead of blind copying, they appear to engage in frequent contract tailoring. Instead of chasing the origins of contract terms, they focus primarily on current practices. And instead of overlooking mistaken additions to contract boilerplate, they demonstrate a thorough understanding of the language used in their contracts.[47]

Although the modifications of the *pari passu* clause have been 'modest' and have only 'occurred at the margins', the authors conclude that sovereign bond contracts are not static and that even the *pari passu* clause has been revised in subtle ways over time. However, they do admit that major shifts in sovereign debt contract provisions can be driven by historical events, such as financial crises, rather than 'lawyer ingenuity'.[48] Their discussion does not, however, lead us any closer to establishing the content of the *pari passu* clause, whether the narrow or the broad interpretation.

---

[43] ibid 30–31.
[44] ibid.
[45] ibid 5.
[46] Weidemaier and others (n 21) 18, see also 5.
[47] ibid 73.
[48] ibid 95–96.

86 INTERCREDITOR EQUITY RULES BY DOMESTIC LAW

As described in this section, several writers have given an account of rather complex developments of the use of the clause from secured to unsecured credits and from domestic to cross-border credit instruments. Moreover, several different explanations of the intention behind and the practical use of the *pari passu* clause have been presented. Regardless of the discussions on the origin of the *pari passu* clause in sovereign bonds and the background for the development of its form and use, it is difficult to conclude what effect these findings may have on the interpretation of the present-day *pari passu* clause. Courts may establish the content of a modern clause regardless of history, theories about its origin, and the motivation of early drafters. The next subsection will therefore examine more recent case law discussing the proper construction of the *pari passu* clause.

4.2.3 Recent case law

4.2.3.1 *Elliott Associates v Banco de la Nacion and Peru*

The discussion regarding the content of the *pari passu* clause has not only taken place among legal scholars but also in courts. Various creditors have argued in different jurisdictions that, as a result of the *pari passu* clause, sovereign states should be prevented from making payments to creditors without paying litigating creditors on a pro rata basis (the broad interpretation).

Elliott Associates v Banco de la Nacion and Peru was the first case to discuss the meaning of the *pari passu* clause in the context of sovereign debt.[49] Banco de la Nacion (hereafter, Nacion) is a Peruvian public sector bank which had issued bonds on the international markets, guaranteed by the Peruvian government. Nacion defaulted on its bonds and Peru sought to restructure the bonds with its creditors.[50] Elliott Associates (hereafter, Elliott), a US hedge fund, purchased bonds issued by Nacion right before the restructuring. Peru was unwilling to pay Elliott as, unlike the majority of other creditors, it refused to accept Peru's restructuring offer and demanded to be paid in full in accordance with the original contract. Elliott sued Nacion in the courts of New York and secured a judgment declaring its right to full payment.[51] When it sought to enforce its right, it discovered a lack of assets to attach in the United States and was therefore forced to resort to the courts of several other countries in its search for attachable property.

While Peru was not willing to pay Elliott, it planned to pay its other creditors who had agreed to the restructuring. The payment was supposed to be transferred via

---

[49] *Elliott Associates, LP v Republic of Peru* 12 F Supp 2d 328 (SDNY 1998). There are several cases between the same parties in many of the cases that will be discussed in this chapter. To avoid confusion, the references related to the cases discussed in this chapter will contain more information compared to cases discussed in other chapters.

[50] ibid at 334–35.

[51] In the first instance, the District Court dismissed Elliott's suit on the ground that it violated the champerty law in s 489 of the New York Judiciary Law. However, the Second Circuit Court of Appeals reversed the District Court's judgment: *Elliott Associates, LP v Banco De La Nacion* 194 F 3d 363 (2d Cir 1999). Upon remand, the District Court granted a judgment in favour of Elliott, see *Elliott Associates, LP v Banco De La Nacion* 194 FRD 116 (SDNY 1999).

Euroclear in Belgium. Elliott now brought the case to Belgian courts arguing that payments by Peru violated the equal treatment principle in the *pari passu* clause contained in the bond. An affidavit from Professor Lowenfeld at the New York University School of Law supported this view that the *pari passu* clause in lending documents, including lending documents of sovereigns, provide that a debtor must pay all creditors rateably when it makes a payment to any of the creditors.[52]

The Brussels Court of Appeals found Professor Lowenfeld's argument convincing. As a result, in September 2000, Elliott obtained a restraining order that prohibited its financial agent (Chase Manhattan) and Euroclear from paying any interest on Peru's bonds.[53] The court stated that

> [t]he basic agreement regulating the reimbursement of the Peruvian foreign debt, also indicates that the different creditors enjoy a 'pari passu clause', which has a result that the debt should be paid down equally towards all creditors in proportion to their claim.[54]

Peru was prevented from paying the creditors who had accepted the restructuring but as it did not want to default on this restructured debt it settled with Elliott for the full contractual claim.[55] In the wake of the Belgian court's decision in the *Elliott* case, various hedge funds tried to reproduce Elliott's strategy against Peru and benefit from the broad interpretation of the *pari passu* clause. Cases were brought in several jurisdictions, such as California, New York, the United Kingdom, and Brussels, without these cases providing any significant clarification.[56] Most of the cases were unsuccessful, but no explicit rulings contradicted the actual *Elliott* ruling and its articulation of the *pari passu* clause. Argentina was the biggest target in these lawsuits with the biggest default in history (at that time). For a decade, Argentina steadily refused to pay those creditors who did not restructure their debt. This changed with *NML v Argentina*, discussed in the following section.

---

[52] In an affidavit, Professor Lowenfeld stated: 'I have no difficulty in understanding what the pari passu clause means: it means what it says—a given debt will rank equally with other debt of the borrower, whether that borrower is an individual, a company or a sovereign state. A borrower from Tom, Dick, and Harry can't say "I will pay Tom and Dick in full, and if there is anything left over I'll pay Harry." If there is not enough money to go around, the borrower faced with a pari passu provision must pay all three of them on the same basis.' He is quoted in Buchheit and Pam (n 25) 878.

[53] C.A. Bruxelles, 8e ch, 26 septembre 2000, *Elliot Associates, LP* (No 2000/QR/92, unreported) (Belgium).

[54] ibid. The translated quote is taken from Rodrigo Olivares-Caminal, 'The *Pari Passu* Clause in Sovereign Debt Instruments: Developments in Recent Litigation' (BIS Paper, Bank for International Settlements 2013) 124.

[55] William Bratton, 'Pari Passu and a Distressed Sovereign's Rational Choices' (2004) 53 Emory Law Journal 823, 824.

[56] *Red Mountain Finance, Inc v Democratic Republic of Congo* CD Cal (District Court 2001) (California); *Kensington International Ltd v Republic of the Congo* (2003) unreported (High Court), approved by CA at [2003] EWCA Civ 709 (UK); *Kensington International, Ltd v BNP Paribas SA* No 03602569 (NY Sup Ct 2003) (New York); *Republic of Nicaragua v LNC Investments and Euroclear Bank S.A.*, R.K. 240/03 (Brussels Commercial Ct 11 September 2003) (Belgium); *Macrotecnic Int'l Corp v Republic of Argentina*, No 02 Civ 5932 (TPG) (SDNY 2004) (New York). See also Kupelyants (n 15) 244–46; Olivares-Caminal (n 19) 87.

4.2.3.2 *NML v Argentina*

The debate over the content and the consequences of the *pari passu* clause was revived by the New York District Court orders issued in *NML v Argentina* in 2011 and 2012.[57] The Argentine sovereign debt litigation has its roots in bonds issued by Argentina in the 1990s. After Argentina defaulted on its debt in 2001, it managed to get the holders of some 93% of the relevant bonds to agree, in 2005 and 2010, to exchange their bonds for new ones.

Argentina continued to make payments to holders of the exchange bonds, but did not make any payments to those who still held the defaulted bonds. In fact, the Argentine Parliament adopted legislation prohibiting the State from repaying holdout creditors (the Lock Law).[58] In 2010, a number of these holdout creditors, led by NML Capital Ltd ('NML') (a unit of Elliott Management Corp),[59] brought proceedings against Argentina in the Southern District Court of New York, pursuing full payment under the defaulted bonds.[60]

In 2011, the District Court held that Argentina had violated the equal treatment provision (the *pari passu* clause) of the bond, by (i) lowering the rank of claimants' bonds 'when it made payments currently due under the Exchange Bonds, while persisting in its refusal to satisfy its payment obligations currently due under [claimants'] Bonds', and (ii) when it enacted a law that prohibited the government from repaying the holdout creditors.[61] The claimants then sought a remedy for Argentina's breach of the *pari passu* clause and in 2012 the District Court issued an injunction obliging Argentina to make a 'rateable payment' to NML whenever it paid any amount due on the Exchange Bonds.[62] An amended injunction prohibited 'all parties involved, directly or indirectly, in advising upon, preparing, processing, or facilitating any payment on the Exchange Bonds' and from 'aiding and abetting' any effort to make payments to the Exchange Bonds without also making a 'rateable payment' to NML.[63] The *pari passu* injunction was appealed first to the 2nd Circuit Court of Appeals, who confirmed the District Court's orders, and later to the US Supreme Court.[64] In June 2014, the Supreme Court refused to hear Argentina's appeal without any further comment and thereby rendered the lower court's decision on both issues final.[65]

---

[57] See especially *NML Capital, Ltd v Republic of Argentina* No 08-cv-6978 (TPG) (SDNY 7 December 2011); No 08-cv-6978 (TPG) (SDNY 21 November 2012); 727 F 3d 230 (2d Cir 2013).

[58] Law 26,017 in 2005 (Argentina).

[59] Matt Levine, 'Pari Passu, Blobs and Fortune Cookies', *Bloomberg.com* (8 April 2017) <https://www.bloomberg.com/opinion/articles/2017-08-04/pari-passu-blobs-and-fortune-cookies> accessed 13 March 2022.

[60] According to Argentina's Financial Agency Agreement of 19 October 1994, the bonds were governed by the laws of the State of New York and conferred jurisdiction to the Courts of New York City in respect of any action brought by a bondholder arising out of or based on the bonds or the Financial Agency Agreement (FAA).

[61] *NML Capital, Ltd v Republic of Argentina* (n 57). Argentina also re-enacted the Lock law in Law 26,547 in 2009 and Law 26,866 in 2013, which barred Argentina from awarding bondholders who had filed a lawsuit any settlement worth more than the prior exchange offers.

[62] *NML Capital, Ltd v Republic of Argentina* No 03 Civ. 8845 (TPG) (SDNY 23 February 2012).

[63] *NML Capital, Ltd v Republic of Argentina* No 08-cv-6978 (TPG), s 2(a), 2(e) (SDNY 21 November 2012).

[64] *NML Capital, Ltd v Republic of Argentina* (n 57); cert. denied *Republic of Argentina v NML Capital, Ltd* 134 S Ct 2819 (2014).

[65] The Supreme Court ruled against Argentina despite interventions by the US Executive and the governments of Brazil, France, and Mexico, among others, each of which insisted that the *pari passu* clause could

Some questions were left open by the 2nd Circuit's decision. It was particularly unclear whether it was based on a context-specific and textual reading of the *pari passu* clause or on the *pari passu* clauses in general, implying that the 2nd Circuit's decision might have a major impact on other sovereign debt contracts that contained that type of clause.

The 2nd Circuit's judgment gave holdout creditors a right to be paid at the same rate, relative to the respective debt obligations, and at the same time as those who had agreed to reschedule. The judgment as such is in accordance with the broad interpretation of the *pari passu* clause. It does not state that Argentina has an obligation to pay its creditors at a certain time, but rather that Argentina must pay the holdout creditors *if* it pays the creditors who have accepted the restructuring.[66]

By giving NML what seemed to be a victory on the *pari passu* clause interpretation, the court held the drafters of the bond contract and Argentina responsible for the difficult situation they were in. The Argentine *pari passu* clause contained the word 'payment' in the second sentence. Additionally, it had implemented the above-mentioned Lock law. According to the judgment, Argentina could have avoided the result by eschewing the payment language and not enacting legislation altering the legal ranking of the bonds. Last, it has been argued that the result in *NML v Argentina* concerning the rateable payment requirement was the result of a particular situation where Argentina had demonstrated recalcitrant behaviour in connection with both its restructuring and the lawsuit.[67]

4.2.3.3 *Knighthead v BNYM* (England)

In 2014, after the rateable payment injunction in *NML v Argentina* became effective, Argentina transferred a sum corresponding to the payment due to some of the bondholders who had accepted the restructuring (the Euro exchange bondholder). The sums were transferred to an account that the Bank of New York Mellon (BNYM), the trustee of the Euro exchange bonds, held with Banco Central de la Republica de Argentina. Due to the rateable payment injunction, BNYM did not forward the payment to the Euro bondholders, which triggered a default on Argentina's performing debt. NML nevertheless returned to the New York District Court complaining that Argentina had 'defiantly and contemptuously' violated the judge's order by transferring these funds to BNYM.[68] In August 2014, the court found that the transfer of money from Argentina to the trustee BNYM was 'illegal and a violation of the Amended February 23 Orders

---

not be construed to require full payment to the holdouts. Gelpern, 'The Importance of Being Standard' (n 21) 31; see also IMF, 'Strengthening the Contractual Framework' (n 23) 9.

[66] The *pari passu* clause which promises equal ranking without reference to payment was assumed not to result in a payment injunction until another US court accepted a copycat complaint against Grenada in 2013. The case left open the possibility that even a *pari passu* clause without the payment wording may support an injunction. The court ordered the case to proceed to trial on the assumption (even though just for the sake of argument) that Grenada's *pari passu* clause was 'similar' to Argentina's *pari passu* clause which did contain the payment wording. The case was, however, settled without a definitive ruling. *The Export-Import Bank of the Republic of China v Grenada* No. 13 Civ. 1450 (HB) 5 (SDNY 19 August 2013). See also Gelpern, 'The Importance of Being Standard' (n 21) 33.

[67] See, among others, Kupelyants (n 15) 245.

[68] As quoted in *Knighthead Master Fund LP & Others v The Bank of New York Mellon* [2014] EWHC 3662 (EWHC) [12].

[the *pari passu* injunction]'.[69] Furthermore, the order stated that BNYM's retention of the funds in its account pursuant to the court's order should

> not be deemed a violation of the Amended February 23 Orders [the pari passu injunction]. BNY[M] shall incur no liability under the Indenture governing the Exchange Bond or otherwise to any person or entity for complying with this Order and the Amended February 23 Orders.[70]

The Argentine default and the latter statement led to a new round of legal action, this time brought by Euro bondholders against BNYM, in the English courts.

The restructured Euro-denominated bonds were governed by English law and Argentina irrevocably submitted these securities to the jurisdiction of the courts of England. This is why the Eurobond holders sought a declaration by the English High Court of Justice that, amongst other things, as a matter of English law, an order of a foreign court is ineffective in varying a contract governed by English law. In other words, the purpose of the declaration was to establish that the New York District Court's injunction provided no defence to a claim to enforce the terms of the trust indenture, which was subject to English law, including the obligation to transfer the Euro funds to the Euro bondholders.

In November 2014, Newey J adjourned the application for the declarations sought to 'give Holdout Creditors the chance to put forward any arguments they might wish in opposition to it'.[71] However, none of the holdout creditors from the US proceedings sought to participate.[72] In the adjourned hearing, held in December 2014, Richards J declined to make the declaration. He deemed that the question should be kept open because it would 'serve no useful purpose' insofar as it amounted to 'a declaration that the trustee would be in breach of trust unless it had a defence'.[73] Both Justices did, however, comment on the effect of the foreign order on English contract law and on the District Court's balancing of interests when construing the rateable payment injunction. First, Newey and Richards JJ were both sceptical about the District Court's statement that the trustee was absolved from any liability as long as it acted in accordance with the injunction. Richards J stated:

> [i]t is highly arguable that the terms of section 5.2(xvi) and (xx) [of the trust indenture] would relieve the trustee of its obligations under the trust indenture to the extent that they were prohibited from performing them by the injunction. It is also arguable that where a trustee is subject to a legal inhibition, preventing it from performing its obligations as trustee, that too can provide a defence to a claim for breach of trust under general principles of law....[74]

---

[69] *NML Capital, Ltd v Republic of Argentina* No 08-cv-6978 (TPG) (SDNY 21 August 2014), item 1 of the order.
[70] ibid, item 4 of the order.
[71] *Knighthead Master Fund LP & Others v The Bank of New York Mellon* (n 68) [28].
[72] *Knighthead Master Fund LP & Others v The Bank of New York Mellon* [2015] EWHC 270 (EWHC) [45].
[73] ibid [49].
[74] ibid.

Second, the Justices also expressed more general scepticism towards the underlying premises of the District Court's injunction. Regarding the Euro-denominated payments that Argentina made to BNYM and the role of the BNYM as the trustee of the Euro bondholders, Newey J stated:

> It can, perhaps, be observed that if, as the Indenture and securities suggest, money paid to the Bank by the Republic in discharge of its obligations under the Exchange Bonds is held on trust for the second defendant and, ultimately, the bondholders, the present position is rather unfortunate, albeit explicable by the understandable concern of the United States Courts that their orders should be obeyed: the bondholders (who, or whose predecessors, will already have had to agree to take far less than the face value of the FAA [the original] Bonds that they will once have held) would be liable to be prevented indefinitely from obtaining access to money that had been due to them contractually and to which they would now be beneficially entitled.[75]

Along the same lines, and on the same subject, Richards J stated in his judgment: 'More problematic is the state of "paralysis", as leading counsel for both the claimants and the trustee described it, in the operation of the trust caused by the injunction.'[76]

In the quotations from the judgments, when referring to the effects of the New York District Court's rateable payment injunction, concern is raised about the fairness of the injunctive measures with respect to the creditors who have accepted the restructuring and who have already taken on losses.

Knighthead v BNYM sheds light on the differences in interpretation of the *pari passu* clause and the use of third party injunctions to enforce such clauses in sovereign debt cases under New York and English laws. When commenting on the District Court's orders, the English High Court limits itself to criticizing the consequences of the rateable payment injunction. Therefore, *Knighthead v BNYM* does not help clarify the District Court's interpretation of the *pari passu* clause directly. For the same reasons, because the judges only explicitly look at the consequences of the injunction, one may claim that the High Court's criticism sheds little light on the actual content of the *pari passu* clause under English law.[77] That said, a rateable payment interpretation of the *pari passu* clause and a pro rata payment injunction will *de facto* have the same consequences. As such, when the judges criticize the consequences of the District Court's injunction, this indicates that the English courts would be unlikely to construe the *pari passu* clause itself to encompass a pro rata payment obligation.

For some, this may not come as a surprise. In 2005, the Financial Markets Law Committee (FMLC)[78] had already stated that, as a matter of English law, the pro rata

---

[75] *Knighthead Master Fund LP & Others v The Bank of New York Mellon* (n 68) [18].
[76] *Knighthead Master Fund LP & Others v The Bank of New York Mellon* (n 72) [46].
[77] Romain Zamour, '*NML v. Argentina* and the Ratable Payment Interpretation of the *Pari Passu* Clause' (2013) 38 Yale Journal of International Law Online 55, 60.
[78] The Financial Markets Law Committee is a UK registered charity established for the purposes of education and the advancement of the understanding of financial markets law. It aims to identify issues of legal uncertainty affecting wholesale financial markets, including inconsistencies between draft law or regulations and market practice, and to make proposals for resolving them. See FMLC, 'About the FMLC' (*Financial Markets Law Committee*, no date) <http://fmlc.org/about-the-fmlc/> accessed 11 March 2022.

interpretation of the *pari passu* clause was incorrect and the 'ranking' interpretation was the proper alternative.[79] The basis for the conclusion of the FMLC was, first, that, in a literal sense, the language of the clauses emphasized the rank of the claims and not the *pari passu* payment. Additionally, other provisions typically found in sovereign debt obligations, which require equal payment, suggest that the *pari passu* clause was not intended to require equal payment. Both of these arguments comply with the principles of English contract construction, where the words used must be given their ordinary and natural meaning, and should be considered in the context of the entire transaction. Second, the FMLC claimed that English case law does not provide for a pro rata payment interpretation. Third, and related to the *consequences* of the 'rateable payment' interpretation, the FMLC argued that the pro rata payment interpretation 'would offend the "business commonsense" principle used by English courts when construing a contract',[80] because it would be prejudicial not only to debtors but also to creditors, by making it impracticable for all creditors to sustain the debtor's business if only one of them objected. This third argument against a pro rata interpretation of the *pari passu* clause is also valid when arguing against the legality of a pro rata injunction, as the *consequences* of a pro rata remedy construed in the same way as the injunction in *NML v Argentina* would *de facto* have the same consequences as a pro rata interpretation of the *pari passu* clause.

In sum, despite the fact that *Knighthead v BNYM* does not discuss the *pari passu* clause directly, it can be read as indirect confirmation that the clause does not imply a pro rata payment obligation under English law. The statements of the FMLC also support this conclusion.

4.2.3.4 *Ajdler v Province of Mendoza*
In 2017, a New York District Court had the opportunity to discuss the *pari passu* clause in *Ajdler v Province of Mendoza*.[81] The background of this case is that the Argentine Province of Mendoza (the Province) issued bonds in 1997 which it sought to restructure in 2004, through an optional bond exchange offer. On 23 August 2004, the Province announced that it would no longer make the scheduled interest payments on the bonds and would only make payments on the new bonds issued pursuant to the exchange offer. A majority of the bondholders accepted the bond exchange, but the bondholder Ajdler (the claimant) did not participate.[82]

On 1 March 2017, Ajdler commenced an action alleging breach of the indenture agreement due to the Province's failure to make principal and interest payments on the bonds in accordance with the contract since March 2004. Ajdler also claimed that the Province's payments of interest and principal on the restructured debts violated the relevant indenture's terms and conditions, which require that the bonds 'rank pari passu among themselves and at least pari passu in priority of payment with all other

---

[79] FMLC, 'Analysis of the Role, Use and Meaning of *Pari Passu* Clauses in Sovereign Debt Obligations as a Matter of English Law' (n 26) 2.
[80] ibid.
[81] *Ajdler v Province of Mendoza* No 17-CV-1530 (VM), 2017 WL 3635122 (SDNY 2017).
[82] See overview of the background of the case in the appeal before the second circuit, *Ajdler v Province of Mendoza* 890 F3d 95, 2–7 (2d Cir 2018).

present and future unsecured and unsubordinated Indebtedness'.[83] In the action, Ajdler was seeking monetary, injunctive, and declaratory relief.

In his latter claim, Ajdler relied on the *pari passu* interpretation of *NML v Argentina*. The district judge (who was not the same as in the *NML v Argentina* case) held that *NML v Argentina* was a 'truly extraordinary' case that was unlikely to apply to many cases involving *pari passu* clauses in the future:

> In NML Capital, the court found that Argentina violated the pari passu clause of the FAA Bonds because the President's declaration of a 'temporary moratorium' on principal and interest payments on more than $80 billion of its public external debt including the FAA Bonds' and the Argentine legislature's enactment of the Lock Law and Lock Law Suspension were extraordinary acts undertaken to subordinat[e] the ... FAA Bonds to the Exchange Bonds and lower ... the ranking of the ... FAA Bonds below the Exchange Bonds.[84]

The court further underlined that, contrary to *NML v Argentina*, the only alleged violation of the *pari passu* was that the Province had paid principal and interest on the other bonds. The court deemed this to be 'insufficient to state a claim of breach of pari passu' and declined to block payments on Mendoza's new (restructured) bonds.[85]

Ajdler v Province of Mendoza may have contributed to clarifying and modifying the interpretation of the *pari passu* clause in *NML v Argentina* when underlining that, contrary to the *NML* case, there were no extraordinary circumstances. It is, however, somewhat early to conclude whether this is a permanent change in the jurisprudence in New York courts. For instance, what may constitute extraordinary circumstances is still to be further developed. Moreover, the case has not been appealed, which makes it easier for other courts to come to a contradictory finding in future cases.

After the *Elliott* case, scholars, practitioners, international institutions, and governments reacted negatively to the pro rata payment interpretations. Despite this, the wording of the *pari passu* clause was not amended to avoid similar interpretations in the future.[86] Several explanations have been provided that may contribute to explain this lack of change.[87] When the pro rata payment interpretation was repeated in *NML v Argentina*, it provoked strong and critical reactions but this time changes to the *pari passu* clause were initiated and actively promoted by several key actors in

---

[83] ibid at 4.A

[84] *Ajdler v Province of Mendoza* (n 81) 23.

[85] ibid at 26. The court referred to previous case law as well: *NML Capital, Ltd v Republic of Argentina* (n 57) 247. ('[W]e have not held that a sovereign debtor breaches its pari passu clause every time it pays one creditor and not another'); *White Hawthorne v Argentina*, No 16-Civ-1042 (TPG), 2016 WL 7441699, 3 (SDNY 2016) ('Non payment on defaulted debt alone is insufficient to show breach of the pari passu clause.')

[86] Some reaction came after the Elliott ruling and a similar ruling against Nicaragua which was later overturned on unrelated grounds: Belgium enacted legislation shielding Euroclear from injunctions. (The Belgian legislation will also be discussed in Section 4.4). In addition, there were early signs of resistance against the pro rata payment interpretation in the United Kingdom, for instance when a court in London declined to interpret the *pari passu* clause in the Congo's debt contracts. *Kensington International Ltd v Republic of the Congo* (n 56), approved by CA at [2003] EWCA Civ 709. For a description of the statute, see National Bank of Belgium, 'Financial Stability Review 2005' (23 June 2005) 162–63.

[87] See, for example, Stephen J Choi and G Mitu Gulati, 'Contract as Statute' (2006) 104 Michigan Law Review 1129.

the sovereign debt market. These reactions and changes, which will be discussed in the next section, may contribute to clarifying the meaning of the *pari passu* clause in sovereign debt instruments in the future, to a greater extent than current case law has managed.

4.2.4 Contractual reform: Governmental and market reactions to the rateable payment interpretation in *NML v Argentina*

There is clear evidence that not all market participants approved of the New York District Court's rateable payment injunction and the possible pro rata interpretation of the *pari passu* clause. In the aftermath of the judgments in *NML v Argentina*, the International Capital Market Association (ICMA)[88] published a new standard *pari passu* clause for inclusion in the terms and conditions of sovereign debt securities. The new standard clause is intended to facilitate future sovereign debt restructurings and specifies that

> the Issuer shall have no obligation to effect equal or rateable payment(s) at any time with respect to any such other External Indebtedness and, in particular, shall have no obligation to pay other External Indebtedness at the same time or as a condition of paying sums due on the Notes and vice versa.[89]

In October 2014, the Executive Board of the IMF also supported widespread use of this modified *pari passu* clause in international sovereign bonds as a means to 'enhance legal certainty and consistency across jurisdictions'.[90] In 2015, a G20 communiqué called for the inclusion of this strengthened *pari passu* clauses in future bonds. China has also publicly stated its support for the change:

> We must continue to promote orderly restructuring of sovereign debt, including inserting strengthened contract provisions into newly issued and existing sovereign bonds, as well as incentivising strengthened co-ordination between government and debtors.[91]

---

[88] ICMA has, as of October 2019, more than 580 members drawn from both the buy and sell sides, made up of issuers (including sovereign issuers), primary and secondary market intermediaries, asset managers, investors, and capital market infrastructure providers. Its activities include promoting best market practice through the development of standard documentation, which is normally sent to its membership for consultation before publication. See, in general, ICMA, 'About ICMA' (*International Capital Market Association*, no date) <https://www.icmagroup.org/About-ICMA/> accessed 12 March 2022.

[89] ICMA, 'Standard Aggregated Collective Action Clauses (CACs) for the Terms and Conditions of Sovereign Notes' (International Capital Market Association August 2014).

[90] IMF, 'IMF Executive Board Discusses Strengthening the Contractual Framework in Sovereign Debt Restructuring' (Press release no 14/459, *International Monetary Fund*, 10 June 2014) <https://www.imf.org/en/News/Articles/2015/09/14/01/49/pr14459> accessed 13 March 2022.

[91] Elaine Moore and Gabriel Wildau, 'China Eyes Revamp of Sovereign Bonds', *Financial Times* (4 November 2016) <https://www.ft.com/content/b35681b6-fc1b-11e5-b3f6-11d5706b613b> accessed 14 March 2022.

The promotion of the non-pro rata payment approach to the *pari passu* clause by influential financial institutions in the aftermath of *NML v Argentina* is likely to lead to an increased implementation of an amended *pari passu* clause in future sovereign bond issuances.[92] There may already be signs of such a development. Between October 2014 and the end of 2018, almost 90% of all new issuances of sovereign bonds have included a modified *pari passu* clause explicitly providing for non-pro rata payment interpretation.[93] More specifically, the inclusion of modified *pari passu* clauses is slightly more common for new issuances under New York law compared to those under English law. One explanation for this is that market participants believe that English courts are unlikely to follow the *NML v Argentina* approach and interpret the *pari passu* clause as requiring that the issuer make rateable payments to creditors.[94] Euro area sovereigns have generally not included modified *pari passu* clauses in their issuances.[95]

4.2.5 Prevalence of variations of the *pari passu* clause—practical issues

Both the official sector and market actors reacted negatively to the rateable payment interpretation put forward in *NML v Argentina*. Alternative *pari passu* standard clauses, which explicitly exclude a pro rata payment obligation, were created, actively promoted, and to a great extent implemented in new international bond issuances. However, a significant number of outstanding bonds still do not contain the modified *pari passu* clause. At the end of October 2018, approximately 60% of outstanding international sovereign bonds do not include the modified *pari passu* clause.[96] The stock not containing the modified clause is slowly declining. The IMF reports that the maturity profile of the outstanding stock without modified clause indicates that approximately 31% of these bonds will mature in more than 10 years. About 50% of these are below investment grade.[97]

The *pari passu* clause that causes the most discussion and is most likely to open up to a broader (pro rata) payment interpretation is the variation which refers to payment. The numbers referred to above, which are provided by the IMF, do not identify whether the *pari passu* clauses contain a payment wording or not. According to Weidemaier and others, almost half of the bonds issued since 2000 included the payment language found in the Argentine bond discussed in *NML v Argentina*.[98]

---

[92] See Anna Gelpern, 'A Sensible Step to Mitigate Sovereign Bond Dysfunction' (RealTime Economic Issues Watch blog, *Peterson Institute for International Economics*, 29 August 2014) <https://www.piie.com/blogs/realtime-economic-issues-watch/sensible-step-mitigate-sovereign-bond-dysfunction> accessed 11 March 2022.
[93] IMF, 'Fourth Progress Report' (n 10) 6.
[94] As discussed in the sections above, the Financial Markets Law Committee (FMLC) took the view that the interpretation of the *pari passu* clause by the New York courts was unlikely to be followed by the English courts. See FMLC, '*Pari passu* clauses: Analysis of the Role, Use and Meaning of *Pari Passu* Clauses in Sovereign Debt Obligations as a matter of English Law' (n 26). See also IMF, 'Fourth Progress Report' (n 10) 5–6.
[95] FMLC, '*Pari passu* clauses: Analysis of the Role, Use and Meaning of *Pari Passu* Clauses in Sovereign Debt Obligations as a matter of English Law' (n 26).
[96] IMF, 'Fourth Progress Report' (n 10) 7.
[97] ibid.
[98] Weidemaier and others (n 21) 11.

While it is unlikely that any *pari passu* clause will be interpreted as a pro rata payment obligation under English law, the situation under New York law is more unsettled. Although *Ajdler v Province of Mendoza* seems to have modified the broad *pari passu* finding in *NML v Argentina*, it remains somewhat unclear whether the clauses containing a payment wording may still oblige a sovereign debtor to make a pro rata payment in certain extraordinary circumstances in the future. Currently, approximately 70% of the bonds maturing in more than ten years are governed by New York law. It is this stock of bonds where the risk of a pro rata payment interpretation is greatest.[99] The extent to which this outstanding stock of debt will provide for a pro rata payment interpretation will depend, in large part, on how courts interpret *pari passu* clauses in future litigation.

4.2.6 Preliminary conclusions

This chapter has made it clear that there are two main interpretations of the *pari passu* clause: the payment interpretation and the ranking interpretation. The objectives behind the various *pari passu* clauses are equal treatment across typically unsecured creditors, to ensure that the relative negotiated position of creditors is not deviated from. Nevertheless, it is not self-evident what kind of equal treatment the clause guarantees.

According to the ranking interpretation, creditors have a right not to be legally subordinated to other (unsecured) creditors. If the debtor state is not able to pay all its creditors on the respective due dates, one creditor cannot challenge the lack of or delayed payment by reference to the state paying other creditors. The creditor's contractual right to payment is maintained, but it has few tools except economic power to ensure that it is paid back at the same time as its co-creditors. This means that minority holdout creditors cannot enforce their right to payment in accordance with the contract terms to the detriment of the majority of bondholders, potentially disturbing a debt restructuring. Under the ranking interpretation, the sovereign debtor is provided with greater flexibility to decide the repayment schedule of its creditors. When there is a lack of insolvency mechanisms and clear ranking rules, the ranking interpretation cannot prevent abuse by the debtor state, nor can it guarantee that repayment will remain independent of the political and economic strength of a creditor. Indeed, the debtor state may selectively choose to default on some creditor claims over others.

The payment interpretation provides a creditor with the right to a pro rata payment, at the same time as other equal ranking creditors are paid. In this case, the rights of individual creditors are stronger than under the ranking interpretation, though this is partly dependent on the enforcement measures available to the creditor. As demonstrated by *NML v Argentina*, injunctions inhibiting other creditors from receiving their payments have been effective. According to the payment interpretation, the right of an individual creditor can be used to the detriment of the majority of creditors, because it can use the majority as leverage. If holdout creditors are not paid, nor are the

---

[99] IMF, 'Fourth Progress Report' (n 10) 7.

majority creditors who have already accepted restructuring. This reduces the willingness of creditors to participate in restructurings. It also gives the state considerably less flexibility to design and implement a debt restructuring that results in a sustainable debt burden.

This chapter has shown that in spite of thorough analyses of variations in the wording of the clause, of the origin of the clause, and of case law, it is difficult to establish *one* interpretation of the *pari passu* clause. What is possible is to examine the prevalence of certain types of *pari passu* clauses and detect tendencies in the reasoning in case law. Anna Gelpern describes the current *pari passu* clause, post *NML v Argentina*, in the following descriptive manner:

> The pari passu compromise reached in response to Argentina's pari passu saga was a redrafted [ICMA] clause that clarified what it did not mean [equal ranking and not pro rata payment], and judicial opinions that whittled the application of pari passu down to Voldemort.[100]

What she refers to is firstly the broadly supported amendment of the ICMA's standard *pari passu* clause, explicitly providing for a ranking interpretation. Second, she refers to a tendency—at least in the United States—for courts to interpret vague *pari passu* clauses more narrowly and closer to the ranking interpretation. In sum, there seems to be a move, politically and legally, towards interpreting the *pari passu* clause according to the ranking interpretation.

Last, it should be mentioned that although the wording of a *pari passu* clause varies, this cannot fully explain why the interpretation of the *pari passu* clause differs so fundamentally between courts and across jurisdictions. The *consequences* of the outcome of the various interpretations seem to have been conclusive factors in the discussed judgments under New York law and English law, respectively. Although the New York District Court uses the terms 'justice' and 'public interest' as policy considerations constituting legal arguments in favour of a specific result, they appear to be mere labels the courts use for their respective interpretations, so as to legitimize their conclusions. Moreover, *NML v Argentina* and *Knighthead v BNYM*, interpreting New York and English law respectively, chose to put the emphasis on different underlying values and objectives when interpreting identical contract clauses. English courts have emphasized that a payment interpretation, in particular when combined with enforcement measures, may have a disruptive effect, negatively disturbing the rights to payment of non-holdout creditors. As the ranking interpretation seems to have prevailed, this latter underlying argument or objective is likely to have been the most important among the actors in the sovereign debt market. This interpretation deliberately seeks to enable sovereign debtors to design a restructuring that allows for differential treatment of creditors, in terms of payment order.

---

[100] Anna Gelpern, 'Imagine Riding the Ceteris Pari-Bus into the Sunset ... in Argentina' (Blog, *Credit Slips: A discussion on credit, finance, and bankruptcy*, 11 July 2019) <https://www.creditslips.org/creditslips/2019/11/imagine-riding-the-cetris-pari-bus-into-the-sunset-in-argentina.html> accessed 12 March 2022.

4.3 Collective Action Clauses and Exit Consent— Intercreditor Equity and Majority Decisions

4.3.1 Introduction

There are no national or international rules regulating sovereign insolvency. Fundamentally, a debtor state has to renegotiate its debt contracts with its various creditors on a voluntary basis in order to restructure its debts. Such renegotiations are challenging because they can easily fall victim to collective action problems, which may effectively hinder sustainable resolution of a debt crisis (see Section 1.4). Today, sovereign debt restructurings are typically implemented through the exercise of majority powers, in particular based on so-called collective action clauses (CACs) and exit consent. CACs typically enable the majority of bondholders, in agreement with the sovereign debtor, to bind the minority creditors to a restructuring agreement. Exit consent is a technique by which creditors, as part of an exchange offer, consent to the amendment of provisions in the exchanged debt instrument (the original debt instrument) in order to make these debts less attractive to creditors who may seek to hold out.[101] Both are contractual techniques allowing majority decisions to bind minority creditors in certain respects. These techniques are currently the most important tools available to curb collective action problems and improve chances of a successful restructuring.[102]

Because CACs and exit consent enable the majority of bondholders, in agreement with the sovereign debtor, to bind the minority creditors to a restructuring, their use may result in the oppression of minority creditors. A restructuring implemented by use of these contractual techniques can sometimes be characterized by the use of coercive and expropriatory measures, leading disgruntled minority creditors to call on courts to intervene claiming that a certain application of a CAC or exit consent is invalid.[103]

This chapter examines the extent to which a court can interfere with the implementation of a restructuring enabled by CACs or exit consent on the grounds that the majority has abused its powers. It discusses whether a majority decision can be abusive in terms of the dissenting minority creditors as such ('minority protection'), but also whether majority decisions that provide for preferential treatment of classes of creditors may result in courts finding a majority decision invalid ('discriminatory majority decisions'). The analysis mainly discusses majority decisions under English and New York law, as these jurisdictions are the two main jurisdictions for international (foreign law issued) bonds.[104]

Section 4.3.2 presents the main features of CACs and exit consent, while Section 4.3.3 discusses the relevance of domestic case law for establishing the threshold for

---

[101] See Lee C Buchheit and G Mitu Gulati, 'Exit Consents in Sovereign Bond Exchanges' (2000–01) 48 UCLA Law Review 59, 62, 66.
[102] Rodrigo Olivares-Caminal and others, *Debt Restructuring* (2nd edn, Oxford University Press 2016) 720.
[103] Kupelyants (n 15) 209–10.
[104] See Section 1.4.1.

protection of minority creditors. Section 4.3.4 sets out the legal basis for the exercise of judicial scrutiny of majority decisions. Sections 4.3.5–4.3.7 examine the substantive rules which may potentially provide minority creditors with protection in the context of debt restructurings implemented by means of majority votes. Section 4.3.8 discusses whether CACs can be exploited by the debtor state and minority creditors to implement a discriminatory restructuring.

4.3.2 General features of exit consent and CACs

The use of CACs and exit consent in a sovereign debt context are two market-based techniques that originated in corporate bond practice. They were developed as a response to the holdout problem described in Section 1.3. In a restructuring, both techniques are typically complemented by the use of contractual term enhancements.[105]

As mentioned above, exit consent is a contractual technique where a specified majority or supermajority of creditors exercises its power, as a part of an exchange offer, to amend the terms of the old debt instrument. The aim is to make the old instruments less attractive to potential holdout creditors and thereby create an incentive for all (other) creditors to capitulate and accept the restructuring.[106] When using the exit consent technique, the sovereign debtor's exchange offer is normally conditioned on a minimum threshold of creditor acceptance and the amendments to the terms of the original debt instrument are performed once the required majority has been obtained.[107]

CACs comprise a range of contract clauses, also found in sovereign bonds (typically in the prospectuses of bonds), which seek to coordinate bondholder action to ensure efficient restructurings.[108] They include majority action (majority voting by creditors); no-action clauses (bondholders cannot accelerate or take action against the debtor without the consent of a specified proportion of the creditors); collective representation (appointment of a trustee or other representative or committee on behalf of the creditors); and sharing clauses (pro rata sharing of recoveries of a defaulting debtor).[109] The most central of these is the majority action clause, which allows for a supermajority of creditors to approve restructuring terms and bind dissenting minority bondholders.[110]

---

[105] Olivares-Caminal and others (n 102) 720.
[106] To be effective, exit amendments to the old bonds must impair the secondary market value of those bonds after the exchange, reduce the likelihood of the bonds eventually being repaid, or make it harder for a holdout creditor to pursue legal remedies against the issuer. The prospect of being left with such a weakened bond might push a bondholder to accept the restructuring because they may not want to risk the majority of bondholders agreeing to the offer and approving the amendments, so weakening the non-exchanged bonds. It is therefore a classic prisoners' dilemma, likely to be aggravated in cases where the bonds are widely dispersed and the holders have no effective way to communicate with each other. See Buchheit and Gulati, 'Exit Consents in Sovereign Bond Exchanges' (n 101) 69.
[107] Olivares-Caminal and others (n 102) 729.
[108] Olivares-Caminal (n 19) 111; Olivares-Caminal and others (n 102) 721.
[109] Olivares-Caminal (n 19) 111. See also Philip R Wood, 'The Origins and Future of Non-Discrimination in Sovereign Bankruptcies: A Comment' (2014) 9 Capital Markets Law Journal 293, 295.
[110] Lee C Buchheit and Mitu Gulati, 'The Argentine Collective Action Clause Controversy' (2020) 15 Capital Markets Law Journal 464, 464.

Concerning both exit consent and CACs, there are typically various categories of provisions that, according to the terms of the debt instruments themselves, can be amended with the consent of a specified majority of bondholders. In some jurisdictions, such majority requirements may also be defined in domestic law. To simplify somewhat, these terms can be divided into three groups: (i) payment-related terms; (ii) clauses that indirectly affect payment terms (eg applicable law, events of default and acceleration rights); and (iii) clauses not included under the two previous categories, such as jurisdictional immunity, financial covenants, listing requirements, etc.[111]

CACs are not a new phenomenon, not even in sovereign bond contracts, and have traditionally been included in sovereign bonds governed by English and Japanese law.[112] The design of CACs has, however, evolved over time. The first generation of CACs were first introduced in in corporate bonds governed by English law in 1879.[113] These CACs permitted a specified supermajority (typically 75% of the outstanding principal) to amend the terms of the debt instrument with binding effect on the dissenting bondholders.

Normal practice in this first generation of CACs was that changes to payment terms could be voted by a supermajority of bondholders (typically 75% of the outstanding principal) and this would bind a potential holdout minority.[114] These CACs became commonplace in both corporate and sovereign bonds governed by English law in the late nineteenth and twentieth centuries, but remained uncommon in US jurisdictions.[115] For a long time, amendments to the financial terms in sovereign issues under New York law required unanimous agreement.[116] The US market thus moved in the opposite direction to the English market. The reason was the adoption of 1939 Trust Indenture Act in which the US Congress decided to ban the use of CACs in corporate bonds issued to the public in the United States, because it preferred the process to be conducted under the supervision of a bankruptcy judge.[117] Even though the Act was limited to corporate bonds, the practice migrated to sovereign bonds.[118] The

---

[111] Olivares-Caminal and others (n 102) 729.

[112] IMF, 'Strengthening the Contractual Framework' (n 23) 17.

[113] According to Buchheit and Gulati, the English lawyer Francis Beaufort Palmer is the self-acclaimed father of the clause, see Buchheit and Gulati, 'The Argentine Collective Action Clause Controversy' (n 110) 464.

[114] See Buchheit and Gulati, 'Exit Consents in Sovereign Bond Exchanges' (n 101) 29, 48 and n 10; Andrew Yianni, 'Resolution of Sovereign Financial Crises - Evolution of the Private Sector Restructuring Process' [1999] Financial Stability Review 78, 80–81; Buchheit and Gulati, 'The Argentine Collective Action Clause Controversy' (n 110).

[115] Buchheit and Gulati, 'The Argentine Collective Action Clause Controversy' (n 110) 465.

[116] IMF, 'Strengthening the Contractual Framework' (n 23) 17. See also Antonia E Stolper and Sean Dougherty, 'Collective Action Clauses: How the Argentina Litigation Changed the Sovereign Debt Markets' (2017) 12 Capital Markets Law Journal 239, 243.

[117] The Act required unanimity if amendments were to be made to the payment terms under a publicly issued corporate bond, cf Rule 316(b) of the Trust Indenture Act of 1939 (US). See also Stolper and Dougherty (n 117) 243. Until 2003, the German law involved a similar prohibition in § 12(3) Gesetz über Schuldverschreibungen aus Gesamtemissionen (SchVG) v. 31.07.2009, BGBl. I 2009, p. 2512, see Jeannette Abel, *The Resolution of Sovereign Debt Crises: Instruments, Inefficiencies and Options for the Way Forward* (1st edn, Routledge 2019) 75.

[118] Robert B Gray, 'Collective Action Clauses' in (UNCTAD 2005) Proceedings of 4th inter-regional debt management conference and WADMO conference 43, 44.

prohibition in corporate bonds seems to have influenced several American lawyers to think that the clauses were contrary to public policy in general.

Buchheit and Gulati argue that this misconception was not corrected until 2002 following the Argentine bond default of December 2001.[119] At this time, the US Treasury Department revived the idea of using CACs as the principal tool to reduce the risk of aggressive holdout creditors that could delay or derail sovereign bond restructurings.[120] The rationale of prohibiting CACs in corporate bonds was not valid for sovereign bonds, because foreign sovereigns would not be subject to the supervision of a US bankruptcy judge. On the initiative of the USA, the G10 countries commissioned a group of experts in 2002 to draft a model collective action clause suitable for use in sovereign bonds governed by New York law. The model CACs designed by this group of experts represents the second generation of CACs. The design built on the existing standard used in English law, but provided greater protection for minority bondholders and was also adapted for procedures familiar to the US bond market.[121] Since 2003, there has been a significant increase in the implementation of CACs in New York governed sovereign bonds.[122]

A sovereign state's bonds are typically divided into multiple issuances or 'series' (with different maturities, interest rates, etc). In both the first and second generation of CACs, voting was confined to particular series of bonds, which left the sovereign vulnerable to individual bondholders with a blocking position within a particular series of bonds.[123] The third generation of CACs sought to remedy the weaknesses resulting from series voting. Mexico and Uruguay were frontrunners in this regard implementing so-called *aggregated* CACs that enabled holders of different series of bonds to vote together as a single class.[124] The challenge with such aggregated voting is an increased risk that the majority will implement disadvantageous terms at the expense of minority bondholders. In an attempt to make a balanced clause and reduce the risk of majority abuse, Uruguay chose a two-tier (sometimes called a two-limb) system. The Uruguay clause required an affirmative vote from the holders of 85% of the outstanding principal of all series of affected bonds and a vote of 66.66% of each affected series of bonds.[125] The two-tier system is a core characteristic of the third generation of CACs.

There is some debate as to why there has been an increase in the implementation of CACs in sovereign bonds.[126] Some argue that it is a result of the efforts of the official

---

[119] Buchheit and Gulati, 'The Argentine Collective Action Clause Controversy' (n 110) 465.
[120] ibid.
[121] See G10, 'Report of the G-10 Working Group on Contractual Clauses' (26 September 2002); Buchheit and Gulati, 'The Argentine Collective Action Clause Controversy' (n 110) 465.
[122] Anna Gelpern, 'Sovereign Debt: Now What?' (2016) 41 (Special edition on sovereign debt) Yale Journal of International Law Online 45, 68. For an elaboration of the development of CACS, see G10 (n 122); IMF, 'Strengthening the Contractual Framework' (n 23); W Mark C Weidemaier and G Mitu Gulati, 'A People's History of Collective Action Clauses' (2013) 54 Virginia Journal of International Law 51.
[123] ILA, 'Report of the Sovereign Bankruptcy Study Group' (77th Biennial Conference of the International Law Association, Johannesburg, South Africa, no date) 11–12 <https://ila.vettoreweb.com/Storage/Download.aspx?DbStorageId=2423&StorageFileGuid=f8a1fb00-b287-4094-bb00-ffb6b3c93c6a> accessed 13 March 2022.
[124] Buchheit and Gulati, 'The Argentine Collective Action Clause Controversy' (n 110) 466.
[125] ibid.
[126] See, in general, Buchheit and Gulati, 'The Argentine Collective Action Clause Controversy' (n 110).

sector, such as the IMF and the G20, pushing for more efficient and sustainable contract practice in sovereign bonds with respect to debt restructurings. Others claim that market actors themselves have found CACs attractive. Regardless of its origin, many argue that there was momentum for reform of bond contracts to ease the restructuring procedure for sovereign debtors in the aftermath of the initiative by the IMF to establish a Sovereign Debt Restructuring Mechanism (SDRM) in the early 2000s.[127] The initiative was vetoed by the United States, in particular, and the 'softer' and more market-friendly approach, which consisted of promoting the implementation of CACs in sovereign bonds, gained acceptance. Argentina's difficult debt restructuring in 2005 and 2010 and the years of litigation which followed, brought by the creditors who refused to take part in the restructuring, is also likely to have contributed to an increase in CACs in sovereign bonds.[128] In addition, the fact that the success of the restructuring in Greece in 2012 (see Section 5.4) was due to the implementation of CACs may also have contributed to further increase the focus on this specific contractual technique as a means of resolving sovereign debt crises and easing debt restructuring.

The two latter debt restructurings (in Argentina and in Greece) also contributed to the development of a fourth generation of CACs. As discussed in Section 4.2, Argentina faced (and contributed to) a very messy restructuring due to a minority of aggressive holdout creditors. It was also clear that Greece would not have been able to implement a debt restructuring based on a Uruguay-style two-tier aggregated CAC; stronger restructuring incentives were needed. In 2014, the US Treasury invited financial and legal experts representing sovereign issuers, investor institutions, and official sector actors to prepare a new model CAC—an enhanced aggregated CAC. The result was a new model CAC promulgated by the International Capital Markets Association (ICMA) in August 2014.

The ICMA model CAC permitted modifications to the important terms of a sovereign bond, so-called Reserved Matters, in three possible ways:

1. pursuant to a series-by-series vote with a 75% voting threshold;
2. on an aggregated basis by a two-limb vote with a 66.66% vote of the entire aggregated pool of bondholders and a 50% vote within each series of the aggregated pool; and
3. pursuant to a single 75% vote of the entire aggregated pool of bondholders, if the proposed modification was Uniformly Applicable to all affected series.

Today, core international financial institutions, major financial jurisdictions and key market actors see this fourth generation of CACs as the main solution to inefficient sovereign debt restructurings that fail to achieve long-term debt sustainability (see Section 1.4). International institutions, such as the ICMA, the IMF, and the G20, recommend implementation of this CAC in sovereign bonds to stop minority creditors

---

[127] See Anne O Krueger and Sean Hagan, 'Sovereign Workouts: An IMF Perspective' (2005) 6 Chicago Journal of International Law 203.

[128] See also Astrid Iversen, 'The Future of Involuntary Sovereign Debt Restructurings: *Mamatas and Others v Greece* and the Protection of Holdings of Sovereign Debt Instruments under the ECHR' (2019) 14 Capital Markets Law Journal 34, 50.

from refusing to participate in debt restructuring that majority creditors find optimal and so promote a more efficient debt restructuring process.[129]

Since 1 January 2013, it has also become mandatory to implement CACs in sovereign bonds issued by Euro area countries with a maturity above one year (Euro area Model CAC).[130] The initial Euro area Model CACs allowed for voting across series, but still required a certain (though lower) majority within each series (a two-limb voting procedure). This provides a weaker incentive for creditors to participate in restructuring than the aggregated standard.[131] In December 2018, the Heads of State in the Eurogroup approved a number of measures in relation to the European Stability Mechanism Treaty reform, which aimed to complete the Banking Union and to further strengthen the Economic and Monetary Union and the ESM. On 27 January and 8 February 2021, ESM member countries signed the Agreement Amending the ESM Treaty. The revised ESM Treaty envisages the introduction of single-limb CACs as of 1 January 2022.[132]

A feature of the fourth generation CACs that is closely connected to the implementation of a restructuring is the 'uniform applicability' provision. Not all CACs that provide for majority voting contain such a provision. However, the ICMA standard single-limb CAC (alternative 3. above) provides that restructuring offers must satisfy the uniform applicability condition: that is, the debtor must offer all bondholders in the aggregate pool the same restructuring terms.[133] Providing an identical offer to all sovereign bondholders may not always lead to an optimal restructuring outcome, or benefit the bondholders as a whole, but it is meant to prevent harm to minority creditors. Uniform applicability conditions are further discussed in Section 4.3.3.

The rest of the discussion in this chapter assumes, unless otherwise specified, that the required creditor consent to amend the terms of the original bonds (exit consent) or to implement a restructuring based on CACs is valid. In other words, the majority decisions are *intra vires*. Even when exit consent or the implementation of a CAC fulfils statutory or contractual majority requirements, care must be taken to ensure that the majority do not abuse their power to discriminate against the minority or any specific groups within the minority.

---

[129] See IMF, 'IMF Executive Board Discusses Strengthening the Contractual Framework in Sovereign Debt Restructuring' (n 90). See also Gelpern, 'The Importance of Being Standard' (n 21) 20.

[130] For an examination of the 2012 Euro Model CAC, see, for example, Astrid Iversen, 'Holdout Creditor Litigation: An Assessment of Legislative Initiatives to Counter Aggressive Sovereign Debt Creditor Litigators' (University of Oslo Faculty of Law Research Paper, 6 February 2015).

[131] The aggregated standard was suggested by the ICMA after a thorough consultation process including international institutions and market actors. For details on the revised ICMA standard, see ICMA, 'Standard Aggregated Collective Action Clauses (CACs)' (n 89). For differences between the ICMA standard and the Euro area standard, see Gelpern, 'Sovereign Debt: Now What?' (n 123); Chanda DeLong and Nikita Aggarwal, 'Strengthening the Contractual Framework for Sovereign Debt Restructuring—the IMF's Perspective' (2016) 11 Capital Markets Law Journal 25.

[132] https://www.esm.europa.eu/sites/default/files/migration_files/esm-treaty-amending-agreement-21_en.pdf. The single-limb CAC was not implemented without debate. See Theresa Arnold and others, 'The Ridiculous Drama in Rome Over Proposals to Reform the ESM Treaty' (*Oxford Law Faculty*, 12 October 2019) <https://www.law.ox.ac.uk/business-law-blog/blog/2019/12/ridiculous-drama-rome-over-proposals-reform-esm-treaty> accessed 10 March 2022.

[133] ICMA, 'ICMA Sovereign Bond Consultation Paper' (December 2013). See also Gelpern, 'The Importance of Being Standard' (n 21) 20–21.

4.3.3 Equal treatment requirements in *pari passu* and uniform applicability clauses

Majority voting provisions can directly influence the issue of intercreditor equity in general and discrimination in particular. A first question is whether a restructuring implemented through majority voting can provide preferential treatment to certain creditors and not to others, if all creditors were promised *pari passu* treatment in their bond terms. Case law has not discussed the *pari passu* clause from this angle, but Kupelyants argues that any restructuring that differentiates between two groups of creditors without defensible reasons, as was the case in *Redwood*, is likely to be in breach of the *pari passu* clause. He argues that the assessment would be similar to the 'like circumstances' standard applied in World Trade Organization (WTO) cases and investment treaty arbitration (see Section 5.3). The test here is whether similarly situated creditors have received the same treatment or have been treated differently. In practice, this is a challenging test. Creditors (and debtors) may endlessly justify why certain creditors ought to receive differential treatment.[134] Kupelyants suggests that a *pari passu* clause would require rateable payment to all creditors in situations where bondholders were not presented equal exchange offers at the restructuring stage. As such, this approach goes further than claiming that the *pari passu* clause is a matter of legal ranking.[135]

A clause with a similar effect—but with a more certain application than Kupelyants' *pari passu* interpretation—is the so-called uniform applicability clause. This clause typically forms an integral part of fourth generation CACs. As mentioned earlier, in Section 4.3.2, the ICMA standard single-limb CAC provides that restructuring offers must be uniformly applicable to all bondholders. In other words, the debtor must offer the same restructuring terms to all bondholders subject to aggregation.[136]

Providing an identical offer to all sovereign bondholders may not always lead to an optimal restructuring outcome or benefit the bondholders as a whole. The ICMA did not seek to benchmark a form of net present value loss across the different series of bonds being restructured because they believed that would be too complex to both develop and apply.[137] As discussed in Section 1.3, restructuring may be more complicated if a sovereign debtor is not able to design an exchange offer that differentiates between different types of creditors.[138] Both Zandstra and Gelpern argue that the ICMA single-limb voting procedure affords flexibility by allowing for differential treatment among bondholders through sub-aggregation. This means that a sovereign debtor can differentiate among groups of issuances by offering different instruments

---

[134] Kupelyants (n 15) 250.
[135] ibid. Kupelyants' view hereby partially conflicts with the findings in Section 4.2 discussing the *pari passu* clause.
[136] ICMA, 'ICMA Sovereign Bond Consultation Paper' (n 134). See also Gelpern, 'The Importance of Being Standard' (n 21) 20–21.
[137] ICMA, 'ICMA Sovereign Bond Consultation Paper' (n 134) para 9. See also Kupelyants (n 15) 242.
[138] For criticism of the practice of conducting separate votes for different groups of bondholders so as to ensure flexibility for the sovereign debtor and reduce the risk of blocking positions, see IMF, 'Strengthening the Contractual Framework' (n 23) 22–23.

to different groups of bondholders under a single-limb procedure, so long as the uniformly applicability requirement is met within each group.[139] The sovereign debtor can do this by activating the provisions separately in respect of two or more series of bonds drawn from the larger group of all series of bonds that may be aggregated. These sub-aggregated transactions can proceed simultaneously.[140]

It should be mentioned that, as with all contract provisions, uniform applicability provisions may come in many forms. It is possible to draft them in a way that seeks to ensure that no sub-aggregation is allowed, or even that different types of bonds issuances or different types of debts instruments are given equal or similar restructuring offers. When uniform applicability provisions are not drafted in line with international standards, their proper interpretation can be difficult to establish and they may become an easy target for litigation.[141]

4.3.4 CACs and the risk of abuse by minority creditors

In 2020, both Argentina and Ecuador experienced severe economic challenges and managed to restructure their bonded debts. While there have not yet been any real-life experiences with debt restructuring under the enhanced ICMA CACs with single-limb voting, the recent restructurings in Argentina and Ecuador provided the first test cases for the use of the enhanced ICMA CACs with two-limb voting in international bonds.[142]

The market haircuts were 41% the case of Ecuador and 50% in the case of Argentina.[143] In the case of Ecuador, over 98% of creditors participated in the restructuring, resulting in 100% participation after the use of CACs. Over 93% of creditors consented to the Argentinian exchange, resulting in over 99% participation. Despite the high participation, the restructuring revealed weaknesses in the design and functioning of the enhanced ICMA CACs that were not thought through at the time of

---

[139] Deborah Zandstra, 'New Aggregated Collective Action Clauses and Evolution in the Restructuring of Sovereign Debt Securities' (2017) 12 Capital Markets Law Journal 180, 196–97. See Gelpern, 'The Importance of Being Standard' (n 21) 20–21.

[140] Zandstra (n 140) 196 gives the example that 'the sovereign could aggregate its first, second, and third bond issues, the holders of which would vote together, whether on a single- or two-limb basis, and, separately, aggregate its fourth, fifth, and sixth bond issues, the holders of which would also vote together'.

[141] One example of such a provision is found in the Argentine bonds issued after 2016 under President Macri, see Prospectus for the Republic of Argentina (14 March 2017). At the time of issuance, Argentina also had other outstanding bonds that were issued in debt exchanges in 2005 and 2010 during Kristina Kirchner's presidency. One question is whether a sovereign debtor can restructure one type of bond while leaving the other type of bonds untouched. The design of this provision and the question of equal treatment of various creditors in a future Argentine debt restructuring is discussed in a series of blog posts on creditslips.org: W Mark C Weidemaier and G Mitu Gulati, 'Can Argentina Discriminate Against Bonds Issued Under Macri?' (Blog, *Credit Slips: A discussion on credit, finance, and bankruptcy*, 11 April 2019) <https://www.creditslips.org/creditslips/2019/11/can-argentina-discriminate-against-bonds-issued-under-macri.html> accessed 15 March 2022; Gelpern, 'Imagine Riding the Ceteris Pari-Bus into the Sunset ... in Argentina' (n 100).

[142] IMF, 'The International Architecture for Resolving Sovereign Debt Involving Private-Sector Creditors—Recent Developments, Challenges, and Reform Options' (Policy paper, 23 September 2020) 25–27.

[143] In a sovereign debt context, a haircut refers to the size of creditor losses in a debt restructuring typically due to reduction in the interest rate, face value, granting of grace periods, or an extension of the maturity date.

drafting. Both debtor countries proposed fixes to these challenges and ICMA is considering making amendments in their model CACs.

In advance of the restructuring, the debtor states were afraid that a restructuring attempt would fail because it might not meet the required threshold in the series-by-series vote when applying its two-limb CAC.[144] Both states therefore adopted legal strategies, announced in their respective exchange offer prospectuses.[145] While both states adopted the so-called re-designation strategy, Argentina in addition sought to implement a 'Pac Man' strategy. In short, redesignation means that the debtor can create a new and, in its own view, more ideal voting pool of creditors under a two-limb procedure, even after the exchange offer has been closed and the votes have been counted. Creating a new and more ideal voting pool maximizes a debtor's possibility to force the participation of holdout creditors that might otherwise undermine procedural fairness and the integrity of the restructuring.[146] The 'Pac-Man' strategy is used in situations where the debtor restructures a selection of its bonds with the support of less than an overall supermajority of creditors. After concluding an initial exchange offer (restructuring), a debtor may launch one or more subsequent exchange offers. The aim of the subsequent offer would be to bind those creditors who had refused to participate in the initial exchange. To do this, the debtor state would aggregate the already restructured bonds with (a subset of) the remaining unrestructured bonds (creating a new voting pool) and use a single-limb CAC. As explained earlier, in a single-limb CAC, only an aggregate voting threshold need be met and no per-series voting is required. The idea is that the debtor would offer slightly better terms compared to the initial exchange to convince the creditors with new bonds to consent to the subsequent exchange as well. If the aggregate voting threshold is met, the creditors holding out from the initial exchange offer would be bound in this subsequent offer regardless of their support in a particular series.

When Argentina made it clear in the prospectuses that they intended to use these legal strategies in their restructurings, some creditors claimed that redesignation and Pac Man strategies were not in accordance with the ICMA standard.[147] Creditors were

---

[144] The Argentine CAC actually contained a single-limb CAC, but due to specific circumstances in the Argentine offer, they deemed it unlikely that they would be able to implement a restructuring under the single-limb CAC and chose the two-limb CACs instead. See Buchheit and Gulati, 'The Argentine Collective Action Clause Controversy' (n 110) 470.

[145] Republic of Argentina Prospectus Supplement, 21 April 2020, S-11, 12 <https://www.sec.gov/Archives/edgar/data/914021/000119312520188103/d935251d424b5.htm> accessed 27 February 2022; Invitation Memorandum, The Republic of Ecuador, Solicitation of Consents to Certain Amendments to the Bonds of the Republic of Ecuador listed below (collectively, the 'Eligible Bonds') and Invitation to Exchange Eligible Bonds for New Securities of the Republic of Ecuador (the "New Securities")', 20 July 2020 <https://sec.report/lux/doc/101823707/> accessed 27 February 2022.

[146] IMF, 'The International Architecture for Resolving Sovereign Debt Involving Private-Sector Creditors' (n 143) 25.

[147] Ecuador's largest bondholder group consisted of many of the same institutions as those who participated in Argentina's restructuring. The bondholders did not, however, react negatively in the Ecuadorian context. Clark and Lyratzakis argue that there are two reasons for this. First, even though Ecuador's bonds are governed by New York law, they did not restrict redesignation. Ecuador's indentures included the ICMA CACs recommended for bonds issued under English law which, as explained previously, do not impose the same 'finality' condition on designation as the New York law version. More importantly, Ecuador's restructuring offer was the outcome of a negotiated process with the country's largest creditor group, and was designed to attract the support of a supermajority of Ecuador's bondholders in a two-limb CAC process. See, in general, discussion in Ian Clark and Dimitrios Lyratzakis, 'Towards a More Robust Sovereign

less concerned with Ecuador's exchange offer because its redesignation strategy would help achieve a majoritarian restructuring. If the 'Pac Man' strategy is used repeatedly, however, and in combination with the redesignation strategy, a consenting minority of bondholders can in theory force the majority of bondholders to participate in a debt restructuring.[148] Shortcomings in the design of the 2014 ICMA CACs allow for 'Pac Man' and redesignation strategies to be used and these can be exploited by debtors who are unwilling or unable to build the requisite consensus with their private creditors.[149]

If we look at the requirements in the enhanced ICMA CAC, it is clear that a sovereign debtor has the freedom to choose the method used to obtain bondholder approval. If an aggregated voting method is chosen, the debtor state also has freedom to choose which series of bonds are included in the aggregate voting pool.[150] Buchheit and Gulati describe the two-limb voting procedure in the ICMA CACs as having an 'all or nothing' feature: once the debtor state has chosen which series of bonds to aggregate in a restructuring voting, that choice is final for the purposes of that offer.[151] If one of the series in the second limb does not achieve the required majority when voting, the entire offer fails. Consequently, if an issuer wished to exclude one or more series of bonds from the aggregate voting pool *after* the offer has been launched, it would have to give all holders notice of this decision and either (i) give participating holders a period in which to withdraw their tenders if they felt the change was material to their decision to participate or (ii) relaunch the offer with the amended voting pool.[152] The rationale of the 'all or nothing' feature of the two-limb ICMA CACs is to ensure that the bondholders know the context in which they are voting in favour or against a restructuring offer. A core part of this context is knowledge about which series of bonds (and which bondholders) are in the aggregated pool of a specific restructuring offer. This may influence the bondholders' decision of whether there is a risk of subsequent holdout litigation or other political or financial risk associated with the restructuring offer. In other words, if some of the debtor state's bonds are excluded from the restructuring or provided with differential treatment, this is material information that the bondholder ought to be informed of before they have to vote.[153]

Debt Restructuring Architecture: Innovations from Ecuador and Argentina' (2021) 16 Capital Markets Law Journal 31.

[148] ibid 24.
[149] IRC Task Force on IMF and global financial governance issues, 'The IMF's Role in Sovereign Debt Restructurings' (Occasional Paper Series, 14 September 2021) 37.
[150] The relevant text of the ICMA standard CAC intended for use in bonds governed by New York law states: 'The Issuer shall have the discretion to select a Modification Method for a proposed Reserve Matter Modification and to designate which Series of Debt Securities will be included in the aggregated voting for a proposed Cross-Series Modification; provided, however, that once the Issuer selects a Modification Method and designates the Series of Debt Securities that will be subject to a proposed Cross-Series Modification, those elections will be final for purposes of that vote or consent solicitation.' See ICMA, 'Standard Aggregated Collective Action Clauses (CACs)' (n 89). As Buchheit and Gulati point out in their article, this language did not appear in the ICMA model CAC intended for use in bonds governed by English law even though the two models were supposed to be substantively identical (Buchheit and Gulati, 'The Argentine Collective Action Clause Controversy' [n 110] 468, n 10).
[151] Buchheit and Gulati, 'The Argentine Collective Action Clause Controversy' (n 110) 468.
[152] ibid.
[153] ibid 469.

Argentina did not, as explained above, choose any of these approaches in their exchange offer prospectuses, but rather a third alternative. In a first exchange offer, the two debtor states would apply the two-limb ICMA CAC and thus seek bondholders' consent to an amendment of the bond terms removing the 'all or nothing' feature of the two-limb CACs altogether. This enabled the implementation of a subsequent exchange offer applying the single-limb CAC option, which could potentially bind holdout creditors from the first exchange offer.

In the end, both Argentina and Ecuador accepted to include clauses in the new bonds issued in the restructuring that would limit the use of these legal techniques in a future restructuring of the bonds.[154] The limitations were that: in future restructurings, re-designation of voting pools will only be permitted if (i) bondholders are given five business days after the exchange offer closes to withdraw their votes, or (ii) the offer is approved by holders of more than 66.66% of the aggregate principal amount of the originally designated pool.[155] Moreover, the debtor can only use the 'Pac Man' technique if, in the first round of restructuring, holders of more than 75% of the aggregate principal amount of all bonds included in the original restructuring offer accept the deal. If the first-round restructuring does not meet this threshold, the debtor state must wait at least 36 months before using a single-limb vote to cram down remaining holdouts. Several academics and international finance institutions suggest that, with these limitations, the legal techniques can be sound restructuring tools that can provide strong incentives for a sovereign to engage constructively with its private creditors.[156]

In the context of intercreditor equity, it must be underlined that, in the case of the 2020 Argentine debt restructuring, the problem with the use of redesignation and 'Pac Man' was *not* that creditors voting in favour of a restructuring could force holdout creditors to participate in a restructuring on poorer condition than themselves. In this case, sovereign bonds with single-limb and two-limb voting structures coexisted. The use of the 'Pac Man' strategy required the second exchange offer to be uniformly applicable. When designing the second exchange offer, Argentina had to take into consideration the uniform applicability requirement envisaged in the single-limb ICMA CACs and ensure that the holders of all affected bond series got the same exchange terms or menu of exchange options.[157] In other words, the bonds in the series that were able to reject the first exchange offer would have had to be given the same restructuring terms as the bondholders who initially accepted the first restructuring offer.[158] However, as sovereign bonds contain different formulations of CACs—both with regards to the possibility of implementing redesignation and 'Pac Man' strategies, but also in terms of uniform applicability requirements—the combination of the two

---

[154] IMF, 'The International Architecture for Resolving Sovereign Debt Involving Private-Sector Creditors' (n 143) 25.

[155] ibid.

[156] IRC Task Force on IMF and global financial governance issues (n 150) 37. For a more detailed record of these issues and specific fixes, see Clark and Lyratzakis (n 148); Buchheit and Gulati, 'The Argentine Collective Action Clause Controversy' (n 110); Andrés de la Cruz and Ignacio Lagos, 'CACs at Work: What Next? Lessons from the Argentine and Ecuadorian 2020 Debt Restructurings' (2021) 16 Capital Markets Law Journal 226.

[157] IRC Task Force on IMF and global financial governance issues (n 150) 37.

[158] Buchheit and Gulati, 'The Argentine Collective Action Clause Controversy' (n 110) 471.

strategies may be used by other debtor countries to provide creditors with differential treatment.

4.3.5 Relevance of case law from domestic law

There is limited case law examining the minimum threshold for treatment of minority creditors connected to CACs and the use of exit consent in sovereign debt restructuring. The following section will therefore mainly discuss case law concerning ordinary market-based restructuring of corporate debts.

This chapter could also have chosen to look at ordinary insolvency proceedings involving corporations. However, as mentioned above, domestic insolvency proceedings do not apply to sovereign debt and sovereign debt restructurings. Moreover, ordinary insolvency proceedings are to a large degree unsuitable for comparison with sovereign debt restructuring. By insolvency proceedings, I refer to both liquidation and restructuring proceedings that are overseen by a domestic court system. The liquidation proceeding constitutes the cornerstone of general insolvency law. To generalize somewhat, when liquidation proceedings are initiated, an initial right to enforce claims against the company's pool of available assets is transformed into a right to receive distributions from this same pool in accordance with a statutorily determined hierarchy of priority.[159] Liquidation proceedings mostly involve the end of the entity under liquidation and distribution of its property. A state cannot be liquidated and its property cannot be distributed to its creditors. Domestic insolvency law concerning liquidation is therefore less relevant as a basis for comparison in this chapter.

Restructuring proceedings are a part of national insolvency law that produce legal effects more closely resembling those of sovereign debt restructuring. Although they vary across jurisdictions, restructuring proceedings can be placed somewhere between the classic state-based approach of court-ordered liquidation and the purely market-based approach of privately negotiated 'debt work-outs'.[160] Legislation (and related case law) concerning restructuring proceedings demonstrates that majority decisions are a common and widely accepted tool to minimize holdout problems and permit an orderly rearrangement of debt. It shows that there is nothing illegal or unusual in a majority using its contractual amendment power in a multi-creditor debt instrument to protect its own interests.[161] Examining the threshold of what types of interference with minority creditors rights are accepted in statutory restructuring proceedings could potentially also contribute to shedding light on what will be deemed acceptable in purely market-based contractual restructurings, as those implemented in the context of sovereign debt. However, the fact that a legislator has chosen to regulate these restructuring procedures in law, in addition to the existence of a pure market-based

---

[159] Sjur Swensen Ellingsæter, 'Creditor Priority and Financial Stability: A Study of the Emergence and Rationales of the Creditor Hierarchy in EU and EEA Bank Insolvency Law' (PhD, University of Oslo 2020) 31.
[160] ibid.
[161] Buchheit and Gulati, 'Exit Consents in Sovereign Bond Exchanges' (n 101) 29–30.

approach, speaks against comparing them to an out-of-court and market-based debt restructuring, such as that applicable to sovereign debt.

For these reasons, the case law most relevant to sovereign debt restructuring is that concerned with market-based solutions to financial distress for legal (and natural) persons in domestic law. Such market-based restructurings take place outside of insolvency proceedings, through privately negotiated solutions, within the limits of contract and company law. Transaction costs and other coordination problems related to restructuring negotiations may prevent creditors from reaching a result acceptable to all parties involved and may be an obstacle to reaching the most desirable (or most sustainable) restructuring agreement.[162] Even within this market-based approach, one must be cautious about drawing absolute parallels between the contractual discretion of majority bondholders of sovereign bonds and majority decisions in the context of corporate debt restructuring. After all, a sovereign debtor is fundamentally distinct from a corporation. Nevertheless, consideration of such issues may enlighten us as to the extent to which a court is willing to interfere with a majority decision based on contractual rights.

4.3.6 Judicial scrutiny of majority decisions

Sovereign bonds are commercial contracts. It must therefore be assumed that bondholders are conscious of the risk that the terms of the bond issue may be modified when subscribing to an issue containing a CAC or other majority voting provision allowing for exit consent.[163] Accordingly, commercial debt instruments such as bonds are normally enforced in accordance with a plain reading of their terms in sovereign debt litigation. Courts are generally reluctant to find obligations with regard to majority bondholders other than those explicitly expressed in the debt instrument itself.[164] Some have argued that courts should not exercise review of contractual discretion of majority power in commercial cases at all since this may create uncertainty and opportunism, as well as increasing costs; the regulation of abuses of contractual discretion should be left to the market.[165] Having established this, it must be said that sovereign bonds may be silent as to the exact limits of the majority's discretion to implement contractual amendments. There are also a number of cases where courts have been called on by dissatisfied minority creditors and which have concluded that majority creditors do not have unrestrained discretion to adopt resolution and contract amendments that bind the minority.

Before discussing the substance and threshold of protection of minority creditors in a debt restructuring based on CACs and exit consent, we first need to determine who is the proper respondent for a claim that a restructuring based on a CAC is discriminatory: the sovereign debtor or the majority bondholders? While it is the majority

---

[162] Ellingsæter (n 160) 31.
[163] *Allen v Gold Reefs of West Africa* [1900] 1 Ch 656, 678.
[164] Carmine D Boccuzzi and others, 'Defences' in Rosa M Lastra and Lee C Buchheit (eds), *Sovereign debt management* (Oxford University Press 2014) 111–13. See also Kupelyants (n 15) 215.
[165] Kupelyants (n 15) 268. See also Keegan S Drake, 'The Fall and Rise of the Exit Consent' (2013–14) 63 Duke Law Journal 1589, 1622–23.

bondholders who decide on a restructuring, the sovereign debtor normally initiates the restructuring and puts forward a concrete offer. English (as well as some US) case law seems to take contrasting positions on this question in *ex post* challenges to sovereign debt restructurings.[166] Under English law, actions are often framed against the majority bondholders who ultimately make the decision whether or not to restructure the debt. In the United States, on the other hand, these types of claims are usually targeted against the debtor in distress seeking to restructure its debts.[167] A finding of potential joint liability of the debtor and the majority bondholders requires a fact-specific enquiry, which will largely depend on the degree of complicity between the two respondent actors.[168]

A second issue to consider is the legal basis for courts to intervene and exercise judicial scrutiny over potentially abusive contractual majority powers. Kupelyants holds that the source of such judicial power to assess contractual discretion is not completely clear under English law. Nevertheless, he convincingly argues that the most likely legal basis for judicial scrutiny would be an implied term based on common law rules that require the majority to act in good faith in the best interests of the creditors (bondholders) as a whole.[169] This good faith approach, as will be discussed below, is not likely to be applicable under New York law, as the District Court has gone so far as to deny the existence of any good faith obligation in the relations between the minority and majority bondholders.[170]

Building on case law concerning shareholder and multi-party debt instruments, both Woods and Kupelyants refer to two separate principles underpinning the valid exercise of majority powers that are relevant in the context of intercreditor equity.[171] These principles are (i) that the majority acted in good faith (ie were not motivated solely by malice or vindictiveness) and (ii) that there was no unjust oppression of the minority so as to constitute a fraud, for example, by a discriminatory decision denying the minority an advantage.[172] While both categories are closely related, case

---

[166] Kupelyants (n 15) 210.
[167] In English law, see *Northern Assurance Company Ltd v Farnham United Breweries Ltd* [1912] 2 Ch 123. In US law, see *Katz v Oak Industries Inc* 508 A 2d 873 (Del Ch 1986). One exception where the court holds that the majority bondholders have a good faith obligation towards minority bondholders is *Hackettstown National Bank v DG Yuengling Brewing Co* 74 F 110 (2d Cir 1896). See Kupelyants (n 15) 210.
[168] Kupelyants (n 15) 214.
[169] In all, he suggests three possible sources. The first approach is based on a textual argument. The plain language of debt instruments typically allows for a majority of bondholders to 'modify' or 'amend' the rights and obligations of all bondholders. One may argue that these words do not encompass majority votes that 'extinguish' or 'destroy' the rights of the minority. Second, some courts may imply terms in fact to be able to constrain the abusive implementation of majority powers. This approach is also challenging because it has to establish the necessity of implication under English law on implied terms in fact. The third is the good faith approach discussed in the following. ibid.
[170] See *Aladdin Hotel Co v Bloom* 200 F 2d 627 (8th Cir 1953); *Yucyco, Ltd v Republic of Slovenia* 984 F Supp 209 (SDNY 1997). See also William Bratton and G Mitu Gulati, 'Sovereign Debt Reform and the Best Interest of Creditors' (2004) 57 Vanderbilt Law Review 1, 66–69.
[171] Philip R Wood, 'Syndicated Credit Agreement: Majority Voting' (2003) 62 The Cambridge Law Journal 261, 262–63; Kupelyants (n 15) 218–22. Building on Wood's categorization, Kupelyants draws up a structure illustrating possible challenges to a sovereign debt restructuring implemented by majority resolution, which are applicable to both CACs and exit consent. Wood summarizes the case law on creditor voting clauses, mainly in the context of bond issues, when combined with the case law on shareholder voting, voting on corporate schemes of arrangement, and the like.
[172] In total, both refer to four principles underpinning the valid exercise of majority powers. The two other principles are first, that the majority decision has to be *intra vires*, meaning that the exercise of

law concerning shareholders' rights provides authority for the assertion that good faith with regard to companies would encompass cases where all of the bondholders have an interest in a specific restructuring. In other words, case law suggests that a court's assessment must look at whether the majority decision benefits the group of bondholders as whole. The category of unjust oppression of minority creditors that constitutes fraud, on the other hand, covers cases where the restructuring causes the interests of one group of bondholders to conflict with those of another group of bondholders.[173] When examining to what extent courts under English and New York law may exercise judicial scrutiny over majority decision affecting intercreditor equity, the following sections adopt this distinction. First, Section 4.3.7 assesses the subjective good faith standard which assesses whether creditors as a whole have an interest in a specific restructuring. Subsequently, Section 4.3.8 discusses unjust oppression or fraud with regard to a minority, such as discrimination against all (or groups of) minority creditors.

4.3.7 Minority protection—good faith as a standard for majority decisions

Katz v Oak Industries, a 1986 case from Delaware (United States), sheds light on key features of the question of protection of the minority in a debt restructuring decided by the majority creditors.[174] In this case, creditors who agreed to exchange their old securities for new ones also consented to amendments of the governing indentures that would, among other things, strip away all financial covenants that were binding for the securities that dissenting minorities still held. The dissenting minority bondholders challenged the legality of the majority vote in the Delaware Chancery Courts. The claimants argued that the exit consent and the exchange offer were 'coercive' and violated the debtor's (Oak's) contractual obligation to act in good faith with respect to its bondholders.[175]

In *Katz v Oak Industries*, Chancellor Allen disagreed with the claimants. He agreed that the exit consent would remove 'significant negotiated protections' from holders of Oak's outstanding debt securities and could have adverse consequences for debtholders who chose not to exchange their bonds in the restructuring offer. Chancellor Allen then underlined that the relationship between a corporation and its debtholders is contractual in nature and that there are no implicit fiduciary responsibilities on the part of the corporation. Moreover, it was not determinative whether

majority powers was within the terms of the power of the majority described in contract or statutes; second, that there are no secret advantages to some creditors to procure their votes, eg bribes. (Wood [n 172] 262–63; Kupelyants [n 15] 218–22).

[173] *Citco Banking v Pusser's Ltd* [2007] BCC 205 [18]. While the *Citco* case refers to shareholders, the following systematization refers to bondholders. See also Kupelyants (n 15) 220.
[174] *Katz v Oak Industries Inc* (n 168).
[175] *Assénagon Asset Management SA v Irish Bank Resolution Corporation Ltd* [2012] EWHC 2090 (EWHC) [5]. *Katz v Oak Industries Inc* (n 168) did not direct any claims against the majority bondholders, as was the case in *Assénagon* (discussed in later in this section, see text accompanying n 197ff). In *Assénagon*, the court found that the majority bondholders' participation in the bond exchange constituted an abuse of their contractual majority rights which enabled them to bind the minority to a variation of the bond terms.

the restructuring was coercive, but rather whether the coercion was wrongful.[176] Lastly, the Chancellor held that the appropriate legal test for determining whether Oak breached an obligation to deal fairly and in good faith with its bondholders was to ask whether the parties who negotiated the terms of the relevant instruments could have forbidden the action that took place if they had foreseen the exchange offer.[177] The answer in this particular case was that the minority bondholders could not have forbidden it, and therefore the exit consent was not illegal.

This case was decided by a Delaware court. Buchheit and Gulati argue that the so-called boilerplate doctrine should give New York judges a basis for following Delaware's approach to this issue. This doctrine contends that market participants have a strong interest in seeing a uniform and predictable interpretation of standard provisions in commercial contracts ('boilerplate' provisions). When New York courts interpret such provisions, great weight is given to relevant decisions in other jurisdictions. This is particularly the case, Buchheit and Gulati argue, when market participants can be presumed to have been aware of those other decisions but did not change their documentation practices in a way that might suggest disagreement with a prior judicial interpretation of a boilerplate clause.[178] Since this 1986 judgment, exit consents and later CACs have been the subject of considerable attention in legal journals, and both contractual techniques have been used in several corporate bond exchanges. If the drafters of debt instruments have not altered their approach to clauses allowing for majority amendments and therefore also exit consent as discussed in *Katz v Oak Industries*, the boilerplate doctrine should give New York judges a basis for following the Delaware court's approach to the issue.[179]

In *Katz v Oak Industries*, the court rejected the applicant's claim that majority creditors had violated an implied duty of good faith and fair dealing toward the co-creditors who chose not to restructure but to hold on to their old debt instruments.[180] The applicant's argument has some support in earlier decisions that were prepared to infer such duties when debtholders acted together with the borrower to harm other creditors.[181] However, other legal sources support *Katz v Oak Industries* and indicate the opposite solution. For trust indentures that must be qualified under the Trust Indenture Act of 1939, the Act requires a disenfranchisement of voting by bondholders 'owned by any obligor ... or by any person directly or indirectly controlling or controlled by or under direct or indirect common control with any such obligor'.[182] Similarly, the federal Bankruptcy Code forbids 'insiders' from voting on whether a reorganization plan will be accepted by impaired creditors.[183] Apart from such arrangements with a debtor clearly designed to impair the rights of minority creditors, US courts have been reluctant to find implicit intercreditor duties in corporate debt

---

[176] *Katz v Oak Industries Inc* (n 168) 879–80.
[177] ibid at 880.
[178] Buchheit and Gulati, 'Exit Consents in Sovereign Bond Exchanges' (n 101) 18. See, for example, *Morgan Stanley & Co v Archer Daniels Midland Co* 570 F Supp 1529, 1542 (SDNY 1983).
[179] Buchheit and Gulati were somewhat more cautious in their 2002 publication on CACs: Lee C Buchheit and G Mitu Gulati, 'Sovereign Bonds and the Collective Will' (2002) 51 Emory Law Journal 1317, 1346.
[180] Buchheit and Gulati, 'Exit Consents in Sovereign Bond Exchanges' (n 101) 20.
[181] See, for example, *Hackettstown National Bank v DG Yuengling Brewing Co* (n 168).
[182] TIA, s 316.
[183] US Bankruptcy Code 11 USC, s 1129(a)(10) (US).

instruments. Buchheit and Gulati argue that creditors should not rely on a vague sense of implicit intercreditor duties when they enter into multiple lender transactions. If a particular debt instrument provides each creditor with a right to vote on certain types of amendments to the terms, only very extraordinary circumstances seem to justify courts disregarding such a majority vote under New York law.[184] This is also in line with Wood's findings that case law in the US declines to imply overriding covenants of good faith and fair dealing into bonds, regardless of whether a restructuring is somewhat coercive, if the bondholders did not negotiate the protection in the first place.[185]

In English law, a majority decision must benefit the affected debtors as a whole. The generality of this principle is described in *British America Nickel Corporation v MJ O'Brien*.[186] In this judgment, Viscount Haldane describes the relationship between creditors in a multiholder debt instrument under English law by comparing their position with voting powers to amend the debenture to the position of shareholders voting to amend articles of association:[187]

> There is, however, a restriction of such powers when conferred on a majority of a special class in order to enable that majority to bind the minority ... the power given must be exercised for the purpose of benefiting the class as a whole and not merely individual members only.[188]

The basis for the application of this principle in relation to powers conferred on majorities to bind minorities is traditionally described as arising from general principles of law and equity, and by way of implication.[189]

The above quoted part of the *British America* case focusing on the purpose of benefiting the class as a whole was cited with approval in *Redwood Master v TD Bank*.[190] In *Redwood*, the borrowing company was facing financial problems and sought to restructure its syndicated debts by using exit consent. The syndicated loan was composed of three facilities (tranches), of which two (A and B) had colliding interests. The

---

[184] Buchheit and Gulati, 'Exit Consents in Sovereign Bond Exchanges' (n 101) 21–22. In a case from a New York State Court in 1985, *Crédit Français v Sociedad* 128 Misc 2d 564 (NY Sup Ct 1985), the judge held that banks in a syndicated loan owed each other implicit fiduciary duties. The case has been heavily criticized and distinguished and is unlikely, according to Buchheit and Gulati, to be followed by other courts in the future. See Buchheit and Gulati, 'Exit Consents in Sovereign Bond Exchanges' (n 101) 22. See also Lee C Buchheit and Ralph Reisner, 'The Effect of the Sovereign Debt Restructuring Process on Inter-Creditor Relationships' (1988) 1988 University of Illinois Law Review 493, 502–04; Lee C Buchheit, 'Is Syndicated Lending a Joint Venture?' (1985) 4 International Financial Law Review 12.
[185] Philip R Wood, *Principles of International Insolvency*, vol 1 (The Law and Practice of International Finance Series, 2nd edn, Sweet & Maxwell 2007) para 20-060.
[186] That principle was applied to the relationship of shareholders in a limited company, both in *Ebrahimi v Westbourne Galleries Ltd* [1973] AC 360 (House of Lords) 381 by Lord Wilberforce, and in *O'Neill v Phillips* [1999] 1 WLR 1092, 1098–101 by Lord Hoffmann, in relation to the statutory remedy for unfairly prejudicial conduct. The same principle was applied to the power of a majority of debenture holders to modify the terms of the debenture issue so as to bind a minority in *British America Nickel Corporation Ltd v O'Brien* [1927] AC 369; repeated in *Redwood Master Fund and Others v TD Bank Europe Ltd and Others* [2002] EWCH 2703 (EWHC) [92].
[187] *British America Nickel Corporation Ltd v O'Brien* (n 187).
[188] ibid at 371. See also *Assénagon* (n 176) [43].
[189] *Allen v Gold Reefs of West Africa* [1900] 1 Ch 656, 671.
[190] *Redwood* (n 187) [92].

exit consent entailed that the debtor could draw from a revolving facility to prepay outstanding loans under one of the facilities, so that only some lenders, including the minority creditors who were claimants in the case, were net contributors. In other words, the risk of the debt was transferred to these minority creditors.[191] The majority of the creditors were able to force the holders of facility A, through the use of exit consent, to advance an additional sum to the debtor by drawing down the A tranche while writing off their own debt. In other words, only some lenders, including the minority creditors who were claimants in the case, were net contributors and the risk of the debt was transferred to these minority creditors.[192] The claimants (consisting of facility A creditors) argued that the majority creditors had not acted in good faith because they had discriminated against A-facility creditors as a class and enriched themselves through the A-facility creditors' funds.

Rimer J held that the purpose of majority voting powers could be restricted where such powers were motivated by bad faith towards the minority creditors. The standard of bad faith has a high threshold as Rimer J referred to situations where majority resolutions are passed in an act of vindictiveness or malice towards the claimant.[193] Moreover, Rimer J's reasoning indicated that proof that a resolution has been promoted for reasons of vindictiveness or malice towards the claimant (minority creditor) may be sufficient to enable the minority claim to succeed, since it can then be argued that its object is to do harm to the minority creditors as a whole.[194] In this sense, the question of bad faith is relevant to the assessment of whether a majority resolution is for the benefit of the creditors as a whole. In the case at hand, however, Rimer J concluded that the facts did not indicate that any such vindictive or malicious purpose was present (no 'subjective bad faith' was found).[195] Despite certain coercive factors, Rimer J found the majority decision to be guided by the objective of obtaining a successful debt renegotiation and improving the situation of the lending syndicate as a whole.

In a more recent case from 2012, *Assénagon Asset Management v Irish Bank Resolution Corporation*, the court concluded that implementation of an exit consent clause was illegal.[196] This case demonstrates that there is indeed a limit to the types of majority decision that can be imposed on minority creditors and perhaps helps to nuance the seemingly high threshold for what is deemed majority abuse in *Redwood*. *Assénagon* concerned a debtor (issuer of bonds) who attempted to convince its bondholders to accept a restructuring offer. In 2010, the Irish Bank launched an exchange offer that gave holders of notes the right to exchange their original notes for new ones, pursuant to a trust deed governed by English law. By accepting the restructuring offer, the holders of the notes were also required to vote in favour of a resolution at a bondholder meeting which would amend the payment terms of the original notes. As a result, those who refused the restructuring offer would have their principal reduced

---

[191] See also Matthew Padian and Jonathan Porteous, 'Carrots and Sticks: Limits on Majority Creditors' Rights to Bind a Minority' [2017] Butterworths Journal of International Banking and Financial Law 22, 23.
[192] See also ibid.
[193] *Redwood* (n 187) [85].
[194] ibid.
[195] ibid.
[196] *Assénagon* (n 176).

to EUR 0.01 per EUR 1,000. The claimant, who did not accept the exchange deal, challenged the exit consent on three different legal grounds. The reason most relevant in the context of this book is that the exit consent constituted an abuse of power, more specifically an unfair and oppressive act by the majority.[197]

In his judgment, Briggs J agreed with the claimants and held that the majority decision was both oppressive and unfair against the minority as it imposed upon a defined minority the expropriation of their notes and did not confer any conceivable benefit or advantage on the bondholders as whole. The majority resolution therefore constituted an abuse of power, not by the debtor bank, but by the noteholders who, although not affected by it, had voted for it.[198] In justifying his conclusion, Briggs J also pointed to the fact that the majority voting was exercised solely to the detriment of the bondholders which had not exchanged their notes.[199] As such, the conclusion was in line with the aforementioned and well-established principle that the authority conferred upon the majority, which enables them to bind a minority, must be exercised for the purpose of benefiting the class as a whole and not any individual alone.[200]

Assénagon should not be interpreted as forbidding all use of exit consent that imposes less favourable consequences on minority creditors who reject an associated exchange offer and thereby incentivizes participation in a restructuring.[201] Rather, it is a question of establishing the acceptable level of coercion using the exit consent mechanism.[202] It remains to be seen where this line will be drawn in various circumstances in the future. Some central features that may be useful for future assessments. First, in *Assénagon*, there was a substantial disparity between the value offered to those who accepted the exchange offer and voted in favour of the resolution, and those who did not. Second, the remaining minority creditors' right to nominal payment was in practice expropriated through the majority vote. And finally, the design of the exit consent only served the purpose of threatening and punishing holdout creditors and did not contribute to improving the economic situation for a whole class of creditors, as the restructuring offer was designed separately from the exit consent.

The contrasting outcome in *Redwood* concerning the threshold for general minority abuse can be explained by that fact that the debt in *Redwood*, which was modified through the exercise of majority powers, was in the form of syndicated loans. The

---

[197] The first claim was that the exit consent was *ultra vires*: that it went beyond the powers conferred on the majority of bondholders under the terms of the trust deed. The claimant argued that the terms did not permit the issuer to expropriate the old notes for a nominal amount. The court rejected this claim. The second claim was that the resolution had procedural flaws and that certain bondholders who held notes beneficially for the issuer should have been disenfranchised according to the terms of the trust deed. The court upheld this claim.

[198] *Assénagon* (n 176) [70]. The claimants referred to the *British America Nickel Corporation Ltd v O'Brien* (n 187), in particular at 371.

[199] Briggs J emphasized: 'The exit consent is, quite simply, a coercive threat which the issuer invites the majority to levy against the minority, nothing more or less. Its only function is the intimidation of a potential minority based upon the fear of any individual member of the class that, by rejecting the exchange... he (or it) will be left out in the cold.' (*Assénagon* [n 176] [84]).

[200] ibid [43].

[201] ibid [69].

[202] The court rejected the argument that the problem of coercion is cured by providing clear and express disclosure on this issue. In doing this, it recognized that there seemed to be some misapprehension among market participants and legal practitioners.

members of the syndicate could therefore collaborate more easily to increase their bargaining power. It is possible that the highly deferential bar for finding oppression of the minority might not apply to the same extent to bondholders (such as in *Assénagon*) who are more dispersed and more challenging to coordinate.[203]

Two additional factors are likely to influence whether a majority decision will fall under the concept of 'in good faith for the benefit of the bondholders as a whole': the overall rate of bondholders' support for the restructuring and the extent of the reduction in creditors' rights.[204]

4.3.8 Discriminatory majority decisions

Sovereign debt restructurings lack an established priority structure to determine the order in which the claims of unsecured creditors should be satisfied. The question here is whether a minority creditor can attack a sovereign debt restructuring on the grounds that a certain group of creditors has been afforded preferential treatment. The question may also be formulated as one concerning when such discrimination becomes unfair.[205]

Case law indicates that the US courts are not particularly concerned with the formalistic question of classes of creditors to the same extent that English courts have been. This type of question concerning discrimination seems less relevant to US law.[206] The following sections will therefore focus primarily on English law.

Redwood—the English law case discussed in the previous section—sheds light on this question of discriminatory majority decisions. More specifically, Rimer J examined the minority creditors' discrimination claim, asking whether there was objective bad faith on the side of the majority creditors. In this case, the syndicated loan was divided into three separate classes. However, Rimer J indicated that an absence of classes would not necessarily be a bar to a potential discrimination claim.[207] In other words, the three classes were not decisive since Rimer J would have reached the same conclusion had the minority creditors been in the same class as the majority creditors. Rimer J held that the majority had acted for the benefit of the whole syndicate and that '[the] agreement of the majority lenders to this particular disparity as part of the means of achieving the overall reduction was, in my view, a commercial decision to which they were perfectly entitled to come'.[208] According to this reasoning, Rimer J focused on the fact that the syndicated loan was a commercial contract, drafted by professionals, and that it expressly provided for the right of two-thirds of the creditors to modify the loan agreement. He continued by holding that he could not imply a term whereby the majority of creditors had a duty to act for the benefit of all creditors as they all had

---

[203] Kupelyants (n 15) 271.
[204] ibid.
[205] ibid 237.
[206] See, for example, *Marblegate Asset Mgt v Educ Mgt Corp* 111 F Supp 3d 542 (SDNY 2015), reversed on other grounds in *Marblegate Asset Mgt v Educ Mgt Finance* 846 F 3d 1 (2d Cir 2017). See also analyses in Kupelyants (n 15) 238 or, generally, 237–250.
[207] See also Padian and Porteous (n 192) 23.
[208] *Redwood* (n 187) [107], [111].

different interests. Majority clauses were designed precisely to enable a majority to bind a minority, regardless of whether a class of creditors could claim that the decision was not for its benefit. *Redwood* seems to depart from earlier case law as it applies a stricter interpretation of the principle of equal treatment of bondholders. Previous cases were more inclined to find that the minority had been discriminated against when a restructuring excluded certain creditors from the restructuring.[209]

The discretion of the majority was not left unconstrained, however. Rimer J emphasized that the majority could not amend terms in a way that was 'manifestly disadvantageous, discriminatory or oppressive' with regard to the minority creditors or which clearly indicated that the decision had 'been motivated by dishonest considerations inconsistent with a proper exercise of the power for the purpose for which it was intended'.[210] Where the limit is drawn in various circumstances is challenging to articulate in the abstract. As mentioned above, in some situations it can be financially sound to provide preferential treatment to local rather than foreign banks in a sovereign debt restructuring. In other situations, it may be sound to provide local creditors with preference over foreign creditors, or vice versa. Moreover, there are economic considerations which support treating international financial institutions and lenders of last resort, such as the IMF and certain financial EU institutions, preferentially in debt restructurings.[211] These are all examples of preferential treatment (whether through preferential terms or through being excluded from the restructuring process completely) of groups of creditors that, under certain circumstances, would be financially sound for the creditors as a whole. It can be argued that under the deferential test set out in *Redwood*, differential treatment of such groups of creditors under specific circumstances are unlikely to be struck down by courts.[212]

4.3.9 Preliminary conclusion

CACs and exit consent are both contractual tools that make it more difficult for a dissenting minority of creditors to disturb a debt restructuring. At the same time, CACs and exit consent deprive minority creditors of contractual rights through the use of majority votes and the result can, in certain circumstances, be discriminatory and constitute an abuse of majority powers. First, whether or not the various creditors are guaranteed the same terms in a restructuring depends on the formulation of CACs and other contractual terms related to the debt instrument. In particular, the uniform applicability clause requires that the sovereign debtor offer all affected creditors the same restructuring terms if the restructuring relies on CACs for its implementation. As such, the clause forces creditors with different characteristics and preferences, roles, and objectives to participate in a restructuring on equal terms. Nevertheless,

---

[209] Kupelyants (n 15) 237–40. Kupelyants more generally argues that it would go against the general thrust of English law if creditors could attack a sovereign debt restructuring on the grounds that a certain group of creditors was accorded preferential treatment. See also Wood (n 32) vol 3, p, para 16-047.
[210] *Redwood* (n 187) [105].
[211] See, in general, Section 1.2.
[212] Kupelyants (n 15) 237, 240.

the sovereign debtor retains a certain degree of flexibility; it may differentiate between various groups of creditors by sub-aggregating votes into different classes.

Second, court-developed rules in domestic law may protect minority creditors from majority abuse. The discretion that courts grant state debtors and/or majority creditors to design and implement a debt restructuring by means of majority votes (CACs or exit consent) is wide under both New York and English law, but not absolute. Section 4.3.7 has established that, under English law, majority powers in the context of restructuring are not unlimited; they must benefit the debtors as a whole.[213] This principle can be said to express the general benchmark for assessing the legality of the powers of the majority when making contractual amendments to the terms of a debt instrument that also binds the dissenting minority creditors.[214] Such majority powers cannot be motivated by bad faith (or a lack of good faith), such as vindictive or malicious purposes. In *Redwood*, this was described as 'subjective bad faith'. *Redwood* also discussed the question of 'objective bad faith'. This encompasses situations where the restructuring causes the interests of one group of bondholders to conflict with those of other groups of bondholders. The question is whether a creditor can attack a sovereign debt restructuring on the grounds that a group of creditors has been accorded preferential treatment. In other words, when does discrimination become unfair? In a debt restructuring, creditors often have different (and sometimes conflicting) interests. A rule that obliged majority creditors to take into consideration the interests of all creditors would make CACs and exit consent ineffective tools to overcome collective action problems and would even challenge the system of debt restructurings as such. Consequently, the principle under English law that a restructuring implemented through majority powers must benefit the debtors as a whole does not imply that it is prohibited to vote in favour of a restructuring arrangement that treats some creditors better than others.

The threshold for minority protection under English law is high. Under New York law, it is highly unlikely that a claim based on a good-faith obligation in relations between minority and majority bondholders will be accepted by courts if a particular debt instruments provides each creditor with a right to vote for certain types of amendments to the terms.[215]

There are several objectives behind the high threshold for providing protection and deferential court scrutiny. First, relaxing the terms of a debt instrument may be preferable to forcing the sovereign debtor into open default. Purchasers of a sovereign debt instrument will know from the outset that it contains a majority voting clause. Moreover, judging from the prevalence of such clauses in sovereign debt instruments, most creditors view this flexibility as desirable.[216] Second, some have argued that, in commercial cases, the courts should give up jurisdiction to review contractual discretion altogether. The reason is that the uncertainty associated with judicial scrutiny creates opportunism and increases costs, as well as leaving the regulation of abuses

---

[213] See *British America Nickel Corporation Ltd v O'Brien* (n 187) 373; *Assénagon* (n 176) [72]; *Greenhalgh v Arderne Cinemas* [1951] Ch 286, 291.
[214] Kupelyants (n 15) 216–17.
[215] Bratton and Gulati (n 171) 66–69; Wood (n 186) vol 1, p para 20-060.
[216] Buchheit and Gulati, 'Exit Consents in Sovereign Bond Exchanges' (n 101) 13–14.

of contractual discretion to markets.[217] Third, the power of the courts to conduct a fairness review in statutory restructuring procedures for companies and municipalities relies on statutory rules. Where such a statutory regime of judicial scrutiny does not exist (ie for sovereign debtors), it can be argued that the parties to a contract containing CACs should freely enjoy the majority powers provided for in the contract. Allowing for extensive judicial scrutiny in such situations might upset the contractual balance that has been negotiated between the parties.[218] An argument to the contrary might assert that, precisely because there are no statutory rules to fall back on, there is a need for more thorough court supervision. The special nature of sovereign debt restructurings may justify an extra layer of protection or at least a minimum review of the exercise of majority powers.[219] Though it should also be noted that even when courts have a statutory obligation to oversee a restructuring, they seem to be rather deferential in their approach.[220] It is therefore questionable how strong this argument for an extra layer of protection actually is.

One can ask whether minority creditors should be able to escape the terms of the restructuring binding all creditors if no protections have been built into the text of the debt instrument, for example in the CAC itself.[221]

4.4 Vulture Fund Legislation

4.4.1 Introduction

This section concerns national legislation in different jurisdictions which aims to reduce aggressive minority creditor behaviour—so-called vulture fund behaviour—by limiting certain of these creditors' contractually negotiated rights. In short, vulture funds purchase debt on the secondary market at very low prices when a country is in economic distress and on the brink of default, with the intent of suing, or threatening to sue, to recover the full amount.[222]

The relevance of this legislation to the question of intercreditor equity is twofold. On the one hand, the legislation interferes with only some of the creditors' contractual rights and one can argue that this constitutes inferior treatment compared to other creditors. On the other hand, as will be shown, the aim is to force certain minority creditors to receive the same treatment in terms of relative repayment as creditors who have voluntarily accepted a restructuring or a debt cancellation.

---

[217] Kupelyants (n 15) 268; Drake (n 166) 1622–23.
[218] Kupelyants (n 15) 271.
[219] See, for example, Buchheit and Gulati, 'Sovereign Bonds and the Collective Will' (n 180) 1338–39.
[220] Kupelyants has examined court discretion to sanction schemes of arrangements under English law and concludes that courts are reluctant to interfere with the reasonableness of schemes of arrangement, except for situations concerning procedural irregularities. See Kupelyants (n 15) 272.
[221] ibid 268.
[222] See definition in Ian Townsend, 'Debt Relief (Developing Countries) Bill [Bill 17 of 2009-10]' (Research briefing, 25 February 2010) para 1.2. See also African Development Bank Group, 'Vulture Funds in the Sovereign Debt Context' (*afdb.org*, African Development Bank Group 17 April 2019) <https://www.afdb.org/en/topics-and-sectors/initiatives-partnerships/african-legal-support-facility/vulture-funds-in-the-sovereign-debt-context> accessed 10 March 2022.

It is the current system of sovereign debt restructuring—where there are no legally binding bankruptcy mechanisms for sovereign states and debt restructuring is based on voluntary renegotiation of the loan terms—that has allowed for the development of a vulture fund business model. Legal proceedings concerning sovereign debt are challenging, because a sovereign state is protected by sovereign immunity rules. Today, rules concerning immunity from execution constitute the main obstacle for creditor claims against states.[223] Ordinary creditors do not have the resources to litigate for full payment, because the search for attachable property is expensive and time-consuming, often entailing multiple court cases around the world. Consequently, debt restructurings are generally the main tool by which a sovereign debtor can resolve its solvency problems and creditors can be repaid, at least in part.[224] However, some specialized creditors have the resources to pursue litigation and use this as a business strategy, holding out on restructuring and instead claiming full payment under the original loan agreement. Investment funds that specialize in such strategies are sometimes called 'distressed debt funds' or 'vulture funds'. The latter term clearly signals an ethical condemnation of the funds' business practices.

The triggering cause and the objective behind vulture fund legislation may vary to some degree across jurisdictions. The common denominator is, first, the concern that vulture fund activity undermines the current restructuring system for states, challenging serious debt crisis resolutions efforts and the ability of debtor states to reach sustainable debt levels. Vulture funds take advantage of the difficult situations in which heavily indebted states find themselves to make disproportionate profits. They buy (at a steep discount) when the debtor state is defaulting (or on the verge of defaulting) and later claim the face value. The funds then take legal action just when the economic situation of the debtor state is improving. The amounts involved are generally significant and the vulture funds' action jeopardizes economic improvement while the financial situation of the debtor state is still fragile. Second, the action of vulture funds also deprives states in difficult financial situations of sums necessary for their development and the wellbeing of their populations. Third, vulture fund activity disrupts the collective debt restructuring efforts. Fourth, (highly indebted) sovereign debtors who are the victims of vulture funds do not always have adequate legal assistance to defend themselves in the courts seized by the funds, typically far from their territory. Sometimes debtor countries do not even appear and are sentenced by default. Having to defend themselves in numerous and complex disputes can be a serious inconvenience for the states concerned.[225]

The argument in favour of vulture fund activities, though it has lost ground in the past decade, is that they contribute to disciplining sovereign debtors.[226] Admittedly, some debtor states are in a state of poor governance and widespread corruption. As a result, development aid is diverted to the benefit of leaders and does not benefit the people. These situations should clearly be fought. Nevertheless, there seems to be an

---

[223] Iversen, 'Holdout Creditor Litigation' (n 131) 18–28.
[224] Astrid Iversen, 'Solvency II and Sovereign Bonds' in Mads Andenas and others (eds), *Solvency II: A Dynamic Challenge for the Insurance Market* (Il Mulino 2017) 126.
[225] See, for example, discussion in Belgian Constitutional Court: C.C., 31 mai 2018, n° 61/2018, B.10.3.1.
[226] See, for example, discussion in European Parliament Committee on Development, 'Report on Enhancing Developing Countries' Debt Sustainability' (2016).

emerging consensus that these situations do not justify the activities of vulture funds and that their action only further aggravates the situation of the debtor state.[227]

The following three sections discuss legislation in Belgium, in the United Kingdom, the Isle of Man and Jersey, and in France, which aims to discourage disruptive litigation initiated by vulture funds in the context of intercreditor equity.

4.4.2 Belgium

In 2008, Belgium became the first country to pass a law against vulture funds. It aimed to safeguard 'funds disbursed towards development cooperation and debt relief' from vulture funds' actions.[228] The legislation was adopted in response to a number of cases brought before national courts by vulture funds seeking to seize funds allocated to developing countries under official development assistance programmes.[229] The law ensures that funds and assets earmarked for international cooperation or for public development aid cannot be attached or assigned. The legislation also covers loans granted by Belgium to foreign countries and institutions.

On 12 July 2015, the Belgian federal parliament adopted a new vulture fund law by a large cross-party majority.[230] The objective of the law was to further prevent vulture funds from resorting to litigation in Belgium. More specifically, it provides a legal framework for avoiding the accrual of 'illegitimate advantages' to holdout creditors. That is, a vulture fund can no longer secure through litigation more than the amount they paid when they bought the junk debt at a discount price on secondary markets. An illegitimate advantage is defined as a 'manifest disproportion between the amount claimed by the creditor and the notional face value of the debt'.[231] Article 2, fourth paragraph of the law provides additional criteria to clarify what constitutes an illegitimate advantage. At least one of the following conditions must be met for the law to be applicable:

- the debtor state was insolvent or at imminent risk of default at the time the debt was bought;
- the creditor is established in a tax haven (defined by reference to the lists maintained by the Financial Action Task Force, the Organisation for Economic Cooperation and Development (OECD) or the Belgian official blacklist);

---

[227] See discussion in C.C., 31 mai 2018, n° 61/2018 (n 226), B.11.5, referring amongst other things to the discussion in the Belgian parliament.

[228] Loi du 6 avril 2008 (Belgium).

[229] Ten lawsuits were lodged against the Democratic Republic of the Congo in 2007 alone. Devi Sookun, *Stop Vulture Fund Lawsuits: A Handbook* (Commonwealth Secretariat 2010) 90–91.

[230] Loi du 12 juillet 2015 relative à la lutte contre les activités des fonds vautours (Belgium). On 28 August 2015, Belgium also amended Art 1412 of its Code Judiciaire, which governs sovereign immunity from attachment, see Loi insérant dans le Code judiciaire un Art. 1412 (Belgium).

[231] Article 2 second paragraph of loi du 12 juillet 2015 relative à la lutte contre les activités des fonds vautours (Belgium). In French, the second paragraph reads: '*La recherche d'un avantage illégitime se déduit de l'existence d'une disproportion manifeste entre la valeur de rachat de l'emprunt ou de la créance par le créancier et la valeur faciale de l'emprunt ou de la créance ou encore entre la valeur de rachat de l'emprunt ou de la créance par le créancier et les sommes dont il demande le paiement.*'

- the creditor refused to participate in a debt restructuring agreement;
- the creditor has a track record in this type of litigation;
- the creditor has abused the weakness of the debtor to negotiate a manifestly unfair debt restructuring agreement;
- full repayment of the creditor's claim would have a significant impact on the state's public finances and could have an adverse effect on the economic and social welfare of the debtor state's population.[232]

The law also extends to foreign arbitral awards so that they cannot be enforced in Belgium.

In March 2016, the hedge fund known for its litigation against Argentina, NML Capital Ltd, sought annulment of this legislation before the Constitutional Court of Belgium, claiming that the new law was unconstitutional.[233] NML alleged violation of Articles 10, 11, and 16 of the Constitution, read alone or in conjunction with a number of other international obligations,[234] including Article 1 of the First Additional Protocol to the European Convention on Human Rights (ECHR) (right to protection of property) (1st Protocol to the ECHR) and Regulation (EU) No 1215/2012 (Brussels I Recast).[235] Articles 10 and 11 of the Constitution concern equal treatment or non-discrimination, while Article 16 concerns the protection of the right to property.

In a ruling on 31 May 2018, the Belgian Constitutional Court rejected NML's claims and upheld the country's vulture fund law. The court found the law not to violate the right to property or prohibitions against discrimination in the constitution, nor did it violate Belgium's corresponding EU and international commitments.

As mentioned above, NML claimed that the law arbitrarily determined that some claims were legitimate whereas others were illegitimate by wrongfully discriminating between creditors affected by the legislation and other creditors. In response to this, the court underlined that the principle of equality and non-discrimination (which includes a prohibition against treating differently situated persons equally) does not preclude a difference in treatment between categories of persons, provided this is based on objective criteria and is reasonably justified. In considering this, one must take into account the purpose and the effect of the measures taken. The court stated that the principle of non-discrimination is violated only where there is no reasonable relationship of proportionality between the means employed and the aim pursued. The court thereafter referred to the legislator's justification for implementing the law, namely

---

[232] See also Jan Van de Poel, 'New Anti-Vulture Fund Legislation in Belgium: An Example for Europe and Rest of the World' (Blog, *Eurodad*, 5 December 2015) <https://www.eurodad.org/new_anti_vulture_fund_legislation_in_belgium> accessed 15 March 2022.
[233] C.C., 31 mai 2018, n° 61/2018 (n 226) (concerning an action for annulment of the loi du 12 juillet 2015 relative à la lutte contre les activités des fonds vautours, introduced by NML Capital Ltd, an investment fund registered on the Cayman Islands).
[234] NML Capital Ltd alleged violation of Arts 10, 11, and 16 of the Belgian Constitution, read alone or in conjunction with Arts 6 and 13 ECHR; Art 1, 1st protocol ECHR; Arts 49 and 56 TFEU; Art 16 EU Charter; Regulation (EC) No 593/2008 (Rome I); Regulation (EC) No 1215/2012 (Brussels I Recast); Art 23 Belgian Constitution; Art 1134 Belgium Civil Code; and with the 'principle of legal certainty'.
[235] Regulation (EU) No 1215/2012 of the European Parliament and of the Council of 12 December 2012 on jurisdiction and the recognition and enforcement of judgments in civil and commercial matters [2012] OJ L341/1, 1–32 (European Union) (hereafter Brussels I Recast).

that it seeks to hinder the speculative practice in which creditors acquire a sovereign debt contract of a heavily indebted country on the verge of default, on the secondary market, and at very low prices.[236] Moreover, such creditors speculate based on a potential improvement in the debtor's situation, the existence of sizeable assets, or the granting of aid or other sums that could be seized. The court also underlined that the law is intended only to impede the activities of certain categories of persons who redeem their sovereign debt claims. It is not intended to regulate the action of the original creditor more generally or that of creditors on the secondary market who pursue a profit deemed legitimate. Hence, it is not intended to prevent normal transactions in the secondary market, including those of creditors and sovereign debtors. The court concluded that this justified the differential treatment provided for by the vulture fund legislation.[237]

The Constitutional Court's considerations were bound to the constitutional provisions regarding protection of property and non-discrimination. Regarding the alleged violation of Brussels I Recast, the court limited itself to establishing that the legislation was not discriminatory because creditors who have obtained a foreign judgment against a sovereign debtor are no better or worse off than creditors who have obtained such a ruling from a Belgian court. Whether or not the Belgian vulture fund law infringes Brussels I Recast remains therefore unanswered.

4.4.3 The United Kingdom, the Isle of Man, and Jersey

In 2010, the UK Parliament passed the Debt Relief (Developing Countries) Act 2010. The background for the adoption of this Act was the UK government's commitment to granting debt relief to heavily indebted poor countries (HIPC) in the aftermath of it chairing the G8 meeting in 2005. The meeting culminated in the Multilateral Debt Relief Initiative (MDRI), which involved the International Development Association, the IMF and the African Development Fund cancelling USD 49 billion in debt to the world's poorest countries that had completed (or would complete) the HIPC Initiative.[238] The legislative initiative to implement vulture fund legislation was taken in response to vulture funds that sought to take advantage of the international debt relief provided by the HIPC Initiative and the MDRI, which had put certain debtor countries in a better economic position to pay off other debt obligations. Aggressive holdout creditors commenced lawsuits against different HIPC before the courts of England and Wales, in which they claimed full repayment under the original loan agreements, as they stood prior to the HIPC debt relief initiative.[239]

The adopted Debt Relief (Developing Countries) Act prevents vulture funds from making massive profits out of debt restructuring in developing economies subject to

---

[236] C.C., 31 mai 2018, n° 61/2018 (n 226), B.10.3.1.
[237] Especially C.C., 31 mai 2018, n° 61/2018 (n 226), B.10.3 and B.10.4.
[238] 'Multilateral Debt Relief Initiative—Questions and Answers' (*International Monetary Fund*, 28 July 2017) <https://www.imf.org/external/np/exr/mdri/eng/index.htm> accessed 30 April 2022.
[239] One such lawsuit took place in England in 2007: *Donegal International v Republic of Zambia [2007] EWHC (Comm)* [2007] EWHC 197 (EWHC). See also Iversen, 'Holdout Creditor Litigation' (n 131) 33; Sookun (n 230) 88.

the HIPC Initiative by putting a cap on the amount that a litigating creditor can obtain through a lawsuit or settlement. The legislation was designed to ensure that all creditors provide their share of debt relief under the HIPC Initiative.[240] The capped amount is hence equal to the amount that would otherwise be recoverable if the debt were reduced in accordance with the HIPC Initiative. The Act regulates the total amount recoverable from a claim based on a contract conferring jurisdiction on UK courts (even if the law applicable is the law of a country outside the United Kingdom); the total amount recoverable under a claim based on a contract subject to UK law anywhere in the world; and the execution of a foreign judgment or award concerning HIPC debt within the United Kingdom.[241]

The Act had a sunset clause introduced primarily to review evidence of the impact of the legislation, but on 16 May 2011 the Act became permanent.[242] The Isle of Man (a self-governing British Crown dependency) and Jersey enacted legislation that mirrored the UK legislation in both form and substance in December 2012 and March 2013, respectively.[243]

4.4.4 France

On 8 November 2016, the French Parliament approved legislation aimed at enhancing legal protection of the property of foreign states. The law inserted new provisions in the *Code des procédures civiles d'exécution (Code of Civil Procedure of Enforcement)*, including specific provisions aimed at protecting foreign states against vulture funds.[244]

Article 59 consists of general provisions concerning the protection of the foreign state's property, which to a great extent reflects the 2004 United Nations Convention on Jurisdictional Immunities of States and Their Property.[245] Article 60 protects the property of foreign states specifically against vulture funds. Under this article, measures of constraint can be authorized by a judge only if very restrictive conditions are met. The courts cannot authorize any measures against the property of a state initiated by the holder of a sovereign debt instrument if the following conditions are met:

---

[240] See, in general, Townsend (n 223).
[241] See also Iversen, 'Holdout Creditor Litigation' (n 131) 34.
[242] While there were no sovereign debt cases in court in the Isle of Man, Jersey had experienced vulture fund litigation. In 2011, New York hedge fund FG Hemisphere sued the Democratic Republic of Congo in Jersey courts. In the summer of 2012, the Jersey courts ruled against FG Hemisphere's attempt to sue a state-owned mining company for USD 100 million on a USD 3 million debt. See Amber Przybysz, 'Anti-Vulture Fund Legislation Introduced in Jersey as One Vulture Swoops in on Argentina' (Blog, *Blog the Debt*, 22 October 2012) <https://jubileeusa.typepad.com/blog_the_debt/2012/10/anti-vulture-fund-legislation-introduced-in-jersey-as-one-vulture-swoops-in-on-argentina-.html> accessed 14 March 2022.
[243] Heavily Indebted Poor Countries (Limitation on Debt Recovery) Act 2012 (Isle of Man); Debt Relief (Developing Countries) Law 2013 (Jersey).
[244] The legislation was revised following the introduction of the Loi n° 2016-1691 du 9 déc 2016 relative à la transparence, à la lutte contre la corruption et à la modernisation de la vie économique [Law n° 2016-1691 of 9 Dec 2016 on transparency, anti-corruption, and modernization of economic life] JO du 10 déc 2016 (France).
[245] The conditions in the law largely reflect Arts 18, 19, and 21 of the United Nations Convention on Jurisdictional Immunities, which has been ratified by France but is not yet in force.

- the debtor state was on the OECD list of recipients of official development when issuing its debt instrument;
- the creditor acquired the debt instrument while the debtor state was in default on this instrument or had proposed a change to the term of the debt obligation (a restructuring);
- the default on or restructuring of the debt obligation had been initiated less than 48 months earlier (at the time the holder of the obligation sought to obtain an order or motion), or a restructuring agreement had been accepted by creditors representing at least 66% of the principal amount of eligible claims.

Despite acceptance of a debt restructuring by more than 66% of the creditors, a holdout creditor can still go to court to seek provisional enforcement measures against property owned by a foreign state for sums whose total amount is less than or equal to the amount he would have obtained if he had accepted the restructuring proposal.

A judge may change the 48-month time limit to 72 months in the case of manifestly abusive behaviour by the holder of the debt obligation.

On 8 December 2016, the French Constitutional Council held that Articles 59 and 60 of the new legislation were constitutional and compliant with the right to respect for private property as well as the right to obtain the execution of court decisions (as assessed in light of the 1789 Declaration of the Rights of Man and of the Citizen).[246]

4.4.5 Preliminary conclusions

The vulture fund legislation discussed in Section 4.4 are similar insofar as they all put a cap on the total amount a holdout creditor may be repaid when suing (or seeking to enforce a judgment) for payment under a sovereign debt obligation.

France and the United Kingdom limit the scope of their legislation to the debt of developing countries, though the United Kingdom defines these more narrowly as they are restricted to certain developing countries (HIPC). The justification for differential treatment therefore has an additional element: the safeguarding of money taxpayers spend on development aid and the international community's fight for development and the eradication of poverty. The Belgian law applies a more general test when considering which creditors (or, more specifically, which creditor claims) are deemed to seek an illegitimate advantage and misuse the system. It was enacted while taking into account the special burden that developing countries experience when facing vulture fund litigation, but at the same time it attempts to deal with the problem as a more general systemic risk issue. In sum, all three examples of vulture fund legislation identify certain acts of (minority) creditors whose interests are deemed less honourable. In these cases, they limit creditors' freely negotiated contractual rights, with the aim of honouring the crisis resolution measures adopted by sovereign debtors, co-creditors, and the international community.

---

[246] C.C., 8 décembre 2016, n° 2016-741 (France).

The legislation interferes with the contractually agreed payment rights of holdout creditors. Vulture fund legislation that effectively hinders holdout creditors from claiming full payment under the debt instrument and instead forces them to accept the same relative economic losses as those borne by creditors voluntarily participating in a restructuring creates a few issues with regards to intercreditor equity.

Legislation that seeks to distinguish legitimate and non-legitimate holdout creditors using rules that appeal to discretionary considerations are more prone to legal challenge by holdout creditors for being discriminatory. The rationale for implementing vulture fund legislation is, as in the Belgian case, likely to be justified and accepted as legitimate. In concrete cases, holdout creditors limited by Belgian-style legislation may still bring suits arguing that they have been unduly categorized as a vulture fund with illegitimate reasons to reject a restructuring when compared to other creditors. International organizations, such as the IMF, are to an increasing extent supporting the use of national legislative initiatives to counter aggressive holdout creditors. It is therefore likely that more countries will implement various types of vulture fund legislation in the future. It is equally likely that there will be an increase in creditor litigation related to such new legislation.

5
International Law Protection of Creditors Holding Debt Instruments Governed by Domestic Law

5.1 Introduction

Contracts between states and private persons are normally not concluded by states in their capacity as subjects of public international law, but by virtue of their private autonomy (see Sections 2.2.2 and 2.2.3). These types of contracts are typically governed by domestic law. However, this does not imply that international law is irrelevant in the context of sovereign debt obligations governed by domestic law. International law can restrict the way in which a sovereign debtor treats its private creditors (even where they hold debt instruments governed by domestic law) during a sovereign debt restructuring in several ways.[1]

First, sovereign debtors may be obliged to treat their creditors according to minimum standards under customary international law, which contains rules on due treatment of foreigners and their property. This is normally referred to as the 'international minimum standard' and is discussed in Section 5.2.[2] Second, a sovereign debtor may have promised a certain standard of treatment to its creditors in an international treaty.[3] Rights in international investment agreements (IIAs) are discussed in Section 5.3, while Section 5.4 examines requirements under the European Convention on Human Rights (ECHR). Creditors have no specific rights to be treated equally by sovereign debtors under customary international law, IIAs, or the ECHR. However, all these rules potentially provide creditors with a certain level of protection against discriminatory treatment. Whether or not a general principle of law, in accordance with Article 38(1)(c) of the ICJ Statute, is emerging, which might provide creditors with certain forms of protection from discriminatory treatment, will be discussed in Section 7.2.1.

International law subjects may also hold debt instruments governed by domestic law. Creditors of domestic law governed debt instruments who are themselves subjects

---

[1] Ursula Kriebaum and August Reinisch, 'Property, Right to, International Protection' in Rüdiger Wolfrum (ed), *Max Planck Encyclopedia of Public International Law* (Oxford University Press 2019) s A.1.

[2] Art 38(1)(b) of the Statute of the International Court of Justice 3 Bevans 1179, 59 Stat 1055, TS No 993, 3 Bevans 1179, 59 Stat 1055, TS No 993 (United Nations 1945) (hereafter ICJ Statute). See also Matthias Herdegen, *Principles of International Economic Law* (2nd edn, Oxford University Press 2016) 85; Irmgard Marboe and August Reinisch, 'Contracts between States and Foreign Private Law Persons' in Rüdiger Wolfrum (ed), *Max Planck Encyclopedia of Public International Law* (Oxford University Press 2019) para 35.

[3] In accordance with Art 38(1)(a) of ICJ Statute. See also Marboe and Reinisch (n 2) para 35.

Intercreditor Equity in Sovereign Debt Restructuring. Astrid Iversen, Oxford University Press. © Astrid Iversen 2023.
DOI: 10.1093/oso/9780192866905.003.0006

of international law are not normally protected by the international law provisions discussed below (such as IIAs, human rights treaties, or the minimum standard under customary international law).

In each of the following three sections (5.2–5.4), we will first consider *whether* the rights of creditors are protected under the different regimes that govern sovereign debt restructurings. The discussion will then shift to examine *to what extent* creditors are protected (substantive protection) and how this protection relates to the question of intercreditor equity.

5.2 The International Minimum Standard—Intercreditor Equity in Customary International Law

5.2.1 Introduction

Under public international law, a state is free to decide whether it will permit foreigners and foreign investments into its territory.[4] Once admitted and established, foreigners and their assets enjoy a certain level of protection under the rules of diplomatic protection.[5] These rules follow from customary international law and guarantee foreigners and their property a certain level of due treatment, which is referred to as the 'international minimum standard'.[6]

The minimum standard is a substantive standard that limits the state's conduct vis-à-vis a foreign party independently of, or in addition to, the governing domestic law and international treaty protection.[7]

In the last 100 years or so, there have been numerous examples of foreigners who have demanded that they, or their property, be treated in accordance with the international minimum standard. Nevertheless, the exact content of the minimum standard in international law, including its level of protection, is subject to debate. In fact, some even dispute the existence of such a standard.[8] This chapter discusses whether the minimum standard provides foreign creditors with any rights to equal or preferential treatment in a sovereign debt restructuring. It also explains why the minimum standard in the area of sovereign debt is currently underdeveloped and may have become less relevant.

---

[4] James Crawford, *Brownlie's Principles of Public International Law* (8th edn, Oxford University Press 2012) 612–13; Herdegen (n 2) 411.

[5] Herdegen (n 2) 411.

[6] ibid 85. See also Crawford (n 4) 612–16; Roland Kläger, *'Fair and Equitable Treatment' in International Investment Law* (Cambridge Studies in International and Comparative Law, Cambridge University Press 2011) 50.

[7] Stephan W Schill, 'The Impact of International Investment Law on Public Contracts' in Mathias Audit and Stephan W Schill (eds), *Transnational Law of Public Contracts* (Bruylant 2016) 6.

[8] Kläger (n 6) 50. See also Edwin M Borchard, *The Diplomatic Protection of Citizens Abroad* (Banks Law Publishing Co 1914) 497, 515, 517–18; Rodrigo Polanco, *The Return of the Home State to Investor-State Disputes: Bringing Back Diplomatic Protection?* (Cambridge International Trade and Economic Law, Cambridge University Press 2019) pt I, ch A.

5.2.2 Types of claims covered by diplomatic protection

In 1914, Borchard wrote that diplomatic protection of citizens abroad 'is a comparatively modern phenomenon in the evolution of the state, in constitutional and in international law'.[9] He argued that, due to the bonds of citizenship, a state has a duty to watch over its citizens abroad and intervene when their rights are violated. Borchard did not mention the rights of these citizens under the jurisdiction of the host state. Rather, he referred to an 'international minimum standard' of rights that foreigners (and their property) should enjoy in a foreign country under customary international law.[10]

In its 2006 Draft Articles on Diplomatic Protection, the International Law Commission (ILC) defined 'diplomatic protection' as

> the invocation by a State, through diplomatic action or other means of peaceful settlement, of the responsibility of another State for an injury caused by an internationally wrongful act of that State to a natural or legal person that is a national of the former State with a view to the implementation of such responsibility.[11]

The International Law Commission's (ILC) definition of diplomatic protection has become part of customary international law.[12]

Normally, after the exhaustion of local remedies, the private contracting party can request that its home state pursue a claim for breach of this standard through inter-state negotiations and inter-state dispute settlement, such as before an international court or arbitral tribunal.[13] This raises the question, in the context of a sovereign debt restructuring, of what the minimum standard of treatment of a foreign creditor requires, in particular with regard to equal or preferential treatment. Does the minimum standard even cover such situations?

Protection of foreigners and their property under customary international law is not limited to movable and immovable property. Several arbitral tribunals have confirmed that intangible rights, including contractual rights, are also protected.[14] One of the cases confirming this is the *Norwegian Shipowners' Case*, in which the United States had requisitioned a number of ships, including contracts to build 15 hulls

---

[9] Borchard (n 8) 497.
[10] ibid 515, 517–18.
[11] Art 1 of ILC *Diplomatic Protection: Titles and Texts of the Draft Articles on Diplomatic Protection Adopted by the Drafting Committee on Second Reading* UN Doc A/CN4/L684 (United Nations 2006).
[12] Freya Baetens, 'Diplomatic Protection' in Rainer Grote and others (eds), *Max Planck Encyclopedia of Comparative Constitutional Law* (Oxford University Press 2017) para A.2.
[13] Schill (n 7) 6. On the protection of contracts under customary international law, see Frederick A Mann, 'State Contracts and State Responsibility' (1960) 54 American Journal of International Law 572; Robert Y Jennings, 'State Contracts in International Law' (1961) 37 Yearbook of International Law 156.
[14] For example *Norwegian Shipowners' Claims (Norway v United States of America)* (1922) I RIAA 307 (Permanent Court of Arbitration 1922) (hereafter *Norwegian Shipowners' Claims*); *Certain German Interests in Polish Upper Silesia (Germany v Poland)* (Merits) (1926) PCIJ Series A no 7 (hereafter *German Interests in Polish Upper Silesia*); *Oscar Chinn (United Kingdom v Belgium)* (Judgment) (1932) PCIJ Series A/B no 61 (hereafter *Oscar Chinn*). See also Kriebaum and Reinisch (n 1) s C.2; Michael Waibel, *Sovereign Defaults before International Courts and Tribunals* (Cambridge University Press 2011) 201–02.

(ships) which were being constructed by American Shipbuilders. The arbitral tribunal held that 'the contracts were the property, or created it' and stated that physical property is just one of the elements or aspects of 'property' under the domestic law of the United States, Norway, and other states. The tribunal concluded that the requisitioning of these contracts by the United States was a transfer of property implying a 'cancellation or "destruction" of the *Jura in personam* or *in rem*'.[15] This was equivalent to the taking of private property.[16] Furthermore, the tribunal found in favour of a legal claim in the *Venezuelan Preferential Case* despite the fact it originated in contract rather than in tort. 'The refusal to pay an honest claim is no less a wrong because it happens to arise from an obligation to pay money instead of originating in violence offered to persons or property.'[17]

Despite the fact that contractual rights are protected under customary international law, it is a hotly debated question amongst scholars whether sovereign debt instruments and creditors in a debt restructuring are protected under the minimum standard.[18] Schreuer has stated that 'the law of expropriation proceeds not from a traditional concept of tangible property but from a broad concept of economic rights that are necessary for the investor to pursue its business successfully'.[19] According to Feilchenfeld, debts are property rights that are protected under international law.[20] Borchard was of the view that international arbitral tribunals should decline jurisdiction or exercise more careful scrutiny over sovereign debt compared to ordinary contractual claims.[21] He justified this by arguing that claims arising out of the unpaid bonds of a government held by a citizen of another state are different from contract claims arising out of contracts between a citizen abroad and a foreign government, such as those arising out of supply of material for the execution of public works and the exercise of concessions.[22] Similar to Borchard, Drago viewed sovereign debt as special by drawing an analogy to paper money, since bonds, too, are put into circulation.[23] Change of the value of paper money is the domain of a state's monetary sovereignty and is not protected by international law. Drago argued that this was also the

---

[15] *Norwegian Shipowners' Claims* (n 14) 334.
[16] ibid. *Oscar Chinn* (n 14) and *German Interests in Polish Upper Silesia* (n 14) repeat this approach.
[17] John Bassett Moore, *History and Digest of the International Arbitrations to Which the United States Has Been a Party* (Government Printing Office 1898) 3649. See Section 3.4 for further discussion of the case.
[18] Waibel (n 14) 204–06.
[19] Christoph Schreuer, 'The Concept of Expropriation under the ETC and Other Investment Protection Treaties' (2005) 2 Transnational Dispute Management 1, para 64.
[20] Ernst H Feilchenfeld, 'Rights and Remedies of Holders of Foreign Bonds' in *Bonds and Bondholders: Rights and Remedies, with Forms* (Burdette Smith Co 1934) vol 1, 203.
[21] Edwin M Borchard, 'Contractual Claims in International Law' (1913) 13 Columbia Law Review 457, 458, 494.
[22] ibid 457–60, 476. One of the reasons, according to Borchard, is that '[i]n the latter case, the government has entered into relations with a definite person; in the former, bonds usually being payable to bearer and negotiable by mere delivery, the State never knows prior to presentation for payment to whom it is indebted'. Moreover, he argues that the distinction is important because 'there is far less reason for governmental intervention to secure the payment of defaulted bonds of a foreign government than there is in the case of breaches of concession and similar contracts' (ibid 458, 476). Borchard also argued that sovereign bonds did not fulfil the fourth typical feature of an 'investment', which required the activity of the foreigner to be associated with a commercial undertaking. See also Waibel (n 14) 204.
[23] Luis M Drago, 'State Loans in Their Relation to International Policy' (1907) 1 American Journal of International Law 692, 695, 725. See also Waibel (n 14) 204.

case for sovereign bonds. Hall did not agree that there was a distinction between sovereign debt and other contractual claims:

> Fundamentally ... there is no difference in principle between wrongs inflicted by breach of a monetary agreement and other wrongs for which the state as itself the wrongdoer, is immediately responsible. The difference which is made in practice [through diplomatic protection] is in no sense obligatory; and it is open to governments to consider each case by itself and to act as seems well to them on its merits.[24]

Waibel has comprehensively analysed practice from arbitral tribunals and claims commissions from before the First World War, the interwar period, and after the Second World War. He is sceptical of the view that sovereign debt claims constitute expropriable property under customary international law.[25] He argues that before the First World War, creditors (through the diplomatic protection of their governments) failed to obtain compensation before arbitral tribunals and mixed claims commissions in the majority of cases. There were a few exceptions, but, in general, claims commissions declined 'pure' creditor claims. Some tribunals declined compensation to creditors because there was no clear causation between a governmental expropriation of a commercial undertaking and the injury suffered by the creditor. The tribunals defined such injury suffered by the creditor as only indirect. The reason was that creditor claims raised particular issues of causation and attribution under the secondary rules on state responsibility. The reluctance to accept creditor claims also extended to claims commissions.[26] Waibel admits that a certain shift can be observed in the interwar period but argues that consistency in the claims practice on creditor claims continued to be lacking. He points out one change: namely that secured debt claims began to receive international protection. However, most of the time, unsecured creditors were still without an international law remedy.[27] In general, Waibel argues that it is difficult to establish whether mixed claims commissions and foreign claims commissions have accepted or declined compensation for a sovereign debt claim based on a breach of the minimum standard in customary international law or based on their own more narrow and case-specific protocols and constituting treaties.[28]

Another factor which makes it challenging to establish whether in fact diplomatic protection and the minimum standard cover sovereign debt disputes is that home states exercise exclusive control over the rights of their nationals in the international legal sphere. Moreover, the exclusive prerogative of the state of nationality of an individual to provide diplomatic protection is exercised on a discretionary basis.[29] In

---

[24] William Edward Hall, *A Treatise on International Law* (JB Atlay ed, 5th edn, Clarendon Press 1904) 280–81.
[25] Waibel (n 14) 204–06.
[26] ibid 169.
[27] ibid.
[28] The reason for this is that they have not clearly distinguished their basis for accepting jurisdiction (the treaty provision, whether it was common to extend diplomatic protection in the specific area or international law), nor the basis for deciding the substantive question of the case concerning compensation. ibid 182.
[29] Baetens (n 12) paras A.1, A.2. Domestic constitutional law may provide citizens with a right to diplomatic protection and it may do so outside the areas where international law does. In her contribution, Baetens also provides a comparative overview of constitutional protection.

other words, the natural or legal person does not have a right to diplomatic protection under international law. Indeed, the state can settle, waive, or modify the claims of its nationals by international agreement when negotiating with the host state, with whom its nationals have contracted.[30] Consequently, a state's decision to extend diplomatic protection has often been explained by political rather than legal factors, which has made it challenging to properly examine the legal basis for a minimum standard.

The above discussion indicates that the conclusion as to whether a contractual claim for payment under a sovereign debt instrument is protected property in customary international law is in flux.

5.2.3 Substantive protection

Assuming sovereign debt claims are covered, the question is the extent to which creditors are protected in a restructuring. It should be clear that the 'wrongful act' that gives a state the right to extend diplomatic protection to its nationals, and which is referred to in Article 1 of the ILC's Draft Articles on Diplomatic Protection, is not limited to cases concerning a direct breach of an international law obligation. Private parties contracting with another state can request that their home state to exercise diplomatic protection and pursue the private claim against the host state at the international level.[31] In the *Serbian Loans Case*, the Permanent Court of International Justice (PCIJ) made it clear that customary international law allows a home state to exercise diplomatic protection on behalf of its citizens even if the contractual relationship between the host state and the foreign private party was exclusively governed by domestic law.[32] In other words, the minimum standard considers, in principle, the contractual relations between the host state and the private party, and the relation between the host state and the foreigner's home state as independent systems. The former relationship is represented by the sovereign debt contract and is typically governed by domestic law. The latter relationship is governed by international law. What the minimum standard in customary international law offers is some substantive protection to foreign private parties' rights under a contract governed by domestic law. The availability of this protection presupposes that the breach of the contract or the change made to the governing law constitutes an independent tort under international law vis-à-vis the foreigner's home state. A consequence of the aforementioned distinction is that not all breaches by a sovereign debtor of the contract terms of a debt instrument or changes in the domestic background law to that contract automatically constitute a violation of international law.[33]

In basic terms, the minimum standard is violated if the contracting state party fully or partially expropriates the contractual rights, interferes with them in an arbitrary manner, or commits an independent breach of international law through a denial of

---

[30] See also Schill (n 7) 7.
[31] ibid 6.
[32] Case concerning the Payment of Various Serbian Loans Issued in France (*France v Kingdom of the Serbs, Croats and Slovenes*) (Judgment) (1929) PCIJ Series A no 20, para 5 (hereafter *Serbian Loans Case*).
[33] Schill (n 7) 7.

justice in its domestic courts. Moreover, the protection under the minimum standard in customary international law is limited to sovereign acts interfering with a contract and does not encompass breaches of contract based on a state's commercial activity.[34] A debt restructuring implemented through coercive governmental acts, such as a change in domestic legislation, is likely to interfere with the contractual rights of a creditor, as it typically entails prolongation of the maturity, a cut in interest rate, and sometimes also a reduction in the nominal value of the instrument. Additionally, if the restructuring is implemented in a way that discriminates between foreign creditors in an arbitrary manner, it could be argued that this breaches the minimum standard. Borchard, for example, has written that 'nothing produces so immediate a diplomatic protest as actual discrimination in the treatment of nationals of the protecting state by a foreign debtor, and in this respect equality of treatment may be said to be an unwritten financial tradition and practice'.[35] Discrimination based on nationality was not the only basis for states taking on claims from its nationals at the international level. Borchard also mentions that measures which favour one group of foreigners over others, or which give preference to internal creditors over external creditors, or short-term creditors over long-term creditors, or one bond issue over another, could also give rise to diplomatic protests.[36]

5.2.4 Preliminary conclusion

There have been a number of instances where states have extended diplomatic protection to nationals holding sovereign debt claims in the past hundred years or so, in informal and formal negotiations with sovereign debtor states, as well as with states of private co-creditors.[37] Sovereign debt claims have also been the subject of international disputes in various claims commissions and tribunals throughout history.[38] Nevertheless, overall, states have historically been relatively reluctant to exercise diplomatic protection on behalf of their citizens' economic contractual interests, such as a claim by a private creditor against a sovereign debtor concerning an alleged breach of the minimum standard. This is a factor that has contributed to making it challenging to establish the content of the minimum standard for the treatment of creditors holding sovereign debt. During the time of absolute immunity, creditor states actively encouraged a quasi-judicial avenue to avoid being pressured by bondholders into using diplomatic relations as a means of promoting private creditors' claims. Sovereign debtor countries were also keen to keep creditor governments at a distance. Arbitration was often considered a preferable alternative to diplomatic pressure. In the second half of the nineteenth century and up until the interwar period, arbitration clauses for sovereign debt disputes were still

---

[34] ibid 7–8.
[35] Edwin M Borchard, *State Insolvency and Foreign Bondholders*, vol 1 (Yale University Press 1951) 261.
[36] ibid 262.
[37] ibid 265.
[38] See, in general, Borchard (n 35) vol 1, p; Waibel (n 14).

popular. With the rise of restrictive sovereign immunity from the 1970s onwards national courts started to hear sovereign debt cases and arbitration clauses in private loan contracts and bonds became less common.[39] In domestic courts, the minimum standard and customary international law are not normally the basis for sovereign debt claims (or any other claims). As such, there is little new case law to help establish to what extent a contractual claim to payment, such as a sovereign debt obligation, is protected under the minimum standard. Even less practice exists to establish whether creditors may have a claim concerning intercreditor equity. The minimum standard in general, and in the area of sovereign debt in particular, is therefore an underdeveloped standard.

The importance of the minimum standard to sovereign debt claims has decreased with the aforementioned transition to restrictive immunity, under which domestic courts have started to accept jurisdiction over sovereign debt related disputes. The development of modern investment law has also made the customary minimum standard less important. In parallel with the development of sovereign immunity rules, there has been a revival of investment arbitration for state contracts more generally. As discussed in Section 2.2.3, whereas states have been willing to immunize loan contracts by subjecting them to the laws of another state, they have not generally been willing to do this with investment contracts. Consequently, there has been a greater need for IIAs protecting foreign investors from unilateral changes made to contract obligations by the host state. Controversy over the existence and potential content of the minimum standard has also contributed to this situation. As a result, the regulation of investments has in practice been left mainly to the host state and customary international law rules have rarely been involved.[40] Today modern international investment law is dominated by treaties substituting for the traditional customary international law rules on the protection of foreign property.[41] The development of IIAs, discussed in Section 5.3, has also given foreign private parties contracting with sovereign states more opportunities to pursue legal disputes concerning their treatment directly, without relying on the diplomatic intervention of their own state.

The substantive protection of foreign investors under IIAs largely depends on the wording of the relevant treaty. The following section discusses whether sovereign debt instruments are protected in IIAs and what substantive protection is potentially provided that may influence the question of intercreditor equity in a sovereign debt restructuring.

---

[39] Waibel (n 14) 157–58, 163, 167; Borchard (n 21) 481. For official lending, arbitration clauses are sometimes still included in loan agreements. Multilateral development banks, such as the World Bank and the Inter-American Development Bank, insert arbitration clauses into their lending agreements, but in fact they have never invoked them. The main reason is that default on official debts normally leads to restructuring negotiations and multilateral development banks normally have other means to encourage debtor countries to pay. See Waibel (n 14) 162.
[40] Kläger (n 6) 55.
[41] Kriebaum and Reinisch (n 1) s C.

5.3 International Investment Agreements (IIAs)

5.3.1 Included protection and jurisdiction over sovereign debt claims

Section 5.3 discusses whether IIAs limit a sovereign debtor's liberty to design and implement a debt restructuring by providing foreign creditors with a right to equal or preferred treatment in a sovereign debt restructuring. As of 2019, 2,658 IIAs are in force and some 900 international investment tribunal decisions have been made.[42] The investment treaty provisions discussed in this chapter are: the most favoured nation (MFN) standard, the national treatment (NT) standard, and expropriation and the right to fair and equitable treatment (FET). First, Section 5.3.1 discusses whether sovereign debt instruments are protected under IIAs.

The objective behind IIAs is to protect foreign investments.[43] The first question is whether sovereign debt instruments fall under a specific treaty's definition of an investment. Modern treaty practice typically defines 'investment' in very broad terms and examples of what falls under the definition are listed in the specific IIA.[44] Many IIAs explicitly refer to contractual rights and the payment of money or other claims with an economic value. A typical formulation in an IIA regarding included investments is 'bonds, debentures, other debt instruments, and loans'.[45] This wording does not make it clear whether sovereign debt, which is rather different to ordinary corporate debt, is covered by such terms.

In *Abaclat v Argentina*, the arbitral tribunal found that state bonds qualified as a protected investment. The tribunal based its conclusion on the wording of the bilateral investment treaty (BIT) between Argentina and Italy, which stated that protected investments included 'obligations, private or public titles or any other right to performances or services having economic value, including capitalized revenues'.[46] In *Postova Banka v The Hellenic Republic*, another tribunal found that the Greek government bonds held by a Slovak bank and later restructured under Greek legislation were not covered by the BIT between Slovakia and Greece.[47] The tribunal highlighted the fact that while the BIT's definition of investment was formulated broadly, it did not, in contrast to the *Abaclat* case, contain references to 'public' bonds. These cases show

---

[42] UNCTAD, 'World Investment Report 2019: Special Economic Zones' (World Investment Reports, 6 December 2019) 19.
[43] There are two streams of authority for protection of foreigners and their assets under international law. One is based on the practice and jurisprudence of diplomatic protection and the other is based on the generic standards in numerous BITs as applied in tribunal decisions. Crawford (n 4) 607–08.
[44] Herdegen (n 2) 444.
[45] See the US Model BIT (2012) and Art 9.1 of the Trans-Pacific Partnership Agreement (TTP). See also ibid.
[46] Art 1(1)(c) of the BIT.
[47] See *Poštová banka, a.s and Istrokapital SE v Hellenic Republic* No ARB/13/8 (International Centre for Settlement of Investment Disputes 9 April 2015) (hereafter *Postova Banka v Greece*). Art 1(1) of the Slovakia–Greece BIT stated that protected investment 'means every kind of asset and in particular, though not exclusively, includes ... c) loans, claims to money or to any performance under contract having a financial value'. The article is quoted in Herdegen (n 2) 445.

that the wording of the BIT is decisive when deciding whether a specific IIA protects sovereign bonds or not.[48]

For a creditor to be able to enjoy her rights, it is necessary to establish whether a tribunal has jurisdiction over sovereign debt disputes. Some investment tribunals accept jurisdiction on the basis that an IIA defines a sovereign debt instrument as an investment.[49] Others require a so-called double review. This means that it is not sufficient to establish that sovereign debt instruments are covered by the IAA; it must also be shown that the tribunal has jurisdiction over a specific sovereign debt claim according to its own constituting rules.[50] This is the case for the International Centre for Settlement of Investment Disputes (ICSID), the tribunals of which are the most frequently used fora for the settlement of investment disputes. Article 25(1) of the ICSID Convention states that the jurisdiction of tribunals established within its framework is limited to disputes 'arising directly out of an investment'. It is unclear whether sovereign debt instruments fall under the scope of Article 25(1). The ICSID Convention gives no definition of the term 'investment' and two conflicting approaches have become dominant both in practice and in scholarly writings. One approach seeks to establish the ordinary meaning of the term 'investment' based on an interpretation of the ICSID Convention and international law generally (the objective approach). The alternative is to approach the issue on the basis of the definition of 'investment' found in the applicable IIA (the subjective approach). Those applying an objective approach have argued that what constitutes an investment in the sense of Article 25 should be decided based on the character of the transaction.[51] In other words, typical elements decide the core meaning of 'investment' and determine the outer limits of an ICSID tribunal's jurisdiction. The exact content of the core, and how flexible these characteristics are, remains the subject of debate.[52] The *Fedax v Venezuela* decision described five criteria constituting the basic features of an investment: 'a certain duration, a certain regularity for profit and return, assumption of risk, a substantial commitment, and significance for the host State's development'.[53] Four of these features were repeated in *Salini v Morocco*—the regularity for profit and return was left out—and have become known as the 'Salini criteria'.[54] The Salini criteria have been referred to by a number

---

[48] Herdegen (n 2) 446. Some agreements, such as the Comprehensive Economic and Trade Agreement (CETA) between Canada and the European Union, are clearer and specifically address non-payment or restructuring of public debt (cf Arts 8(1), 8(3) and Annex 8-B: Public Debt of CETA).

[49] Giuseppe Bianco, 'Restructuring Sovereign Debt Owed to Private Creditors. The Appropriate Role for International Law' (PhD, University of Oslo 2017) 218. See also Daniella Strik, 'Investment Protection of Sovereign Debt and Its Implications on the Future of Investment Law in the EU' (2012) 29 Journal of International Arbitration 183, 185–86.

[50] Waibel (n 14) 212.

[51] In *Salini Costruttori S.pA v Morocco* No ARB/00/4, para 57 (International Centre for Settlement of Investment Disputes 23 July 2001), the tribunal argued that jurisdiction is dependent on the transaction's character, meaning elements that typically constitute an investment. See also Waibel (n 14) 228.

[52] According to Waibel (n 14) 231, Schreuer originally introduced five typical elements of 'investments': (i) certain duration, (ii) regularity of profit and return, (iii) risk sharing, (iv) substantial commitment, and (v) significance for the host state's development.

[53] *Fedax NV v Republic of Venezuela* No ARB/96/3, para 43 (International Centre for Settlement of Investment Disputes 11 July 1997).

[54] *Salini v Morocco* (n 51). See n 52 for Schreuer's five typical elements of 'investments'. See Christoph H Schreuer, *The ICSID Convention: A Commentary* (1st edn, Cambridge University Press 2001) para 122; See also Waibel (n 14) 231.

of subsequent arbitral tribunals.[55] Nevertheless, the debate concerning whether the objective approach (based on the Salini criteria) or the subjective approach to jurisdiction is more appropriate remains unsettled.

This debate is also at centre of discussions about whether sovereign debt instruments fall under ICSID's jurisdiction. ICSID tribunals have varied in their approaches to whether and on what grounds they will accept jurisdiction over disputes related to sovereign debt instruments. In *Fedax v Venezuela*, the tribunal regarded the promissory notes that were issued by Venezuela and assigned by another company to Fedax as an 'investment'. The tribunal held that promissory notes were not like volatile capital since, as mentioned above, they have 'a certain duration, a certain regularity for profit and return, assumption of risk, a substantial commitment, and a significance for the host State's development'.[56] Moreover, the promissory notes contributed substantially to Venezuela's treasury. Consequently, the tribunal found that the promissory note satisfied the basic features of an investment and accepted jurisdiction.[57]

ICSID tribunals' acceptance of jurisdiction over sovereign debt claims has been criticized. Waibel is one of the main critics, arguing that purchases of sovereign bonds fail to display the typical features of an investment required by Article 25(1) of the ICSID Convention. He notes that sovereign debt instruments are typically repaid with regularly scheduled interest payments and payment of principal on maturity. Regularity of profit and return is hence likely to be present for sovereign debt instruments. However, Waibel questions whether sovereign bonds qualify as an investment because: (i) they do not necessarily significantly contribute to the host state's development; (ii) the duration of the activity is not substantial enough; and (iii) holding sovereign debt instruments does not sufficiently involve risk sharing. He further argues that a territorial link with the host country and an association with a commercial undertaking should be relevant characteristics when discussing whether sovereign debt instruments constitute an investment. For these reasons, Waibel concludes that characteristics of a sovereign bond resemble those of an ordinary commercial transaction and thus sovereign bonds should not be treated as investments under Article 25 of the ICSID Convention.[58]

In the above-mentioned *Abaclat v Argentina* case concerning an Argentine debt restructuring, the ICSID tribunal concluded that sovereign bonds amounted to an investment under the BIT in question and accepted jurisdiction on this basis (the subjective approach).[59] *Abaclat v Argentina*, and two similar cases in which jurisdiction

---

[55] See, for example, *Global Trading Resource Corp and Globec International, Inc v Ukraine* No ARB/09/11 (International Centre for Settlement of Investment Disputes 1 December 2010), in particular para 43.

[56] *Fedax v Venezuela* (n 53) para 43.

[57] For criticism of the tribunal for accepting jurisdiction in this case, as well as in *Ceskoslovenska Obchodni Banka, AS v Slovak Republic* No ARB/ 97/4 (International Centre for Settlement of Investment Disputes 24 May 1999), see Michael Waibel, 'Opening Pandora's Box: Sovereign Bonds in International Arbitration' (2007) 101 American Journal of International Law 711, 719–22.

[58] Waibel (n 14) 250–51.

[59] *Abaclat and others v Argentine Republic* No ARB/07/5, para 387 (International Centre for Settlement of Investment Disputes, 4 August 2011). This view derives support from some ICSID decisions arguing that the *Salini* test provides useful guidance, but does not create any jurisdictional requirements. For example, the tribunal in *Biwater Gauff (Tanzania) Ltd v United Republic of Tanzania* No ARB/05/22, para 312 (International Centre for Settlement of Investment Disputes, 24 July 2008) took this view: 'there is no basis for a rote, or overly strict, application of the five *Salini* criteria in every case. [They] are not fixed or mandatory as a matter of law. They do not appear in the ICSID Convention.' See also Waibel (n 14) 228.

over sovereign debt restructuring disputes was accepted, have caused increased concern among policymakers and scholars because they regard investment arbitration as an inappropriate forum for sovereign debt related disputes.[60]

The core of the critique is grounded in the fact that sovereign debt instruments differ from traditional foreign investments. This critique is similar to that raised by Waibel against ICSID tribunals accepting jurisdiction in sovereign debt related disputes. In more general terms, these commentators are worried that investment arbitration is not fit to assess the ambit of regulatory powers of the host state (the sovereign debtor) in taking measures in response to an existing debt crisis. The concern is that the investment tribunal will consider the rights of non-cooperative creditors in a negotiated sovereign debt restructuring in an overly narrow manner.[61] For example, investment tribunals accepting jurisdiction may lead to contractual forum selection clauses and substantive contract clauses in the sovereign bond being disregarded. The reason for this is that, in international investment law, contractual obligations and treaty obligations are essentially two separate spheres. Investment tribunals will primarily assess whether there is a breach of an investment agreement, not a breach of contract.[62] Debt restructurings typically include a reduction in the nominal value of the debt instrument or prolongation of the maturity of the bonds. Such 'haircuts' may violate several core provisions of IIAs, including FET and MFN treatment (further discussed in Section 5.3.2).[63]

Since the rise of the critical discussions regarding whether investment tribunals are the right to treat claims related to sovereign debt restructurings, some IIAs have addressed this concern directly. According to the United Nations Conference on Trade and Development (UNCTAD), 39% of IIAs concluded between 2011 and 2016 adapted the definition of an investment to exclude debt. In the older generations of IIA, only 3% excluded debt instruments from the definition of investment and the majority had a broad definition of assets.[64] Sovereign debt instruments can be excluded from the definition of investment in different ways. First, an IIA can use a positive or negative

---

[60] *Ambiente Ufficio S.pA and others v Argentine Republic* No ARB/08/9 (International Centre for Settlement of Investment Disputes, 8 February 2013); and *Giovanni Alemanni and Others v Argentine Republic* No ARB/07/8 (International Centre for Settlement of Investment Disputes 17 November 2014) are the two other cases concerning sovereign debt restructurings taking a similar approach to *Abaclat v Argentina* (n 59). Both examined in which state's territory an investment was made, based on which state benefitted from the investment. *Alemanni v Argentina* took a slightly different approach. The tribunal argued that the payments made by the underwriting banks at the time of the issuance of the bond would have qualified as investment. *Abaclat, Ambiente Ufficio,* and *Alemanni* all considered that the different legal operations of a sovereign debt instrument should be seen as an economic whole. They also concluded that the location of the investment was the jurisdiction issuing the sovereign bond because the funds were to be used for the benefit of the sovereign debtor. Dissenting opinions in both disputes took a different view underlining the remoteness between the sovereign debtor and the bonds it had issued, on one hand, and the securities and their holders on the other hand. See dissenting opinion by George Abi-Saab in *Abaclat v Argentina* and Santiago Torres Bernárdez in *Ambiente Ufficioi v Argentina*. For a broader analysis of the interpretation of what qualifies as an investment under the respective BITs, see Bianco (n 49) 225–32. See also Yuefen Li, 'How International Investment Agreements Have Made Debt Restructuring Even More Difficult and Costly' (South Centre Investment Policy Brief, February 2018).
[61] See, for example, Matthias Goldmann, 'Foreign Investment, Sovereign Debt and Human Rights' in Ilias Bantekas and Cephas Lumina (eds), *Sovereign Debt and Human Rights* (Oxford University Press 2018).
[62] See, for example, discussion in Bianco (n 49) ch 2c; Waibel (n 57).
[63] Li (n 60) 4.
[64] ibid 7.

list of assets to exclude debt instruments. Second, an IIA can apply an enterprise-based definition and only recognize those investors who directly own and control an enterprise. India's model BIT takes this approach and defines an enterprise as entities with 'real and substantial business operations' in the host country with 'substantial and long-term commitment of capital' and a 'substantial number of employees in the territory of the host state'.[65] Other IIAs have given sovereign debt special treatment by having a special annex to prevent investor claims on 'negotiated debt restructuring'.[66] Such terms typically provide that as long as sovereign debtors take into account NT and MFN standards when carrying out debt restructuring and the implementation is accepted by 75% (or another defined percentage) of bondholders, claims against a debt restructuring are not allowed.

In *Postova Banka*, the ICSID tribunal seems to have taken some of the criticism concerning the inappropriateness of investment arbitration for dealing with sovereign debt claims into account. In fact, it explicitly and extensively considered the specific legal characteristics of sovereign debt and found it did not have jurisdiction. It did so by concluding that sovereign bonds did not fall under the definition of 'investment' in the relevant BIT. In addition, however, the tribunal discussed—and in the end rejected—the idea that sovereign bonds fall under the definition of an 'investment' in the ICSID Convention, were an objective standard to apply.[67]

In sum, it is still unsettled whether and to what extent ICSID tribunals will accept jurisdiction over disputes involving a sovereign debt instrument and a related debt restructuring. Whether an IIA includes sovereign debt instruments must be decided on a case-by-case basis. Assuming an IIA includes debt instruments, Section 5.3.2 examines the substantive protection offered to foreign creditors that is relevant for intercreditor equity issues.

5.3.2 Substantive protection

5.3.2.1 National treatment and most favoured nation
The NT standard and the MFN standard may both protect sovereign bondholders from discriminatory treatment based on nationality.[68] The NT and MFN principles have no basis in customary international law and rest on international agreements alone. However, they are both common features in investment treaties.[69]

Under the NT standard, the host state (the sovereign debtor) is obliged to give the same treatment to foreign creditors as it gives to national creditors in like situations. It protects against *de jure* as well as *de facto* discrimination. In a sovereign debt restructuring, NT clauses may oblige the debtor country to grant the same treatment

---

[65] ibid and n 28. See also Kavaljit Singh, 'The India–US Bilateral Investment Treaty Will Not Be an Easy Ride' (*East Asia Forum*, 2 October 2015) <https://www.eastasiaforum.org/2015/02/10/the-india-us-bilateral-investment-treaty-will-not-be-an-easy-ride/> accessed 14 March 2022.
[66] Li (n 60) 7, n 29. See for instance Peru–Singapore FTA, Art 10.18 'Public Debt'; United States–Uruguay BIT, Annex G 'Sovereign Debt Restructuring'; China–Peru FTA, Chapter 10, Annex 8 'Public Debt'.
[67] *Postova Banka v Hellenic Republic* (n 47) paras 351–371.
[68] Waibel (n 14) 273.
[69] Herdegen (n 2) 450.

to foreign creditors as to domestic creditors or, more generally, to all creditors if they are in a like situation. MFN clauses allow foreign bondholders to benefit from more favourable privileges granted to third country creditors. As with the NT standard, the application of the MFN clause requires that respective bilateral situations be comparable.[70] The meaning of comparable situations is discussed below.

First, it may be useful to briefly reiterate why a sovereign debtor might want to differentiate between creditors based on their country of origin or nationality in a debt restructuring. As discussed in Sections 1.2 and 1.3, there are economic arguments in favour of, as well as an actual practice of, treating certain sectors of domestic creditors preferentially in a sovereign debt restructuring. This practice could potentially violate an NT standard. The aim of such preferential treatment is typically to protect key domestic banks and financial institutions and in so doing prevent a further deepening of the economic crisis and promote economic stability.[71] That being said, sovereign debtors may also have less honourable justifications for treating domestic creditors preferentially, because it may affect the likelihood of the sitting government being re-elected. There are fewer obvious reasons why a sovereign debtor would want to treat creditors from certain jurisdictions preferentially compared to creditors from other foreign jurisdictions (except for foreign policy considerations). It is therefore easier to imagine a restructuring breaching an NT standard than an MFN standard.

As mentioned above, both the MFN and the NT standards require that the creditors find themselves in like situations to have a right to require that the sovereign debtor treat them equally with national or third-state creditors.[72] What should be considered like situations? Amongst the most clearly articulated test for 'like circumstances' is the *Pope & Talbot* statement that 'the treatment accorded a foreign owned investment protected by Article 1102(2) should be compared with that accorded domestic investments in the same business or economic sector'.[73]

Subsequent investment tribunal cases seem to support the 'same business or economic sector' test as the determining criterion in establishing likeness.[74] The test stems from World Trade Organization (WTO) law and the logic is that entities in

---

[70] ibid 452.
[71] See Anna Gelpern and Brad Setser, 'Domestic and External Debt: The Doomed Quest for Equal Treatment' (2003–04) 35 Georgetown Journal of International Law 795, 813. See also Youngjin Jung and Sangwook Daniel Han, 'Sovereign Debt Restructuring under the Investor-State Dispute Regime' (2014) 31 Journal of International Arbitration 75, 88–89.
[72] Freya Baetens, 'Discrimination on the Basis of Nationality: Determining Likeness in Human Rights and Investment Law' in Stephan W Schill (ed), *International Investment Law and Comparative Public Law* (Oxford University Press 2010) 298. This was to be expected as many investment treaties contain a 'joint' clause on non-discrimination which requires both national and most-favoured nation treatment. Also, the likeness test does not differ depending on the subject matter at hand. Some NT and MFN clauses explicitly state that the treatment is to be given 'in like circumstances'. However, adding this phrase does not make a difference for the application of non-discrimination clauses. ibid 298, 307.
[73] *Pope & Talbot Inc v Canada*, UNCITRAL/NAFTA, Award on the Merits of Phase 2 (10 April 2001), para 78. See also Arwel Davies, 'Group Comparison vs. Best Treatment in International Economic Law Nondiscrimination Analysis' in Andrea K Bjorklund (ed), *Yearbook on International Investment Law & Policy 2014–2015* (Oxford University Press 2016) 164.
[74] See, for example, *Marvin Feldmann v Mexico* No ARB(AF)/99/1 (International Centre for Settlement of Investment Disputes 16 December 2002); *Methanex Corporation v United States of America*, UNCITRAL, Final Award of the Tribunal on Jurisdiction and Merits (3 August 2005); *S.D. Myers, Inc. v Government of Canada*, UNCITRAL/NAFTA, Partial Award (13 November 2001). See Baetens (n 72) 300, 307.

the 'same business or economic sector' should be compared because they are likely to be in a strong competitive relationship.[75] If this is correct, there can be a violation of an NT standard when domestic investors (competing with a foreign investor) are protected. An alternative view is to focus on the entities under the 'same business or economic sector' approach instead of the competitor perspective. The justification for focusing on entities is that some entities are likely to raise the same regulatory concerns.[76] In other words, the argument is that, regardless of whether two entities are in a strong competitive relationship, similar (non-competitive) investors in the same economic sector should be comparable. This logic can be expanded. The argument would then be that the 'same business or economic sector' test may not always be an appropriate starting point because entities in entirely different sectors may also raise the same regulatory concerns.[77] Different arbitral tribunals diverge as between broad and narrow definitions of the 'same business or economic sector' test. However, none have elaborated on this issue or identified criteria of likeness other than 'same business or economic sector'.[78]

In the context of sovereign debt instruments, it can make sense to claim that all creditors of a sovereign debtor are in the 'same business or economic sector'. When purchasing sovereign bonds, investors compete in terms of making the highest profit and, in the context of a debt restructuring, all creditors potentially 'compete' with regard to receiving the best restructuring terms. At the same time, official creditors such as development banks and international lenders of last resort would typically not be in the same business as private law creditors purchasing sovereign bonds for profit. However, some creditors may be private law entities established under the domestic law of a foreign jurisdiction to serve a public function. It would be more challenging to examine which of these creditor institutions would be in a comparable situation to that of more ordinary commercial creditors. A number of other distinctions between creditors are imaginable, such as consumer or retail investors versus, for example, professional investors, institutional investors, and high-risk funds. The question is still whether the likeness between them, whether as competitors or as entities, is strong enough for a creditor to claim equal treatment. If the creditors hold similar debt instruments, the debt instruments can be acquired on the secondary market, and are purchased for profit, these are presumably strong arguments in favour of concluding that the creditors are in like situations. In sum, standards are vague and there is a lack of practice concerning sovereign debt related claims in international investment law. It is therefore difficult to firmly conclude what constitutes similar situations for creditors in the context of MFN and NT.

---

[75] This seems to follow from *SD Myers v Canada* (n 74) para 251, where the tribunal noted that the claimants were 'in a position to take business away from its Canadian competitors'. See also Davies (n 73) 164.

[76] Nicholas DiMascio and Joost Pauwelyn, 'Nondiscrimination in Trade and Investment Treaties: Worlds Apart or Two Sides of the Same Coin?' (2008) 102 American Journal of International Law 48, 75–76, 85.

[77] See, for example, Davies (n 73) 164–65. Davies' main argument is that there can be an investment law NT violation when there is inexplicably different treatment of a claimant and domestic investments which operate in different business sectors, but whose activities raise the same regulatory concerns. He holds that there can be a violation even though there is no protection of, or competitive advantage for, the better treated domestic investment because they are in a different sector to the claimant.

[78] Baetens (n 72) 300.

It should be noted that discriminatory treatment may sometimes be justified under the MFN and NT standards of protection. When assessing whether the alleged discriminatory state measures, such as a debt restructuring, violate the NT or MFN standards, tribunals take into account the circumstances justifying the debt restructuring and why differential treatment is necessary to protect the public interest.[79] There are therefore arguments in favour of allowing preferential treatment under the NT and MFN standards of certain official creditors with public purposes as well as domestic creditors who are systemically important to the domestic economy.

Waibel suggests that the NT standard is unlikely to be violated in a sovereign debt restructuring. He explains that sovereign debtors often do not know the identity of their bondholders and therefore their nationalities, due to the fact the bonds are continuously resold on the secondary market. Moreover, an intermediary may hold sovereign bonds so that the beneficiary owner is unknown to the sovereign debtor. For these reasons, Waibel argues that 'even if a country desired to treat bondholders unequally, purposeful discrimination against foreign bondholders within a single bond issue, while theoretically possible, is exceedingly difficult as a practical matter'.[80] The same logic may also be applied to MFN standards.

However, Waibel's argument can be challenged, since it assumes that NT and MFN standards are violated only when the host state intends to discriminate.[81] The question of intent, however, remains to be settled. Baetens, for example, has analysed practice and argues that the majority of tribunals do not consider discriminatory intent to be a prerequisite in order to find that investors are in a like situation.[82]

Another controversial issue related to the MFN and NT standards is whether the host state, according to the principle of national treatment, is obliged to treat the foreign investor no less favourably than the national investor in general or whether it requires the best treatment accorded to any national investor.[83] In some cases, it has been assumed that any regulatory treatment of a foreigner that is less favourable than the treatment given to a national is a result of the investor's nationality.[84] If this standard is applied, debtor states' freedom to choose to treat some creditors preferentially is further restricted.

5.3.2.2 Expropriation
Expropriation is a core element of IIAs.[85] Although some scholars question whether sovereign debt instruments are capable of being expropriated,[86] the question of

---

[79] ibid 301.
[80] Waibel (n 57) 740.
[81] ibid. See also Jung and Han (n 71) 87.
[82] The majority of tribunals did not consider discriminatory intent to be a prerequisite to a likeness finding. See Baetens (n 72) 300. See also Herdegen (n 2) 450.
[83] Herdegen (n 2) 452.
[84] This was the case in for example *SD Myers v Canada* (n 74) para 250. This less favourable treatment could only be accepted under the NT standards if the sovereign debtor's (the host state) measures 'have a reasonable nexus to rational government policies that 1) do not distinguish on their face or de facto' between foreign and domestic creditors, and 2) do not otherwise 'undermine the liberalizing objective' of the investment treaty. See Baetens (n 72) 303. Her analysis refers to *Pope & Talbot v Canada* (n 73) para 78.
[85] Waibel (n 14) 278; Herdegen (n 2) 471.
[86] See discussion in Section 5.2.2.

whether rules concerning expropriation cover sovereign debt instruments is primarily a question of the applicable definition of 'investment' in the IIA.[87] For the sake of this discussion, it will be assumed that sovereign debt instruments are covered by the relevant IIA.[88]

Foreign investors have historically been vulnerable to land and property seizures, as well as expulsion from the host state.[89] Over time, expropriation as a standard of protection has come to be interpreted increasingly broadly, particularly in relation to so-called indirect expropriation. For example, arbitral tribunals in the context of the North American Free Trade Agreement (NAFTA) have included not only direct property takings, but 'covert or incidental interference with the use of property, which [deprives] the owner ... of the use or reasonably-to-be-expected economic benefit of property'.[90]

The main elements that have been crystallized through arbitral practice, and which may help determine whether a government engages in indirect expropriation action or exercises legitimate regulatory authority, are:[91] (i) the severity of the interference caused by the restructuring for the creditor (the economic impact); (ii) the effect on the investor (and not the intent or the aim pursued by the host state);[92] (iii) violation of the legitimate expectations of the investor by host states; and (iv) the balancing of the demands of the general interest of the community and the requirements of the protection of the rights of the individual (proportionality).[93]

Various actions by a sovereign debtor related to a debt restructuring may constitute direct or indirect expropriation under an IIA. A debt restructuring typically entails

---

[87] August Reinisch, 'Expropriation' in Peter Muchlinski and others (eds), *The Oxford Handbook of International Investment Law* (Oxford University Press 2008) 410. Case law from courts and tribunals does not always clearly explain whether they based their decisions on customary international law notions of property or on treaty definitions of investments contained in BITs or other investment instruments. Reinisch nevertheless notes that the various legal bases may frequently be decisive for the judicial and arbitral decisions reached. Many BITs contain broad definitions of what constitutes an 'investment' and it is generally accepted that expropriation may also affect intangible assets of economic value to an investor, such as contractual rights. See ibid.

[88] See *Norwegian Shipowners' Claims* (n 14); *Oscar Chinn* (n 14); *Certain German Interests in Polish Upper Silesia* (n 14). See also Waibel (n 57) 743, critically discussing whether sovereign debt instruments can be expropriated. He states that '[b]ecause they typically define investments to include contractual rights, BITs lend considerable support to the view that rights arising from a contract are potentially susceptible to expropriation, and in much the same way as tangible property'.

[89] Rachel D Thrasher and Kevin P Gallagher, 'Mission Creep: The Emerging Role of International Investment Agreements in Sovereign Debt Restructuring' (2015) 6 Journal of Globalization and Development 257, 268–69.

[90] *Metalclad Corporation v United Mexican States* No ARB(AF)/91/1, para 103 (International Centre for Settlement of Investment Disputes 30 August 2000). On the topic of indirect expropriation, see also OECD, '"Indirect Expropriation" and the "Right to Regulate" in International Investment Law | READ Online' (OECD Working Papers on International Investment, September 2004).

[91] Reinisch (n 87) 438–39, 444–48.

[92] Reinisch notes, however, that clear evidence of intent to expropriate may assist tribunals in their assessment of the facts. By referring to case law, he holds that the effect on the investor is the main criterion. Whether qualification of an action as indirect expropriation should only consider the negative effect of a state measure on the investment ('sole effect doctrine') or also the intent or the aim pursued by the host state, is viewed by some as a controversial issue. ibid 444–47. See also Herdegen (n 2) 472.

[93] Reinisch suggests that such a balancing approach may be regarded as 'inherent in the test relied upon by many investment arbitral tribunals' and more recent arbitral awards in particular have shown this to be true. See Reinisch (n 87) 450.

a partial cancellation of a claim (a 'haircut') where the formal title is not transferred or the exchange of a debt instrument for a new debt instrument of lower value. A restructuring may interfere with creditors' expectations and typically causes creditors to suffer substantial deprivation of the value of their investments, thereby amounting to indirect expropriation.

It is clear that not all types of state acts that result in economic loss for a creditor amount to expropriation.[94] Whether a sovereign debt restructuring constitutes an indirect expropriation must be established on a case-by-case basis.[95] When and why a specific debt restructuring will be deemed expropriation under a particular IIA is a broad question and beyond the scope of this chapter.[96] Here, I wish simply to consider whether unequal treatment of creditors in a restructuring may influence the assessment of whether or not it is expropriation and thereby offers protection. In addition to the factors listed above, it seems to be agreed that discriminatory effects and/or a discriminatory intent is relevant when establishing whether governmental action constitutes indirect expropriation.[97] It must be noted that discriminatory treatment is just one of several elements and simply contributes to tipping the conclusion in the direction of establishing expropriation. As Reinisch argues, discriminatory intent or effect only serves as a subsidiary or additional element evidencing indirect expropriation. As such, it must be distinguished from other discriminatory state measures contrary to investment standards, such as MFN and NT standards discussed above.[98] It can be argued that non-discriminatory adjustment measures that affect domestic and foreign creditors alike reduce the chances of triggering a restructuring state's international responsibility.[99]

The public policy arguments and economic rationales in favour of treating some creditors preferentially (despite a prohibition on discrimination)—those mentioned in the section on NT and MFN standards—are also likely to be applicable in the context of expropriation claims. There is little arbitral practice concerning discrimination as part of an expropriation claim related to sovereign debt restructurings. The extent to which a sovereign debtor will be allowed to treat certain creditors preferentially for public purposes (such as achieving sustainable debt levels) without effective compensation is unclear.

It should be noted that several arbitral awards seem to support the view that only state acts may constitute expropriation.[100] In *Waste Management v Mexico*, the tribunal

---

[94] Waibel (n 14) 278.
[95] Crawford (n 4) 622. See also Herdegen (n 2) 472.
[96] It should nevertheless be mentioned that some BITs include specific debt restructuring annexes, which limit treatment obligations on public debt to MFN and NT, see for example the Chile–US FTA and the Uruguay–US BIT. See Waibel (n 14) 272.
[97] Reinisch (n 87) 450–51.
[98] ibid.
[99] Without necessarily affecting the outcome, others approach the question of expropriation and discrimination/ preferential treatment slightly differently holding that IIAs require that expropriation is only carried out: (i) for a public purpose; (ii) in a non-discriminatory manner; and (iii) on payment of prompt, adequate, and effective compensation. The question of discrimination is here an integral part of examining whether an expropriation is legitimate, because differential treatment of some creditors may be justified and may therefore not constitute discrimination. This is for example in line with Art 1110 NAFTA. See, for example, Thrasher and Gallagher (n 89) 268.
[100] Waibel (n 14) 279–80.

held that the Mexican government's failure to pay relevant fees to the foreign investor under a concession contract did not amount to indirect expropriation because the investor retained control and use of its property at all times and was able to service its customers and earn collection fees from them.[101] Moreover, the tribunal held that 'an enterprise is not expropriated just because its debts are not paid or other contractual obligations towards it are breached', in particular when there is no outright repudiation of the transaction.[102] The tribunal further held that the Mexican government entered into the concession contract in its private capacity and the default on its contract obligation was not of a public nature.[103] This indicates that, on the one hand, a default on bonds in a private capacity will not qualify as expropriation; on the other hand, a coercive public-natured repudiation of sovereign bonds may qualify as such. The question that remains to be assessed on a case-by-case basis is which acts of a sovereign debtor are of a public nature and which are not. With regards to sovereign debt restructuring, the relevant question is whether a private corporation could have successfully carried out such a restructuring or whether the government used specific regulatory, administrative, or governmental powers to implement its debt restructuring. This indicates that restructuring implemented by CACs—the most common contractual majority-voting tool—would not lead to finding of an expropriation. Consequently, creditors may have difficulties in claiming that they have been discriminated against in an expropriation if co-creditors implemented it through a majority vote.

5.3.2.3 Fair and equitable treatment

FET is an autonomous standard of investment protection included in the vast majority of IIAs, though formulations vary.[104] Some IIAs specify that FET refers only to the recognition of basic due process requirements and explicitly states that it does not grant 'additional substantive rights' to investors. Others specify the content of the FET standard by listing examples.[105] Due to its abstract formulation and/or the listing of a non-conclusive set of examples, the exact content of the obligation is subject to ongoing debate. To a large extent, the particular circumstances of each case shape the interpretation of the FET standard. This is evident from the fact-driven approach often taken by arbitral tribunals resulting in lengthy descriptions of fact in their awards. Doctrinal treatment of the FET standard is for the same reason typically far from illuminating.[106] Nevertheless, certain patterns of argument concerning the FET standard have emerged from arbitral awards. In short, the core of the FET standard, as developed in practice, protects legitimate commercial expectations and encompasses

---

[101] *Waste Management, Inc v United Mexican States* No ARB (AF)9/00/3, para 159 (International Centre for Settlement of Investment Disputes 30 April 2004). See also Waibel (n 57) 745.

[102] *Waste Management v Mexico* (n 101) para 160.

[103] In para 155, the tribunal states for example that 'the question is whether the combined conduct of Mexican public entities had an effect equivalent to the taking of the enterprise, in whole or substantial part. In considering this question it is necessary to distinguish between the measures affecting Acaverde as a whole and those concerning particular contractual rights under the Concession Agreement.' (ibid para 155).

[104] Crawford (n 4) 616.

[105] Thrasher and Gallagher (n 89) 268. See also UNCTAD, 'Fair and Equitable Treatment: A Sequel' (UNCTAD Series on Issues in International Investment Agreements II, February 2012) 82.

[106] Kläger (n 6) 115.

procedural and substantive requirements. In general schematic terms, the standard covers: (i) legitimate commercial expectations, (ii) non-discrimination, (iii) fair procedure, (iv) transparency, and (v) proportionality.[107]

Exploring the threshold for when a sovereign debt restructuring may breach the FET standard on a general basis is beyond the scope of this book. Waibel discusses a number of FET-standard claims that may arise in relation to a coercive sovereign debt restructuring. The process leading up to the bond exchange may, for example, lack transparency and undermine the legitimate expectations of the creditors. Further, a take-it-or-leave-it exchange offer may violate due process, since it disappoints investors' legitimate expectations with respect to the restructuring. The restructuring itself may not have been carried out in good faith. Moreover, to enable a debt restructuring, the debtor state may have transformed the business environment profoundly, to the detriment of the creditors. For example, it may have undermined the legal framework of the sovereign bonds.[108]

The main question relevant to this book is the extent to which discrimination between creditors in a sovereign debt restructuring influences the finding of a breach of the FET standard. It is sometimes thought that FET provides an absolute standard of protection and that this standard exists irrespective of how the state treats other investors.[109] However, and as mentioned above, discriminatory behaviour can also be considered unfair or inequitable, and thereby provide foreign creditors with protection under the FET standard. The fact that treaties usually contain express discrimination clauses does not rule this option out.[110] That said, the relation between FET treatment and the prohibition of discriminatory treatment is not settled. Some tribunals have found that the FET standard generally prohibits discriminatory treatment of foreign investors.[111] This approach is probably too broad. In particular, the non-discrimination standard that forms part of the FET standard should not be confused with the MFN or NT standards. While these standards deal with nationality-based discrimination, the non-discrimination requirement in the FET standard appears to prohibit discrimination that specifically targets a foreign investor on other manifestly wrongful grounds such as gender, race or religious belief, or other types of conduct that amount to a 'deliberate conspiracy ... to destroy or frustrate the investment'.[112]

---

[107] ibid 117–19. To a certain extent, the elements which legal scholars choose to focus on, or which they use to describe the content of the FET standard, vary. For example, Schill lists legality; administrative due process and denial of justice; non-discrimination; legitimate expectations; stability, predictability, and consistency; transparency; and proportionality and reasonableness. (Marc Jacob and Stephan W Schill, 'Fair and Equitable Treatment: Content, Practice, Method' in Marc Bungenberg and others (eds), *International Investment Law: A Handbook* (C.H. Beck/Hart/Nomos 2015) 717). UNCTAD (n 105) 61 lists legitimate expectation; manifest arbitrariness; denial of justice; due process; discrimination; abusive treatment and the role of investor conduct. Schefer refers to legitimate expectations through establishment of a transparent and predictable legal and business framework. (Krista Nadakavukaren Schefer, *International Investment Law: Texts, Cases and Materials* (3rd edn, Edward Elgar 2020) 355). See also Waibel (n 14) 293.

[108] Waibel (n 14) 296.

[109] Jacob and Schill (n 107) 731.

[110] ibid.

[111] UNCTAD (n 105) 81. See, for example, *Waste Management v Mexico* (n 101) para 98; *CMS Gas Transmission Company v The Republic of Argentina* No ARB/01/8, para 287 (International Centre for Settlement of Investment Disputes 12 May 2005).

[112] *Waste Management v Mexico* (n 101) para 138. Also, in *Grand River Enterprises Six Nations Limited and others v United States*, UNCITRAL, Award (12 January 2011), the tribunal held that 'neither Art. 1105 [of the NAFTA agreement] nor the customary international law standard of protection generally prohibits

It is nevertheless possible that a debt restructuring will violate the FET standard if it openly discriminates (whether *de jure* or *de facto*) against a creditor on the grounds of nationality and there is no legitimate justification for the measure.[113] In other words, arbitral tribunals will not just compare the types of treatment accorded to different creditors but will also examine whether the action of the sovereign debtor involves arbitrariness or harassment.[114]

5.3.3 Preliminary conclusion

The definition of 'investment' in a particular agreement determines whether creditors holding sovereign debt instruments are protected under an IIA. Whether various investment tribunals will accept jurisdiction over a dispute arising from a sovereign debt instrument and sovereign debt restructurings depends on the rules of the tribunal. More specifically, the debate is ongoing as to whether ICSID tribunals should accept jurisdiction over disputes arising out of sovereign debt instruments and debt restructurings.

The most relevant IIA clauses in an intercreditor equity context are the NT and MFN clauses, the expropriation clause and the FET clause. The NT and MFN standards may both protect sovereign bondholders from discriminatory treatment based on nationality. Both standards require that the creditors find themselves in similar situations to national or third-state creditors, respectively, to have a right to equal treatment by the sovereign debtor. IIAs and investment tribunals do not provide a clear answer as to what constitutes like circumstances. The most clearly articulated likeness test is whether the two investors belong to the 'same business or economic sector'. In the context of sovereign debt instruments, there are strong arguments in favour of claiming that creditors of the sovereign debtor are in the same business or economic sector. At the same time, a number of distinctions between various types of

---

discrimination against foreign investments'. For instance, Art 8.10 para 2 of the Comprehensive Economic and Trade Agreement (CETA) lists, among other things, 'manifest arbitrariness; targeted discrimination on manifestly wrongful grounds, such as gender, race or religious belief' and 'abusive treatment of investors, such as coercion, duress and harassment' as factors that should be taken into account in determining a violation of the FET standard. See also UNCTAD (n 105) 82.

[113] UNCTAD (n 105) 82. In *Alex Genin, Eastern Credit Limited, Inc and AS Baltoil v The Republic of Estonia* No ARB/99/2, paras 368, 369, 371 (International Centre for Settlement of Investment Disputes 25 June 2001), the tribunal emphasized that 'customary international law does not ... require that a state treat all aliens (and alien property) equally, or that it treats aliens as favourably as nationals'. Moreover, the tribunal only considered it a violation of FET if the investor was 'specifically targeted' or if the differential treatment amounted to bad faith. See also Jacob and Schill (n 107) 732.

[114] See, for example, *SD Myers v Canada* (n 74) para 263; *Ronald S. Lauder v Czech Republic*, UNCITRAL, Final Award (3 September 2001), paras 237ff, 293–295; *Nykomb Synergetics Technology Holding AB v Latvia*, SCC Arbitration Institute, Award (16 December 2003), para 4.3.2; *CMS Gas v Argentina* (n 111) para 290; *Saluka Investments BV v Czech Republic*, UNCITRAL, Partial Award (17 March 2006), paras 307, 460; *Parkerings-Compagniet AS v Lithuania* No ARB/05/08, paras 280, 287ff (International Centre for Settlement of Investment Disputes 11 September 2007). It has also been found that non-discrimination is not compromised by Art 1105(1) NAFTA in, for example, *Methanex v USA* (n 74) paras 144 et seq. See also Kläger (n 6) 117.

creditors can be made. Due to the vagueness of the NT and MFN standards and the lack of sovereign debt related practice, future case law will be decisive in terms of how the standard will shape sovereign debtor restructuring in the future.

Various actions by a sovereign debtor related to a debt restructuring may constitute direct or indirect expropriation under an IIA, due to the fact that they may interfere with creditors' expectations and will typically cause creditors to be substantially deprived of the value of their investments. There seems to be agreement that discriminatory effects and/or intent are relevant when establishing whether a governmental action constitutes indirect expropriation. However, it is important to note that discriminatory treatment is one of several elements and will simply tip the conclusion in the direction of establishing unlawful expropriation. Finally, only state acts may cause expropriation. This implies that creditors may have difficulties in claiming that they have been discriminated against in an expropriation if it results from a creditor majority vote.

The FET standard, as developed in practice, protects legitimate commercial expectations and encompasses procedural and substantive requirements. The relationship between FET treatment and the prohibition of discriminatory treatment is not settled. In a restructuring, the standard is likely to provide fundamental protection for creditors against discrimination and arbitrariness in the restructuring process. In particular, it is likely to protect against discrimination that specifically targets an investor on manifestly wrongful grounds other than nationality (covered by MFN and NT standards) such as gender, race or religious belief, or other types of conduct that amount to a deliberate conspiracy to destroy or frustrate the investment.

5.4 ECHR—Protection of Property and the Prohibition Against Discrimination

5.4.1 Introduction

A sovereign debt restructuring may give rise to a non-discrimination claim under Article 14 of the ECHR, in conjunction with Article 1 of the First Protocol to the ECHR, which protects the right to property.

A sovereign debt restructuring typically involves rescheduling payment of interest rates and/or final repayment, cutting the interest rate, or reducing the nominal value of the debt, all of which will typically entail economic loss for the creditors. A sovereign debtor may implement a debt restructuring by using more or less coercive methods, in particular where there is a risk of holdout behaviour by the creditors.[115] This can give rise to creditor claims of expropriation under Article 1 of the First Protocol to the ECHR, which protects the right to property. The question discussed in this section is what differential treatment of creditors is allowed under the ECHR in a debt restructuring with coercive elements.

---

[115] Such as retroactively adopting laws governing the debt contract, restructuring using CACs or exit consent, or threatening to default.

The European Court of Human Rights (ECtHR) follows a specific methodology when assessing whether certain state measures, such as a restructuring, violate the ECHR's prohibition on discrimination. First, it addresses whether the claim falls within the scope of protection of the ECHR. Section 5.4.2 discusses how sovereign debt instruments are protected under the ECHR. Second, the ECtHR typically assesses whether a violation of a substantive right has taken place. Whether a restructuring amounts to an interference with a creditor's possessions under Article 1 of the First Protocol is not the main topic of this book. Although the non-discrimination rules in Article 14 of the ECHR are not freestanding, it is not necessary to establish an actual breach of the corresponding provision (such as Article 1 of the First Protocol to the ECHR) to 'activate' ECHR protection from discrimination. Nevertheless, to present a fuller picture, Section 5.4.3 presents the main elements used in assessing creditors' rights to the free enjoyment of their possessions in relation to a debt restructuring. Third, the ECtHR considers whether there is inequality of treatment in the enjoyment of an ECHR right and subsequently examines whether this differential treatment violates Article 14.[116] This is the main concern of this section and will be discussed in Section 5.4.4.

5.4.2 Covered protection

Article 1 of the First Protocol to the ECHR guarantees 'the peaceful enjoyment of ... possessions', protection against deprivation of 'possessions', and against disproportionate measures of control over 'the use of property'. The first question is whether holding sovereign debt instruments constitutes a 'possession' in accordance with Article 1 of the First Protocol.

The ECHR does not define the terms 'possession' or 'property' and the ECtHR has refrained from providing a general definition in practice. According to the jurisprudence of the ECtHR, two types of 'possessions' are covered by the first sentence of Article 1 of the First Protocol: (i) existing property rights and (ii) existing claims to money or performance with a financial value,[117] provided that the holder has a legitimate expectation of fulfilment.[118] The ECtHR's jurisprudence establishes that sovereign bonds fall within the latter category.[119] In *Mamatas and others v Greece* (*Mamatas*), a case concerning the treatment of creditors in the 2012 Greek debt

---

[116] Baetens (n 72) 293.
[117] Waibel (n 14) 182. Waibel also notes that the wide definition of possessions under Art 1 of the First Protocol of the ECHR is not necessarily co-extensive with the protection of property under general international law, outside the regional European context.
[118] ibid 182–83. Also, in *Kopecký v Slovakia*, App no 44912/98, 7 January 2003 (ECtHR), para 35 c), the tribunal said '"[p]ossessions" can be either "existing possessions" or assets, including claims in respect of which the applicant can argue that he or she has at least a "legitimate expectation" of obtaining effective enjoyment of a property right'. See also Ursula Kriebaum and Christoph Schreuer, 'The Concept of Property in Human Rights Law and International Investment Law' in Stephan Breitenmoser and others (eds), *Human Rights, Democracy and the Rule of Law:* Liber amicorum *Luzius Wildhaber* (Nomos 2007) 6–7.
[119] See, for example, *Mamatas and Others v Greece*, App no 63066/14, 64297/14 and 66106/14, 21 July 2016 (ECtHR). The ECtHR does not distinguish between ordinary bonds and sovereign bonds but takes a general approach to the legitimate expectation of the enjoyment of a claim to money or performance with a financial value. See also *Malysh and Others v Russia*, App no 30280/03, 11 February 2010 (ECtHR).

restructuring, the ECtHR explained that because bonds mature, and the nominal value of the bond in principle must be repaid, creditors have a legitimate expectation of fulfilment. That government bonds are traded on capital markets where their value fluctuates did not change this conclusion. According to the terms of the Greek bond, in this particular case, the holders were entitled to repayment at maturity. The ECtHR therefore concluded that the debt instruments fell within the meaning of a 'possession' in the first sentence of Article 1 of the First Protocol.[120]

5.4.3 Protection of property

As established in the previous section, creditors holding sovereign debt instruments are in principle protected from interference with their enjoyment of the right related to the sovereign bond under Article 1 of the First Protocol of the ECHR. Under this Article, the state may nevertheless restrict or control the use of property, but any interference must pursue a legitimate aim and the measures applied must be proportionate to the aim pursued. This implies that the state must strike a fair balance between the general interest of the community and the fundamental rights of the individual.[121]

Which state measures leading up to or implementing a debt restructuring constitute an interference with creditors' possessions? In *Malysh v Russia* (*Malysh*), six creditors holding Russian Urozhay 90 bonds (domestic debt) held that the failure of the Russian government to provide for payment under the bonds amounted to a violation of Article 1 of the First Protocol. The relevant debts were excluded from the main restructuring and only settled by special federal law, and the Russian government thereafter delayed implementation of the special settlement year after year. In *Malysh*, the ECtHR held that Russia's legislation and extensive delay of any payment constituted an interference. The ECtHR concluded that the state had violated Article 1 of the First Protocol because between 1995 and 2009 it had taken no steps to satisfy the claims arising out of the bonds.[122]

Mamatas concerned, as mentioned above, the restructuring of Greece's debt in 2012. The question at stake was whether an involuntary bond exchange, leading to a 53.5% loss in the nominal value of the bonds, constituted a violation of the bondholders' rights to protection of their property pursuant to Article 1 of the First Protocol. The involuntary restructuring was enabled by legislation making it mandatory to retroactively implement CACs in all sovereign bonds subject to Greek law. As mentioned above, CACs enable a specific majority of bondholders to bind the minority of bondholders to a debt restructuring.[123] In *Mamatas*, the ECtHR held that Greece had interfered with the creditors' possessions through its legislation but, as discussed below, it rejected the creditors' overall claim. Both *Malysh* and *Mamatas* considered an involuntary restructuring enabled by legislation. While *Malysh* concerned the lack of implementation (and thus lack of payment) following a forced restructuring, in

---

[120] *Mamatas v Greece* (n 119) para 90.
[121] ibid para 96.
[122] *Malysh v Russia* (n 119) paras 85–86.
[123] The Greek parliament enacted the Greek Bondholder Act.

Mamatas, Greece had implemented its restructuring and fulfilled its restructured payment obligations. All debt restructuring with coercive elements imposed by the state, and which interfere with the contractual rights of the creditor, are likely to constitute an 'interference' with a creditor's possession in a sovereign bond under the ECHR.

For an 'interference' to be legal under the ECHR, it must be implemented for legitimate reasons. A debt restructuring implemented purely to ease or escape an economic burden will fail to meet this criterion, but a restructuring as a response to an economic crisis to achieve economic stability will typically be a legitimate aim. In *Malysh*, the ECtHR accepted Russia's general argument that difficult financial conditions could justify strong limitations on compensation to bondholders and that 'defining budgetary priorities in terms of favouring expenditures on pressing social issues to the detriment of claims with a purely pecuniary nature was a legitimate aim in the public interest'.[124] Similarly, in *Mamatas*, the ECtHR held that Greece had acted legitimately in taking steps to maintain the economic stability of the country and seek a restructuring of public debt in the general interest of society.[125]

Further, for a state's interference to be accepted, the measures applied have to be proportional to the aims pursued (crisis resolution and economic stability). In this regard, the design of the restructuring is decisive, in particular the scale of losses it imposes on its creditors compared to how much restructuring is actually needed for the state to reach a sustainable level of debt. In addition, the tools and methods used to implement the debt restructuring can be important factors. For instance, in *Mamatas*, the ECtHR pointed to the fact that CACs were a common contractual tool on the international money market and not an exceptional means of executing a debt restructuring.[126] Also, the fact that the involuntary bond exchange reduced the nominal value of the bonds by 53.5% was not in itself sufficient to establish that the measure was not proportionate or constituted an excessive burden for the applicants.[127] In the ECtHR's opinion, the reference point for assessing the loss suffered should take into account the Greek economic situation at the time, as this reflects the true market value at the time of interference with the possession and the gain investors actually could expect from the bonds.[128] Furthermore, the bondholders could have sold their securities on the market up until a certain date before the debt exchange. In other words, the ECtHR looked at the alternatives available to bondholders who might wish to avoid the interference. It also considered the state's alternatives, concluding that, if CACs had not been implemented, the bondholders would have had to reach a consensus and Greece would probably not have been able to restructure its debts at all.[129]

---

[124] *Malysh v Russia* (n 119) para 80. See also *Mamatas v Greece* (n 119) paras 103–104; Waibel (n 14) 186.
[125] Through the bond exchange operation, the Greek authorities managed to reduce Greek debt by approximately EUR 107 billion. And, while the interest payments scheduled for 2012 were initially estimated at EUR 17.5 billion, they dropped to EUR 12.2 billion following the bond exchange and remained under EUR 6 billion in 2013. *Mamatas v Greece* (n 119) paras 103–104.
[126] CACs have been included in all new Euro area government securities with a maturity above one year. CACs are furthermore standard in government bonds subject to English law and are recommended in sovereign bonds by ICMA, the IMF, and the G20.
[127] *Mamatas v Greece* (n 119) para 110.
[128] ibid.
[129] ibid para 116.

The practice of the ECtHR has established that states enjoy a wide margin of appreciation when it comes to regulating social policy, particularly in the wake of the 2008 financial crisis. This wide margin of appreciation also includes the enactment of laws to balance state expenditure and revenue deemed necessary to achieve the desired social policy. The *Mamatas* case demonstrates that this wide margin also extends to the design and implementation of crisis resolution measures concerning sovereign bonds for states in financial crisis, even if it involves forced measures that interfere with the right to protection of property under Article 1 of the First Protocol of the ECHR.[130]

To summarize, because states are granted a wide margin of appreciation when implementing crisis resolution measures, it may prove difficult to establish that a sovereign debt restructuring implemented in response to a severe economic crisis violates the ECHR's right to protection of property. In *Mamatas*, a 53% reduction in nominal value was accepted by the ECtHR. Moreover, the fact that the economic loss of the creditor cannot be equalled with the reduction of the nominal value of the debt also makes it difficult for creditors to establish that an expropriation that breaches the ECHR has taken place. The *Malysh* case shows, however, that a debtor state is not completely free to implement crisis resolution measures that leave creditors without any real rights over their possessions.

5.4.4 Prohibition against discrimination

5.4.4.1 General

Article 14 of the ECHR prohibits discrimination 'on any ground such as sex, race, colour, language, religion, political or other opinion, national or social origin associated with a national minority, property, birth or other status'.[131] ECtHR case law has clarified that the Article not only covers these listed grounds of discrimination but more generally prohibits situations in which 'states treat differently persons in analogous situations'[132] and situations in which states (without an objective and

---

[130] The ECtHR typically reasons that, as the decision to enact laws to balance state expenditure and revenue will commonly involve consideration of political, economic, and social issues, national authorities are in principle—according to the ECtHR's practice—better placed than an international tribunal to choose the most appropriate means of achieving this. The ECtHR should therefore not intervene unless the measures prove to be manifestly without reasonable foundation. *Mamatas v Greece* (n 119) para 88. The original judgment (in French) states: '*La Cour rappelle en outre qu'elle a déjà construit une jurisprudence relative à la marge d'appréciation des États dans le contexte de la crise économique qui sévit en Europe depuis 2008 et plus particulièrement en relation avec des mesures d'austérité prises par voie législative ou autre et visant des couches entières de la population ... Dans ce contexte, la Cour rappelle aussi que les Etats parties à la Convention jouissent d'une marge d'appréciation assez ample lorsqu'il s'agit de déterminer leur politique sociale. L'adoption des lois pour établir l'équilibre entre les dépenses et les recettes de l'Etat impliquant d'ordinaire un examen de questions politiques, économiques et sociales, la Cour considère que les autorités nationales se trouvent en principe mieux placées qu'un tribunal international pour choisir les moyens les plus appropriés pour parvenir à cette fin et elle respecte leurs choix, sauf s'ils se révèlent manifestement dépourvus de base raisonnable....*'

[131] Protocol No 12 to the ECHR will not be discussed in this book. Protocol No 12 provides for a general prohibition on discrimination. The current non-discrimination provision of the ECHR is of a limited kind because it only prohibits discrimination in the enjoyment of one or the other rights guaranteed by the ECHR. The Protocol removes this limitation and guarantees that no-one shall be discriminated against on any ground by any public authority.

[132] *Thlimmenos v Greece*, App no 34369/97, 6 April 2000 (ECtHR), para 44.

reasonable justification) 'fail to treat differently persons whose situations are significantly different'.[133]

It is important to note that if likeness between groups of creditors is established and it is coupled with different treatment, it will not automatically constitute a breach of the non-discrimination standard.[134] According to the ECtHR's case law, Article 14 sets up a test to distinguish between differential treatment that is allowed and that which is not.[135] The structure of the examination of differential treatment is similar to the test discussed for interference with property under Article 1 of the First Protocol of the ECHR. First, the allegedly discriminatory state measure must pursue a legitimate aim and correspond to a pressing social need. Second, the measure must be proportionate.[136] Third, the ECtHR has recognized that states enjoy a certain margin of appreciation in assessing 'whether and to what extent differences in otherwise similar situations justify a different treatment' or equal treatment in the case of different situations.[137] The scope of the margin of appreciation varies with different 'circumstances, the subject matter and its background'.[138]

Out of the listed grounds for discrimination in Article 14, nationality is perhaps the most probable factor in a restructuring, due to the fact that sovereign debtors may have economic justifications for treating foreign creditors differently to domestic creditors.[139] Whether preferential treatment based on nationality violates the ECHR is discussed in the following section together with the general question of the circumstances in which differential treatment of similarly situated creditors and like treatment of differently situated creditors in a sovereign debt restructuring violates Article 14.[140]

5.4.4.2 Like circumstances

When analysing the scope of the ECHR's protection against differential treatment in similar circumstances and similar treatment in different circumstances, the important question is: what constitutes like circumstances or analogous situations? The ECHR does not provide an elaborate answer to this question. *Lithgow v United Kingdom* is a key case in this regard. In this case, the ECtHR explained that the likeness test is a safeguard for 'persons ... who are "placed in analogous situations" against discriminatory

---

[133] ibid para 44. In certain circumstances, it is the absence of differential treatment to correct an inequality that may, without a reasonable and objective justification, constitute a violation of the Article (see, among others, ibid). In *Mamatas v Greece* (n 119) paras 130–132, the court also highlighted the fact that general policy measures that have disproportionately prejudicial effects on a group of people can be considered discriminatory even if they do not specifically target this group and there is no discriminatory intent. It is the government who has the burden of proof when proving that differential treatment was justified.

[134] Baetens (n 72) 294.

[135] ibid 293.

[136] ibid 296. See, for example, *Lithgow and Others v United Kingdom*, App nos 9006/80, 9262/81, 9263/81, 9265/81, 9266/81, 9313/81, 9405/81, 8 July 1986 (ECtHR), para 177, where the ECtHR stated that even though a differential measure has a legitimate aim, it will still be regarded as discriminatory if 'there is no reasonable relationship of proportionality between the means employed and the aim sought to be realized'.

[137] *Gaygusuz and Turkey (intervening) v Austria*, App no 17371/90, 16 September 1996 (ECtHR), para 42.

[138] *Inze v Austria*, App no 8695/79, 28 October 1987 (ECtHR), para 41. See also Baetens (n 72) 296–97.

[139] See Sections 1.1–1.3 in this book and Gelpern and Setser (n 71) 795.

[140] Regardless of alleged grounds for discrimination, the ECtHR applies the same type of assessment of whether a state measure, such as a restructuring, violates Art 14 ECHR. See, for example, Baetens (n 72) 293.

differences of treatment'.[141] Although this provides a starting point, the ECtHR's case law fails to establish clear general criteria for what constitutes similar circumstances.

As mentioned above, it follows from the practice of the ECtHR, that differential treatment may be justified under Article 14 in certain circumstances.[142] The ECtHR will often first assess whether the applicants and the group with whom they compare themselves are in like circumstances. Only then will it consider whether discriminatory measures may be justified. Differential treatment that does not pursue a 'legitimate aim' and for which there is no 'reasonable relationship of proportionality between the means employed and the aim sought to be realized' cannot be justified and will violate the prohibition against discrimination.[143] Under this approach, the legitimacy of the aim pursued, the proportionality of the measure, and the state's margin of appreciation do not influence the assessment of whether a situation is to be considered as like or not.[144] However, in some cases, the ECtHR is less clear about the described division and conflates the consideration of whether there are like circumstances and whether differential treatment may be justified.[145] This explains why it is difficult to establish general criteria for what constitutes similar circumstances.

Although a likeness test and the elements justifying discrimination are different concepts, it seems that the ECtHR often discusses the need for and the proportionality of specific measures without first firmly establishing whether the applicant and the group with which the applicant is compared are in like situations or not. Sometime a likeness may be silently assumed, but the discussion of whether the relevant measures have a legitimate aim, are necessary and proportionate makes up the main part of the ECtHR's assessment. This seems to be the case, especially where the outcome is that no violation is found.[146] Whether something is a like situation under the ECHR is to a large extent based on fact. Instead of seeking objective criteria for what constitutes like circumstances then, it may be just as informative to look at the context in which an allegedly discriminatory measure is implemented and examine which measures differentiating between creditors are accepted and which are not.[147]

In the context of sovereign debt restructuring, the legal persons whose likeness will be assessed are all creditors of a sovereign debtor. Many of the creditors even hold debt instruments with identical contractual terms and may be holders of bonds from the same issuance. Thus there are already key factors indicating that creditors are in a similar situation. The next section discusses case law that may shed light on whether all creditors of a sovereign debtor are comparable and which potentially discriminating measures may have a legitimate aim and be deemed necessary and proportionate.

---

[141] See *Lithgow v UK* (n 136) para 177; *Van der Mussele v Belgium*, App no 8919/80, 23 November 1983 (ECtHR); *Fredin v Sweden*, App no 12033/86, 18 February 1991 (ECtHR).
[142] For example, in *Lithgow v UK* (n 136) para 177, where the ECtHR stated that Art 14 does not forbid every difference in treatment 'in the exercise of the rights and freedoms recognized by the Convention'. Rather, '[i]t safeguards persons (including legal persons) who are placed in analogous situations against discriminatory differences of treatment'.
[143] See *Gaygusuz v Austria* (n 137) paras 41–42.
[144] Baetens (n 72) 294.
[145] See, for example, *Mamatas v Greece* (n 119).
[146] This was also the case in *Mamatas v Greece* (n 119), which is discussed further in Section 5.4.4.3.
[147] Baetens (n 72) 309–10.

5.4.4.3 Case law—differential treatment in a sovereign debt context
5.4.4.3.1 Preferential treatment not provided by contract or background law
The only ECtHR case directly discussing discrimination in relation to a sovereign debt restructuring is the previously mentioned *Mamatas* case. In this case, the minority creditors who were forced to participate in the restructuring argued that they had been (inversely) discriminated against because they had been treated equally with other creditors in violation of Article 14 of the ECHR and Article 1 of the First Protocol. The ECtHR held, as discussed, that Greece had not breached the bondholders' right to protection of property because it found that the interference with the property right was proportionate and legitimate. As there was interference with the creditors' property rights, it is still possible to conclude that discrimination under the ECHR had taken place.

In their reverse discrimination claim, the applicants asserted that they were a different type of creditor and in a different situation compared to those who had voluntarily accepted the restructuring. They argued that they were private individuals, including small investors (usually with capital of less than EUR 100,000), holding bonds with a shorter life expectancy and without the level of professional insight legal entities in the financial market might have. As such, they argued that they should be treated differently from the bigger institutional creditors who voted in favour of the restructuring.

The ECtHR rejected the applicants' arguments.[148] First, the ECtHR noted that it would be difficult to identify the persons who should allegedly receive special treatment and thus be exempted from the bond exchange. In part, because the Greek economic crisis had resulted in a highly volatile bond market where sovereign bonds were traded at high frequency, but also because this is the state of the current dematerialized and intermediated global financial market. In general, an attempt to locate bondholders would lead to a prolonged restructuring process, which could hurt the economy of the state even more. Second, even if the bondholders could have been located, the ECtHR stated that it would still have been difficult to draw up specific criteria to legitimately differentiate between the types of creditors: between natural and legal persons or between professional and nonprofessional investors. It is particularly so, the ECtHR held, because the rights enshrined in the bond contract did not (and normally do not) provide reasons for differentiating between bondholders based on status. Nor did the bonds give any guidance regarding what factors should determine different statuses. Third, an announcement exempting specific categories of bondholders from restructuring would likely have led to a massive transfer of bonds to the exempted categories, which might have jeopardized the restructuring agreement.[149]

The applicants' arguments, which rested on consumer protection-like considerations, were rejected both because it was difficult to ascertain that the creditors were in fact consumer-like investors and because there was a legitimate and pressing social need to implement restructuring.[150] On a more general level, the case indicates that it

---

[148] *Mamatas v Greece* (n 119) paras 135–139.

[149] As the consequence would have been that the holders of non-exempted bonds would have had to take a much more drastic haircut to achieve the same reduction in public debt.

[150] In the EU, consumer-like investors are more likely to hold sovereign debt instruments through investment funds or pension funds rather than directly from the sovereign debtor and so could address claims

is an uphill battle for creditors claiming to have the right to special treatment, when this has no basis in background law or in the contract.

In the *Mamatas* case, the ECtHR did not explicitly state that the applicants were in a non-similar situation that required different treatment and thereafter examine whether there were legitimate reasons for not providing such treatment. Instead, it went directly to the assessment of whether the implementation of the alleged discriminatory measures had an 'objective or reasonable justification' in general.[151] Consequently, this case shows that it is difficult to extract objective criteria that can be applied to determine what constitutes similar circumstances. Rather, this case relates more squarely to the issue of which measures providing creditors with differential treatment are accepted and which are not. In the context of this assessment, the ECtHR held that states have a wide margin of appreciation to interfere and regulate for the sake of a public good, including economic crisis resolution and economic stability. By looking to what was contractually agreed when considering whether the various creditors were similarly situated, the ECtHR sought to anchor the wide margin of appreciation provided to the state in the bond terms, thereby taking a contractual market-based approach.

In the case, the ECtHR emphasized the fact that the method used to implement the restructuring was the majority voting procedure, similar to that of CACs, which had just been made mandatory in new sovereign bond issuances in the Euro area and in general was widely accepted by market participants. This indicates that the ECtHR is likely to accept differential treatment implemented through the use of CACs. One might wonder whether majority voting procedures must be identical to the dominant market standard in order to be accepted by ECtHR (and, if so, how this standard should be determined).[152] Is it a specific standard, such as the Euro area model CAC or the International Capital Market Association's (ICMA) standard CACs, applicable at any given point in time? Several arguments speak against a conclusion that the ECtHR refers to only one type of majority voting procedure as legitimate. After all, the Greek majority voting procedure required a lower majority compared to the Euro area model CACs. Moreover, the Greek restructuring allowed for voting across series (aggregation) in a more liberal manner than that envisaged in the initial design of the Euro area model CAC (valid at the time of the case) as well as the then applicable ICMA standard CACs (the new aggregated ICMA standard had not yet been developed). The ECtHR nonetheless accepted the Greek legislation providing for majority voting.

---

concerning economic loss to the fund. If a consumer purchases a sovereign bond and argues that she was not well-informed about the risks or should receive preferential treatment it is more likely that she will have a claim against the bank who sold her the investment product, for not sufficiently informing her about the risk related to the product.

[151] *Lithgow v UK* (n 136) para 116.
[152] Against this view, it can first be argued that Greece's majority voting had a lower threshold and was aggregated across series, and was therefore much more debtor friendly than the Euro model CACs. And it was still accepted by the ECtHR. This indicates that the court refers to the method as such and not the exact design of the majority voting provision. Second, it is not at all clear what the existing market standard is. One may argue that the Euro model CAC in force at a certain time is the market standard in Europe. At the same time, one should keep in mind that ICMA, the IMF, and the G20 have promoted a stricter standard than the one that has been in force in the Euro area for several years and that market practices have developed independently of Euro area legislation.

Accorinti v ECB (Accorinti) is another case that discussed the contractually agreed terms in order to assess whether any bondholders had been discriminated against in a debt restructuring. This case concerned equal treatment rights under the EU Charter and was brought before the Court of Justice of the European Union (CJEU).[153] CJEU judgments based on the EU Charter do not have any bearing on the ECtHR. However, Article 52 of the EU Charter provides that insofar as it contains corresponding rights to that of the ECHR, 'the meaning and scope of those rights shall be the same as those laid down by the said Convention [ECHR]'. It may therefore be of interest to examine the extent to which the CJEU emphasized the contractual provisions compared to the ECtHR in the *Mamatas* case.

Accorinti concerned the question of the ECB's holdings of Greek sovereign bonds during the country's 2012 restructuring. Again, the applicants claimed they had been discriminated against. They argued that the principle of equal treatment of private creditors within the meaning of Articles 20 and 21 of the EU Charter was violated when the ECB concluded the exchange agreement of 15 February 2012 with Greece. The agreement exempted the ECB from partaking in ordinary debt restructuring on the same terms as the other bondholders. Similar to Article 14 of the ECHR, Article 21 of the EU Charter provides creditors with a right to equal treatment if they are similarly situated and to distinct treatment (unless equal treatment is objectively justified) when the creditors are differently situated. When considering whether creditors are similarly situated, the CJEU held that the aim and objective of the creditors must be taken into account—and in particular public interest objectives. It thereafter noted that the ECB's purchase of bonds was part and parcel of their monetary policy programme, an objective that is clearly distinct from that of other private creditors.[154] The CJEU therefore rejected the argument that all individuals who acquired Greek bonds, whether private savers or creditors of Greece, could be compared with the ECB and hence enjoyed equal rights.[155] This justified, in the view of the CJEU, the ECB's exemption from the debt restructuring. It was necessary for the ECB to be given preferential treatment for it to be able to maintain its function in the long run. In *Accorinti*, differential treatment was accepted despite the fact that all creditors were regulated by identical contractual terms, including the *pari passu* clause.[156] Under the EU Charter, the private law instrument was found not to be decisive when interpreting the public law threshold for equal treatment.

Mamatas and *Accorinti* differ in their approach to how much weight should be put on the bond terms when deciding whether the respective claimant creditors are in

---

[153] The CJEU is divided into two courts: the Court of Justice and the General Court. The former deals with requests for preliminary rulings from national courts and certain actions for annulment and appeals. The latter deals with rules on actions for annulment brought by individuals, companies, and EU governments. For simplicity, the book uses the term CJEU when discussing cases from both courts.

[154] *Accorinti and Others v European Central Bank* [2015] ECLI:EU:T:2015:756 [90].

[155] ibid [88], [89].

[156] ibid [91] states: '[a]lthough, under the applicable private law, when purchasing State bonds those central banks, like the private investors, acquired the status of creditors of the issuing and debtor State, that single point in common cannot justify their being regarded as being in a comparable, or indeed identical, situation to that of those investors. In fact, such an approach, taken solely from the viewpoint of private law, does not take account of either the legal framework of the operation involving the purchase of those bonds by the central banks or the public-interest objectives.'

similar situations compared to 'the other' creditors in the restructuring. They are, however, similar in the sense that they both take a comprehensive approach to their assessment, focusing on the legitimacy and the proportionality of the measure—the restructuring—and whether or not preferential (*Accorinti*) or equal (*Mamatas*) treatment can be justified under the EU Charter and the ECHR respectively. Moreover, both seek to safeguard the negotiated crisis resolution and the established debt restructuring agreement.

5.4.4.3.2 Nationality-based discrimination
As mentioned in the Introduction, nationality-based discrimination is one of the grounds specifically prohibited in Article 14 of the ECHR. In *Gaygusuz v Austria*, the ECtHR extended limited discretion to states to grant differential treatment based on nationality. In the case, the Turkish claimant (Gaygusuz) had been refused a pension benefit under the Austrian Unemployment Insurance Act. The applicant had contributed to the Austrian welfare scheme on equal terms as Austrian citizens throughout his working life. However, Austria argued that the relevant benefits were restricted to Austrian citizens. The ECtHR held that Article 14 was violated as nationality was the only reason given for differential treatment. The ECtHR noted that only 'very weighty reasons' could justify ECHR-compatible differential treatment based exclusively on the ground of nationality.[157]

The earlier mentioned *Lithgow v UK* can be interpreted as moderating the strict approach adopted in *Gaygusuz*. This case concerned proceedings arising from the nationalization of seven companies. The majority of the companies concerned were not listed on the stock exchange, so compensation was assessed on the basis of a hypothetical stock exchange quotation.[158] The applicants claimed, among other things, that they had not been adequately compensated and that the nationalization constituted a breach of their right to protection of property under Article 1 of the First Protocol of the ECHR. The applicants further claimed that to treat general principles of international law as inapplicable to expropriation by a state of property belonging to its own nationals would permit differential treatment on the ground of the nationality, which would be incompatible with Article 14 in conjunction with Article 1 of the First Protocol. The basis for the applicants' claim was the second sentence of Article 1 of the First Protocol, which refers to general principles of international law. The court rejected this view by referring to the ECHR preparatory works. However, it did also note that there could be good reasons to draw a distinction between nationals and non-nationals:

> Especially as regards a taking of property effected in the context of a social reform or an economic restructuring, there may well be good grounds for drawing a distinction between nationals and non-nationals as far as compensation is concerned. To begin with, non-nationals are more vulnerable to domestic legislation: unlike nationals, they will generally have played no part in the election or designation of its authors nor have been consulted on its adoption. Secondly, although a taking of property must

---

[157] *Gaygusuz v Austria* (n 137) paras 41–42 [internal quotations omitted]. See also Baetens (n 72) 283.
[158] *Lithgow v UK* (n 136) para 37.

always be effected in the public interest, different considerations may apply to nationals and non-nationals and there may well be legitimate reason for requiring nationals to bear a greater burden in the public interest than non-nationals.[159]

This indicates that the ECHR allows for differential treatment based on nationality, if the justification is 'objective and reasonable'.

As discussed in Sections 1.1–1.3 of the book in particular, there are several sound and legitimate reasons for providing national or foreign creditors with preferential treatment in a restructuring. The most common reason may be that protecting national financial institutions increases the chances of economic recovery and stability (the opposite of the discrimination discussed in *Lithgow v UK*). Depending on the design of the debt restructuring, differential treatment based on nationality may be both a legitimate and a proportionate measure. In today's global market, however, it is arguable how strong this argument actually is. After all, non-resident creditors may hold debt governed by domestic law (denominated in either local or foreign currency) and resident creditors may hold foreign-currency denominated, foreign law debt. Nevertheless, one should not reject the idea that a sovereign debtor may have access to an overview of creditors based on nationality and that differential treatment on this basis could reduce the overall losses the creditors, as a group, might need to bear for a sovereign debtor to reach a sustainable level of debt. Therefore, and as Baetens argues, if all nationality-based differential treatment were prohibited, it would lead to unreasonable results.[160]

5.4.4.3.3 Discrimination between different legislative state measures over time
In the *Lithgow* case just discussed, some applicants also claimed that they had been discriminated against in violation of Article 14 and Article 1 of the First Protocol of the ECHR due to the fact that they had been treated differently to owners of undertakings nationalized under earlier legislation. The ECtHR did not discuss whether the applicants were in an analogous situation to the persons deprived of their possessions under earlier legislation. The court held that the difference complained of did not raise any issues under Article 14, because '[p]arliaments of the Contracting States must in principle remain free to adopt new laws based on a fresh approach'.[161]

This issue is also relevant for debt restructurings. It is not uncommon for sovereign debtors to implement several debt restructurings over time if a debt crisis is not solved by the first restructuring, typically because the number of participating creditors is relatively low. This was the case, for example, in Argentina following the 2001 debt crisis, when the Republic defaulted on approximately USD 100 billion within 152 series of outstanding bonds.[162] In 2005, Argentina made an exchange offer with respect to the bonds in default that were subject to foreign law. Approximately 76% of the bondholders accepted the offer. In 2010, Argentina launched a second debt

---

[159] ibid para 116.
[160] Baetens (n 72) 293.
[161] *Lithgow v UK* (n 136) para 187.
[162] Eugenio Bruno, 'Argentina Debt—The Settlement Clause' (SSRN Scholarly Paper, 17 December 2013) 1.

restructuring, which took the participation level to 93% of the debt in default as of 2001.[163] A debt restructuring agreement may contain contract clauses prohibiting the sovereign debtor from granting preferential treatment to certain creditors in a subsequent restructuring, such as Most Favoured Creditor clauses or Rights Upon Future Offers (RUFO) clauses. Additionally, as was the case in the Argentine 2005 restructuring, the sovereign debtor may promise in legislation not to reopen or to provide better restructuring terms to holdout creditors in the future.[164] However, the *Lithgow* case indicates that differential treatment of creditors in a future restructuring implemented through legislation will not violate the ECHR prohibition on discrimination.

5.4.5 Preliminary conclusion

A sovereign debt restructuring can give rise to a discrimination claim under Article 14 of the ECHR in conjunction with Article 1 of the First Protocol to the ECHR, which protects the right to property, in particular if the restructuring is implemented using coercive tools.

The ECHR prohibits a wide spectrum of discriminatory treatment of legal persons who are in analogous situations. Regardless of the alleged grounds for discrimination, the ECtHR applies the same type of approach to assess whether a state measure, such as a restructuring, violates Article 14 of the ECHR.

In theory, a creditor must first show that they have received less favourable treatment than a comparable creditor or creditor group (or have received equal treatment while being in a different situation). If this is accepted, a sovereign debtor can still argue that the differential treatment had a legitimate aim and was proportionate. When the ECtHR assesses this—whether there is a causal link between the measure (the discriminatory treatment of creditors) and its legitimate objective (debt crisis resolution and economic stability)—it seems to be satisfied with evidence of a reasonable or rational nexus and does not require a strict necessity test.[165]

The determination of whether circumstances are alike is to a great extent fact-based and it is difficult to establish objective criteria to determine what constitutes likeness. Instead of basing its decisions on precise descriptions of the creditors that are in analogous situations, the ECtHR has taken a broader approach, allowing states proportional differential treatment if it is for legitimate policy purposes.[166]

States' margin of appreciation to grant preferential treatment in a sovereign debt restructuring may vary according to the type of discriminatory treatment. For example, if differential treatment is found to be based *only* on nationality, case law suggests that it will be more difficult to justify the measure when compared to other characteristics that describe the aims and objectives of the creditor. Moreover, there is some authority

---

[163] Bruno (n 162).
[164] Argentina enacted the Lock Law (Art 2 of Law No 26,017), which prohibited reopening of the debt exchange offer to non-participating bondholders. In 2010, however, the Lock Law was suspended to enable the second debt exchange. See Martin Guzman, 'An Analysis of Argentina's 2001 Default Resolution' (2020) 62 Comparative Economic Studies 701, 10.
[165] See also Baetens (n 72) 314.
[166] ibid 315.

in favour of taking into account whether or not the contract terms in the debt instrument provide for differential treatment of different types of creditors. For example, when the ECtHR rejected the argument based on consumer protection-like considerations, it referred to the fact that this protection had no basis in background law or in the contract (among other things).

In general, there are numerous legitimate reasons and proportionate measures to justify discriminating between creditors, even when they hold similar or the same type of sovereign debt instruments. The degree of urgency and the gravity of a situation, as well as the complexity of the implementation of a restructuring itself, seem to influence the state's margin of appreciation. The more grave and complex a situation, the more leeway the state seems to be given to design restructuring measures and the higher the chances the court will accept the state's justification for preferential treatment. Alternatively, one might read the ECtHR's practice as evidence that the court is willing to go further to find circumstances that distinguish the applicant from the group with whom they compare themselves in grave economic (or other) crisis situations and so justify the differential treatment.

6
Interconnected and Conflicting Rights

6.1 Introduction

When a sovereign debtor is faced with payment difficulties, it is forced to decide how much it is able to pay and which creditor it will prioritize and pay first. Similarly, in cases where a debt restructuring is deemed necessary, the debtor state must decide how to treat different types of creditors.

Chapters 3–5 have treated intercreditor equity rights arising out of or in relation to debt instruments governed by some domestic law, separate from those governed by international law. Chapter 3 analysed intercreditor equity rules applicable to debt instruments governed by international law. Intercreditor equity rules in domestic law, which are first and foremost applicable to debt instruments governed by domestic law, were examined in Chapter 4. Chapter 5 discussed international law protection of creditors holding debt instruments governed by domestic law. A question that has been left somewhat open—or has been treated only implicitly—in Chapters 3–5 is how intercreditor equity rights stemming from debt instruments governed by international law relate to intercreditor equity claims stemming from debt instruments governed by some domestic law. Moreover, the discussions in Chapters 3–5 have, to some extent, assumed that the debt instruments governed by international law are held by creditors who are subjects of international law and that creditors holding debt instruments governed by domestic law are held by subjects governed by domestic law (only).[1] In reality, the ownership of debt instruments, on the creditor side, is more complex. International law subjects—states and international organizations—may purchase commercial debt instruments governed by some domestic law. Again, the question arises of how potential intercreditor equity rights of an international creditor may affect intercreditor equity rights contained in its debt instruments governed by domestic law.

A debtor state's need to prioritize between creditors encompasses both debt instruments governed by domestic law and international law. This chapter therefore discusses and seeks to clarify how intercreditor rights in international law and intercreditor rights in domestic law relate to each other and how potential *de jure* and *de facto* conflicts between intercreditor equity rights stemming from the different spheres may be solved. Section 6.2 examines how intercreditor equity rules in domestic law may interfere with intercreditor equity rules stemming from international law. Section 6.3 discusses the reverse situation: how intercreditor equity rights

---

[1] The main exception is Chapter 5, which discussed international law protection of creditors holding debt instruments governed by domestic law. These international law rules affecting intercreditor equity are established by states and provide private persons of these states with certain rights. In other words, states have—in various ways—chosen to make international law a part of domestic law of the creditor.

Intercreditor Equity in Sovereign Debt Restructuring. Astrid Iversen, Oxford University Press. © Astrid Iversen 2023.
DOI: 10.1093/oso/9780192866905.003.0007

stemming from international law may interfere with intercreditor equity rights stemming from domestic law.

Not only can sovereign debtors be faced with conflicting intercreditor equity obligations but creditors too can end up in situations where they are subject to conflicting creditor obligations. The main reason is that international law subjects, such as states and international organizations, who have rights and obligations under international law may purchase commercial debt instruments governed by domestic law. The relevant question that arises in this scenario is how the potential intercreditor equity rights of an international creditor may affect intercreditor equity rights and obligations contained in a debt instrument governed by domestic law. Section 6.4 examines official sector holdings of domestic law governed sovereign bonds, more specifically the holdings of the European Central Bank (ECB). The chapter is thus a case study of a situation in which a creditor's intercreditor equity obligations in international law (EU primary law) and a contract provision in domestic law potentially conflict and how such conflicts can be solved.

The following sections do not purport to treat questions of interconnected rights exhaustively. Rather, they seek to draw up the legal starting points for assessments of how intercreditor equity rights stemming from international and domestic law relate to each other and discuss some cases where these issues may occur or in fact have occurred in cases before a court. What will become clear is that not all conflicts between intercreditor equity rights and obligations can be solved. Both sovereign debtors and creditors may face situations where intercreditor equity obligations conflict *de jure* or *de facto*. In these cases, they may be forced to violate one obligation in order to be able to fulfil another.

6.2 Domestic Law Interference with Creditor Rights in Debt Instruments Governed by International Law

The first question is whether an intercreditor equity right stemming from domestic law can interfere with or alter a creditor right in international law governed debt instrument.

The starting point is that domestic law is incapable of *de jure* interfering with or excusing a breach of international law. This means that an intercreditor equity right stemming from domestic law cannot alter intercreditor rights under international law. From the debtor state's perspective, the consequence is that its obligation to pay under a sovereign debt instrument governed by some domestic law cannot excuse a state's payment obligations under international law. There are exceptions to this. As discussed in earlier chapters, international law provides several venues for individuals to elevate their domestic law claims to the realm of international law, in particular through diplomatic protection (Chapter 3) and through treaty-based rights for private domestic law creditors (Chapter 5). Nevertheless, potential recognition of these claims at the level of public international law—whether through judgments or awards from international courts and tribunals or through settlements in international agreements—will receive the same status as all other obligations under international law in accordance with the equality rule (see Section 3.2).

Moreover, factors at the domestic law level can interfere with the *de facto* or *de jure* rights to preferred treatment of creditors who are subjects under international law and who have a claim governed by international law.[2] First, a domestic court can issue orders that impede financial transactions between international law creditors and a sovereign debtor. These include repayment of a creditor claim in relation to a sovereign debt instrument (governed by international law) that has a preferred status under international law. The reason is that, in most jurisdictions, a money judgment can be enforced against the property of a debtor.[3] Hence, there is a risk that a money payment on its way to an international law creditor for the settlement of an international law governed debt obligation can be attached—by means of an order from a domestic court—by another of the sovereign debtor's creditors.[4] One example demonstrating such an interference is one of the many cases between, among other claimants, NML Capital Ltd and Argentina.[5] In this case, holdout creditors from the restructurings following the Argentine economic crisis in the early 2000s (the claimants) sought to attach Argentine funds to fulfil their outstanding claims against Argentina. More specifically, the holdout creditors sought to attach certain funds, held in one of the Argentine Central Bank's accounts at the Federal Reserve Bank of New York, that were allegedly meant to be used to repay the Republic's debts to the International Monetary Fund (IMF). The court concluded that the money held by the Argentine Central Bank in this account was shielded from attachment by the provisions in the US Foreign Sovereign Immunities Act of 1976 (FSIA). In this case, sovereign immunity rules hindered the commercial creditor's attempt (based on a domestic law claim) to impede payment to the IMF (a payment obligation governed by international law). However, not all payments or all parts of a payment route (through various intermediaries) to a creditor who is an international person will necessarily be immune.[6] Under other circumstances, such an attempt at *de facto* interference in an international law payment claim may be possible.

A second factor originating in domestic law that can interfere with an intercreditor equity right under international law relates to the *pari passu* clause and how it may interfere with *de facto* preferred creditor status. The clause guarantees that unsecured creditors are treated equally and is commonly found in sovereign debt instruments (bonds) governed by domestic law. The clause is thoroughly discussed in Section 4.2. The question here is whether this contract clause also requires a sovereign debtor to treat creditors holding international debt instruments on an equal footing with creditors holding domestic debt instruments. The role and function of the *pari passu* clause in ordinary corporate insolvency cases under domestic law is well established. It is less clear how the clause operates in sovereign debt instruments, but two approaches

---

[2] See Rutsel Silvestre J Martha, *The Financial Obligation in International Law* (Oxford University Press 2015) 510.
[3] See, however, Section 2.4 on sovereign immunity.
[4] See also Martha (n 2) 510.
[5] *EM Ltd v Republic of Argentina* 473 F 3d 463 (2d Cir 2007).
[6] By relying on sovereign immunity rules, the Court avoided actually having to consider whether the IMF's right to payment under international law would affect the right of the private creditors to attach property as a means to fulfil a domestic law debt obligation, under New York law. Nevertheless, it constituted an attempt at a *de facto* interference in an international law payment claim.

exist. Under the first approach, the *pari passu* clause is considered to guarantee that all—typically external—unsecured debt ranks equally. The second, and more expansive, interpretation is that the clause, in addition to barring legal subordination, also precludes the debtor from paying certain creditors without at the same time paying pro rata other creditors on the defaulted contract.[7] Again, one of the cases from the long-running dispute between NML Capital Ltd and the Republic of Argentina provides an example.[8] The relevant case was also discussed in Section 4.2.3.2. In short, the case concerned a hedge fund which held defaulted Argentine sovereign bonds.[9] A restructuring of these sovereign bonds had been attempted a decade earlier, but NML Capital Ltd had refused to take part and had instead chosen to sue for full payment under the original bonds. At the core of this lawsuit was the interpretation of the *pari passu* clause. For the most part, the court seemed to agree with NML Capital Ltd's claim and issued an injunction in conformity with the payment interpretation of the *pari passu* clause stating that the debtor state could choose to default on all creditors or to pay all—both holdout creditors and creditors who accepted to restructure the debt—rateably.

This gave rise to the question whether the injunctive relief obtained by the holdout creditors also encompassed payments to multilateral creditors. Martha notes that the reasoning underlying this decision could be extended to payments to international finance institutions, such as the IMF, and undermines the institution's *de facto* preference.[10] Gulati and Boudrau express a similar concern.[11] They argue that there is a risk that *NML v Argentina* will imply that sovereigns cannot pay some unsecured debtors while neglecting to pay other holders of unsecured debt, unless clear legal priority separates those bondholders. Moreover, they argue that de facto preferred creditor status—like the one enjoyed by multilateral financial institutions, such as the IMF— 'simply no longer cuts it'.[12]

In the judgment, the Court limits itself to treating the questions raised by the claimants.[13] Nevertheless, the Court touched upon this issue:

> We are not called upon to decide whether policies favoring preferential payments to multilateral organizations like the IMF would breach pari passu clauses like the one at issue here. Indeed, plaintiffs have never used Argentina's preferential payments to the IMF as grounds for seeking ratable payments. Far from it; they contend that 'a sovereign's de jure or de facto policy [of subordinating] obligations to commercial unsecured creditors beneath obligations to multilateral institutions like the IMF would not violate the Equal Treatment Provision for the simple reason that

---

[7] Martha (n 2) 511.
[8] *NML Capital, Ltd v Republic of Argentina* No 08-cv-6978 (TPG) (SDNY 21 November 2012); 727 F 3d 230 (2d Cir 2013).
[9] See *NML Capital, Ltd v Republic of Argentina* (n 8).
[10] Martha (n 2) 513.
[11] Melissa Boudreau and G Mitu Gulati, 'The International Monetary Fund's Imperiled Priority' (2014) 10 Duke Journal of Constitutional Law & Public Policy 119.
[12] ibid 146.
[13] It should be noted that NML had little interest in going after IMF funds because Argentina had already paid off all its obligations to the IMF, see ibid 121.

commercial creditors never were nor could be on equal footing with the multilateral organizations.[14]

By referring to the claimant's argument, it could be argued that the Court indirectly seemed to support the view that commercial creditors and multilateral organizations (such as the IMF) would never be on equal footing under New York law.

As discussed in Section 4.2, the support for the payment interpretation of the *pari passu* clause is weakened, as are the risks related to it. The theoretical possibility of domestic courts interpreting a covenant of a debt instrument as prohibiting payment to creditors of debt instruments governed by international law—and issuing an injunction to enforce it—is still alive and therefore a valid concern. That being said, it is important to note that, regardless of whether a domestic court finds that a contract provision prohibits payment or preferential treatment of debt instruments governed by international law under domestic law, this does not affect a sovereign debtor's payment obligations under public international law. As discussed in Section 3.2, it follows from the PCIJ case, *Société commerciale de Belgique*, that a sovereign debtor cannot justify non-fulfilment of a public international law obligation (non-payment of a debt regulated by international law) to a multilateral creditor or another state based on the *pari passu* clause or domestic law in general.[15]

6.3 International Law Interference with Creditor Rights in Debt Instruments Governed by Domestic Law

How international law may affect or interfere with the rights of creditors holding debt instruments governed by domestic law depends on the law of the forum and the governing law of the debt instrument.[16] Whether intercreditor equity rights stemming from international law supersede an intercreditor equity right in domestic law and can even excuse a breach of a domestic intercreditor equity right will therefore vary across jurisdictions.

Both cases discussed in Section 6.2 are examples of how domestic law may potentially interfere *de facto* with payment obligations under international law. However, they are also relevant when examining how creditor rights arising from international law governed debt instruments relate to or interfere with creditor rights in domestic law governed debt instruments. The first case asked whether holdout creditors could attach money held by the Argentine Central Bank, when these sums had been set aside to pay the IMF.[17] To answer this question, the court would have had to consider

---

[14] *NML Capital, Ltd v Republic of Argentina* 699 F 3d 246, para 260 (2d Cir 2012).
[15] Société commerciale de Belgique (*Belgium v Greece*) (Judgment) (1939) PCIJ Series A/B no 78 (hereafter *Société commerciale de Belgique*), para 20.
[16] On the topic of incorporation and interpretation of international law in various jurisdictions, see, for example, Dinah Shelton, *International Law and Domestic Legal Systems: Incorporation, Transformation, and Persuasion* (Oxford University Press 2011). For a view that goes beyond the monist–dualist dichotomy when describing the relationship between international law and domestic law, see, for example, Janne E Nijman and André Nollkaemper, *New Perspectives on the Divide Between National and International Law* (Oxford University Press 2007).
[17] *EM Ltd v Republic of Argentina* (n 5).

whether, as a matter of New York law, the IMF's right to payment under international law superseded the right of the private creditors to attach property as a means to fulfil a domestic law debt obligation. However, by relying on sovereign immunity rules to reject the holdout creditors' claim, the court avoided actually having to answer this question.

The second case discussed above concerned the interpretation of the *pari passu* clause, where the court had forbidden Argentina from paying certain creditors without also paying the holdout creditors on a pro rata basis.[18] The question relevant to this section is whether Argentine payments to the IMF (an obligation governed by public international law) breached the *pari passu* clause in a domestic law governed bond. If the court had dwelled on the question, it would have had to consider whether the IMF in fact had preferred creditor status in international law and thereafter whether this preferred status superseded contractual obligations.

A similar question is whether an acquired status as a preferred creditor of a claim under international law may affect a previously existing debt obligation governed by domestic law that contains a *pari passu* clause. That is, can an undertaking governed by international law be construed as a violation of a contract obligation governed by domestic law? In the described situation, a creditor holding the domestic law governed bond would potentially have an action against the debtor on the basis of breach of contract under the proper law of the loan agreement and subject to the scope of the underlying loan agreement. Whether such a claim succeeds depends, as earlier established, on the interpretation of the contract, the law of the forum where the suit is brought, and the relevant rules on immunity.[19]

There are several techniques in domestic law applied by domestic courts to make domestic law compatible with international law. As discussed in Chapter 5, international law may provide an extra layer of intercreditor equity rights for private individuals holding debt instruments governed by domestic law (eg through international investment treaties, human rights treaties such as the European Convention on Human Rights (ECHR), and the minimum standards in customary international law). Such international protection will typically form part of the domestic law requirements that a sovereign debtor is obliged to respect when implementing a sovereign debt restructuring.

There may be intercreditor equity conflicts between creditors holding debt instruments governed by international law and creditors holding debt instruments governed by domestic law that cannot be interpreted to be consistent with one another. One example may be the aforementioned situation where a later acquired status as a preferred creditor of certain claims under international law may violate a *pari passu* clause in a previously existing debt obligation governed by domestic law. In this scenario, the sovereign debtor who has extended a preferred status to the international creditor is forced to breach either its international law obligations or its domestic law obligations.

Borchard offers a pragmatic solution for sovereign debtors facing such conflicting obligations; he holds that sovereign debt instruments owed to other states are in a preferred position. The reason, he argues, is that violations of obligations arising out of

---

[18] *NML Capital, Ltd v Republic of Argentina* (n 14).
[19] Martha (n 2) 512, n 92.

contractual relations between governments and private individuals entail different legal consequences compared to contracts between states that are governed by international law. He explains this in the following manner:

> While mere default on a governmental loan contract with private individuals is not a breach of international law and becomes a matter of international concern only if the home state of the injured creditor, invoking an exceptional ground, espouses their claim and brings diplomatic pressure upon the defaulter, non-payment of a debt incurred by one state toward another amounts to an international delinquency exposing the wrongdoer to the appropriate sanctions of the international law.[20]

Borchard explains that a state cannot be required to sacrifice its independent existence to the preservation of its credit with private nationals of another state. It therefore follows, he argues, that 'no objections can be raised against a debtor state's fulfilling its international law obligations in times of financial difficulties, in preference to obligations owing to foreign individuals'.[21]

It is not obvious that Borchard's approach is beyond criticism. The economic and reputational consequences can be detrimental for sovereign debtors who default on debt obligations governed by domestic law. In addition, the international investment regime and protection under the ECHR has grown since Borchard's work was published and states are now commonly sanctioned at the international level for violations of domestic debt obligations. The choice of whether to honour a debt obligation governed by domestic law or a debt obligation governed by international law is more likely to depend on other economic, political, and legal factors influencing the particular sovereign debtor.[22]

6.4 Conflicting Creditor Obligations—A Case Study of the ECB's Holdings of Domestic Law Governed Sovereign Bonds

6.4.1 Introduction

To some extent, the discussions in Chapters 3–5 have assumed that the debt instruments governed by international law are held by creditors who are subjects of international law and that creditors holding debt instruments governed by domestic law are held by subjects governed by domestic law only.[23] In reality, the ownership of debt

---

[20] Edwin M Borchard, *State Insolvency and Foreign Bondholders*, vol 1 (Yale University Press 1951) 350. He mainly discusses foreign bondholders and not domestic bondholders, without this necessarily affecting the statement.

[21] ibid.

[22] See Section 2.5.2, which discusses why debtor states should prioritize payment obligations to international lenders of last resort.

[23] The main exception is Chapter 4, which discussed international law protection of creditors holding debt instruments governed by domestic law. These international law rules affecting intercreditor equity are established by states and provide private persons of those states with certain rights. In other words, states have—in various ways—chosen to make international law a part of domestic law of the creditor.

instruments is more complex. In particular, one complicating factor is that official sector institutions, such as multilateral creditors, which are subjects of international law, may purchase commercial debt instruments governed by domestic law.

The question that arises when such creditors hold debt instruments governed by domestic law are similar to those discussed in the two foregoing sections: how do intercreditor equity rules stemming from international law relate to intercreditor equity rules stemming from domestic law? The difference is that the previous sections focused on how a sovereign debtor must balance domestic law rules and international law rules concerning intercreditor equity when implementing a debt restructuring, while this section concerns challenges that certain creditors face when forced to balance intercreditor equity rules stemming from the two legal spheres.

Chapter 3 concluded that no creditors have a preferred status under customary international law and that such a right only can be acquired through an act of will. Moreover, it is clear that the ECB does not claim to have acquired such a preferred creditor status with regard to its holdings of sovereign bonds.[24] There are, however, other rules in international law that may result in an indirect requirement to treat the ECB preferentially. The following section discusses the ECB's holding of sovereign bonds and whether the institution's obligations under international law—and more specifically the Treaty of the Functioning of the European Union (TFEU)—conflicts with intercreditor equity rights under domestic law.

6.4.2 The ECB's obligations and the TFEU

As a starting point, multilateral finance institutions holding debt instruments subject to domestic law will find themselves in the same position and are bound by the same contract provisions as all other creditors. However, two rules in particular in primary EU law can be problematic and may challenge this starting point when the ECB acquires sovereign bonds. First, Article 123(1) TFEU holds that

> [o]verdraft facilities or any other type of credit facility within the European Central Bank or with the central banks of the Member States … in favour of central governments … shall be prohibited, as shall the purchase directly from them by the European Central Bank or national central banks of debt instruments.

This is commonly referred to as the prohibition against monetary financing of EU Member States.[25]

Second, Article 125(1) TFEU provides that '[t]he Union … [or a] Member State shall not be liable for or assume the commitments of central governments, … of another

---

[24] See Section 3.5.4.2. The European Stability Mechanism (ESM) does not claim preference for the Secondary Market Support Facility (SMSF). It is also clear that the two ECB programmes that allow the purchase of sovereign bonds—the Outright Monetary Transactions (OMTs) and the Public Securities Purchase Programme (PSPP)—are not intended to have preferred status in a restructuring.

[25] It also prohibits the financing of 'Union institutions, bodies, offices or agencies, central governments, regional, local or other public authorities, other bodies governed by public law, or public undertakings of Member States'.

Member State'. This clause constitutes a prohibition against bailing out a Member State (the no-bailout clause).

Several cases have been brought before the Court of Justice of the European Union (CJEU) against the ECB to challenge the legality of its programmes. Cases have also been brought against the European Stability Mechanism (ESM), another finance institution that purchases sovereign bonds on the secondary market. These cases shed light on the legality of ECB programmes.

The legality of the ESM's lending practices and purchase of sovereign bonds under EU law was first challenged in *Pringle v Ireland*.[26] The applicants claimed, among other things, that the lending breached the no-bailout clause in Article 125 TFEU. They expressed consternation at ESM lending practices, under which the money of other Euro area countries was being used to help Member States in financial trouble. The CJEU found that Article 125 TFEU did not prohibit the '[European] Union or the Member States from granting any form of financial assistance whatever to another Member State'.[27] The court insisted that purchasing bonds on the secondary market does not thereby make the ESM responsible for the debt of an ESM member owed to that creditor.[28]

The legality of the ECB's crisis programmes has also been challenged in court. In *Gauweiler v Deutcher Bundestag*, the applicants claimed that the ECB's Outright Monetary Transactions (OMT) programme constituted monetary financing and, hence, violated Article 123(1) TFEU.[29] The CJEU found that the OMT programme did not violate primary EU law. The court held that Article 123(1) TFEU prohibited all financial assistance by the ECB to a Member State, but underlined that it 'does not preclude, generally, the possibility of the ECB purchasing from the creditors of such a State, bonds previously issued by that State' on the secondary market.[30] The court further held that the purchases must be considered in the context of the ECB's objectives and its mandate to implement sound monetary policies in the Euro area. The court accepted that the ECB could purchase bonds on the secondary market because this was considered a legitimate monetary policy tool, which served the objectives of the ECB. It underlined, however, that such purchases could not go so far as to undermine the effectiveness of the prohibition in Article 123(1) TFEU. The court stated that 'when the ECB purchases government bonds on secondary markets, sufficient safeguards must be built into its intervention to ensure that the latter does not fall foul of the prohibition of monetary financing in Art. 123(1) TFEU'.[31]

The ECB's programme allowing the purchase of sovereign bonds on the secondary market (PSPP) was challenged before the CJEU in *Weiss v ECB*.[32] The case concerned a request for a preliminary ruling under Article 267 TFEU from the German Bundesverfassungsgericht. The main questions concerned whether the PSPP violated the prohibition against monetary financing enshrined in Article 123(1) TFEU

---

[26] *Thomas Pringle v Government of Ireland and Others* [2012] ECLI:EU:C:2012:756.
[27] ibid [130].
[28] ibid [141].
[29] *Peter Gauweiler and Others v Deutscher Bundestag* [2014] ECLI:EU:C:2015:400.
[30] ibid [95].
[31] ibid [102].
[32] *Heinrich Weiss and Others v European Central Bank* [2018] ECLI:EU:2018:1000.

and whether the ECB had acted *ultra vires* in establishing and implementing the programme. First, the CJEU found that establishing and implementing the PSPP did not exceed the ECB's mandate, which according to Articles 127(1) and 282(2) TFEU is to implement monetary policy to maintain price stability.[33] Second, the court considered the implementation of PSPP to be proportionate, since the PSPP did not manifestly go beyond what was necessary to achieve its objective.[34] This decision applied both to the timing and the volume of the programme. Third, the court concluded that the PSPP decision did not infringe the prohibition on monetary financing. The CJEU underscored that the PSPP did not have an effect equivalent to that of a direct purchase of government bonds from the public authorities and bodies of the Member State,[35] nor did the programme lessen the impetus of member states to follow a sound budgetary policy.[36] By referring to the *Gauweiler* case (concerning OMT), the CJEU further held that, in principle, the legality of the purchase of government bonds on secondary markets by the ECB is not open to question. The validity of a specific programme, such as the PSPP, was said to depend on the guarantees surrounding it. The CJEU held that the guarantees described in the *Pringle* case were sufficient. As a consequence, the PSPP did not violate Article 123(1) TFEU.[37]

The implementation of debt restructuring represents the point where the issue of bailout or monetary financing is most acute. However, none of the aforementioned cases explicitly dealt with the question of whether the ECB, or its specific bond acquisitions (and extensions of ordinary loans), should enjoy a preferred status in a potential debt restructuring.[38] The fact that the Court did not discuss the issue of restructuring might be interpreted as acceptance of the risk that the ECB must bear any economic losses that befall it. In the cases discussed above, the CJEU noted that when Euro institutions facilitate credit, extend loans and purchase sovereign bonds on secondary markets, debtor countries are expected to repay their loans in line with the underlying contracts and according to ordinary market practice. At the same time, the CJEU admits that these activities do come at a risk, including the possibility that the creditor will not be repaid. However, this risk of loss is inherent in the market and is equal for all market actors, private as well as public (international law) investors. Even though the court did not discuss the ECB's preferred creditor status directly, it did reject the argument that the mere existence of this risk in the discussed activities should result in the bond acquisitions being prohibited under Articles 123(1) and 125(1) TFEU.

---

[33] See discussion in ibid [46]–[70].
[34] ibid [79]–[99].
[35] ibid [101]–[128].
[36] ibid [129]–[144].
[37] The court also rejected the claim that PSPP was not compatible with Art 123(1) TFEU because it allowed the ESCB (i) to hold bonds purchased until maturity and (ii) to purchase bonds at a negative yield. ibid [145]–[158].
[38] In *Weiss v ECB*, the German Bundesverfassungsgericht asked 'whether it is compatible with Art. 4(2) TEU and Art. 123 and 125 TFEU for a decision of the ECB to provide for the entirety of the losses that might be sustained by one of the central banks following a potential default by a Member State to be shared between the central banks of the Member States, in a context in which the scale of those losses would make it necessary to recapitalise that central bank'. However, the court found the question inadmissible, as at the current stage it remained hypothetical. See ibid [159]–[167].

6.4.3 The ECB's participation in debt restructurings

What happens when the risk of the sovereign debtor being unable to perform on its sovereign bonds actually materializes? *Accorinti v ECB* from 2015 sheds light on the difficulties the ECB may encounter if and when a restructuring of the bonds it holds is attempted. *Accorinti* concerned the question of the ECB's holdings of Greek sovereign bonds affected by the 2012 restructuring.[39] The case was brought to the CJEU by holders of Greek bonds. The applicants argued that EU law had been breached when the ECB (and the national central banks) concluded the exchange agreement of 15 February 2012 with Greece, which exempted the bank from partaking in ordinary debt restructuring on the same terms as other bondholders.[40] More specifically, they argued that Article 123(1) TFEU—the prohibition against monetary financing—was violated because the ECB did not suffer losses on the same basis as private creditors, but rather concluded a preferred exchange agreement. The CJEU rejected the claim because, as mentioned, the exchange agreement was precisely intended to avoid the involvement of the ECB in the restructuring of Greek public debt. On the contrary, the Court stated that such unconditional involvement could have been classified as an intervention, as it would have had an effect equivalent to that of the direct purchase of state bonds by those central banks, which is prohibited by Article 123 TFEU.[41] As a result, this decision indicates that the CJEU may view an ECB vote (or that of another Euro area central bank) in favour of restructuring as a violation of EU primary law.[42]

On this point, the CJEU's line of argument in *Accorinti* may appear to conflict with the previously discussed cases, particularly *Gauweiler* and *Weiss*. To reiterate, in their constituent documents or by more informal means, the ECB has insisted that it agrees to be treated equally with other bondholders in accordance with the bond terms. Moreover, the case law discussed above concluded that the design of the programmes was not in violation of EU law. As a consequence, they could be taken to support (or at least accept) the idea that the ECB, when holding sovereign bonds, may be treated as an equal with regard to other privately held debt. There is an interpretation that might help align *Accorinti* with the previously discussed case law: while the ECB formally accepts *pari passu* treatment, this does not imply that the Euro area system allows it to *voluntarily* vote in favour of a debt restructuring.[43] The *Accorinti* case indicates that voluntarily writing down claims on these bonds could violate the prohibition against monetary financing (Article 123 TFEU, Article 21 ECB Statute). To avoid voting against restructuring and jeopardizing the successful implementation of a crisis resolution measure, the ECB may seek a preferential restructuring deal (or to be exempted

---

[39] *Accorinti and Others v European Central Bank* [2015] ECLI:EU:T:2015:756.
[40] The case is further discussed in Section 5.4.4.3, as the applicants also claimed, unsuccessfully, that the principle of equal treatment of private creditors was violated in the restructuring.
[41] *Accorinti v ECB* (n 39) [114].
[42] For further discussion about the ECB and whether participation in a debt restructuring may violate Art 123(1) TFEU, see Sebastian Grund and Filip Grle, 'The European Central Bank's Public Sector Purchase Programme (PSPP), the Prohibition of Monetary Financing and Sovereign Debt Restructuring Scenarios' (2016) 41 European Law Review 781, 798–99.
[43] ibid.

from the restructuring), as it did in the Greek restructuring example. Under this interpretation, *Accorinti* forces the ECB to seek *de facto* preferred treatment.

In sum, the main finding by the CJEU in *Pringle*, *Gauweiler*, and *Weiss* is that the various official ECB programmes involving the acquisition of bonds on the primary and secondary markets do not, as such, constitute a bailout or transfer of money to the debtor state. The programmes do not therefore violate Articles 123(1) or 125(1) TFEU. In the cases mentioned above, the court did however state that, *when* the relevant institutions facilitate credit, extend loans, and purchase sovereign bonds on secondary markets, they must ensure sufficient safeguards in their design for it to be in conformity with EU law. The circumstances in which and the extent to which the ECB can be treated equally with other creditors when a debtor cannot service all its debts as they fall due or seeks to implement a debt restructuring remains to be clarified by future case law. The *Accorinti* case did indicate that the ECB may violate EU law, in particular Article 123(1) TFEU, if it participates in debt restructuring, at least insofar as it actively votes in favour of it if a CAC is activated.

Following a strictly legal interpretation, it is true that the ECB does not claim preferential treatment insofar as it follows and is bound by the contract terms of the debt instruments on equal terms with other bondholders. It can nevertheless be argued that it is somewhat misleading to say that the ECB accepts equal treatment, if it is *de facto* forced to be a permanent holdout creditor in majority voting procedures where CACs are activated.

An ECB policy of always voting against restructuring may constitute a significant disruptive element in a crisis-struck state's endeavour to implement resolution measures. Knowing that these institutions will not vote in favour of a restructuring may make it easier for other holdout creditors to block a successful debt restructuring. The particular legal framework that regulates the ECB's operations forces it to seek to avoid debt restructurings. By potentially being obliged to vote against restructuring, the ECB may even undermine its own objectives to maintain financial and monetary stability in the Euro area. It also risks undermining the objective behind the mandatory implementation of CACs in Euro countries. CACs are currently the most important mechanism in the EU to solve collective action problems—the situation in which minority creditors can insist on preferred treatment—and ease debt restructuring (see Section 4.3).

This ECB example demonstrates the consequences of an uncoordinated framework for sovereign debt crisis resolution with disparate rules affecting intercreditor equity. The ECB has chosen a pragmatic solution to the challenge encountered in a situation where it is bound by both domestic and international law rules that each seem to pull in opposite directions. However, and as has been discussed in the previous sections in the context of sovereign debtors' obligations, there may be a situation where creditors who are international law subjects but who also act on the private law market will have to choose between violating a domestic law obligation or an international law obligation.

7
Systemic Challenges and the Future of Intercreditor Equity Disputes

7.1 Introduction

The topic of intercreditor equity forms part of a broader debate concerning the legal framework governing sovereign borrowing and debt crisis resolution. A core element of this debate centres on the design of the current legal framework for sovereign debt restructuring and whether it is equipped to solve debt crises in a satisfactory manner. My hope is that analyses of the functioning of one type of rule, as that done in this book, may serve to shed light on risk factors and weaknesses within the regulatory framework at large, and thereby contribute to the broader debate.

This chapter starts by discussing the compatibility of intercreditor equity rules with public policy considerations, defined as a debtor state's need to reach a sustainable debt burden and ensure monetary and financial stability (Section 7.2).[1] This includes a discussion of how the current design of the legal framework governing sovereign debt shapes the functioning of intercreditor equity rules, both individually and together. Different chapters of the book have already touched upon the question of intercreditor equity rules and the surrounding legal frameworks' compatibility with public policy considerations indirectly. Section 7.2.1 categorizes the various intercreditor equity rules to assess the extent to which they share underlying objectives and pull in the same direction. It finds that the risk of rules directly conflicting is not acute. Nevertheless, the underlying objectives are not sufficiently coherent to actively decrease the risk of intercreditor conflicts and increase the chances of reaching a sustainable debt restructuring agreement. Section 7.2.2 turns to discuss the debtor state's room for manoeuvre to provide creditors with differential treatment in a restructuring, with the aim of ensuring sustainable debt restructuring. Section 7.2.3 continues by discussing the debtor state's room for manoeuvre within the broader legal framework. More specifically, it looks back at the rules concerning governing law, the jurisdiction of courts, and sovereign immunity discussed in Chapter 2 and examines the extent to which debtor states are prevented from using their sovereign powers to dampen intercreditor disputes and manage a debt crisis. Section 7.2 concludes that there is limited room for improvement of intercreditor equity rules to reduce intercreditor equity conflicts and thereby contribute to improving the chances of successful debt restructuring. As long as the overall design of the legal framework governing sovereign debt is fragmented and dominated by market solutions, intercreditor equity disputes will continue to pose a risk to sustainable debt crisis resolution.

---

[1] See discussion on sustainable debt restructurings in Section 1.4.2.

Intercreditor Equity in Sovereign Debt Restructuring. Astrid Iversen, Oxford University Press. © Astrid Iversen 2023.
DOI: 10.1093/oso/9780192866905.003.0008

Section 7.3 explores the potential developments that may reduce intercreditor equity disputes in the future and so improve the overall legal framework governing sovereign debt. Section 7.3.1 examines whether a general principle of international law in line with Article 38(1)(c) of the International Court of Justice (ICJ) Statute is emerging. Such a principle may work as a tool of cohesion, contributing to pushing the interpretation of intercreditor equity rules in the same direction and thereby creating a more coherent legal framework.[2] Last, Section 7.3.2 offers some concluding remarks. More specifically, it discusses the need for (and the likelihood of) more comprehensive legal reforms that effectively deal with intercreditor equity disputes, diverging intercreditor equity rules, and the challenges they pose to sustainable debt crisis resolution.

7.2 Systemic Challenges

7.2.1 Fragmentation and diverging objectives

The various chapters of this book have made it clear that states acquire credit from creditors who are subjects of public international law as well as domestic law and they have payment obligations that stem from debt instruments governed by both domestic and international law. A number of rules belonging to different sub-areas of law—such as domestic contract law, international investment law, and international human rights law—influence creditors' intercreditor equity rights in the context of sovereign debt restructuring.

From a creditor's point of view, it can be hard to get an overview of the relevant intercreditor rights applicable to their particular situation. It is also challenging to foresee which rights other creditors have and how they may use these rights to negotiate or litigate to obtain a preferential restructuring deal. From a debtor state's perspective, it can be difficult to get an overview of the relevant intercreditor equity rights and obligations of its various creditors. As a result, the restructuring process is less predictable. Legal uncertainty regarding these questions increases the level of conflict in debt restructuring, drags out the restructuring process, prolongs sovereign debt crises, inflicts unnecessary losses on the creditor group as a whole, and contributes to higher borrowing costs for states.[3]

Hopefully, in clarifying the content and scope of core intercreditor equity rights and obligations applicable in the context of sovereign debt restructuring, Chapters 3–5 will help reduce the level of conflict in future sovereign debt restructurings and increase the chances of achieving sustainable outcomes. Despite detailed and thorough knowledge of the various rules and requirements, however, there remains a risk that some

---

[2] Mads Andenas and Ludovica Chiussi, 'Cohesion, Convergence and Coherence of International Law' in Mads Andenas and others (eds), *General Principles and the Coherence of International Law*, vol 37 (Queen Mary Studies in International Law, Brill Nijhoff 2019) 33–34.
[3] On the issue of 'too little, too late', see IMF, 'Sovereign Debt Restructuring—Recent Developments and Implications for the Fund's Legal and Policy Framework' (Policy paper, 26 April 2013). See also Brett House and others, 'Sovereign Debt Restructurings: The Costs of Delay' (10 April 2017). See also Section 1.4.2 of this book.

of the intercreditor equity rules pertaining to different sub-areas of law will pull in different directions or will be directly contradictory.

Chapter 6 made it clear that not all conflicts between intercreditor equity rights and obligations can be solved. Both sovereign debtors and creditors may face situations where intercreditor equity obligations conflict *de jure* or *de facto*. They may be forced to choose between violating one obligation to be able to fulfil another. These situations further increase the potential for intercreditor conflict and further complicate the restructuring process. However, it is not evident that all intercreditor equity rules will conflict. Sections 7.2.1.1–7.2.1.3 examine the extent to which the various intercreditor equity rules discussed in Chapters 3–5 share underlying objectives and pull in the same direction, thereby reducing intercreditor conflict and increasing the chances of reaching a sustainable restructuring outcome. There, I argue that intercreditor equity rules, broadly speaking, can be divided into two categories: (i) ranking rules, and (ii) non-discrimination rules extending protection to creditors or curbing creditor rights based on the creditor's aims and objectives. In the following, these two categories will be examined separately.

7.2.1.1 Ranking and preference rules

The first type of rules, defined as ranking rules, are sometimes also referred to as rules of preference in the literature.[4] However, these are not equivalent to ranking rules found in domestic corporate insolvencies. The reason is that in a situation where a sovereign debtor faces severe economic problems, it never risks being dissolved. Nor is there a pool of state assets to distribute to creditors. In the context of sovereign debt, ranking (or preference) rules refer to whether or not creditors have: (i) priority in payment (in the temporal sense) if there are not sufficient resources to cover all debt obligations as they fall due; (ii) the right to a preferential restructuring agreement; or (iii) the right to be exempted from a debt restructuring altogether. The term is therefore less strict compared to domestic insolvency law because it does not provide for a clear ladder of priority. The international law rules discussed in Chapter 3 belong to this first category of rules (the equality rule, subordination agreements, preference, and security positions). There are normally no ranking provisions in domestic statutes that are applicable to the relationship between creditors holding various sovereign debt obligations.[5] The *pari passu* clause and the uniform applicability clause, that can be found in bonds governed by domestic law and analysed in Section 4.2, can also be categorized as ranking rules (this categorization would fit both a ranking interpretation and a payment interpretation of the *pari passu* clause).

---

[4] Because the two types of rules may overlap to a certain extent, the various types of rules can be placed on a continuum where the two archetypes of rules are on opposite sides of the continuum.

[5] In some countries, the constitution requires that the repayment of public debts, in particular foreign loans, be prioritized. For example, during the European sovereign debt crisis of 2011–2013, some nations faced with rising borrowing costs adopted commitments to treat bondholders as priority claimants. That is, if there were a shortage of funds, bondholders would be paid first. Spain enshrined in its constitution a strong commitment to give absolute priority to public debt claimants (Section 135.3 of the Constitution of the Kingdom of Spain). See G Mitu Gulati and others, 'When Governments Promise to Prioritize Public Debt: Do Markets Care?' (2020) 6 Journal of Financial Regulation 41, 42.

The ranking (or preference) rules found in international law provide for a customary equality rule—that all debt obligations under international law are independent of each other and rank equally—and exemptions require an express act of will. *De jure* subordination, preference, and security positions in a sovereign debt instrument are, in the main, established through a treaty (or a passive *de facto* acceptance of a subordinated position by certain creditors). In a similar vein, in debt instruments governed by domestic law, the *pari passu* clause and the uniform applicability clause related to majority voting provisions (collective actions clauses (CACs) and exit consent) regulate intercreditor equity questions in voluntary and negotiated agreements (see Chapter 4).

These ranking rules do not provide preferential or equal treatment for specific groups of creditors based on certain characteristics, nor do they advocate any particular values or 'pull' creditor behaviour in any particular direction. Their objective is simply to provide for a system of ranking or preference for creditors who have purchased or negotiated a certain position. They promote any relative ranking solution that market actors are capable of agreeing on and pricing in. The idea is that the market, consistent with classical liberalism and based on the principle of party autonomy, will best solve issues that arise when a sovereign debtor is unable to fulfil all debt claims as they fall due, such as who should be paid first, who should participate in a debt restructuring, and how to solve the debt crisis itself.

7.2.1.2 Non-discrimination rules related to creditors' aims and objectives

The other category of intercreditor equity rules extends protection to creditors or curbs creditor rights based on certain creditor characteristics or objectives. The decisive factor for whether these rules regulate intercreditor equity issues is whether the basis for discrimination is an interest worthy of protection or one that should be curbed. The objective behind the rules in this category, and whether they pull in the same direction, is discussed in the following.

7.2.1.2.1 Vulture fund legislation

The objective of vulture fund legislation, as discussed in Section 4.4, is to curb certain undesirable creditor behaviour. The legislation seeks to avoid what the respective legislators have perceived to be a challenge to sound sovereign debt restructuring processes: minority holdout creditors purchasing distressed or defaulted debt and then suing (or threatening to sue) the sovereign debtor to obtain full payment under the original loan agreement. As such, the legislation targets free-riders who profit from debtor countries' economic crises. The legislation distinguishes between creditors whose behaviour and aims are legitimate and those whose behaviour and aims are not. It limits the contractual rights of the creditors that belong to the second category. The aim is to honour the debt crisis resolution measures of sovereign debtors, co-creditors, and the international community. It is the legislation itself that defines what is perceived as legitimate. The design of the legislation, including the tools chosen to deal with the problem, varies from one country to another. However, the underlying aim of such legislation—to curb speculative holdout behaviour—is shared.

7.2.1.2.2 Protection of minority creditors from discrimination
CACs and exit consent are contractual tools that make it more difficult for a dissenting minority of creditors to disturb debt restructuring. These clauses may therefore play a similar role to vulture fund legislation. At the same time, the use of majority votes can enable abuse of majority powers and result in discrimination against minority creditors. The aim of the intercreditor equity rules related to these majority clauses—uniform applicability clauses[6] and the good faith standard in English law in particular—is not directly to incentivize a successful restructuring agreement. Rather, it is to protect minority creditors from majority abuse in situations where the majority decide on a disadvantageous debt restructuring, for example, which leaves minority bondholders disproportionately affected by restructuring losses. Clearly then, these rules have a different objective to those included in vulture fund legislation. As noted in Section 4.3, the uniform applicability clauses guarantee that the same type of creditors will receive equal restructuring terms. This includes the minority creditors, even when restructuring is implemented by means of a majority vote. Both the uniform applicability clause and the good faith standard can therefore be categorized as non-discrimination clauses. The threshold for ensuring non-discrimination is not comparable: the uniform applicability clause guarantees the same treatment to all creditors involved in a restructuring; the good faith standard potentially forbids certain forms of differential treatment of minority creditors in more extreme situations (see Section 4.3.7).

7.2.1.2.3 IIAs and the ECHR
Creditors who hold debt instruments governed by domestic law may be protected against discrimination by International Investment Agreements (IIAs) as well as the European Convention on Human Rights (ECHR). Article 14 ECHR, read in conjunction with Article 1 of the First Protocol, protects creditors who are subject to the jurisdiction of the sovereign debtor from discrimination in cases where a debt restructuring is implemented on a non-voluntary basis. The most relevant IIA clauses in an intercreditor equity context are the National Treatment (NT) and Most Favoured Nation (MFN) clauses, the expropriation clause, and the Fair and Equitable Treatment (FET) clause (see Section 5.3). All clauses contain a non-discrimination element that provides a foreign creditor with protection in a non-voluntary sovereign debt restructuring.

The discussions in Chapter 5 show that the ECHR and IIAs, in particular the MFN and NT standards, seem to provide for a similar structure of reasoning when assessing whether a creditor has been discriminated against in a restructuring, in violation of the respective international agreements. For both the ECHR and IIAs, the claimant creditor must first prove that their claim falls within the scope of the treaty. Second, the claimant must show that they are part of a group of creditors with similar circumstances. Third, it must be demonstrated that there has been differential treatment. To be more precise, the claimant must prove that they have received less favourable

---

[6] The uniformly applicable clause can be categorized both as a treatment protection as well as a ranking provision.

treatment than a comparable creditor or creditor group. The sovereign debtor state can counter the claim that a creditor has been discriminated against by proving: (i) that treatment was not less favourable, or (ii) that the differential treatment was based on a measure causally related to a legitimate aim and was proportionate.[7]

Another factor that IIAs and the ECHR have in common is that the criteria for determining likeness of circumstances are not well developed. MFN and NT standards in investment law focus on 'like circumstances' such as 'same business or same economic situation', without defining either concept.[8] The ECHR uses similarly vague formulations, such as 'persons who are placed in analogous situations'. Baetens writes—and her description fits with the discussion in Chapter 4—that the reason these likeness tests are underdeveloped is that human rights and investment law to a great extent focus on legitimate aims rather than likeness. This results in a 'negative test' where if two situations *prima facie* appear to be alike, and the state cannot provide a legitimate reason for differential treatment, then likeness is assumed. She concludes that the 'comparator pool' in human rights and investment law is *prima facie* very large, although this likeness can be refuted at a later point in time.[9]

Both the European Court of Human Rights (EctHR) and investment tribunals seem to reject the finding of likeness where they have deemed differential treatment to be justified due to the legitimate aims of the regulations at issue. Courts and tribunals have emphasized that likeness must be determined on a case-by-case basis. However, a general tendency seems to be that the legitimacy of an aim is more likely to be approved if it is part of internationally accepted standards.[10]

Moreover, IIAs and the ECHR also require that two causal links be established under the discrimination test. The first is between the measure and the policy it aims to serve (the legitimate objective); the second is between the measure and the injury. In the context of sovereign debt restructurings, this means that: (i) it has to be shown that differential treatment is part of a restructuring that seeks to ensure debt sustainability, and (ii) a creditor that has been treated differently must prove that the differential treatment has resulted in a particular injury.

The similarity in methods for finding discrimination seem to indicate that the substantive norms in IIAs and the ECHR pull in the same direction. To a certain extent this is true with respect to the prohibition against discrimination based on nationality in the ECHR and the MFN and NT standards in IIAs. However, there are some differences. Baetens has found that human rights dispute settlement bodies, including the EctHR, have allowed proportional differentiations (including those based on nationality) for legitimate policy purposes without an explicit basis in the text of human rights treaties but rather as a factor in determining likeness.[11] This stands in contrast

---

[7] Freya Baetens, 'Discrimination on the Basis of Nationality: Determining Likeness in Human Rights and Investment Law' in Stephan W Schill (ed), *International Investment Law and Comparative Public Law* (Oxford University Press 2010) 308.

[8] ibid 309.

[9] Baetens compares this tendency with trade law, where it seems that to a lesser extent no likeness is assumed *prima facie*. Instead, she argues, 'dispute settlement bodies pick and choose what belongs in the comparator pool' (ibid 309–10).

[10] See, for example, *Pope & Talbot Inc v Canada*, UNCITRAL/NAFTA, Award on the Merits of Phase 2 (10 April 2001), paras 77, 87. See also ibid 313.

[11] ibid 315.

to the more strict discrimination assessment based on nationality that is found in IIAs. The object and purpose of the prohibition against discrimination based on nationality is to create a level playing field for foreigners and nationals. However, the stricter approach to establishing likeness and discrimination, found in international investment law, may increase the risk of ending up with more unreasonable outcomes. An emphasis on legitimate policy purposes and proportionality in the implementation of restructuring measures leaves more leeway to balance the interests of the creditors involved and the public interests pursued by the state.[12] Thus, compared to investment law, the ECHR emphasizes these factors to a greater extent when dealing with discrimination based on nationality. More generally—that is, concerning the whole spectre of protection against discrimination under the ECHR—the degree of urgency, the gravity of a situation, and the complexity of the implementation of restructuring will strongly influence the state's margin of appreciation to implement differential treatment if the aim is legitimate.

The discrimination prohibitions contained in the fair and equitable treatment (FET) standard and the prohibition against unlawful expropriation are both different from the MFN and NT standards discussed above. As a result, they are also less similar to the discrimination prohibition found in the ECHR. Under the expropriation clauses, a state can only expropriate property for legitimate reasons and only when providing full compensation. Involuntary or coercive implementation of a debt restructuring may therefore violate an expropriation clause. However, in contrast to the MFN and NT standards, discriminatory intent or effect only serves as a subsidiary or additional element evidencing indirect expropriation.

The core of the FET standard, as developed in practice, protects legitimate commercial expectations. While non-discrimination forms part of the standard, it should not be confused with the non-discrimination standard found in MFN or NT clauses. The non-discrimination elements in FET prohibit discrimination that specifically targets a foreign investor on other manifestly wrongful grounds such as gender, race or religious belief, or other types of conduct that amount to a 'deliberate conspiracy ... to destroy or frustrate the investment'.[13]

The nationality-based protection in NT and MFN is more expansive than the discrimination element in FET and expropriation clauses. At the same time, it is clear that the three standards can be interrelated. For example, it cannot be completely dismissed that a debt restructuring will violate the FET standard if it openly discriminates against (*de jure* or *de facto*) a creditor based on nationality and there is no legitimate

---

[12] ibid.
[13] *Waste Management, Inc v United Mexican States* No. ARB (AF)9/00/3, para 138 (International Centre for Settlement of Investment Disputes 30 April 2004). Also, in *Grand River Enterprises Six Nations Limited and others v United States*, UNCITRAL, Award (12 January 2011), the tribunal held that 'neither Article 1105 [of the NAFTA agreement] nor the customary international law standard of protection generally prohibits discrimination against foreign investments' (para 209). For instance, Art 8.10(2) CETA, the trade agreement between the EU and Canada, lists, among other things, 'manifest arbitrariness; targeted discrimination on manifestly wrongful grounds, such as gender, race or religious belief' and 'abusive treatment of investors, such as coercion, duress and harassment' as factors that should be taken into account in determining a violation of the FET standard. See also UNCTAD, 'Fair and Equitable Treatment: A Sequel' (UNCTAD Series on Issues in International Investment Agreements II, February 2012) 82.

justification for the measure.[14] Moreover, the discriminatory acts that can contribute to a finding of unlawful expropriation can be related to nationality (MFN and NT standards) or other discriminatory treatment based on factors such as sex, religion, and race, which are covered by the FET standard. The latter, however, are less likely to be relevant in a sovereign debt restructuring context.

To summarize, the minimum standard and the various protections under IIAs all protect foreign investors, but with slightly different approaches. While the MFN and NT strictly prohibit discrimination on the basis of nationality, the FET prohibits a narrower spectrum of discriminatory treatment based on, for example, race, religion, sex, or procedural arbitrariness. Similarly, discriminatory treatment is one element that may lead to a finding of unlawful expropriation. It should be assessed in conjunction with the discrimination standard in FET and MFN/NT. The ECHR protects creditors who are under the sovereign debtor state's jurisdiction from discrimination. The prohibition is broadly formulated and covers differential treatment of similarly situated creditors on a general basis, unless a legitimate and proportionate justification exists.

7.2.1.3 Preliminary conclusion

The grouping of rules into ranking rules and non-discrimination rules may initially seem to indicate that the rules belonging to the respective groups share some common objectives or pull in the same direction, thereby increasing the chances of achieving a sustainable debt restructurings. Such a conclusion would be an oversimplification.

First, the ranking rules do not pull in any particular direction. They do not provide preferred or equal treatment for specific groups of creditors with certain characteristics. Their objective is simply to provide a system of ranking or preference for creditors who have purchased or negotiated a certain contractual position according to market logics.

Second, it is true that the various rules in the second category (non-discrimination rules) partly overlap in the way they seek to protect creditors from discriminatory treatment. Vulture fund legislation limits the ability of holdout creditors to obtain illegitimate advantages in a debt restructuring. IIAs and the ECHR (discussed in Chapter 5), the uniform applicability clause (that often forms part of CACs), and the good faith standard under English law in particular (discussed in Section 4.3) prohibit sovereign debtor states and majority creditors from implementing a coercive debt restructuring that differentiates between creditors based on certain illegitimate considerations. At the same time, it is clear that the different rules in this category protect or promote different values, whether that be protecting human rights or ensuring a level playing field for (and fair treatment of) foreign investors. Moreover, most were not created with the sovereign debt restructuring scenario in mind. Vulture fund

---

[14] *Waste Management v Mexico* (n 13). In *Alex Genin v Estonia*, the tribunal emphasized that 'customary international law does not ... require that a state treat all aliens (and alien property) equally, or that it treats aliens as favourably as nationals'. Moreover, the tribunal only considered it a violation of FET if the investor was 'specifically targeted' or if the differential treatment amounted to bad faith. (*Alex Genin, Eastern Credit Limited, Inc and AS Baltoil v The Republic of Estonia* No. ARB/99/2, paras 368, 369, 371 [International Centre for Settlement of Investment Disputes 25 June 2001]). See also Marc Jacob and Stephan W Schill, 'Fair and Equitable Treatment: Content, Practice, Method' in Marc Bungenberg and others (eds), *International Investment Law: A Handbook* (C.H. Beck/Hart/Nomos 2015) 732.

legislation stands out from the other rules in this category as the only rules designed specifically for debt-related issues and seeking to protect the sustainability of debt restructuring. This also means that vulture fund legislation is therefore more likely to be in conflict with the other rules within this second category. While vulture fund legislation typically interferes with holdout creditors' rights, the other rules all seek to protect creditors who are forced to participate in a debt restructuring against differential treatment. For the same reason—because vulture fund legislation typically interferes with creditors' contractual rights—it is also more likely to conflict with contract-based preferences and ranking positions (ranking rules).

Last, the fact that a sovereign debtor and its creditors have broad freedom to conclude agreements concerning rank and preference through acts of will in relation to debt instruments governed by both domestic and international law, inevitably increases the risk that some of these agreements will conflict with one another.

7.2.2 Debtor states' room for manoeuvre

The challenge to sustainable debt restructuring caused by intercreditor equity rules with divergent objectives may be alleviated if the various intercreditor equity rules allow for a certain amount of flexibility in their application. The examination of the intercreditor equity rules in Chapters 3–5 showed that the rules vary greatly in their ability to accommodate a debtor state's need for wiggle room in implementing a sustainable debt restructuring that allows for the differential treatment of creditors. Table 7.1 summarizes the extent to which the various intercreditor equity rules are sensitive to a debtor state's need to provide creditors with differential treatment in a debt restructuring with the aim of reaching a sustainable outcome.

First, ranking and preference rights—the first of the two categories of intercreditor equity rules defined in Section 7.2.1.1—are relative to a state's resources. One example would be that repayment of creditor X will only happen after creditor Y has been fully repaid. Another example is that repayment of one type of creditor must be made on a pro rata basis. Such rules provide rights that are relative to a state's resources and will not generally curb a debtor state's room for manoeuvre. However, a debtor state's ability to reach a sustainable outcome may be compromised if too many creditors have been promised that they will not be forced to participate in the restructuring or, similarly, if the debtor state's current and future resources have been excessively bound up as security for creditors.

Second, the state's freedom to take into account public policy considerations in the second category of rules—the non-discrimination rules that extend protection to creditors or curb creditor rights based on their aims and objectives—also varies. For some rules, the threshold for a creditor to receive protection against discriminatory treatment is relatively high. This is, for example, the case for the good faith standard in English and New York law. Similarly, the FET standard and the discriminatory component of the expropriation standard under IIAs are likely to have high thresholds in the context of a restructuring. The protection against discriminatory treatment under the ECHR covers a broad spectrum of scenarios but affords a crisis-hit state a wide margin of appreciation to implement crisis resolution measures that

Table 7.1 Intercreditor equity rules & room for manoeuvre to implement crisis resolution

	Intercreditor equity rules	Legal basis	Objective/pull	Ranking/preference rules	Non-discrimination rules (protection based on creditors' aims/objectives)	Subject of protection	Room for manoeuvre
PIL*	Equality rule	Custom	Equality in ranking	x		International law creditor claims	Wide
PIL* & National law	Subordination	Treaty	Subordinate ranking	x		International law creditor claims	Medium
	Preference	Treaty	Preference	x		International law creditor claims	Medium
	Security	Treaty	Preference	x		International law creditor claims	Medium
National law	Pari passu	Contract	Equal treatment Payment	x		Creditors	Narrow
			Equal treatment Ranking	x		Creditors	Wide
	Uniform applicability	Contract	Protects minority creditors	x	x	Minority Creditors	Medium
	Good faith	Domestic law	Protects minority creditors		x	Minority creditors	Wide
	Vulture fund legislation	Domestic law (statutes)	Protects a restructuring (participating creditors and debtor states)		x	Sovereign debtor / participating creditors	Wide

International law protection of bonds governed by domestic law	The minimum standard	Custom	Unsettled			Unsettled
	FET	Treaty	Narrow spectrum of discrimination (religion, sex, race, etc)	x	Foreign creditors/ investors	Medium
	Expropriation	Treaty	General discrimination/ arbitrariness	x	Foreign creditors/ investors	Medium
	MFN/NT	Treaty	Discrimination based on nationality	x	Foreign creditors/ investors	Narrow
	ECHR— discrimination		Prohibits broad spectrum of discrimination	x	Creditors under the debtor state's jurisdiction	Wide

*PIL—Public international Law

treat various creditors differently.[15] Of the rules examined in the book, the MFN and NT in IIAs contain the strictest discrimination standards and will presumably allow for few exceptions. In general, rules containing assessments of proportionality, such as the prohibition against discrimination in the ECHR, are more receptive to debtor states' need to take regulatory measures to solve a debt crisis. Vulture fund legislation is the only type of rule to directly seek to safeguard sustainable debt crisis resolution.

To conclude, while some of these rules allow debtor states the flexibility to provide creditors with differential treatment and so ensure a sustainable outcome in debt restructuring, others do not. When issuing debt instruments, states should carefully take this into consideration. For debtor states with a variety of outstanding debts, it will be difficult to mitigate the challenges caused by conflicting and inflexible intercreditor equity rules. The number of potential intercreditor equity obligations a state must take into consideration decreases a debtor state's room for manoeuvre substantially, as they constitute the limit within which the sovereign debtor must create a restructuring offer.

7.2.3 Sovereign powers and privatized economic crisis resolution measures

When states borrow money, they normally (or ideally) do this for public purposes. A public purpose can be defined as a governmental action that purports to benefit the population as a whole.[16] State acts aimed at ensuring monetary and financial stability, including ensuring sustainable debt levels and solving debt crises, have a clear public purpose. In general, the public purpose activities of states and their various branches are governed by constitutional and administrative law. At the same time, when states borrow money and enter the open market, they may also become subject to private law regulation where rules are typically tailored for actors with commercial intentions and objectives. In such situations, there is a risk of regulatory tension. That is, a debtor state's need (and responsibility) to ensure monetary and financial stability and establish sustainable debt burdens may end up being disregarded when states operate in financial markets where rules are designed for profit maximization.[17]

We also see that, when a sovereign debtor enters the capital market under the current regulatory regime, some of its core sovereign powers in the economic area shift from a public to a private law regime. Chapter 2 discussed the rules concerning

---

[15] See *Mamatas and Others v Greece*, App no 63066/14, 64297/14 and 66106/14, 21 July 2016 (ECtHR) and the discussion in Section 5.4.
[16] 'Public Purpose', *Webster's New World Law Dictionary Online* (no date).
[17] The term 'public policy' is used in a number of contexts with different, yet equally valid, definitions. Broadly speaking, public policy refers to implementation (by a state or government) of measures to maintain order and address the needs of citizens. In this book, the term specifically refers to a debtor state's need to ensure monetary and financial stability, including the implementation of crisis resolution measures to ensure a sustainable debt burden in the long run.

governing law, the jurisdiction of courts, and state immunity. In the absence of a comprehensive legal framework dealing with debt crisis resolution, these rules have the potential to protect debtor states seeking to implement debt crisis resolution measures. More specifically, they influence whether foreign courts will accept jurisdiction over a sovereign debt restructuring dispute and thereby impact a sovereign debtor's room for manoeuvre in designing and implementing a sustainable debt restructuring that—against the will of some—may discriminate between creditors.

If a sovereign debtor is able to choose domestic law as the governing law for its debt instruments, it can rely on the so-called local law advantage, which enables a sovereign debtor to unilaterally amend the terms of the debt instrument through domestic legislation. A sovereign debtor whose debt is governed by its own laws therefore has comparatively greater freedom to treat its creditors in the way it deems fit when seeking to implement a sustainable debt restructuring, regardless of the potentially established rights of creditors to specific treatment. From a sovereign debtor's perspective, letting foreign law govern its debt instruments constrains its sovereign powers to intervene in the economy through legislation for public purposes to solve a debt crisis.

Rules concerning court jurisdiction and sovereign immunity also affect a sovereign debtor's ability to implement economic crisis resolution measures. Although having distinct objectives and designs, both types of rules may preclude foreign courts (on a procedural basis) from assessing the lawfulness of (certain) acts of a debtor state. More specifically, and in the context of sovereign debt, they typically reserve certain non-commercial disputes arising under a debt instrument for courts of the debtor state. Chapter 2 revealed that a foreign court's choice to refer to immunity rules or laws on court jurisdiction when rejecting a sovereign debt related case sometimes seems arbitrary. Moreover, the case law discussed in the same chapter demonstrated that courts have different views on whether economic crisis resolution measures interfering with debt contracts are commercial or state acts (*acts iure gestionis* or *acta iure imperii*). If a foreign court concludes that a crisis resolution measure is a commercial act and therefore accepts jurisdiction, it is likely to provide a debtor state with less deference compared to a domestic court when assessing the legitimacy of the debtor state's implementation of a debt restructuring. This is particularly so if the debtor state has used its sovereign powers to deviate from contractual obligations, such as intercreditor equity rights. The main takeaway from the discussion is that if a foreign court accepts a case related to a sovereign debt restructuring because it is perceived as a commercial issue, it is more likely that a debtor state will be treated like a private actor. Consequently, a foreign court is likely to provide a debtor state with less deference if it has deviated from contractual obligations, including intercreditor equity rights, when implementing a sovereign debt restructuring as a crisis resolution measure.

In short, the shift from a public law sphere to a private law sphere proceeds as follows. If a debt instrument is governed by foreign law, it cannot rely on local law advantage to implement a debt restructuring. Moreover, although this varies between jurisdictions, if the debt instrument is governed by foreign law, a debt restructuring is more likely to be classified as a commercial act in relation to sovereign immunity rules and rules concerning court jurisdiction. Consequently, debtor states are less likely to be able to rely on sovereign powers.

This forces debtor states to rely mainly on private law tools to solve a debt crisis, such as voluntary renegotiation of terms and restructuring based on contractual tools, such as CACs. In a situation where state only has access to private law tools to solve an economic crisis, the crisis resolution tools can be said to have been 'privatized'. This evidently affects the debtor state's room for manoeuvre in implementing crisis resolution measures. The challenge for a sovereign debtor is, of course, that it is not protected by any insolvency procedures, such as those available to corporations or private individuals under domestic law. It is therefore more likely to be challenging to reach a sustainable debt level if the crisis resolution framework is privatized.

7.2.4 Preliminary conclusion

Section 7.2 has established that the objectives of the intercreditor equity rules do not necessarily pull in the same direction and may well conflict with one another. Whether the differences in objectives will lead to a clash between intercreditor equity rights in practice is difficult to establish *ex ante* and must be settled on a case-by-case basis. Further, while some of the intercreditor equity rules allow debtor states the flexibility to treat creditors differently in order to ensure a sustainable debt restructuring, others do not. Both factors constitute a challenge for debtor states who seek to implement a debt restructuring.

Whether the above-mentioned risks will materialize leaving a sovereign debtor unable to secure a sustainable debt restructuring depends on the amount of debt outstanding (the density of intercreditor equity rules), the composition of creditors, the international agreements a creditor is bound by, and the intercreditor equity provisions in the various debt instruments (the flexibility of each of these rules).

When issuing debt instruments in the future, states should carefully consider which intercreditor equity clauses they include in their contracts. Carefully drafting contract clauses will only help so much, as several intercreditor rules are found in domestic legislation, international treaties, or general international law. Moreover, debtor states with significant debt burdens are currently likely to be bound by a great number of varying intercreditor equity rules. It is the number of uncoordinated intercreditor equity obligations a state has to comply with that substantially decreases a debtor state's room for manoeuvre, as these obligations constitute the limit within which the sovereign debtor must create a restructuring offer.

Last, sovereign debtors have limited possibilities to use their sovereign powers to implement crisis resolution measures and should carefully consider issuing debt under local law to increase the room for manoeuvre when implementing crisis resolution measures.

7.3 The Future of Intercreditor Equity Disputes

7.3.1 The emerging general principle of good faith as a cohesion tool

7.3.1.1 Introduction
This section discusses good faith as a general principle of international law, its relevance for sovereign debt restructuring processes, and whether it is developing towards encompassing any of the objectives underlying the intercreditor equity rules discussed in Chapters 3–5.

The argument made here is that 'the general principles of law recognized by civilized nations' found in Article 38(1)(c) of the ICJ Statute have the potential to become a tool of cohesion. They could contribute to helping align the different interpretations of intercreditor equity rules found in domestic and international law, and might thereby forge a more coherent legal framework.[18] Their role as a tool of cohesion is facilitated by the fact that general principles of law can be inferred from domestic law as well as international law.

Section 7.2.1 showed that the intercreditor equity rules discussed in Chapters 3–5 can be divided into two categories: (i) ranking rules, and (ii) non-discrimination rules, extending protection to creditors or curbing creditor rights based on the creditor's aims and objectives. There, I concluded that the two types of rules relate to intercreditor equity in different ways and do not share underlying objectives. The two different categories of rules are therefore unlikely to be able to underpin the same general principles. The section also concluded that, even within the same category, the objectives underlying the different rules tend to vary. This may indicate that the general principles found in Article 38(1)(c) of the ICJ Statute cannot be inferred from the totality of existing intercreditor equity rules or either of the two categories of rules. However, I make the argument in this section that certain elements of the second category of intercreditor equity rules (non-discrimination rules, discussed in Section 7.2.1.2) overlap, which suggests that they may in fact underpin a general principle of good faith. If one also takes into account developments in international soft law, resolutions from international organizations, and a possible policy shift in international finance institutions, there are reasons to argue that a good faith principle relevant for intercreditor equity issues in sovereign debt restructurings may be emerging.

---

[18] Andenas and Chiussi (n 2) 33–34. Though the ICJ Statute addresses the applicable law by the Court, general practice has turned Art 38 into an authoritative statement of the sources of international law. See Robert Y Jennings, 'General Course on Principles of International Law' (1967) 121 Collected Courses of the Hague Academy of International Law, 331; Alain Pellet, 'Article 38' in Andreas Zimmerman and others (eds), *The Statute of the International Court of Justice: A Commentary* (Oxford Commentaries on International Law, 2nd edn, Oxford University Press 2012) 731–870; Gleider I Hernández, *The International Court of Justice and the Judicial Function* (Oxford University Press 2014) 31.

Before analysing whether there may be growing support for a good faith principle which encompasses such objectives, Sections 7.3.1.2 and 7.3.1.3 briefly discuss the theoretical starting points from which a general principle can be derived.

7.3.1.2 Formation of general principles of law

It follows from Article 38(1)(c) of the ICJ Statute that, in carrying out its mandate 'in accordance with international law', the ICJ must apply 'the general principles of law recognized by civilized nations'. It is generally accepted that general principles are a source of international law.[19]

General principles of law can be extrapolated from private law principles in domestic legal orders by means of comparative reasoning.[20] General principles are nevertheless formed within the international legal system.[21] Crawford, for example, has shown that general principles of law are 'a body of international law the content of which has been influenced by domestic law but which is still its own creation';[22] an international tribunal chooses, edits, and adapts elements from other developed systems. Moreover, today there seems to be agreement on the point that general principles of law, falling within the scope of Article 38(1)(c) of the ICJ Statute, may also be formed within the international legal system and do not have to have their origin in national legal systems.[23] To establish whether general principles provide any intercreditor equity rules for creditors in, or in relation to, a debt restructuring, it is necessary to examine relevant domestic and international law rules.

Establishing whether a general principle exists under international law is typically a challenging task. For a general principle of law to exist, it must be widely recognized by states.[24] Concerning general principles of international law that are found in or derived from national legal systems, it is generally accepted in the literature, and it follows from practice, that for a general principle to be recognized, it needs to exist within a sufficiently large number of national legal systems.[25] It must be further determined that it is applicable in the international legal system. This is sometimes referred to as

---

[19] See, in general, Marcelo Vázquez-Bermúdez *First Report on General Principles of Law (for International Law Commission, Seventy-first Session)* UN Doc A/CN4/732 (United Nations 2019) (hereafter *First Report on General Principles*).

[20] Hersch Lauterpacht, 'Private Law Analogies in International Law' (PhD, London School of Economics and Political Science 1926) 47, 61ff. Lauterpacht states that it is private law which gives shape and definite form to these general principles in international law. However, he argues that general principles under international law are not based directly on an analogy from domestic law. Rather, '[i]n the general principles of the universally applied private law they find, in theory and in practice, a system of rules built upon experience and upon infinite intellectual labour. It may or may not be accurate when some authors say that, for instance, the adoption of rules governing fluvial accretion is not analogy to private law, but simply application of common sense. But even granted the accuracy of the statement, it does not say anything else than that it is a rule of private law which embodies here a principle of common sense.' (ibid 63). Root and Phillimore, who were both members of the Committee of Jurists that drafted the ICJ Statute (from the United States and the United Kingdom, respectively), regarded general principles as rules accepted in the domestic law of all civilized states. Their views are referred to in James Crawford, *Brownlie's Principles of Public International Law* (9th edn, Oxford University Press 2019) 32.

[21] *First Report on General Principles First Report on General Principles of Law* (n 19) para 257.

[22] See Crawford (n 20) 32.

[23] *First Report on General Principles First Report on General Principles of Law* (n 19) paras 171, 174.

[24] For a discussion on what is meant by 'civilized nations', see, for example, ibid paras 176–187.

[25] ibid para 167.

'transposition'.[26] How to determine that a principle that is common to national legal systems is also applicable at the international level is a subject of debate.[27] According to both Oppenheim and Crawford, Article 38(1)(c) ICJ Statute must apply the general principles of domestic jurisprudence, in particular of private law, insofar as they are applicable to the relations between states.[28]

Assuming that general principles stemming from international law directly are distinct from those deriving form national laws, recognition may need to be established in a different manner.[29] In the International Law Commission (ILC) Report, Special Rapporteur Marcelo Vázquez-Bermúdez explains that different approaches have been suggested by scholars. Some maintain that the general principles of law under this category emerge through a process of deduction or abstraction from existing rules of international law. The requirement of recognition would then be met because the existing rules are already accepted (or recognized) by states.[30] Others have argued that recognition could take the form of acts of international organizations or other international instruments showing the consensus of states on specific matters, such as General Assembly resolutions.[31] Gaja, for example, holds that the decisive element should be the attitude of states and whether they consider themselves bound.[32]

General principles of international law may have different functions. First, it is a widely held view that general principles of law are a supplementary source of international law in the sense that they serve to fill gaps in treaty-based and customary international law, or to avoid findings of a *non liquet*.[33] Second, in addition to being a direct source of rights and obligations, it has been suggested that general principles of law, may serve as guidelines for interpretation and application of other rules of international law[34] or contribute to reinforce legal reasoning.[35] Third, a more abstract role is, according to the Special Rapporteur, sometimes attributed to them, such that they inform or underlie the international legal system, or that they serve to reinforce its systemic nature.[36] Last, due to the fact the general principles are inferred from both domestic and international law principles, general principles may have a cohesive role.[37] In the context of sovereign debt restructuring, general principles concerning intercreditor equity may, for example, be an interpretative guideline ensuring

---

[26] ibid para 169.
[27] ibid para 229.
[28] See Crawford (n 20) 32.
[29] *First Report on General Principles First Report on General Principles of Law* (n 19) para 171.
[30] See, for example, Paolo Palchetti, 'The Role of General Principles in Promoting the Development of Customary International Rules' in Mads Andenas and others (eds), *General Principles and the Coherence of International Law*, vol 37 (Queen Mary Studies in International Law, Brill Nijhoff 2019).
[31] *First Report on General Principles First Report on General Principles of Law* (n 19) para 173.
[32] ibid.
[33] ibid para 25. See also Andenas and Chiussi (n 2) 10, 14.
[34] Andenas and Chiussi (n 2) 10.
[35] *First Report on General Principles First Report on General Principles of Law* (n 19) para 25.
[36] ibid paras 25–26.
[37] Andenas and Chiussi argue that general principles play a decisive role in international law in at least three different ways: first, principles represent a cohesive force certifying the systemic nature of international law, and 'operate as an "open clause" through which gaps can be filled and new areas of international law can be developed consistently with the existing rules'. Second, principles operate as a 'centripetal force by providing a common ground for interaction between clusters and individual bodies of law, such as international environmental law, international investment law and international human rights law'. Third, they

consistency between disparate rules belonging to different sub-areas of international law. In other words, such a general principle may contribute to pushing the interpretation of intercreditor equity rules in both international and domestic law spheres in the same direction, thereby creating a more coherent legal framework.

7.3.1.3 Good faith and transferability of domestic insolvency principles

A 2019 case concerning a dispute between Argentina and German bondholders before the German Bundesverfassungsgericht (constitutional court) touched upon questions related to sovereign debt restructurings and the formation of general principles under international law.[38] The background for the dispute is the well-known economic crisis in Argentina in the early 2000s and the subsequent debt restructurings in 2005 and 2010. Approximately 7% of the creditors, including the two claimants in the initial proceedings before the regular German courts, refused to participate in the restructuring and ultimately brought an action seeking full payment.

In the case, Argentina argued that there was a general principle in international law providing sovereign debtors with a right to refuse to service their sovereign bonds if holdout creditors asserted their claims in full at the expense of the majority of creditors who had accepted a debt restructuring in the context of a sovereign financial crisis.[39] More specifically, Argentina argued that holdout creditor behaviour can be opposed by a plea of legal abuse of rights based on the universally accepted principle of good faith, which is based on two fundamental principles of national legal orders. These principles are the principle of equal treatment of all creditors and the integrity of an orderly insolvency procedure.[40] Argentina argued that these principles were transferable to the international law management of sovereign debt crises, because in recent decades a decentralized, state-recognized order for the management of sovereign debt crises had emerged at the international level.

The court rejected Argentina's claim. The main argument of the Bundesverfassungsgericht was that the transferability of rules from domestic insolvency laws to the international law plane presupposes the existence of a bankruptcy law regime for sovereign states similar to that existing for corporations in domestic law.[41] This would also be the case for the principle of good faith asserted by Argentina.

---

argue that principles show 'considerable potential to reduce the separation between international law and municipal legal systems'. (Andenas and Chiussi (n 2) 33–34).

[38] BVerfG, v. 03.07.2019, 2 BvR 824/15, Rn. 1-45.
[39] Formally, Argentina claimed that the Bundesgerichshof had failed to comply with the duty to refer a case to the Federal Constitutional Court pursuant to Art 100(2) of the Basic Law (Grundgesetz). More specifically, Argentina claimed that the Bundesgerichtshof should have asked the Federal Constitutional Court whether, under general international law, a sovereign debtor has the right to refuse to service its sovereign bonds if so-called holdout creditors assert their claims in full at the expense of the majority of creditors who accept a debt restructuring in the context of a sovereign financial crisis. See BVerfG 03.07.2019 (n 38), para 18.
[40] BverfG 03.07.2019 (n 38), para 19.
[41] The court also refers to the Bundesverfassungsgerichtt's decision from 2007—the so-called state of necessity ruling. The 2007 case concerned a claim that Argentina was in a state of economic necessity. The declaration of a state of necessity justifies only a temporary refusal of service. In this particular case, the Federal Constitutional Court ruled that there was no general rule of international law which entitled a sovereign debtor to refuse fulfilment on a temporary basis. See BverfG, v. 08.05.2007, 2 BvM 1/03, Rn. 1-95.

The court held that, even assuming that the principle of good faith (creditor equality and the integrity of orderly insolvency proceedings) was a generally accepted principle across jurisdictions, its operation relied on a larger judicial system. In particular, the court found that the transfer of the principle of good faith to the international law plane was dependent on there being an independent supervisory body to ensure compliance with the procedural rules and a careful balancing of the interests of all parties involved, including protection for minority creditors. On this basis, the court concluded that individual principles of insolvency law could not be applied in accordance with Article 38(1)(c) of the ICJ Statute.[42]

The Bundesverfassungsgericht correctly cautioned against the transferability of rules that strictly speaking require the existence of a bankruptcy court to balance the rights and obligations of the parties involved in a debt restructuring. Both international courts and foreign courts are likely to shy away from balancing such interests, including assessing the economic situation of debtor states, since this does not fall under their competences. This is not to say that the strict approach espoused by the court should be generalized and that no rules stemming from domestic insolvency laws are capable of being transferred to the international plane. After all, the court's conclusion in this case concerned a claim that Argentina's obligation to pay the holdout creditor be absolved altogether.[43] The simple fact that a rule stems from domestic insolvency laws should not as such disqualify it from potentially being transferred to the international plane and constituting a general principle of law under Article 38(1)(c) of the ICJ Statute. Some insolvency law rules may function without the whole insolvency law framework found in domestic law and without disturbing the balance of rights between the various parties in a restructuring procedure. Moreover, rules outside the insolvency framework may have the same underlying objectives as insolvency rules and rules found in insolvency laws may have roots outside of insolvency law. Whether a rule is transferrable to the international plane should be based on a thorough case-by-case assessment, regardless of whether the rule at issue belongs to an insolvency framework. This is in line with McNair's approach to the issue of transposition:

> International law has recruited and continues to recruit many of its rules and institutions from private systems of law. Art. 38 (1) (c) of the Statute of the Court bears witness that this process is still active... The way in which international law borrows from this source is not by means of importing private law institutions 'lock, stock and barrel', ready-made and fully equipped with a set of rules. It would be difficult to reconcile such a process with the application of 'the general principles of law'. In my opinion, the true view of the duty of international tribunals in this matter is to regard any features or terminology which are reminiscent of the rules and institutions of private law as an indication of policy and principles rather than as directly importing these rules and institutions.[44]

---

[42] BVerfG 03.07.2019 (n 38), para. 39.

[43] The judgment from the Bundesverfassungsgericht, a domestic court, has very limited bearing on the establishment of international law, but may nevertheless serve as an example in discussing the relevant issues.

[44] *International Status of South West Africa* (Advisory Opinion), separate opinion by Sir Arnold McNair [1950] ICJ Rep 128, 148.

The strict approach adopted in the German case can also be criticized because many rules applicable in a domestic setting are in fact applicable to sovereign debt restructuring already and exist outside any domestic insolvency regime in a narrow sense. This is at least the case for the domestic law intercreditor equity rules discussed in this book. Consequently, it is difficult to argue that domestic intercreditor equity rules have no place in substantiating the good faith principle under international law.

7.3.1.4 An emerging general principle of good faith
It is widely accepted that a general principle of good faith exists under Article 38(1)(c) of the ICJ Statute.[45] The principle manifests itself across numerous regimes in international law.[46] The Vienna Convention on the Law of Treaties (VCLT) highlights its importance in its preamble by noting that 'the principles of free consent and of good faith and the *pacta sunt servanda* rule are universally recognized'.

In international law, the content and meaning of good faith as a general principle of law is broad and defies precise definition. As in domestic law,[47] the general function of the principle is to play a supportive role in legal relationships that expose the parties, typically to a contract, to the influence and discretion of other parties.[48] The good faith principle is meant to reduce the inherent risks that follow from such relationships by requiring mutual trust from the parties.[49] Kolb holds that the good faith principle has three main purposes in this regard: to protect legitimate expectations, prohibit the abuse of rights, and prevent unjustified advantage from unlawful acts.[50]

Although the normativity of good faith and the abuse of rights doctrine in international law seems well established,[51] its application within particular contexts is still debated. The field of sovereign debt restructurings is no exception. Having examined the sources of the content of the general principle of good faith in the foregoing section, the following discussion turns to both domestic and international law sources. Here, I will specifically consider the two first purposes of the good faith principle as outlined by Kolb.

We start by looking back at the first category of intercreditor equity rules (ranking and preference rules). Except for the customary equality rule, what all these rules

---

[45] Crawford (n 20) 34; Matthias Goldmann, 'Putting Your Faith in Good Faith: A Principled Strategy for Smoother Debt Workouts' (2016) 41 (Special edition on sovereign debt) Yale Journal of International Law Online 117, 122. Though the ICJ Statute addresses the law applicable by the Court, general practice has turned Art 38 into an authoritative statement of the sources of international law. See Jennings (n 18) 331; Pellet (n 18) 731–870; Hernández (n 18) 31.
[46] For an overview of the manifestations of good faith in international economic law, see Andreas R Ziegler and Jorun Baumgartner, 'Good Faith as a General Principle of (International) Law' in Andrew D Mitchell and others (eds), *Good Faith and International Economic Law* (Oxford University Press 2015).
[47] See for example the discussion on the good faith principle in English and New York law in Section 4.3.7.
[48] Goldmann (n 45) 124.
[49] ibid.
[50] Robert Kolb, 'Principles as Sources of International Law (With Special Reference to Good Faith)' (2006) 53 Netherlands International Law Review 1, 17–18.
[51] Nuclear Tests Case (*New Zealand v France*) [1974] ICJ Rep 457, para 49; Pulp Mills on the River Uruguay (*Argentina v Uruguay*) [2010] ICJ Rep 14, para 145; Case concerning the Factory at Chorzów (*Germany v Poland*) (Merits) (1927) PCIJ Series A No 17, 15; Trail Smelter Arbitration (*United States v Canada*) (1941) III Rep Int Arbitr Awards 1905; United States—Import Prohibition of Certain Shrimp and Shrimp Products (*India and Other v United States*) [2001] WTO Appellate Body WT/DS58/AB/RW.

have in common is that the respective ranking and preferences are the result of voluntary and negotiated agreements. This voluntary contractual element makes it less likely that these intercreditor equity rules may be transposed into general principles of international law. First, the formulation of each contractually negotiated provision (and position)—even if it is a standard provision—may vary. Second, and most importantly, regardless of the prevalence of the standard clause, the various debt agreements containing the specific ranking and preference clauses are entered into on a voluntary basis and the agreements only bind the contractual parties. These objections are equally true, for example, of the *pari passu* clauses, as was evident from the discussion in Section 4.2: they are voluntary provisions and parties to a sovereign debt agreement can formulate the clauses in a number of different ways, or leave them out entirely. Moreover, it is unclear whether different jurisdictions would interpret similar *pari passu* clauses in the same way. This severely reduces the chances of finding underlying general principles in the *pari passu* clause that might be applicable at the international level. The rest of the rules to be examined belong to the second category of intercreditor equity rules (non-discrimination rules).

Despite several differences, the common feature of the second category of rules is that they aim to hinder various forms of discriminatory treatment (see Section 7.2.1.2). Vulture fund legislation hinders holdout creditors from obtaining illegitimate advantages in a debt restructuring. IIAs and the ECHR, as well as and the uniform applicability clause and the good faith standard, prohibit sovereign debtor states and majority creditors from implementing a coercive debt restructuring that differentiates between creditors based on certain illegitimate considerations, and thereby can be said to abuse their creditor rights. The following sections therefore focuses on these particular objectives when examining whether the general principle of good faith in international law may be relevant to intercreditor equity issues.

7.3.1.4.1 Good faith, the prohibition of the abuse of rights, and majority decisions
When seeking to establish the content of good faith in a debt restructuring context, we may start by looking to domestic law. The principle of good faith is particularly strong in the civil law tradition, but most legal orders recognize that it has a coordinative function for private law relationships.[52] Section 4.3.7 discussed the function of the principle in the context of a debt restructuring impacting intercreditor equity under English and New York law.[53] In short, this section holds that, under English law, the good faith principle in commercial dealings provides that a restructuring implemented through majority powers must benefit the debtors as a whole. However, this does not imply that it is prohibited to vote in favour of a restructuring arrangement that treats some creditors better than others.[54] In English law, the courts have tended to defer to state debtors in restructuring processes implemented by means of majority

---

[52] Goldmann (n 45) 122.
[53] For a discussion on the potential of the good faith principle in New York law to serve as an obligation for creditors to participate in a debt restructuring. See Lee C Buchheit and Mitu Gulati, 'The Duty of Creditors to Cooperate in Sovereign Debt Workouts (with Spanish Translation)' (SSRN Scholarly Paper, 12 June 2021).
[54] See discussion in Section 4.3.7.

votes (CACs or exit consent). It is even more unlikely that an appeal to good faith in the relations between minority and majority bondholders will be accepted by courts under New York law if a particular debt instrument provides each creditor with a right to vote for certain types of amendments of the term.[55] It should be noted that the core of the good faith standard in domestic law is based on majority voting for corporations who are in fact protected from a comprehensive insolvency regime. Its transferability to the international law sphere may hence have important limitations.

A good faith obligation with content similar to that described above could have implications for intercreditor equity issues in a debt restructuring by limiting voting rights in order to protect minority creditors from discrimination. Taking the underlying objectives of the other non-discrimination rules as a starting point, a general principle of good faith in international law could also have implications for intercreditor equity issues in a debt restructuring by limiting the contractual or enforcement rights of holdout creditors on the basis of abuse of rights.[56] This would also be in line with the scope of the good faith principle in general international law as described by Kolb above.[57] Over the past two decades, a number of international soft law principles and resolutions voted by international organizations have referred to good faith in the context of debt restructuring, indicating that the principle may have the latter function.

In 2004, sovereign debtors and private creditors jointly agreed on the 'Principles for Stable Capital Flows and Fair Debt Restructuring in Emerging Market' (hereafter Emerging Market Principles).[58] The principles were also endorsed by the G20 Ministerial Meeting in Berlin that same year. These voluntary principles were a response to the debt crises that primarily hit emerging markets (Asia, Russia, and Latin America) for much of the 1980s, 1990s, and the early 2000s. The Emerging Market Principles have four basics prongs aimed to foster: (i) transparency; (ii) the timely flow of information and close debtor–creditor dialogue and cooperation to avoid debt restructuring; and, where debt restructuring becomes necessary; (iii) a voluntary restructuring process based on good faith; and (iv) the absence of unfair discrimination among affected creditors.[59] In particular, the two last principles are of importance in an intercreditor equity context.

While the Emerging Market Principles insist that restructuring should be voluntary, other principles use slightly stronger language. In 2011, the United Nations Conference on Trade and Development (UNCTAD) issued its Principles on

---

[55] See William Bratton and G Mitu Gulati, 'Sovereign Debt Reform and the Best Interest of Creditors' (2004) 57 Vanderbilt Law Review 1, 66–69; Philip R Wood, *Principles of International Insolvency*, vol 1 (The Law and Practice of International Finance Series, 2nd edn, Sweet & Maxwell 2007), para 20-060.

[56] Mattias Goldmann has argued similarly in Goldmann (n 45).

[57] Kolb (n 50) 17–18.

[58] IIF, 'Principles for Stable Capital Flows and Fair Debt Restructuring in Emerging Markets' (22 November 2004). The Emerging Market Principles are guarded by a Group of Trustees, which includes senior public sector officials and private sector leaders. The Group's mandate is to review the evolution of the international financial system as it relates to emerging markets and other major debtor countries, review the development and implementation of the Principles, and make proposals for modification of the Principles as needed. The Institute of International Finance (IIF) acts as their Secretariat. See https://www.iif.com/Advocacy/Working-Groups-And-Committees

[59] Anna Gelpern, 'Hard, Soft, and Embedded: Implementing Principles on Promoting Responsible Sovereign Lending and Borrowing' in Carlos Espósito and others (eds), *Sovereign Financing and*

Promoting Responsible Sovereign Lending and Borrowing (UNCTAD Principles), which aim to reduce the prevalence of sovereign debt crises, prevent unsustainable debt situations, maintain steady economic growth, and help achieve the Millennium Development Goals, by encouraging responsible sovereign borrowing. Principle no 7 is of key importance. It states that, in circumstances where a sovereign is manifestly unable to service its debts, all lenders have a duty to behave in good faith and in a cooperative spirit so as to reach a consensual rearrangement of those obligations. The principle suggests that reaching a consensual restructuring agreement requires that lenders engage in good faith discussions with the debtor and other creditors to find a mutually satisfactory solution. In this context, then, the good faith obligation entails a duty to negotiate and to ensure a fair outcome to the negotiations, for all parties involved. The explanation to the principles does not provide any guidance as to what a fair outcome is, nor does it clarify whether equal treatment of creditors is necessary for the outcome to be categorized as such. However, it does hold that 'a creditor that acquires a debt instrument of a sovereign in financial distress with the intent of forcing a preferential settlement of the claim outside of a consensual workout process is acting abusively'.[60] The latter is a clear reference to so-called vulture fund activities.

In 2014, these UNCTAD principles were supported by United Nations General Assembly Resolution A/RES/68/304 'Towards the establishment of a multilateral legal framework for sovereign debt restructuring processes'. The General Assembly stressed the importance of establishing a clear set of principles for the management and resolution of financial crises that took into account the obligation of sovereign creditors to act in 'good faith and with a cooperative spirit' to reach a consensual rearrangement of the debt of sovereign states.[61] The resolution specifically refers to the risks related to speculative funds purchasing distressed debt at deeply discounted rates on secondary markets in order to pursue full payment via litigation (vulture fund litigation).

In 2015, the United Nations adopted the Addis Ababa Action Agenda on Financing for Development, which affirms the importance of debt restructurings being 'timely, orderly, effective, fair and negotiated in good faith'.[62] It also refers to the adoption of legislation by certain countries to prevent holdout creditor activity and 'encourage[s] all Governments to take action, as appropriate'.[63]

International Law: The UNCTAD Principles on Responsible Sovereign Lending and Borrowing (Oxford University Press 2013).

[60] The sovereign debtor's responsibilities in this situation are summarized under Principle 15, which states: 'If a restructuring of sovereign debt obligations becomes unavoidable, it should be undertaken promptly, efficiently and fairly.' The wording of the principle is open and 'fairly' can refer to both the process and the outcome. The second bullet point explaining the implications of the principle indicates that the sovereign borrower must communicate with its creditors in a timely fashion and provide necessary information documenting the need to restructure the debt. The explanatory note does not go into detail in explaining how creditors should be treated relative to each other. Restructuring based on majority creditor decisions are recommended.
[61] General Assembly (UNGA) Resolution 68/304 'Towards the establishment of a multilateral legal framework for sovereign debt restructuring processes' A/RES/68/304, 3 (United Nations 9 September 2014).
[62] General Assembly (UNGA) Resolution 69/313 'Addis Ababa Action Agenda of the Third International Conference on Financing for Development' (Addis Ababa Action Agenda) A/RES/69/313, para 98 (United Nations 27 July 2015).
[63] ibid para 100.

The same year, the United Nations General Assembly adopted Resolution 69/319 on the basic principles for sovereign debt restructuring (hereafter UN Principles).[64] The resolution acknowledged the inefficiencies of the current system of sovereign debt restructuring and, in particular, the need to deal with coordination problems amongst creditors. The UN Principles state that sovereign debt restructuring processes should be guided by the principles of sovereignty, good faith, transparency, impartiality, equitable treatment, sovereign immunity, legitimacy, sustainability, and majority restructuring. The objective of the Principles is to balance the rights of creditors with the need for the debtor state to achieve debt sustainability by efficiently minimizing the losses for all parties involved.[65] The UN Principles state that a sovereign has a right to restructure its debts, a right 'which should not be frustrated or impeded by any abusive measures'.[66] This can be read as encouraging the implementation of vulture fund legislation and as a call to courts not to accept abusive claims from holdout creditors.

In March 2017, the G20 countries endorsed, and agreed to promote, the G20 Operational Guidelines for Sustainable Financing (hereafter G20 Guidelines).[67] According to G20 Guidelines, creditors and debtors should commit to the long-term debt sustainability of borrowing countries by facilitating smooth debt restructurings when needed. Creditors should promptly engage with borrowers when borrowers seek a consensual debt restructuring and, when appropriate, creditors should seek to collaborate with other creditors in good faith. In paragraph E (third bullet point), the G20 Guidelines address the challenges posed by non-cooperative and litigating minority creditors. The G20 Guidelines suggest that these minority creditors pose challenges to the financing and debt restructuring processes, especially for the poorest countries that lack the technical capacity to face such legal challenges. Further, the G20 countries committed to exploring enhanced international monitoring of litigation by non-cooperative minority creditors and to taking action as appropriate.

In these examples of soft law principles and resolutions adopted and endorsed both by states and private creditors, good faith seems to imply an obligation to negotiate in a cooperative spirit in debt restructurings. When assessing whether creditors are acting in a cooperative spirit or not, the aim of cooperation should also be taken into account. In a debt restructuring, the aim is typically to solve a crisis and reach a sustainable debt restructuring agreement that is the least burdensome possible for all parties involved. An integral part of such a good faith obligation, then, is to abstain from free-riding on other creditors or seeking an illegitimate advantage at their expense. A concrete example of such an approach can be found in the UN Principles.

Principle 1 states:

---

[64] General Assembly (UNGA) Resolution 69/319 on 'Basic Principles on Sovereign Debt Restructuring Processes' A/RES/69/319 (United Nations 29 September 2015). Despite a clear majority voting in favour, important economic jurisdictions (such as the United States and a number of European countries) voted against the resolution. See discussion in Section 7.3.2.

[65] See, in general, (2016) 41 Yale Journal of International Law (special online edition) for discussion on reform of the current system of sovereign debt restructuring, including how the UN principles can contribute to this.

[66] UNGA Res 69/319, s 1.1.

[67] IMF, 'G20 Operational Guidelines for Sustainable Financing—Survey Results and Policy Recommendation' (31 May 2019) 18 (Annex 1).

A Sovereign State has the right, in the exercise of its discretion, to design its macroeconomic policy, including restructuring its sovereign debt, which should not be frustrated or impeded by any abusive measures....

Moreover, Principle 2 states that:

Good faith by both the sovereign debtor and all its creditors would entail their engagement in constructive sovereign debt restructuring workout negotiations and other stages of the process with the aim of a prompt and durable re-establishment of debt sustainability and debt servicing, as well as achieving the support of a critical mass of creditors through a constructive dialogue regarding the restructuring terms.

The UN Principles 1 and 2, as well as the majority of the soft law principles and resolutions above, can be read as arguing that, under the good faith principle, creditors are not only obliged to *negotiate* in good faith but are obliged not to abuse their right to demand full payment if this will hamper the possibility of reaching a sustainable debt restructuring.

According to Lauterpacht, a common ground between good faith and the abuse of rights doctrine is that they seek to impose limits on the ways in which recognized international rights can be exercised by their holder: they may limit the individualistic use of rights.[68] Lauterpacht's interpretation, read in conjunction with the UN Principles, could support the view that the good faith principle and the abuse of rights doctrine require courts and tribunals to balance the interests of parties exercising their own rights with the damage caused to others. In a sovereign debt context, a possible interpretation is that good faith will prohibit minority creditors from holding out if this risks hampering successful debt restructuring altogether. More specifically, a good faith obligation may prohibit holding out from a debt restructuring supported by a qualified majority. This approach would be in line with the use of CACs, the contract provisions enabling the majority to bind the minority to a debt restructuring.

However, such a broad application of the good faith principle does not seem to have support in domestic law, at least not in central financial jurisdictions. This is evident from the many debt disputes in the courts of New York, England, and Germany.[69] Creditors have not been obliged to participate in debt restructurings where there are no statutory laws or contract terms obliging them to do so.

This approach is exemplified by a 2019 case before the German Bundesverfassungsgericht discussing the implementation of sovereign debt

---

[68] Hersch Lauterpacht, *The Function of Law in the International Community* (first published 1933, Oxford University Press 2011) 286.
[69] For example, *NML Capital, Ltd v Republic of Argentina* No. 08-cv-6978 (TPG) (SDNY 21 November 2012); BVerfG 03.07.2019 (n 38). Moreover, only a handful of jurisdictions have implemented national legislation to curb aggressive holdout creditors who seek to sue debtor states to get full payment instead of participating in debt restructurings (so-called vulture funds). Such legislation is found in the France, Belgium, the United Kingdom, Isle of Man, and Jersey. See Loi du 6 avril 2008 visant à empêcher la saisie ou la cession des fonds publics destinés à la coopération internationale, notamment par la technique des fonds vautours, M.B., 16 May 2008, p. 25594 (Belgium); Loi du 12 juillet 2015 relative à la lutte contre les activités des fonds vautours, M.B., 11 September 2015, p. 57357 (Belgium); Debt Relief (Developing Countries) Act 2010; Debt Relief (Developing Countries) Law 2013 (Jersey); Heavily Indebted Poor Countries (Limitation

restructurings through majority decisions and the formation of general principles under international law.[70] The case concerned a dispute between Argentina and German bondholders. The two claimants, who had refused to participate in the restructuring, brought an action before German courts seeking full payment. Argentina argued that there was a general principle of international law providing sovereign debtors with a right to refuse to service sovereign bonds if holdout creditors asserted their claims in full at the expense of the majority of creditors who had accepted debt restructuring in the context of a sovereign financial crisis.[71] More specifically, Argentina argued that holdout creditor behaviour can be opposed by a plea of legal abuse of rights based on the universally accepted principle of good faith. Further, Argentina claimed that this good faith principle was based on two fundamental principles of national legal orders. The Bundesverfassungsgericht rejected Argentina's claim and held that voluntary participation in debt restructuring was still the basic starting point across a majority of jurisdictions. The court also rejected the argument that a good faith obligation existed in international law which prohibited creditors from jeopardizing a debt restructuring by voting against it. Nor did the court accept that there was a rule under which a majority can bind the minority to a debt restructuring, without a corresponding agreement in the bond conditions or background law.[72]

7.3.1.4.2 Good faith as a standard of legitimate expectations

Although the good faith principle is unlikely to oblige minority creditors to accept a restructuring supported by the majority and give up on their contractual right to payment, the principle may still have a role to play in a sovereign debt context. For example, it may play a guiding role in assessing whether a *treaty* obligation is violated, such as expropriation and interference with property rights under the ECHR or an IIA.

Although not an independent principle under general international law, several investment law decisions apply legitimate expectation standards based on the good faith principle. The tribunals have made it an actionable right within IIA provisions, both under the prohibition of expropriation and under the fair and equitable treatment standard.[73]

---

on Debt Recovery) Act 2012 (Isle of Man); Loi n° 2016-1691 du 9 déc 2016 relative à la transparence, à la lutte contre la corruption et à la modernisation de la vie économique (loi Sapin 2) [Law n° 2016-1691 of 9 Dec 2016 on transparency, anti-corruption and modernization of economic life] JO du 10 déc 2016 (France). See discussion of this legislation in Astrid Iversen, 'Vulture Fund Legislation' (2019) 38 Banking & Financial Services Policy Report.

[70] BVerfG 03.07.2019 (n 38).
[71] BVerfG 03.07.2019 (n 38), para 18.
[72] In its decision, the Bundesverfassungsgericht held that the transferability of rules from domestic insolvency laws to the international law plane presupposes the existence of a bankruptcy law regime for sovereign states similar to that existing for corporations in domestic law, BVerfG 03.07.2019 (n 38), para 19. This strict approach can be criticized. First, whether a rule is transferrable from the domestic to the international plane should be based on a more thorough assessment and on a case-by-case basis, regardless of whether it belongs to an insolvency framework. Second, many rules applicable in a domestic setting are in fact applicable to sovereign debt restructuring already and exist outside any domestic insolvency regime in a narrow sense. On the issue of transposition see for example *International Status of South West Africa* (n 44) 148.
[73] *Técnicas Medioambientales Tecmed, SA v The United Mexican States* No. ARB(AF)/00/2 (International Centre for Settlement of Investment Disputes 29 May 2003). The first time an arbitral tribunal made a general reference to the protection of an investor's expectations. See also *Saluka Investments BV v Czech*

Applying the good faith principle under the legitimate expectations approach means asking whether a particular creditor had legitimate expectations to claim full payment under the original loan terms and hold out from a restructuring. If a creditor bought the debt instrument at a steep discount at a time when it was obvious that the debtor country had severe economic problems or right before economic collapse, it may not be legitimate to expect full repayment.

It can be argued that this application of the good faith principle, taking into account the legitimate expectations of the creditor, is also reflected in ECtHR practice. More specifically, it is reflected in the case concerning the Greek restructuring from 2012—the *Mamatas* case. In this case, Greece implemented a law which retroactively enabled the majority of creditors to bind the minority to a debt restructuring so as to increase the chances of reaching a sustainable debt restructuring. The ECtHR found that Greece had interfered with creditor possession, but found that the restructuring of the public debt represented an appropriate and necessary means of reducing public debt and saving the state from bankruptcy. It emphasized that investing in bonds was never risk-free and that the applicants should have been aware of the risk of a possible drop in the value of their bonds.[74] A legitimate expectations approach allowed for a weighing of interests between holdout creditors, on the one hand, and the debtor state (and its citizens) as well as the other creditors willing to participate in a debt restructuring, on the other hand. It can be argued, then, that the individual rights of creditors—the right to peaceful enjoyment of private property—was limited in *Mamatas* by the good faith and abuse of rights doctrine.

In sum, taking into account legitimate expectations when assessing potential violations of protection standards under IIAs and human rights conventions, in the context of an involuntary debt restructuring, can mitigate claims from at least some holdout creditors. This is one area where the good faith principle can play an important role and contribute to securing sustainable debt restructuring.

It should be mentioned that scepticism with regard to weakening creditor rights exists. And this may be an argument against the existence of a good faith principle in the debt restructuring context. While the great majority of the General Assembly (183 states) voted in favour of adopting the above-mentioned UN Principles on sovereign debt restructuring, they were opposed by several key economic jurisdictions. These states argued that the principles went beyond what can be labelled a pure contractual approach—an approach where improvements to the sovereign debt restructuring regime are based on contract revision only and not on statutory or international law reform.[75] The opposing countries found the principles to be too radical, regardless

---

Republic, UNCITRAL, Partial Award (17 March 2006); Obligation to Negotiate Access to the Pacific Ocean (*Bolivia v Chile*) (Merits) [2018] ICJ Rep 507.

[74] *Mamatas and Others v Greece* (n 15) paras 22, 48–51.
[75] The great majority of the General Assembly acknowledged the need for broader reform—in addition to contractual reforms such as the implementation of CACs—and voted in favour of adopting the Principles. However, a number of influential developed countries were reluctant to take this route: 41 countries abstained and six countries voted against (Canada, Germany, Israel, Japan, the United Kingdom, and the United States). See Martin Guzman and Joseph E Stiglitz, 'A Soft Law Mechanism for Sovereign Debt Restructuring Based on the UN Principles' (Friedrich Ebert Stiftung International Policy Analysis, October 2016) 4.

of the fact that the vote in the General Assembly concerned soft law principles rather than a binding treaty or the establishment of court-like institutions. Nevertheless, the above-mentioned developments in soft law principles and resolutions clearly document growing support for a position condemning holdout creditors that seek to obtain illegitimate advantages in a debt restructuring, putting the successful resolution of debt crises at risk.[76] These developments, together with the second category of non-discrimination rules discussed in Section 7.2.1.2, may underpin an *emerging* general principle of good faith in international law. This could have implications for intercreditor equity issues in the context of debt restructuring, by limiting certain contractual or enforcement rights of holdout creditors on the basis of abuse of rights in more extreme situations.[77]

While a general principle of good faith in international law may emerge with time and so become a tool contributing to more coherent treatment of intercreditor equity issues, it will have clear limitations. The last question, then, is whether other reforms that might deal more efficiently with intercreditor equity disputes, diverging intercreditor equity rules, and the challenges they pose to sustainable debt restructurings are likely to emerge. This is discussed in the final chapter of the book.

---

[76] It is also possible to note a certain policy shift in the attitude of international finance institutions, such as the IMF and the European Central Bank. Increasingly, institutions seem to admit that a subset of creditors that buy distressed debt at a large discount with the intent to recover the full face value through litigation has made restructurings extremely difficult. See IMF, 'The International Architecture for Resolving Sovereign Debt Involving Private-Sector Creditors—Recent Developments, Challenges, and Reform Options' (Policy paper, 23 September 2020); IRC Task Force on IMF and global financial governance issues, 'The IMF's Role in Sovereign Debt Restructurings' (Occasional Paper Series, 14 September 2021) 40–41.

[77] In general, for the development of international law standards in the area of sovereign debt, see Juan Pablo Bohoslavsky and Matthias Goldmann, 'An Incremental Approach to Sovereign Debt Restructuring: Sovereign Debt Sustainability as a Principle of Public International Law' (2016) 41 (Special edition on sovereign debt) Yale Journal of International Law Online 13; Gelpern (n 59).

8
The Outlook for Broader Systemic Reform

8.1 A Case Study on the Need for Reform

One aim of this book has been to go beyond the common platitude that 'equal treatment' is the crux of a successful debt restructuring process. I have shown that equal treatment is an ambiguous concept that is context- and rule-specific, and does not necessarily guarantee a sustainable debt restructuring. As Professor Anna Gelpern has aptly stated: 'Equality is a beautiful ideal constantly crashing into the messy reality of sovereign debt [be it *pari passu* or "uniformly applicable"]. Sometimes you ride into the sunset, sometimes into the ditch.'

The previous chapters of the book have examined the content and scope of intercreditor equity rules in the context of sovereign debt restructurings. They provide a comprehensive and up-to-date analysis of relevant contract clauses, statutory law, and international law, including case law from the European Court of Human Rights (ECtHR) and International Investment Tribunals, decisive for the question of intercreditor equity. By clarifying the content and scope of core intercreditor equity rights and obligations applicable in the context of sovereign debt restructuring, the book may contribute to easing the level of conflict in future sovereign debt restructuring and improving the chances of achieving sustainable debt restructuring.

The book should also be read as cautioning against the shortcomings of the *ad hoc* contract-based regulatory framework governing sovereign debt. This framework contributes to unnecessary sovereign defaults and prolonged crisis resolution processes characterized by uncertainty, which are damaging both for creditors and the debtor country and its citizens. The topic of intercreditor equity is part of a broader debate concerning the legal framework governing sovereign borrowing and debt crisis resolution. A core element of this debate centres on the design of the current legal framework for sovereign debt restructuring and whether it is equipped to solve debt crises in a satisfactory manner. The book does not aim to provide a comprehensive reform proposal for how the broader system of sovereign borrowing ought to be reformed. Nevertheless, analyses of the functioning of one type of rule can shed light on risk factors and weaknesses of the broader regulatory framework and thereby contribute to the broader debate.

The analyses in this book show that, under the current regulatory framework, intercreditor equity rules may conflict with public policy considerations, defined as a debtor state's need to reach a sustainable debt burden and ensure monetary and financial stability. Assessed separately, only a couple of the rules would be considered as problematic in this regard (in particular, certain interpretations of the *pari passu* clause, see Section 4.2). When drafting debt instruments, debtor states could mitigate some of the negative consequences by avoiding specific rules or specific unfortunate formulations of rules. Regardless of such adjustments, the book argues that the challenges posed by intercreditor equity rules are of a broader systemic nature. The *number* of different and uncoordinated intercreditor equity rules that a sovereign debtor state is typically bound by, combined with the *scope* of the rules, may restrict the debtor state's room for manoeuvre to such an extent that it becomes difficult to implement a sustainable debt restructuring. As discussed in Chapter 1, sufficient room for manoeuvre for debtor states to provide preferential treatment to certain creditors may allow for targeted measures that help the crisis-struck economy to recover faster. This, in turn, can benefit creditors, since it increases their chances of being repaid. The described risk—that the parties involved in a debt restructuring are not able to reach a sustainable debt restructuring due to a narrowed policy space—is exacerbated under the current *ad hoc* system for debt crisis resolution. This system is heavily dependent on voluntary participation from creditors and contractual restructuring tools, and the state has limited freedom to use its sovereign powers to solve a debt crisis (see Chapter 2 and Section 7.2.2).

Although there is a growing consensus that the current system of sovereign debt restructurings has several flaws, there is no corresponding agreement on how it should be improved. The reform debate is politicized and polarized. Broadly speaking, there are two opposing camps engaged in academic and policy discussions concerning sovereign borrowing and debt crisis resolution.[1] One side argues that sovereign debt is mainly, or should be, a public regulatory system. This side advocates statutory reform, arguing for binding international rules and a sovereign restructuring mechanism. The other side holds that sovereign borrowing is and should be regulated in accordance with the private contractual approach.[2] This approach is in favour of purely market-based contractual reforms, such as implementing majority voting provisions where the majority of creditors may bind the minority to a restructuring to solve restructuring problems.[3]

Contractual tools, such as Collective Action Clauses (CACs), will indeed contribute to easing a restructuring process where debtor states have limited space for manoeuvre and creditors have conflicting views on how they ought to be treated. In such cases, contractual tools enable the binding of dissenting minority creditors to a restructuring agreement. However, it is unlikely that CACs alone will be able to hinder all future destructive holdout activity: many outstanding bonds lack CACs; the

---

[1] Giuseppe Bianco, 'Restructuring Sovereign Debt Owed to Private Creditors. The Appropriate Role for International Law' (PhD, University of Oslo 2017) 10.

[2] The incremental approach can be perceived as a middle position, where contractual and statutory approaches go hand in hand. This approach argues that international policy processes in informal and formal international institutions pushing for contractual changes in the legal framework of sovereign debt and creating guiding soft law principles for sovereign borrowing and lending, could lead to the emergence of a binding international legal framework for sovereign debt crisis resolution at the international law level. See Juan Pablo Bohoslavsky and Matthias Goldmann, 'An Incremental Approach to Sovereign Debt Restructuring: Sovereign Debt Sustainability as a Principle of Public International Law' (2016) 41 (Special edition on sovereign debt) Yale Journal of International Law Online 13.

[3] The promotion of contractual reform to include strong majority voting provisions such as CACs has been seen as a reaction to, or an effort to defeat an International Monetary Fund (IMF) staff suggestion on establishing a sovereign debt restructuring mechanism (SDRM) in the early 2000s. See, for example, Anna Gelpern, 'Sovereign Debt: Now What?' (2016) 41 (Special edition on sovereign debt) Yale Journal of International Law Online 45.

implementation of enhanced CACs will take a long time; and there is still a chance that holdout creditors may buy up a blocking position across a series that enables them to thwart debt restructuring. Moreover, CACs are currently mandatory only in bonds issued by the Euro area countries and are typically not implemented in other forms of debt instruments.[4] The regulatory framework needs to be complemented with more comprehensive and coordinated crisis resolution tools to ensure more sustainable debt crisis resolution processes.

8.2 COVID-19 and Exogenous Shocks

The global COVID-19 pandemic is the most recent event to expose big gaps in the sovereign debt restructuring architecture. The pandemic has had severe consequences. Millions of lives have been lost. Economic activity globally has been severely disrupted and has pushed over 100 million people into poverty.[5] In 2020, when the pandemic spread globally, it did not trigger a wave of sovereign debt defaults. However, most states borrowed significantly to respond to the pandemic and by 2022 these states are facing higher interest rates and volatile market conditions. In fact, according to the IMF, 2020 saw the largest one-year debt surge since the Second World War, with global debt rising to USD 226 trillion as the world was hit by a global health crisis and a deep recession.[6] A strong and coordinated international response to deal with the increased risk of debt crises has been lacking.

In April 2020, the G20 together with the World Bank announced the Debt Service Suspension Initiative (DSSI). The DSSI would suspend debt payments on a temporary basis to free up debtor states' resources and enable them to spend to fight the negative consequences of COVID-19. In November 2020, the G20 together with the Paris Club announced that they would establish the 'Common Framework for debt treatment beyond the DSSI' (Common Framework).[7] The Common Framework provides eligible

---

[4] It is challenging to find reliable numbers for the prevalence of CACs in outstanding bonds already issued by EU countries. On a global basis, and as of end October 2018, the IMF estimated that approximately 60% of the share of outstanding international sovereign bonds do not include aggregated CACs as recommended by the International Capital Market Association (ICMA), the IMF, and the G20, see IMF, 'Fourth Progress Report on Inclusion of Enhanced Contractual Provisions in International Sovereign Bond Contract' (Policy paper, International Monetary Fund 21 March 2019) 6–7. In 2016, it was reported that approximately 77% of the total outstanding stock of bonds has two-limb aggregated or series-by-series CACs. See IMF, 'Second Progress Report on Inclusion of Enhanced Contractual Provisions in International Sovereign Bond Contracts' (Policy paper, 27 December 2016). See also Astrid Iversen, 'Vulture Fund Legislation' (2019) 38 Banking & Financial Services Policy Report. The prevalence of CACs is also discussed in Section 6.2.3.

[5] According to the World Bank, and counting those who would have otherwise escaped extreme poverty but will not (due to the pandemic), the total COVID-19-induced new poor in 2020 is estimated to be 97 million. Daniel Gerszon Mahler and others, 'Updated Estimates of the Impact of COVID-19 on Global Poverty: Turning the Corner on the Pandemic in 2021?' (Blog, *World Bank Blogs*, 24 June 2021) <https://blogs.worldbank.org/opendata/updated-estimates-impact-covid-19-global-poverty-turning-corner-pandemic-2021> accessed 1 May 2022.

[6] Vitor Gaspar and others, 'Global Debt Reaches a Record $226 Trillion' (*IMF Blog*, 15 December 2021) <https://blogs.imf.org/2021/12/15/global-debt-reaches-a-record-226-trillion/> accessed 1 May 2022.

[7] The terms of 'Common Framework for debt treatment beyond the DSSI' (in G20, 'Statement of Extraordinary G20 Finance Ministers and Central Bank Governors' Meeting (Virtual)' [13 November 2020] 2 (Annex I) <https://www.imf.org/-/media/Files/News/news-articles/english-extraordinary-g20-fmcbg-statement-november-13.ashx> accessed 6 February 2022).

low-income countries severely hit by economic consequences related to COVID-19 with debt restructuring on a case-by-case basis. Both initiatives have been criticized for not including a sufficient number of heavily indebted states, having design flaws, and lacking creditor participation.[8] Some of this criticism goes to the heart of intercreditor conflicts.

In line with the standard practice of the Paris Club,[9] a debt restructuring under the Common Framework requires 'comparability of treatment'.[10] This means that the debtor state is required to seek a restructuring agreement with all lenders that are not part of the Common Framework (bilateral lenders that are non-G20, non-Paris Club members, and private creditors) on the same terms as those provided by bilateral creditors participating in the Common Framework. The purpose of the clause is to ensure equal treatment of creditors and incentivize the participation of creditors that are not a part of the Common Framework initiative. As there are no international debt workout procedures governing sovereign debt, debt restructurings rely mainly on the voluntary participation of creditors.[11] There are no guarantees that these other creditors will in fact accept a restructuring proposed by a debtor state seeking to obtain 'comparability of treatment'.[12]

Despite COVID-19 being an exogenous shock, unrelated to mismanagement of domestic economies, many creditors have been unwilling to provide a moratorium (pause in payments) or restructure outstanding debt burdens two years into the pandemic. The IMF itself has stated that the absence of private sector participation (in particular) in the DSSI has been a challenge, due to the growing share of debt financed by the private sector in developing economies.[13] When large segments of creditors are able to free-ride on a limited number of official-sector creditors, this strongly disincentivizes further debt restructurings by the G20 and Paris Club countries. Engaging non-Paris Club creditors, including private creditors, in a more structured coordination process is an essential step for debt architecture reform. The terms of engagement under the DSSI and the Common Framework are not contributing to shaping a new regime or grounding market expectations. They are simply agreements

---

[8] See, for example, Daniel Munevar, 'The G20 "Common Framework for Debt Treatments beyond the DSSI": Is It Bound to Fail? (II)' (*Eurodad*, 28 October 2020) <https://www.eurodad.org/the_g20_common_framework_for_debt_treatments_beyond_the_dssi_is_it_bound_to_fail_2> accessed 1 May 2022; Iolanda Fresnillo, 'The G20 Debt Service Suspension Initiative: Draining out the Titanic with a Bucket?' (Eurodad Briefing Paper, October 2020).
[9] Paris Club, 'What Does Comparability of Treatment Mean?' (*Paris Club*, no date) <https://clubdeparis.org/en/communications/page/what-does-comparability-of-treatment-mean> accessed 1 May 2022.
[10] See terms of 'Common Framework for debt treatment beyond the DSSI' (in G20 (n 7) 2 (Annex I)).
[11] The voluntary aspect and the fact that, in practice, the Paris Club members do not withdraw their restructuring offer if the debtor does not obtain restructuring on equal terms with private creditors, is also the reason why such clauses have not been treated as true equal treatment obligations in this book.
[12] Moreover, and despite its name (the Common Framework), the initiative is essentially designed to operate on a case-by-case basis. Although a rigid approach that treats all debtor states the same is not desirable, a case-by-case approach comes with the risk of differential treatment both of debtor states and consequently of their respective creditors. This may also challenge the legitimacy of the restructuring tool, increase intercreditor conflict across debtors, and reduce support for the Common Framework from creditors.
[13] In this respect, the Common Framework endorsed by the G20 (see below) would improve debt treatment efficiency in a tailored way for countries with unsustainable debt, along with countries with sustainable debt but facing liquidity issues or high debt vulnerabilities, while supporting fair burden sharing between the official and private sectors.

among a limited number of bilateral creditors and do not purport to create a legal mechanism that can bind or even incentivize private creditors subject to the jurisdiction of the G20 countries. The lack of creditor participation so far increases the pressure for alternative crisis resolution measures. The lack of political will to implement regulatory changes has long and strong roots. Two years into the pandemic, it seems this 'tradition' will endure, despite the momentum for change that was growing.

8.3 Reform and Political Will

Resistance to reform of the legal framework governing sovereign debt is particularly strong with respect to initiatives that go beyond a voluntary contractual approach, especially in jurisdictions of economic importance. This was clear in the early 2000s, when the IMF suggested that a Sovereign Debt Restructuring Mechanism be established. The initiative was vetoed by the United States, among others.[14] A more recent example is the much less comprehensive suggestion contained in the Basic Principles on Sovereign Debt Restructuring, adopted by the UN General Assembly in 2015.[15] Despite a clear majority in favour of adoption, important economic jurisdictions, such as the United States and a number of European countries, voted against the resolution.[16]

It is important to bear in mind that regulatory changes or other state interferences that limit individual creditor rights are always likely to face opposition from some creditors and investors and hence also from jurisdictions where such market actors have significant influence. Both the implementation of CACs and the use of the local law advantage have been subject to the same criticism: the use of the tools will make the cost of default for the debtor too low, which incentivizes debtor states to restructure their debts in situations where it is not strictly necessary. This drives up the cost of borrowing for debtor states (see Sections 2.2 and 4.3, respectively). Many economists have tried to examine whether the market perceives CACs as representing an increased investment risk[17]—because debtor states may seek to restructure debt when it is not strictly necessary—or whether they benefit the sovereign debt framework by providing a more predictable and orderly debt restructuring procedure. To do so, they have analysed whether the implementation of CACs affects bond prices. Some divergence can be seen, but most researchers have found that the difference in bond prices between those which include CACs and those which do not is very limited. In general, it appears that reactions in the financial market to the implementation of these clauses have been minimal.[18]

---

[14] See Anne O Krueger and Sean Hagan, 'Sovereign Workouts: An IMF Perspective' (2005) 6 Chicago Journal of International Law 203.
[15] General Assembly (UNGA) Resolution 69/319 on 'Basic Principles on Sovereign Debt Restructuring Processes' A/RES/69/319, 319 (United Nations 29 September 2015).
[16] See also discussion in Section 7.3.2.
[17] Kay Chung and Michael G Papaioannou, 'Do Enhanced Collective Action Clauses Affect Sovereign Borrowing Costs?' (IMF Working Paper, International Monetary Fund August 2020).
[18] Christoph Grosse Steffen and others, 'Collective Action Clauses in the Euro Area: A Law and Economic Analysis of the First Five Years' (2019) 14 Capital Markets Law Journal 134. See also IMF, 'Fourth Progress Report' (n 4).

Economists have also attempted to calculate the pricing effects of the choice of governing law. For instance, Chamon and others have tested whether sovereign bonds that are governed by foreign law, such as English or New York law, trade at a premium compared to bonds issued under domestic law.[19] They analysed foreign law bonds issued by Euro area countries and traded in the Euro area between 2006 and 2013. Their finding was that a foreign law premium exists, but it only becomes sizable and relevant in periods of debt distress.[20] Their work concluded that the legal features of sovereign bonds matter in periods of distress and for countries with a high risk of default. In sum, the pricing effect of the inclusion of contractual terms influencing the extent to which it is easy to restructure a debt instrument, such as CACs and choice of law clauses, is limited in normal times.[21] The literature also indicates that the governing law has a greater impact on pricing compared to CACs. This may be explained by the fact that a debt restructuring is more predictable when implemented by means of the latter. It is far from obvious that creditors and the market in general would prefer debt instruments governed by foreign law to debt instruments governed by domestic law, if they do not include CAC or similar majority voting provisions that help ease the debt restructuring process.

The preceding paragraphs indicate that it is far from clear that sovereign debtors or creditors holding sovereign debt instruments benefit from a sovereign debt restructuring framework that is reliant mainly on contractual crisis resolution tools. On the contrary, the lack of effective crisis resolution measures may lead the sovereign debtor to default, resulting in no further payments to the creditors. A prolonged and uncertain crisis resolution process is also damaging for creditors.[22] Realizing this, few creditors insist that the right to hold out from restructurings and enforce contractual rights to payment is sacred and an objective that trumps all other considerations. For creditors holding sovereign debt instruments, predictability, limited free-riding opportunities for other creditors, and transparency from debtor states in the process leading up to a restructuring are factors likely to be valued at least as much.[23]

While this book has documented the need for reform, further research is needed to establish how such systemic reforms should take form. A first important step is for

---

[19] Marcos Chamon and others, 'Foreign-Law Bonds: Can They Reduce Sovereign Borrowing Costs?' (ECB Working Paper Series, June 2018).

[20] The authors document a large increase in that premium during the Euro area debt crisis. However, during non-crisis times and in less vulnerable countries, the premium can be slightly negative. They argue that this implies that governments incur a small cost when issuing foreign-law bonds outside of distress episodes (ibid 2).

[21] ibid 3.

[22] On the issue of sovereign debt restructurings that are implemented too late and encompass too little debt, see IMF, 'Sovereign Debt Restructuring—Recent Developments and Implications for the Fund's Legal and Policy Framework' (Policy paper, 26 April 2013). See also Brett House and others, 'Sovereign Debt Restructurings: The Costs of Delay' (10 April 2017); Jerome E Roos, *Why Not Default? The Political Economy of Sovereign Debt* (Princeton University Press 2019).

[23] One example of such a view is the International Capital Markets Association's push for the implementation of an amended CAC. See discussion in Section 4.3 of this book. Another example is the Institute of International Finance (IIF) which, in a letter to the G20 dated 9 April 2021, called for 'an appropriate forum for creditor coordination' and 'increased transparency around all sovereign obligations for all creditors'. (Letter from IIF, 'IIF Letter to the G20 on Common Framework, Debt Transparency, ESG Considerations' [9 April 2021]).

states and other policy-makers to acknowledge the need for broader reforms and not shy away from initiating and taking part in discussions. It is clear that certain states, including several developed economies, have adopted market actors' scepticism with regard to regulatory reform.[24] Despite recurring sovereign debt crises the past decades, policymakers have failed to provide a proper systemic response.[25]

On a general basis, an international treaty governing intercreditor equity—or a strictly regulated priority among various types of creditors—seems politically unfeasible and unnecessarily inflexible. Similarly, the creation of an international bankruptcy court to decide on the outcome of restructurings with binding effect (the burden sharing between a debtor and its creditors as well as between the various creditors) is unlikely to be feasible or desirable. However, there are several middle-ground solutions that can, and ought to, be examined more thoroughly to ensure that debtor states are provided with sufficient room for manoeuvre to successfully implement debt crisis resolution measures, while also ensuring a fair restructuring process and fair restructuring terms for the creditors involved. These might include further improvement of contract terms, increased transparency concerning debts and debtholders, national legislation to further check litigation by aggressive holdout creditors, increased use of creditor committees as a forum for creditors to discuss and negotiate debt restructuring terms, and the creation of an independent forum to facilitate restructuring talks and ensure transparency and access to data.[26]

Important progress on the regulatory framework governing sovereign borrowing and lending has already been made by institutions such as the IMF, the United Nations Conference on Trade and Development, the United Nations Department of Economic and Social Affairs, and the UN General Assembly.[27] Future reform should build on and learn from these processes. It is essential that the institutions driving these processes are not dominated by creditors or purely private actors, so that the legitimacy of the process is ensured and reform outcomes reflect the core interests of states and the well-being of their citizens.

---

[24] See, for example, UNGA Res 69/319, where 183 states voted in favour of adopting the Principles, but were opposed by several key economic jurisdictions because the Principles went beyond what might be called a purely contractual approach.

[25] UNICEF, 'COVID-19 and the Looming Debt Crisis: Protecting and Transforming Social Spending for Inclusive Recoveries' (Innocenti research report, April 2021).

[26] See, for example, general discussion in United Nations, 'Liquidity and Debt Solutions to Invest in the SDGs: The Time to Act is Now' (March 2021). With respect to the debt crisis in the wake of the COVID-19 pandemic, there is some hope that targeted action may be taken to shield governments' assets from their creditors, such as legislative solutions or even a United Nations (UN) Security Council resolution. Chapter VII of the UN Charter gives the Security Council authority to make decisions that are binding on all UN Member States with regard to issues that threaten international peace and security. In 2003, shortly after the collapse of Saddam Hussein's regime, the Security Council adopted Resolution 1483 (2003). Somewhat simplified, the Security Council decided on a stay on enforcement of creditor rights to use litigation to collect unpaid sovereign debt to facilitate a debt restructuring. See Security Council resolution 1483 (2003) [on lifting the economic sanctions on Iraq imposed by resolution 661 (1990)] S/RES/1483(2003) (United Nations 22 May 2003).

[27] The UNCTAD Principles on Promoting Responsible Sovereign Lending and Borrowing were supported by General Assembly (UNGA) Resolution 68/304 'Towards the establishment of a multilateral legal framework for sovereign debt restructuring processes' A/RES/68/304 (United Nations 9 September 2014). See also UNGA Res 69/319.

Bibliography

——, 'Moral Hazard', *Wikipedia* (2022) <https://en.wikipedia.org/wiki/Moral_hazard> accessed 20 December 2022.
——, 'Multilateral Debt Relief Initiative—Questions and Answers' (*International Monetary Fund*, 28 July 2017) <https://www.imf.org/external/np/exr/mdri/eng/index.htm> accessed 30 April 2022.
——, 'Public Purpose', *Webster's New World Law Dictionary Online* (no date).
Abel J, *The Resolution of Sovereign Debt Crises: Instruments, Inefficiencies and Options for the Way Forward* (1st edn, Routledge 2019).
African Development Bank Group, 'Vulture Funds in the Sovereign Debt Context' (*afdb.org*, African Development Bank Group 17 April 2019) <https://www.afdb.org/en/topics-and-sectors/initiatives-partnerships/african-legal-support-facility/vulture-funds-in-the-sovereign-debt-context> accessed 10 March 2022.
Alvik I, 'Statsimmunitet etter norsk rett og folkeretten' in OK Fauchald, H Jakhelln, and A Syse (eds), *Festskrift til Carl August Fleischer, dog fred er ej det bedste* (Universitetsforlaget 2006).
Andenas M and Bjorge E, 'Introduction: From Fragmentation to Convergence in International Law' in E Bjorge and M Andenas (eds), *A Farewell to Fragmentation: Reassertion and Convergence in International Law* (Studies on International Courts and Tribunals, Cambridge University Press 2015).
Andenas M and Chiussi L, 'Cohesion, Convergence and Coherence of International Law' in M Andenas, M Fitzmaurice, A Tanzi, and J Wouters (eds), *General Principles and The Coherence of International Law*, vol 37 (Queen Mary Studies in International Law, Brill Nijhoff 2019).
Arnold T, Panizza U, and Gulati GM, 'The Ridiculous Drama in Rome Over Proposals to Reform the ESM Treaty' (*Oxford Law Faculty Business Law blog*, 12 October 2019) <https://www.law.ox.ac.uk/business-law-blog/blog/2019/12/ridiculous-drama-rome-over-proposals-reform-esm-treaty> accessed 10 March 2022.
Baetens F, 'Discrimination on the Basis of Nationality: Determining Likeness in Human Rights and Investment Law' in SW Schill (ed), *International Investment Law and Comparative Public Law* (Oxford University Press 2010).
Baetens F, 'Diplomatic Protection' in R Grote, F Lachenmann, and R Wolfrum (eds), *Max Planck Encyclopedia of Comparative Constitutional Law* (Oxford University Press 2017).
Bianco G, 'Restructuring Sovereign Debt Owed to Private Creditors. The Appropriate Role for International Law' (PhD, University of Oslo 2017).
BIS Contact group on the legal and institutional underpinnings of the international financial system, 'Insolvency Arrangements and Contract Enforceability' (September 2002).
Blackman JI and Mukhi R, 'The Evolution of Modern Sovereign Debt Litigation: Vultures, Alter Egos, and Other Legal Fauna' (2010) 73 Law and Contemporary Problems 47.
Boccuzzi CD, Brennan MM, and Johnston JH, 'Defences' in RM Lastra and LC Buchheit (eds), *Sovereign Debt Management* (Oxford University Press 2014).
Bohoslavsky JP and Goldmann M, 'An Incremental Approach to Sovereign Debt Restructuring: Sovereign Debt Sustainability as a Principle of Public International Law' (2016) 41 (Special edition on sovereign debt) Yale Journal of International Law Online 13 <https://www.yjil.yale.edu/volume-41-special-edition/> accessed 20 December 2022.

Bohoslavsky JP, 'Has the EU Sacrificed Human Rights on the Altar of Austerity?' (*Equal Times*, no date) <https://www.equaltimes.org/even-in-the-face-of-austerity-and> accessed 8 May 2018.

Bonafè BI, 'State Immunity and the Protection of Private Investors: The *Argentine Bonds* Case Before Italian Courts' (2006) 16 The Italian Yearbook of International Law Online 165.

Borchard EM, *The Diplomatic Protection of Citizens Abroad* (Banks Law Publishing Co 1914).

Borchard EM, 'Contractual Claims in International Law' (1913) 13 Columbia Law Review 457.

Borchard EM, 'International Loans and International Law' (1932) 26 Proceedings of the American Society of International Law at its annual meeting (1921–1969) 135.

Borchard EM, *State Insolvency and Foreign Bondholders*, vol 1 (Yale University Press 1951).

Boudreau M and Gulati GM, 'The International Monetary Fund's Imperiled Priority' (2014) 10 Duke Journal of Constitutional Law & Public Policy 119.

Boudreau MA, 'Restructuring Sovereign Debt under Local Law: Are Retrofit Collective Action Clauses Expropriatory' (2011–12) 2 Harvard Business Law Review Online 164.

Bradley M and Gulati GM, 'Collective Action Clauses for the Eurozone' (2014) 18 Review of Finance 2045.

Bratton W and Gulati GM, 'Sovereign Debt Reform and the Best Interest of Creditors' (2004) 57 Vanderbilt Law Review 1.

Bratton W, 'Pari Passu and A Distressed Sovereign's Rational Choices' (2004) 53 Emory Law Journal 823.

Broches A, 'International Legal Aspects of the Operations of the World Bank' in *Selected Essays: World Bank, ICSID, and Other Subjects of Public and Private International Law* (Martinus Nijhoff 1995).

Brudney V, 'Corporate Bondholders and Debtor Opportunism: In Bad Times and Good' (1992) 105 Harvard Law Review 1821.

Bruno E, 'Argentina Debt—The Settlement Clause' (SSRN Scholarly Paper, 17 December 2013).

Buchheit LC, 'Is Syndicated Lending a Joint Venture?' (1985) 4 International Financial Law Review 12.

Buchheit LC, 'The Negative Pledge Clause: The Games People Play' (1990) 9 International Financial Law Review 10.

Buchheit LC, 'The *Pari Passu* Clause *Sub Specie Aeternitatis*' (1991) 10 International Financial Law Review 11.

Buchheit LC, 'The Search for Intercreditor Parity' (2002) 8 Law & Business Review of America 73.

Buchheit LC, 'Sovereign Debt in the Light of Eternity' in RM Lastra and LC Buchheit (eds), *Sovereign Debt Management* (Oxford University Press 2014).

Buchheit LC, Chabert G, DeLong C, and Zettelmeyer J, 'How to Restructure Sovereign Debt: Lessons from Four Decades' (PIIE Working Paper, 5 June 2019).

Buchheit LC, Chabert G, DeLong C, and Zettelmeyer J, 'The Restructuring Process' in SA Abbas, A Pienkowski, and K Rogoff (eds), *Sovereign Debt: A Guide for Economists and Practitioners* (Oxford University Press 2020).

Buchheit LC and Gulati GM, 'Exit Consents in Sovereign Bond Exchanges' (2000) 48 UCLA Law Review 59.

Buchheit LC and Gulati GM, 'Sovereign Bonds and the Collective Will' (2002) 51 Emory Law Journal 1317.

Buchheit LC and Gulati GM, 'The Argentine Collective Action Clause Controversy' (2020) 15 Capital Markets Law Journal 464.

Buchheit LC and Gulati GM, 'The Duty of Creditors to Cooperate in Sovereign Debt Workouts (with Spanish Translation)' (SSRN Scholarly Paper, 12 June 2021).

Buchheit LC and Pam JS, 'The *Pari Passu* Clause in Sovereign Debt Instruments' (2004) 53 Emory Law Journal 869.
Buchheit LC and Reisner R, 'The Effect of the Sovereign Debt Restructuring Process on Inter-Creditor Relationships' (1988) 1988 University of Illinois Law Review 493.
Burn L, 'Pari Passu Clauses: English Law after *NML v Argentina*' (2014) 9 Capital Markets Law Journal 2.
Carreau D, 'Le rééchelonnement de la dette extérieure des Etats' (1985) 112 Journal du droit international 5.
Chabot B and Gulati GM, 'Santa Anna and His Black Eagle: The Origins of *Pari Passu*?' (2014) 9 Capital Markets Law Journal 216.
Chamon M, Schumacher J, and Trebesch C, 'Foreign-Law Bonds: Can They Reduce Sovereign Borrowing Costs?' (ECB Working Paper Series, June 2018).
Cheng G, Diaz-Cassou J, and Erce A, 'The Macroeconomic Effects of Official Debt Restructuring: Evidence from the Paris Club' (2019) 71 Oxford Economic Papers 344.
Choi SJ and Gulati GM, 'Contract as Statute' (2006) 104 Michigan Law Review 1129.
Chung K and Papaioannou MG, 'Do Enhanced Collective Action Clauses Affect Sovereign Borrowing Costs?' (IMF Working Paper, August 2020).
Clark I and Lyratzakis D, 'Towards a More Robust Sovereign Debt Restructuring Architecture: Innovations from Ecuador and Argentina' (2021) 16 Capital Markets Law Journal 31.
Cordero-Moss G, *International Commercial Contracts: Applicable Sources and Enforceability* (Cambridge University Press 2014).
Council of the EU, 'Eurogroup Report to Leaders on EMU Deepening' (Press release 738/18, 12 April 2018), <https://www.consilium.europa.eu/en/press/press-releases/2018/12/04/eurogroup-report-to-leaders-on-emu-deepening/pdf> accessed 1 November 2019.
Crawford J, *Brownlie's Principles of Public International Law* (8th edn, Oxford University Press 2012).
Crawford J, *Brownlie's Principles of Public International Law* (9th edn, Oxford University Press 2019).
Cruces JJ and Trebesch C, 'Sovereign Defaults: The Price of Haircuts' (CESifo Working Paper Series, 2011).
Cruz A de la and Lagos I, 'CACs at Work: What Next? Lessons from the Argentine and Ecuadorian 2020 Debt Restructurings' (2021) 16 Capital Markets Law Journal 226.
Dang H, 'The Applicability of International Law as Governing Law of State Contracts' (2010) 17 Australian International Law Journal 133.
Davies A, 'Group Comparison vs. Best Treatment in International Economic Law Nondiscrimination Analysis' in AK Bjorklund (ed), *Yearbook on International Investment Law & Policy 2014–2015* (Oxford University Press 2016).
De Witte B, 'Using International Law in the Euro Crisis: Causes and Consequences' (ARENA Working Paper, 2013).
DeLong C and Aggarwal N, 'Strengthening the Contractual Framework for Sovereign Debt Restructuring—the IMF's Perspective' (2016) 11 Capital Markets Law Journal 25.
DiMascio N and Pauwelyn J, 'Nondiscrimination in Trade and Investment Treaties: Worlds Apart or Two Sides of the Same Coin?' (2008) 102 American Journal of International Law 48.
Drago LM, 'State Loans in Their Relation to International Policy' (1907) 1 American Journal of International Law 692.
Drake KS, 'The Fall and Rise of the Exit Consent' (2013–14) 63 Duke Law Journal 1589.
ECB, 'Technical Features of Outright Monetary Transactions' (*European Central Bank*, 9 June 2012) <https://www.ecb.europa.eu/press/pr/date/2012/html/pr120906_1.en.html> accessed 11 March 2022.

214 BIBLIOGRAPHY

ECB, 'Asset Purchase Programmes' (*European Central Bank*, 3 August 2022) <https://www.ecb.europa.eu/mopo/implement/app/html/index.en.html> accessed 11 March 2022.

Ehmke DC, 'Publicly Offered Debt in the Shadow of Insolvency' (2015) 16 European Business Organisation Law Review 63.

Ellingsæter SS, 'Creditor Priority and Financial Stability: A Study of the Emergence and Rationales of the Creditor Hierarchy in EU and EEA Bank Insolvency Law' (PhD, University of Oslo 2020).

Elliott L, Inman P, and Smith H, 'IMF Admits: We Failed to Realise the Damage Austerity Would Do to Greece', *The Guardian* (6 May 2013) <http://www.theguardian.com/business/2013/jun/05/imf-underestimated-damage-austerity-would-do-to-greece> accessed 11 March 2022.

Ellmers B and Gambini A, 'Debt Justice Prevails at the Belgian Constitutional Court: Vulture Funds Law Survives Challenge by NML Capital' (*Eurodad*, 6 May 2018) <https://www.eurodad.org/vulture-funds-blog> accessed 11 March 2022.

ESM, 'EFSF Extends Loan Maturities for Ireland and Portugal' (Press release, *European Stability Mechanism*, 24 June 2013), <https://www.esm.europa.eu/press-releases/efsf-extends-loan-maturities-ireland-and-portugal> accessed 11 March 2022.

ESM, 'Before the ESM' (*European Stability Mechanism*, no date) <https://www.esm.europa.eu/efsf-overview> accessed 11 March 2022.

ESM, 'Explainers' (*European Stability Mechanism*, no date) <https://www.esm.europa.eu/explainers> accessed 11 March 2022.

ESM, 'Lending Toolkit' (*European Stability Mechanism*, no date) <https://www.esm.europa.eu/assistance/lending-toolkit> accessed 11 March 2022.

Eurogroup, 'Statement by the Eurogroup' (Press release, 28 November 2010), <https://www.consilium.europa.eu/uedocs/cms_data/docs/pressdata/en/ecofin/118050.pdf> accessed 14 March 2019.

Eurogroup, 'Eurogroup Statement on the Pandemic Crisis Support' (Press release, 5 August 2020), <https://www.consilium.europa.eu/en/press/press-releases/2020/05/08/eurogroup-statement-on-the-pandemic-crisis-support/> accessed 29 April 2022.

European Commission, 'European Financial Stabilisation Mechanism (EFSM)' (*europa.eu*, no date) <https://ec.europa.eu/info/business-economy-euro/economic-and-fiscal-policy-coordination/financial-assistance-eu/funding-mechanisms-and-facilities/european-financial-stabilisation-mechanism-efsm_en> accessed 11 March 2022.

European Union, 'Court of Justice of the European Union (CJEU)' (*europa.eu*, no date) <https://european-union.europa.eu/institutions-law-budget/institutions-and-bodies/institutions-and-bodies-profiles/court-justice-european-union-cjeu_en> accessed 11 March 2022.

Feilchenfeld EH, 'Rights and Remedies of Holders of Foreign Bonds' in *Bonds and Bondholders: Rights and Remedies, with Forms*, vol 1 (Burdette Smith Co 1934).

Feilchenfeld EH, Elrick E de M, and Judd OG, 'Priority Problems in Public Debt Settlements' (1930) 30 Columbia Law Review 1115.

FMLC, 'Analysis of the Role, Use and Meaning of *Pari Passu* Clauses in Sovereign Debt Obligations as a Matter of English Law' (FMLC Paper, March 2005) <https://fmlc.org/publications/paper-pari-passu-clauses/> accessed 21 December 2022.

FMLC, '*Pari Passu* Clauses: Analysis of the Role, Use and Meaning of *Pari Passu* Clauses in Sovereign Debt Obligations as a Matter of English Law' (April 2015) <https://fmlc.org/publications/report-pari-passu-clauses-13-april-2015/> accessed 21 December 2022.

FMLC, 'About the FMLC' (*Financial Markets Law Committee*, no date) <http://fmlc.org/about-the-fmlc/> accessed 11 March 2022.

Focarelli C, '*Borri v. Argentina*, Request for a Ruling on Jurisdiction, Case No 11225, (2005) 88 Riv Dir Int 856, ILDC 296 (IT 2005), 27th May 2005, Italy; Supreme Court of Cassation' in A

Nollkaemper and A Reinisch (eds), *Oxford Reports on International Law in Domestic Courts* (Oxford University Press 2006).
Fox H and Webb P, *The Law of State Immunity* (Oxford International Law Library, 2nd edn, Oxford University Press 2008).
Fox H and Webb P, *The Law of State Immunity* (Oxford International Law Library, 3rd edn, Oxford University Press 2015).
Fresnillo I, 'The G20 Debt Service Suspension Initiative: Draining out the Titanic with a Bucket?' (Eurodad Briefing Paper, October 2020) <https://www.eurodad.org/g20_dssi_shadow_report> accessed 21 December 2022.
Friedman S, *Expropriation in International Law* (Stevens & Sons 1953).
G10, 'Report of the G-10 Working Group on Contractual Clauses' (26 September 2002) <https://www.bis.org/publ/gten08.htm> accessed 21 December 2022.
G20, 'G20 Finance Ministers and Central Bank Governors Meeting, Fukuoka (Jun. 8–9, 2019)' (Communiqué, *Japanese Ministry of Finance*, June 2019), Communiqué <https://www.mof.go.jp/english/policy/international_policy/convention/g20/communique.htm> accessed 11 March 2022.
G20, 'Statement of Extraordinary G20 Finance Ministers and Central Bank Governors' Meeting (Virtual)' (13 November 2020) <https://www.imf.org/-/media/Files/News/news-articles/english-extraordinary-g20-fmcbg-statement-november-13.ashx> accessed 6 February 2022.
Gaspar V, Medas P, and Perrelli R, 'Global Debt Reaches a Record $226 Trillion' (*IMF Blog*, 15 December 2021) <https://blogs.imf.org/2021/12/15/global-debt-reaches-a-record-226-trillion/> accessed 1 May 2022.
Gelos RG, Sandleris GM, and Sahay R, 'Sovereign Borrowing by Developing Countries: What Determines Market Access?' (IMF Working Paper, 11 January 2004).
Gelpern A, 'Contract Hope and Sovereign Redemption' (2013) 8 Capital Markets Law Journal 132.
Gelpern A, 'Hard, Soft, and Embedded: Implementing Principles on Promoting Responsible Sovereign Lending and Borrowing' in C Espósito, Y Li, and JP Bohoslavsky (eds), *Sovereign Financing and International Law: The UNCTAD Principles on Responsible Sovereign Lending and Borrowing* (Oxford University Press 2013).
Gelpern A, 'A Sensible Step to Mitigate Sovereign Bond Dysfunction' (*PIIE RealTime Economic Issues Watch blog*, 29 August 2014) <https://www.piie.com/blogs/realtime-economic-issues-watch/sensible-step-mitigate-sovereign-bond-dysfunction> accessed 11 March 2022.
Gelpern A, 'Courts and Sovereigns in the *Pari Passu* Goldmines' (2016) 11 Capital Markets Law Journal 251.
Gelpern A, 'Sovereign Debt: Now What?' (2016) 41 (Special edition on sovereign debt) Yale Journal of International Law Online 45.
Gelpern A, 'The Importance of Being Standard' in Legal Issues on Government Debt Restructuring (ECB January 2017) 23.
Gelpern A, 'Imagine Riding the Ceteris Pari-Bus into the Sunset ... in Argentina' (*Credit Slips: A discussion on credit, finance, and bankruptcy*, 11 July 2019) <https://www.creditslips.org/creditslips/2019/11/imagine-riding-the-cetris-pari-bus-into-the-sunset-in-argentina.html> accessed 12 March 2022.
Gelpern A and Setser B, 'Domestic and External Debt: The Doomed Quest for Equal Treatment' (2003–04) 35 Georgetown Journal of International Law 795.
Gerszon Mahler D, Yonzan N, Lakner C, Castaneda Aguilar RA, and Wu H, 'Updated Estimates of the Impact of COVID-19 on Global Poverty: Turning the Corner on the Pandemic in 2021?' (*World Bank Blogs*, 24 June 2021) <https://blogs.worldbank.org/opendata/updated-estimates-impact-covid-19-global-poverty-turning-corner-pandemic-2021> accessed 1 May 2022.

Goldmann M, 'On the Comparative Foundations of Principles in International Law' in C Espósito, Y Li, and JP Bohoslavsky (eds), *Sovereign Financing and International Law: The UNCTAD Principles on Responsible Sovereign Lending and Borrowing* (Oxford University Press 2013).

Goldmann M, 'Putting Your Faith in Good Faith: A Principled Strategy for Smoother Debt Workouts' (2016) 41 (Special edition on sovereign debt) Yale Journal of International Law Online 117.

Goldmann M, 'Foreign Investment, Sovereign Debt and Human Rights' in I Bantekas and C Lumina (eds), *Sovereign Debt and Human Rights* (Oxford University Press 2018).

Gray RB, 'Collective Action Clauses' in Proceedings of Inter-Regional Debt Management Conference and WADMO Conference, Geneva, Switzerland (United Nations Publications 2005) 43.

Grosse Steffen C, Grund S, and Schumacher J, 'Collective Action Clauses in the Euro Area: A Law and Economic Analysis of the First Five Years' (2019) 14 Capital Markets Law Journal 134.

Gruić B and Wooldridge P, 'Enhancements to the BIS Debt Securities Statistics' [2012] BIS Quarterly Review 63.

Grund S, '*Unidentified Holders of Greek Government Bonds v. Greece*, Appeal to Federal Court of Justice, XI ZR 796/16, ILDC 2881 (DE 2017) 19th December 2017, Germany' in A Nollkaemper and A Reinisch (eds), *Oxford Reports on International Law in Domestic Courts* (Oxford University Press 2006).

Grund S, 'Enforcing Sovereign Debt in Court—A Comparative Analysis of Litigation and Arbitration Following the Greek Debt Restructuring of 2012' (2017) 1 University of Vienna Law Review 34.

Grund S, 'Restructuring Argentina's Sovereign Debts – Navigating the Legal Labyrinth' (SSRN Scholarly Paper, 11 December 2019).

Grund S and Grle F, 'The European Central Bank's Public Sector Purchase Programme (PSPP), the Prohibition of Monetary Financing and Sovereign Debt Restructuring Scenarios' (2016) 41 European Law Review 781.

Gulati GM and Buchheit LC, 'Use of the Local Law Advantage in the Restructuring of European Sovereign Bonds' (2018) 3 University of Bologna Law Review 2, 172.

Gulati GM, Panizza U, Weidemaier WMC, and Willingham G, 'When Governments Promise to Prioritize Public Debt: Do Markets Care?' (2020) 6 Journal of Financial Regulation 41.

Guzman M, 'An Analysis of Argentina's 2001 Default Resolution' (2020) 62 Comp Econ Stud 701–38.

Guzman M and Stiglitz JE, 'A Soft Law Mechanism for Sovereign Debt Restructuring Based on the UN Principles' (Friedrich Ebert Stiftung International Policy Analysis, October 2016),

Hall WE, *A Treatise on International Law* (JB Atlay ed, 5th edn, Clarendon Press 1904).

Herdegen M, *Principles of International Economic Law* (2nd edn, Oxford University Press 2016).

Hernández GI, *The International Court of Justice and the Judicial Function* (Oxford University Press 2014).

Hofmann C, 'Sovereign-Debt Restructuring in Europe under the New Model Collective Action Clauses' (2014) 49 Texas International Law Journal 385.

House B, Joy M, and Sobrinho N, 'Sovereign Debt Restructurings: The Costs of Delay' (10 April 2017).

ICMA, 'ICMA Sovereign Bond Consultation Paper' (December 2013).

ICMA, 'Standard Aggregated Collective Action Clauses (CACs) for the Terms and Conditions of Sovereign Notes' (International Capital Market Association August 2014).

ICMA, 'About ICMA' (*International Capital Market Association*, no date) <https://www.icmagroup.org/About-ICMA/> accessed 12 March 2022.

BIBLIOGRAPHY 217

IIF, 'Principles for Stable Capital Flows and Fair Debt Restructuring and 2012 Addendum' (14 November 2004).

IIF, 'Principles for Stable Capital Flows and Fair Debt Restructuring in Emerging Markets' (22 November 2004).

IIF, 'Voluntary Principles for Debt Transparency' (6 October 2019).

IIF, 'IIF Letter to the G20 on Common Framework, Debt Transparency, ESG Considerations' (9 April 2021).

ILA, 'Report of the Sovereign Bankruptcy Study Group' (77th Biennial Conference of the International Law Association, Johannesburg, South Africa, no date) <https://ila.vettoreweb.com/Storage/Download.aspx?DbStorageId=2423&StorageFileGuid=f8a1fb00-b287-4094-bb00-ffb6b3c93c6a> accessed 13 March 2022.

IMF, Interim Committee of the Board of Governors on the International Monetary System, 'Press Communiqué from Thirty-First Meeting, Berlin (West), September 25–26, 1988' (Appendix V to IMF's 1989 Annual Report, *International Monetary Fund*, 26 October 1988), Appendix V to IMF's 1989 Annual Report <https://www.imf.org/external/pubs/ft/ar/archive/pdf/ar1989.pdf> accessed 11 November 2019.

IMF, Interim Committee of the Board of Governors on the International Monetary System, 'Press Communiqué from Thirty-Second Meeting, Washington, April 3–4, 1989' (Appendix V to IMF's 1989 Annual Report, *International Monetary Fund*, 4 April 1989), Appendix V to IMF's 1989 Annual Report <https://www.imf.org/external/pubs/ft/ar/archive/pdf/ar1989.pdf> accessed 11 November 2019.

IMF, 'Sovereign Debt Restructuring—Recent Developments and Implications for the Fund's Legal and Policy Framework' (Policy paper, 26 April 2013).

IMF, 'IMF Executive Board Discusses Strengthening the Contractual Framework in Sovereign Debt Restructuring' (Press release no 14/459, *International Monetary Fund*, 10 June 2014), <https://www.imf.org/en/News/Articles/2015/09/14/01/49/pr14459> accessed 13 March 2022.

IMF, 'Strengthening the Contractual Framework to Address Collective Action Problems in Sovereign Debt Restructuring' (Staff report, 9 February 2014), Staff report.

IMF, 'Second Progress Report on Inclusion of Enhanced Contractual Provisions in International Sovereign Bond Contracts' (Policy paper, 27 December 2016).

IMF, 'Multilateral Debt Relief Initiative—Questions and Answers' (*International Monetary Fund*, 28 July 2017) <https://www.imf.org/external/np/exr/mdri/eng/index.htm> accessed 30 April 2022.

IMF, 'Third Progress Report on Inclusion of Enhanced Contractual Provisions in International Sovereign Bond Contracts' (Policy paper, 15 December 2017).

IMF, 'The Debt Sustainability Framework for Low-Income Countries' (*International Monetary Fund*, 13 July 2018) <https://www.imf.org/external/pubs/ft/dsa/lic.htm> accessed 13 March 2022.

IMF, 'Fourth Progress Report on Inclusion of Enhanced Contractual Provisions in International Sovereign Bond Contract' (Policy paper, International Monetary Fund 21 March 2019).

IMF, 'G20 Operational Guidelines for Sustainable Financing—Survey Results and Policy Recommendation' (31 May 2019).

IMF, 'The International Architecture for Resolving Sovereign Debt Involving Private-Sector Creditors—Recent Developments, Challenges, And Reform Options' (Policy paper, 23 September 2020).

IMF, 'Special Drawing Rights (SDR)' (Factsheet, *International Monetary Fund*, 8 May 2021), Factsheet <https://www.imf.org/en/About/Factsheets/Sheets/2016/08/01/14/51/Special-Drawing-Right-SDR> accessed 13 March 2022.

IMF, 'Glossary of Selected Financial Terms' (*International Monetary Fund*, no date) <https://www.imf.org/external/np/fin/td/Docs/Glossary.pdf> accessed 30 October 2019.

IRC Task Force on IMF and global financial governance issues, 'The IMF's Role in Sovereign Debt Restructurings' (Occasional Paper Series, 14 September 2021).

Iversen A, 'Holdout Creditor Litigation: An Assessment of Legislative Initiatives to Counter Aggressive Sovereign Debt Creditor Litigators' (University of Oslo Faculty of Law Research Paper, 6 February 2015).

Iversen A, 'Solvency II and Sovereign Bonds' in M Andenas, RG Avesani, P Manes, F Vella, and PR Wood (eds), *Solvency II: A dynamic challenge for the insurance market* (Il Mulino 2017).

Iversen A, 'The Future of Involuntary Sovereign Debt Restructurings: *Mamatas and Others v Greece* and the Protection of Holdings of Sovereign Debt Instruments under the ECHR' (2019) 14 Capital Markets Law Journal 34.

Iversen A, 'Vulture Fund Legislation' (2019) 38 Banking & Financial Services Policy Report.

Jacob M and Schill SW, 'Fair and Equitable Treatment: Content, Practice, Method' in M Bungenberg, J Griebel, S Hobe, and A Reinisch (eds), *International Investment Law: A handbook* (C.H. Beck/Hart/Nomos 2015).

Jansen R, 'The European Stability Facility (EFSF) and the European Stability Mechanism (ESM)—A Legal Overview' (no date) 2011 EUREDIA 417.

Jennings RY, 'State Contracts in International Law' (1961) 37 Yearbook of International Law 156.

Jennings RY, 'General Course on Principles of International Law' (1967) 121 Collected Courses of the Hague Academy of International Law.

Jung Y and Han SD, 'Sovereign Debt Restructuring under the Investor-State Dispute Regime' (2014) 31 Journal of International Arbitration 75.

Kläger R, *'Fair and Equitable Treatment' in International Investment Law* (Cambridge Studies in International and Comparative Law, Cambridge University Press 2011).

Kolb R, 'Principles as Sources of International Law (With Special Reference to Good Faith)' (2006) 53 Netherlands International Law Review 1.

Kriebaum U and Reinisch A, 'Property, Right to, International Protection' in R Wolfrum (ed), *Max Planck Encyclopedia of Public International Law* (Oxford University Press 2019).

Kriebaum U and Schreuer C, 'The Concept of Property in Human Rights Law and International Investment Law' in S Breitenmoser, B Ehrenzeller, M Sassoli, W Stoffel, and BW Pfeifer (eds), *Human Rights, Democracy and the Rule of Law: Liber amicorum Luzius Wildhaber* (Nomos 2007).

Krueger AO and Hagan S, 'Sovereign Workouts: An IMF Perspective' (2005) 6 Chicago Journal of International Law 203.

Kupelyants H, *Sovereign Defaults Before Domestic Courts* (Oxford Private International Law Series, Oxford University Press 2018).

Lastra RM, 'The Role of the International Monetary Fund' in RM Lastra and LC Buchheit (eds), *Sovereign Debt Management* (Oxford University Press 2014).

Lauterpacht H, 'Private Law Analogies in International Law' (PhD, London School of Economics and Political Science 1926).

Lauterpacht H, *The Function of Law in the International Community* (first published 1933, Oxford University Press 2011).

Levine M, 'Pari Passu, Blobs and Fortune Cookies', *Bloomberg.com* (8 April 2017) <https://www.bloomberg.com/opinion/articles/2017-08-04/pari-passu-blobs-and-fortune-cookies> accessed 13 March 2022.

Li Y, 'How International Investment Agreements Have Made Debt Restructuring Even More Difficult and Costly' (South Centre Investment Policy Brief, February 2018).

Li Y and Panizza U, 'The Economic Rationale for the Principles on Promoting Responsible Sovereign Lending and Borrowing' in C Espósito, Y Li, and JP Bohoslavsky (eds), *Sovereign Financing and International Law: The UNCTAD Principles on Responsible Sovereign Lending and Borrowing* (Oxford University Press 2013).

Mann FA, 'State Contracts and State Responsibility' (1960) 54 American Journal of International Law 572.

Mann FA, *Further Studies in International Law* (Oxford University Press 1990).

Manuelides Y, 'Using the Local Law Advantage in Today's Eurozone (with Some References to the Republic of Arcadia and the *Mamatas* Judgment)' (2019) 14 Capital Markets Law Journal 469.

Marboe I and Reinisch A, 'Contracts between States and Foreign Private Law Persons' in R Wolfrum (ed), *Max Planck Encyclopedia of Public International Law* (Oxford University Press 2019).

Markakis M, 'European Court of Human Rights Rules on Greek Debt Restructuring' (*Oxford Human Rights Hub*, 30 July 2016) <https://ohrh.law.ox.ac.uk/european-court-of-human-rights-rules-on-greek-debt-restructuring/> accessed 14 March 2022.

Martha RSJ, 'Preferred Creditor Status under International Law: The Case of the International Monetary Fund' (1990) 39 International & Comparative Law Quarterly 801.

Martha RSJ, *The Financial Obligation in International Law* (Oxford University Press 2015).

Moore JB, *History and Digest of the International Arbitrations to Which the United States Has Been a Party* (Government Printing Office 1898).

Moore E and Wildau G, 'China Eyes Revamp of Sovereign Bonds', *Financial Times* (4 November 2016) <https://www.ft.com/content/b35681b6-fc1b-11e5-b3f6-11d5706b613b> accessed 14 March 2022.

Munevar D, 'The G20 "Common Framework for Debt Treatments beyond the DSSI": Is It Bound to Fail? (II)' (*Eurodad*, 28 October 2020) <https://www.eurodad.org/the_g20_common_framework_for_debt_treatments_beyond_the_dssi_is_it_bound_to_fail_2> accessed 1 May 2022.

National Bank of Belgium, 'Financial Stability Review 2005' (23 June 2005).

Nijman JE and Nollkaemper A, *New Perspectives on the Divide Between National and International Law* (Oxford University Press 2007).

Norges Bank, 'About Government Debt' (1 January 2022) <https://www.norges-bank.no/en/topics/Government-debt/About-government-debt/> accessed 14 March 2022.

OECD, '"Indirect Expropriation" and the "Right to Regulate" in International Investment Law | READ Online' (OECD Working Papers on International Investment, September 2004).

Olivares-Caminal R, *Legal Aspects of Sovereign Debt Restructuring* (Sweet & Maxwell 2009).

Olivares-Caminal R, 'The *Pari Passu* Clause in Sovereign Debt Instruments: Developments in Recent Litigation' (BIS Paper, Bank for International Settlements 2013).

Olivares-Caminal R, Kornberg A, Paterson S, Douglas J, Guynn R, and Singh D, *Debt Restructuring* (2nd edn, Oxford University Press 2016).

Ostry JD, Loungani P, and Furceri D, 'Neoliberalism: Oversold? - Instead of Delivering Growth, Some Neoliberal Policies Have Increased Inequality, in Turn Jeopardizing Durable Expansion' (2016) 53 Finance & Development 38.

Padian M and Porteous J, 'Carrots and Sticks: Limits on Majority Creditors' Rights to Bind a Minority' [2017] Butterworths Journal of International Banking and Financial Law 22–24.

Palchetti P, 'The Role of General Principles in Promoting the Development of Customary International Rules' in M Andenas, M Fitzmaurice, A Tanzi, and J Wouters (eds), *General principles and the coherence of international law*, vol 37 (Queen Mary Studies in International Law, Brill Nijhoff 2019).

Paris Club, 'Key Figures' (*Paris Club*, no date) <https://clubdeparis.org/en/communications/page/key-numbers> accessed 8 November 2019.

Paris Club, 'What Does Comparability of Treatment Mean?' (*Paris Club*, no date) <https://clubdeparis.org/en/communications/page/what-does-comparability-of-treatment-mean> accessed 1 May 2022.

Pellet A, 'Article 38' in A Zimmerman, K Oellers-Frahm, CJ Tomuschat, and CJ Tams (eds), *The Statute of the International Court of Justice: A Commentary* (Oxford Commentaries on International Law, 2nd edn, Oxford University Press 2012).

Perera M and Jones T, 'Debt Sustainability Review: Tinkering around the Edges While Crises Loom' (*Bretton Woods Project*, 12 June 2017) <https://www.brettonwoodsproject.org/2017/12/debt-sustainability-review-tinkering-around-edges-crises-loom/> accessed 14 March 2022.

Pohjanpalo K, 'Finland's Collateral Demand Fueled by Greek Bailout Fatigue', *Bloomberg.com* (30 August 2011) <https://www.bloomberg.com/news/articles/2011-08-29/finland-collateral-demand-fueled-by-bailout-fatigue> accessed 14 March 2022.

Polanco R, *The Return of the Home State to Investor-State Disputes: Bringing Back Diplomatic Protection?* (Cambridge International Trade and Economic Law, Cambridge University Press 2019).

Przybysz A, 'Anti-Vulture Fund Legislation Introduced in Jersey as One Vulture Swoops in on Argentina' (*Blog the Debt*, 22 October 2012) <https://jubileeusa.typepad.com/blog_the_debt/2012/10/anti-vulture-fund-legislation-introduced-in-jersey-as-one-vulture-swoops-in-on-argentina-.html> accessed 14 March 2022.

Reinisch A, 'European Court Practice Concerning State Immunity from Enforcement Measures' (2006) 17 European Journal of International Law 803.

Reinisch A, 'Expropriation' in P Muchlinski, F Ortino, and C Schreuer (eds), *The Oxford Handbook of International Investment Law* (Oxford University Press 2008).

Reuter P, *Introduction to the Law of Treaties* (J Mico and P Haggenmacher trs, 2nd edn, Paul Kegan International 1995).

Roberts A and Koskenniemi M, *Is International Law International?* (Oxford University Press 2017).

Roos JE, *Why Not Default? The Political Economy of Sovereign Debt* (Princeton University Press 2019).

Schadler S, 'The IMF's Preferred Creditor Status: Does It Still Make Sense After the Euro Crisis?' (CIGI Policy Brief, 20 March 2014).

Schefer KN, *International Investment Law: Texts, Cases and Materials* (3rd edn, Edward Elgar 2020).

Schill SW, 'The Impact of International Investment Law on Public Contracts' in M Audit and SW Schill (eds), *Transnational Law of Public Contracts* (Bruylant 2016).

Schreuer C, 'The Concept of Expropriation under the ETC and Other Investment Protection Treaties' (2005) 2 Transnational Dispute Management 1.

Schreuer CH, *The ICSID Convention: A Commentary* (1st edn, Cambridge University Press 2001).

Schreuer CH, Malintoppi L, Reinisch A, and Sinclair A, *The ICSID Convention: A Commentary* (2nd edn, Cambridge University Press 2009).

Shaw MN, *International Law* (5th edn, Cambridge University Press 2003).

Shelton D, *International Law and Domestic Legal Systems: Incorporation, Transformation, and Persuasion* (Oxford University Press 2011).

Shleifer A, 'Will the Sovereign Debt Market Survive?' (2003) 93 American Economic Review 85.

Singh K, 'The India–US Bilateral Investment Treaty Will Not Be an Easy Ride' (*East Asia Forum*, 2 October 2015) <https://www.eastasiaforum.org/2015/02/10/the-india-us-bilateral-investment-treaty-will-not-be-an-easy-ride/> accessed 14 March 2022.

Sookun D, *Stop Vulture Fund Lawsuits: A Handbook* (Commonwealth Secretariat 2010).

Stability Mechanism, 'ESM Treaty Reform—Explainer' (*European Stability Mechanism*, no date) <https://www.esm.europa.eu/about-esm/esm-treaty-reform-explainer> accessed 11 March 2022.

Steinkamp S and Westermann F, 'The Role of Creditor Seniority in Europe's Sovereign Debt Crisis' (2014) 29 Economic Policy 495.

Steinsland K, Valvik ME, Nordby KJ, and Strand M, 'Oljefondet stemte nei til Hellas-avtalen', *Aftenposten* (Oslo, 16 March 2012) <https://www.aftenposten.no/okonomi/i/naPJQ/oljefondet-stemte-nei-til-hellas-avtalen> accessed 14 March 2022.

Stolper AE and Dougherty S, 'Collective Action Clauses: How the Argentina Litigation Changed the Sovereign Debt Markets' (2017) 12 Capital Markets Law Journal 239.

Strik D, 'Investment Protection of Sovereign Debt and Its Implications on the Future of Investment Law in the EU' (2012) 29 Journal of International Arbitration 183.

Thrasher RD and Gallagher KP, 'Mission Creep: The Emerging Role of International Investment Agreements in Sovereign Debt Restructuring' (2015) 6 Journal of Globalization and Development 257.

Tomz M and Wright MLJ, 'Do Countries Default in "Bad Times"?' (Working Paper, Federal Reserve Bank of San Francisco 25 May 2007).

Townsend I, 'Debt Relief (Developing Countries) Bill [Bill 17 of 2009-10]' (Research briefing, 25 February 2010).

Trebesch C, Papaioannou MG, and Das US, 'Sovereign Debt Restructurings 1950-2010: Literature Survey, Data, and Stylized Facts' (IMF Working Paper, August 2012).

UN Human Rights Special Procedures (Special Rapporteurs, Independent Experts & Working Groups), 'Open Letter to the IMF' (21 December 2017) <https://www.ohchr.org/sites/default/files/Documents/Issues/Development/IEDebt/Open_Letter_IMF_21Dec2017.pdf> accessed 21 December 2022.

UNCTAD, 'Fair and Equitable Treatment: A Sequel' (UNCTAD Series on Issues in International Investment Agreements II, February 2012).

UNCTAD, 'World Investment Report 2019: Special Economic Zones' (World Investment Reports, 6 December 2019).

UNICEF, 'COVID-19 and the Looming Debt Crisis: Protecting and Transforming Social Spending for Inclusive Recoveries' (Innocenti research report, April 2021).

UNIDO, 'Public Goods for Economic Development' (UNIDO Publication, 2008).

United Nations, 'Liquidity and Debt Solutions to Invest in the SDGs: The Time to Act is Now' (United Nations, March 2021) <https://unsdg.un.org/resources/liquidity-and-debt-solutions-invest-sdgs-time-act-now> accessed 21 December.

Van de Poel J, 'New Anti-Vulture Fund Legislation in Belgium: An Example for Europe and Rest of the World' (*Eurodad*, 5 December 2015) <https://www.eurodad.org/new_anti_vulture_fund_legislation_in_belgium> accessed 15 March 2022.

Van Rompuy H, 'The European Council in 2011' (Publications Office of the European Union January 2012).

Waibel M, 'Opening Pandora's Box: Sovereign Bonds in International Arbitration' (2007) 101 American Journal of International Law 711.

Waibel M, *Sovereign Defaults before International Courts and Tribunals* (Cambridge University Press 2011).

Wautelet P, 'Vulture Funds, Creditors and Sovereign Debtors: How to Find a Balance?' in M Audit (ed), *L'insolvabilité souveraine* (Science Po 2011).

Wautelet P, 'International Public Contracts: Applicable Law and Dispute Resolution' in M Audit and SW Schill (eds), *The Internationalization of Public Contracts* (Bruylant 2013).

Weidemaier WMC, 'Sovereign Debt after *NML v Argentina*' (2013) 8 Capital Markets Law Journal 123.

Weidemaier WMC, 'Restructuring Italian (or Other Euro Area) Debt: Do Euro CACs Constrain or Expand the Options?' (SSRN Scholarly Paper, 4 February 2019).

Weidemaier WMC and Gulati GM, 'A People's History of Collective Action Clauses' (2013) 54 Virginia Journal of International Law 51.

Weidemaier WMC and Gulati GM, 'Can Argentina Discriminate Against Bonds Issued Under Macri?' (*Credit Slips: A discussion on credit, finance, and bankruptcy*, 11 April 2019) <https://www.creditslips.org/creditslips/2019/11/can-argentina-discriminate-against-bonds-issued-under-macri.html> accessed 15 March 2022.

Weidemaier WMC, Scott RE, and Gulati GM, 'Origin Myths, Contracts, and the Hunt for *Pari Passu*' (2011) 38 Law & Social Inquiry 1, 74.

Wood PR, 'Debt Priorities in Sovereign Insolvency' (1982) 1 International Financial Law Review 4.

Wood PR, 'Syndicated Credit Agreement: Majority Voting' (2003) 62 The Cambridge Law Journal 261.

Wood PR, *Conflict of Laws and International Finance*, vol 6 (The Law and Practice of International Finance Series, 1st edn, Sweet & Maxwell 2007).

Wood PR, *International Loans, Bonds, Guarantees, Legal Opinions*, vol 3 (The Law and Practice of International Finance Series, 2nd edn, Sweet & Maxwell 2007).

Wood PR, *Principles of International Insolvency*, vol 1 (The Law and Practice of International Finance Series, 2nd edn, Sweet & Maxwell 2007).

Wood PR, 'Corporate Bankruptcy Law and State Insolvencies' in RM Lastra and LC Buchheit (eds), *Sovereign debt management* (Oxford University Press 2014).

Wood PR, 'The Origins and Future of Non-Discrimination in Sovereign Bankruptcies: A Comment' (2014) 9 Capital Markets Law Journal 293.

World Bank, 'New Reforms to DSF to Provide a Simpler and More Comprehensive Way to Assess Risks to Debt Sustainability' (*World Bank*, 10 February 2017) <https://www.worldbank.org/en/news/feature/2017/10/02/new-reforms-to-dsf-to-provide-a-simpler-and-more-comprehensive-way-to-assess-risks-to-debt-sustainability> accessed 29 February 2020.

Wright MLJ, 'Sovereign Debt Restructuring: Problems and Prospects' (2012) 2 Harvard Business Law Review 153.

Yianni A, 'Resolution of Sovereign Financial Crises—Evolution of the Private Sector Restructuring Process' [1999] Bank of England Financial Stability Review 78.

Zamour R, '*NML v. Argentina* and the Ratable Payment Interpretation of the *Pari Passu* Clause' (2013) 38 Yale Journal of International Law Online 55.

Zandstra D, 'New Aggregated Collective Action Clauses and Evolution in the Restructuring of Sovereign Debt Securities' (2017) 12 Capital Markets Law Journal 180.

Zettelmeyer J, Trebesch C, and Gulati GM, 'The Greek Debt Restructuring: An Autopsy' (2013) 28 Economic Policy 513.

Ziegler AR and Baumgartner J, 'Good Faith as a General Principle of (International) Law' in AD Mitchell, M Sornarajah, and T Voon (eds), *Good Faith and International Economic Law* (Oxford University Press 2015).

Index

For the benefit of digital users, indexed terms that span two pages (e.g., 52–53) may, on occasion, appear on only one of those pages.

abuse of rights *see also* majority voting provisions, abuse of minority rights in
    good faith standard 192, 194, 195–200
    holdout creditors 192, 198, 201–2
    minority creditors 4, 105–9
    vulture fund legislation 123
acta iure gestionis see commercial matters (*acta iure gestionis*)
acts of State (*acta iure imperii*) 54–56
    categorization of the restructuring act 42–43, 44–45, 53–54, 55–56, 187–88
    commercial matters (*acta iure gestionis*) 42–43, 44–45, 53–54, 55–56, 187–88
    mixed activities/continuous transactions 45–53, 54, 55
    Recast Brussels Regulation 34, 35–37, 40
Addis Ababa Action Agenda on Financing for Development 197
alternative crisis management tools 14–15
arbitration 104, 144
    diplomatic protection 132, 134–35
    expropriation clause 145–46
    fair and equitable treatment 146–47
    international investment agreements 28–29, 136–39, 140, 141–42, 144
    vulture fund legislation 123
Argentina, debt restructurings in 21
    Abaclat v Argentina 136–37
    Ajdler v Province of Mendoza 92–94, 96
    amount of money 6
    Argentina v Weltover 46–47
    attachment orders 165, 167–68
    Brussels I Convention 52–53
    collective action clauses (CACs) 101, 102, 105–9
    court cases, number of 6
    discrimination, prohibition of 160–61
    German law 51–52, 192–94, 199–200
    good faith standard 192–94, 199–200
    haircuts 105–6
    holdout creditors 81–82, 88–89, 165–68, 192, 199–200
    IMF, payments to 165–68
    injunctions 165–67
    insolvency principles in domestic law, transferability of 192–94
    Italy 52–53
    Knighthead v BNYM 89–92
    NML v Argentina decision 87, 88–97
    Pac Man strategy 106–7, 108–9
    pari passu clauses 92–94, 96, 165–68
    sovereign immunity 46–47, 51–52, 165, 167–68
attachment orders 165, 209
austerity measures 16–18

Baetens, Freya 143, 160, 180–81
bail-outs 19–20, 170–71, 172, 174
Bank for International Settlements (BIS) 64
Borchard, Edwin M 130, 131–32, 133–34, 168–69
Boudreau, Melissa 67, 166
Buchheit, Lee C 13, 81–83, 84–85, 101, 107, 113–14

CACs *see* collective action clauses (CACs)
Carreau, Dominique 67
Chabot, Benjamin 84–85
challenges *see* systemic challenges
Chamon, Marcos 208
Charter of Fundamental Rights of the EU (CFEU) 32, 158–59
China 44–45, 94

224 INDEX

choice of law
  clauses 33, 34–35, 40
  domestic law 78, 79
  governing law 25, 28–29
  internationalization of state
    contracts 28–30
civil and commercial matters 34, 35–
  36, 37, 40
claims commissions 132, 134–35
coercive measures
  collective action clauses
    (CACs) 98, 182–83
  discrimination, prohibition of 156, 195
  exit consent 98
  expropriation clause 145–46, 181
  fair and equitable treatment 147
  good faith standard 112
  prejudice 19–20
  property, right to 149, 151–52, 156
collateralized public international debt 61–
  62, 63
collective action clauses (CACs) 101, 102,
  105–9
  aggregated CACs 101, 102–3, 104–7
  boilerplate provisions 112–13
  case law, relevance of 109–10
  coercive measures 98, 182–83
  courts, interference of 98
  discriminatory majority decisions 98–99,
    117–19, 179
    exit consent 103, 179
    judicial scrutiny 110–12
    majority voting 104
    preferential treatment 117–18, 119
    Redwood Master v TD Bank 117–18
  domestic law 78, 79
  English law 98, 100–1, 110–12, 117–19
  enhanced CACs 102, 105–6, 107, 204–5
  Euro area Model CAC 103
  European Central Bank 174
  exit consent 103, 109, 110, 113, 118–
    19, 179
  exploitation by debtor states and minority
    creditors 98–99
  expropriation clauses 98, 145, 181
  fourth-generation CACs 102–3, 104
  general features 99–103
  good faith standard 111–18, 119, 195–96,
    199
  governing law 98

haircuts 105–6
holdout creditors 98, 100–2, 106, 108–
  10, 204–5
good faith 199
ICMA Model CAC 106, 108
majority voting procedures 174
ICMA model CAC 102–3, 104–8, 157
  all or nothing features 107–8
  enhanced 105–6, 107
  redesignation strategy 106–7
  Reserved Matters, modification to 102
  uniform applicability clauses 104–5,
    108–9
IMF 101–3
majority decisions, judicial scrutiny
  of 110–12
majority powers, abuse of 98, 103, 110–20,
  179
majority voting provisions 103–4,
  174, 178
market-based approach 99, 109–10
minority creditors 105–20, 179
  abuse, risk of 105–9
  binding to restructuring agreements 98,
    99–103, 110
  case law, relevance of 109
  good faith standard 111–18, 119
  protection 101, 105–9, 110–20, 179
  threshold 109, 119–20
model CACs 101, 102–3, 104–9
New York law 98, 100–1, 111–12, 119
no-action clauses 99
origins 100–1
Pac Man strategy 106–7, 108–9
pari passu clauses 94, 97, 104–5, 178
pricing effects 207–8
property, right to 151–52
Recast Brussels Regulation 36–37
redesignation strategy 106–7, 108–9
retroactivity 151–52
room for manoeuvre 204–5
sharing clauses 99
single-limb CACs 103, 104–5, 106–9
Sovereign Debt Restructuring Mechanism
  (SDRM) 101–2
subordination 60
supermajorities 99–101
sustainable debt restructuring 98, 176–77,
  204–5
two-limb CACs 106

INDEX

uniform applicability clauses 103, 104–5, 108–9, 118–19, 178, 179, 182–83
collective action problems *see* **collective action clauses (CACs); exit consent**
commercial matters (*acta iure gestionis*) 41, 42–54
   acts of State, exclusion of (*acte iure imperii*) 42–43, 44–45, 53–54, 55–56, 187–88
   categorization of the restructuring act 42–43, 44–45, 53–54, 55–56, 187–88
   Jurisdictional Immunities decision (ICJ) 44–45
   mixed activities/continuous transactions 45–53, 54, 55
   Recast Brussels Regulation 33–37, 40
conflicts between debtors-creditors 18–20, 175
conflict of laws *see* **private international law**
contract
   ad hoc regulatory framework 203
   administrative contracts concept 77–78
   consumer contracts 34–35
   debt restructuring as a contract-based tool 3, 14
   diplomatic protection 130–33
   employment contracts 34
   internationalization of state contracts 25–30
   jurisdiction 39
   local law advantage 30–31
   market-based reforms 204
   private law entities 24–30, 77–78
   regulation 203, 204
   standard terms 79, 101, 102–3, 104–9
   sustainable debt restructuring 14
Covid-19 205–7
   Common Framework for debt treatment beyond the DSSI (G20) 205–6
   comparability of treatment 206
   creditor participation, lack of 205–7
   Debt Service Suspension Initiative (DSSI) (G20/World Bank) 205–7
   developing countries 205–7
   G20 205–7
   IMF 206–7
   Pandemic Crisis Support 71
   private law entities 206–7
Crawford, James 26, 29–30, 58–59, 190–91
cultural rights 17–18

currency, inflation of 14–15
customary international law 128, 129–35
   diplomatic protection 130–32, 133–35
   equality rule 58–59
   expropriation 132
   good faith standard 191–92
   international investment agreements 140
   international minimum standard 130–32, 133–35
   most-favoured-nation (MFN) treatment standard 140
   national treatment standard 140
   opinio juris 66–67
   preferred creditor status 63, 64, 65–68, 69, 73, 170
   Serbian Loans case 133
   sovereign immunity 44–45, 53–54
   state practice 66–67
debt restructuring, definition of 8–9
Debt Service Suspension Initiative (DSSI) (G20/World Bank) 205–7
developing countries
   aid, diversion of 121–22
   Covid-19 205–7
   development assistance programmes 122
   emerging market bonds 31
   Emerging Market Principles 196–97
   governing law 78–79
   heavily-indebted countries 124–25, 126, 205–6
   political will 208–9
   vulture fund legislation 122, 124–25, 126
differential treatment 11–12, 153–62, 179–80, 182, 195
diplomatic protection 27–28, 130–35, 164
   arbitral tribunals 132, 134–35
   claims commissions 132, 134–35
   contractual rights 130–33
   customary international law 130–32, 133–35
   definition 130
   expropriation 131–32, 133–34
   ILC Draft Articles 130, 133
   intangible rights 130–32
   international investment agreements (IIAs) 135
   sovereign immunity 134–35
   Venezuelan Preferential decision 130–31

discrimination, prohibition of *see also*
    discrimination, prohibition of
    (ECHR); **nationality discrimination**
  aims and objectives of creditors 178–82
  Emerging Market Principles 196
  equality rule 74
  exit consent 98
  fragmentation 177, 178–83
  good faith standard 111–12, 114–15, 179, 189, 194–96
  international investment agreements 179–82, 195
  majority decisions 98, 103–4, 110–12, 117–19, 179
  minority creditors 179, 195–96
  public policy 183–86
  Redwood Master v TD Bank 117–18
  unsecured creditors 117
  vulture fund legislation 123–24, 127, 178, 182–83, 195
discrimination, prohibition of (ECHR) 153–62
  Accorinti v ECB decision 158–59
  causal links 161, 180
  Charter of Fundamental Rights of the EU 158–59
  coercive elements, restructuring with 156, 195
  collective action clauses (CACs) 157
  consumer protection 156–57, 161–62
  differential treatment 153–62, 179–80, 182, 195
  domestic law 128, 149–62
  ECtHR, case law of 150, 155, 156–62, 180
  fragmentation 177, 179–82
  grounds 153–54
  legislative state measures over time, between different 160–61
  legitimate aims 154, 155–56, 160, 161–62, 179–80
  like circumstances/analogous situations 154–55, 161, 179–81
  Lithgow v UK 154–55, 159, 160
  Mamatas decision 150–53, 156–59, 201
  margin of appreciation 154, 155, 157, 161–62, 180–81, 183–86
  minority creditors 156–57
  nationality discrimination 154, 159–60, 161–62, 180–81
  necessity 155, 161

  objective or reasonable justification 157, 160
  preferred creditor status 154, 156–59, 160–61, 162
  pressing social needs 154
  property, right to 150, 154, 156, 159–61, 179
  proportionality 123–24, 154, 155–56, 158–59, 160, 161–62, 179–81, 183–86
  public international law 128, 149–62
  reverse discrimination 156
domestic law *see also* **domestic legislation**
  collective action clauses (CACs) 98, 182–83
  European Central Bank 164, 169–74
  European Stability Mechanism (ESM) 71, 72, 74
  exit consent 98
  general principles of international law 190, 191–92
  good faith standard 190, 191–92, 194, 195–96, 199–200
  governing law 4–5, 11–12, 24–25, 28–29, 77, 163, 164–67
  insolvency proceedings 10, 109–10, 192–94, 195–96
  interconnected and conflicting rights 4–5, 163–64, 169–70, 174
  interference with creditor rights governed by international law 164–67
  jurisdiction 32–33
  legal status of the creditor 77–80
  local law advantage 30, 31
  pari passu clauses 80–97, 165–67
  preferred creditor status 165–67
  priority, definition of 7
  private law entities, contracts with 24–25, 28–29
  public international law 3–4, 26–28, 57–58, 164–67
  ranking/priority rules 177
  sovereign immunity 43–44, 45–46
  subjects of domestic law 176
  subordination 60, 79–80
  vulture fund legislation 120–27
domicile 34–35
Drago, Luis M 131–32

ECB *see* **European Central Bank (ECB)**
Ecuador 105–8

INDEX

Emerging Market Principles 196–97
English law 5–6, *see also* United Kingdom; vulture fund legislation in United Kingdom
   British America Nickel Corporation v MJ O'Brien 114–15
   Civil Procedure Rules 39–40
   collective action clauses (CACs) 98, 100–1, 110–12, 117–19
   Congreso del Partido decision 47–50
   discrimination, prohibition against 117–18, 154–55, 159, 160
   European Financial Stability Mechanism (EFSM) 70–71
   exit consent 98
   foreign court orders as not being able to vary contracts governed by English law 89–92
   good faith standard 111–12, 114–16, 183–86, 195–96, 199
   governing law 39–40, 78, 79, 89–92
   holdout creditors 89–92
   jurisdiction 39–40, 41
   Knighthead v BNYM 89–92
   Lithgow v UK 154–55, 159, 160
   number of sovereign bonds issued 5–6
   pari passu clauses 83–84, 87, 89–92, 96, 97
   pricing effects 208
   Redwood Master v TD Bank 114–16, 117–18
   service outside the jurisdiction 39–40
   sovereign immunity 44, 47–50, 54, 55–56
equality rule 57, 58–59, 74–76, see also *pari passu* clauses
   customary international law 58–59
   derogations 60, 74–75
   independence of states 58–59
   international responsibility, agreements giving rise to 76
   pacta sunt servanda rule 58–59
   pacta tertiis rule 58–59
   preferred creditor status 63, 74–76
   public international law 57, 58–59, 74–76, 164
   ranking/priority rules 58–59, 72, 178
   secured creditors 62–63
   Société commercial de Belgique decision (PCIJ) 59
   third parties 74–75
   unsecured creditors 62–63, 132
   Venezuelan Preferential decision 75, 76
European Central Bank (ECB)
   bailouts 170–71, 172, 174
   Charter of Fundamental Rights of the EU 158
   collective action clauses (CACs) 174
   crisis programmes, legality of 171
   domestic law governed sovereign bonds, case study on holdings of 164, 169–74
   Accorinti v ECB 173–74
   CJEU, case law of 171–74
   obligations of ECB 170–72
   European Stability Mechanism (ESM), CJEU cases on legality of practices of 171
   European System of Central Banks (ESCB) 72
   Expanded Asset Purchase Programme 73
   holdout creditor, as 174
   monetary financing of EU member states, prohibition against 170, 171–72, 173
   no-bailout clause 170–71
   Outright Monetary Transactions (OMTs) 72–73, 171
   participation in debt restructuring 173–74
   preferred creditor status 2, 69, 72–74, 170, 172–74
   Public Securities Purchase Programme (PSPP) 73, 171–72
   quantitative easing 73
   secondary markets, purchasing on 72–73
   Securities Market Programme (SME) 72–73
   TFEU as conflicting with intercreditor equity rights under domestic law 170–74
European Convention on Human Rights (ECHR) *see also* discrimination, prohibition of (ECHR); protection of property under ECHR
   domestic law 128–29, 149–62
   public international law 128–29, 149–62
   retroactivity 32, 34
European Financial Stability Fund (EFSF) 71, 72

228 INDEX

European Financial Stability Mechanism (EFSM) 69–70, 71
European Stability Mechanism (ESM)
   Banking Union, completion of 103
   CJEU cases on legality of practices 171
   domestic law 71, 72, 74
   European Financial Stability Fund (EFSF) 71, 72
   European Financial Stability Mechanism (EFSM) 69–70, 71
   international lenders of last resort 19–20, 71–72
   macroeconomic adjustments programme 71
   Pandemic Crisis Support 71
   preferred creditor status 64, 69–72, 73–74
   ranking/priority rules 71–72
   reform 103
   rescue fund, as a permanent 71–72
   Secondary Market Support Facility 71
European Union *see also* **Recast Brussels Regulation**
   Brussels I Convention 52–53
   Charter of Fundamental Rights of the EU (CFEU) 32, 158–59
   collective action clauses (CACs) 103, 174
   multilateral financial institutions 69–74
   preferred creditor status 118
   pricing effects 208
exit consent
   acceptance of restructuring 99
   categories 100
   coercive measures 98
   collective action clauses (CACs) 103, 109, 110, 113, 118–19, 179
   courts, interference of 98
   discrimination, prohibition against 98, 103, 179
   domestic law 98
   expropriation 98
   general features 99–103
   good faith standard 112–13, 114–15, 195–96
   governing law 98
   holdout creditors 98, 99
   majority powers, abuse of 98
   minority creditors to a restructuring agreements, binding 98
exogenous shocks 205–7

expropriation clauses 132, 133–34
   coercive measures 145–46, 181
   collective action clauses (CACs) 101, 145–46
   compensation 145, 181
   customary international law 132
   diplomatic protection 131–32, 133–34
   exit consent 98
   fair and equitable treatment (FET) 200
   general principles of international law 159
   good faith standard 200
   haircuts 144–45
   indirect expropriation 144–46, 149, 181
   international investment agreements 136, 143–46, 148–49, 181, 200
   legitimate expectations 144, 149, 200
   majority voting provisions 116
   most-favoured-nation (MFN) treatment standard 145
   national treatment standard 145
   nationality discrimination 145–46, 149, 181–82, 183–86
   preferred creditor status 145
   property, right to 149, 153

fair and equitable treatment (FET) 136, 139, 146–49
   coercive debt restructuring 147
   due process 146–47
   expropriation 200
   good faith standard 147
   interpretation 146–47
   legitimate commercial expectations 146–47, 149
   nationality discrimination 146–48, 149, 181–82, 183–86
   procedural rights 146–47
   substantive rights 146–47
   transparency 146–47
Feilchenfeld, Ernst H 129
Fitzmaurice, Gerald 75, 76
flexibility 183, 186, 188–86
foreign law 11–12, 31, 78–79, 187–88
Fox, Hazel 43
fragmentation 13, 176–83
France *see also* **vulture fund legislation in France**
   administrative contracts concept 77–78
   administrative law 26
fraud 111–12

free riders 20–21, 178, 198
future of intercreditor equity disputes 5, 176, 189–202

G20 Operational Guidelines for Sustainable Financing 198
Gaja, Giorgio 191
Gelpern, Anna 97, 104–5, 203
general principles of public international law
  choice of law 29–30
  emergence 176, 189–97
  expropriation 159
  good faith standard 190–95
  ICJ Statute 57–58
  recognition 190–91
German law
  Argentina, debt restructurings in 51–52, 192–94, 199–200
  general principles of international law 192–94, 199–200
  German Constitutional Court 192–94, 199–200
  good faith 192–94, 199–200
  Greece, 2012 debt restructuring in 50–52
  insolvency principles in domestic law, transferability of 192–94
  sovereign immunity 50–52, 55, 56
good faith standard 189–202
  abuse of rights doctrine 192, 194, 195–200, 201–2
  Addis Ababa Action Agenda on Financing for Development 197
  Assénagon Asset Management v Irish Bank Resolution Corporation 115–16
  British America Nickel Corporation v MJ O'Brien 114–15
  cohesion tool, as 189–202
  collective action clauses (CACs) 111–18, 119, 195–96, 199
  cooperation 196–97, 198–99
  discrimination, prohibition against 111–12, 114–15, 179, 189, 194–96
  domestic law 190, 191–92, 194, 195–96, 199–200
  emergence as a general principle 189–202
  Emerging Market Principles 196–97
  exit consent 114–15, 195–96
  expropriation clause 200
  fair and equitable treatment 147
  formation of general principles of international law 190–95, 199–200
  G20 Operational Guidelines for Sustainable Financing 198
  holdout creditors 192, 199–200, 201–2
  ICJ Statute 189–91, 192–94
  insolvency principles in domestic law, transferability of 192–94, 195–96
  international investment agreements 200, 201
  Katz v Oak Industries 112–14
  legitimate expectations 194, 200–2
  majority decisions 195–200
  minority protection 111–18, 119, 195–96, 199–200
  property, right to 200, 201
  public international law 190–92, 194
  ranking/priority rules 189, 194–95
  Redwood Master v TD Bank 114–16
  soft law 189, 196–99, 201–2
  UN Principles on sovereign debt restructuring 198–99, 201–2
  UNCTAD Principles 196–97
  vindictive or malicious purposes 111–12, 115, 119
  vulture funds 196–97, 198
governing law 3–4, 22–30, 175
  choice of law 11–12, 25, 28–29, 78, 79
  collective action clauses (CACs) 98
  contracts with private law entities 24–30, 77
  domestic law 4–5, 11–12, 24–25, 28–29, 77–127, 163
    European Central Bank 164, 169–74
    public international law 4–5, 57–58, 128–62, 163, 164–69
  equality rule 57, 58–59, 74–76
  European Central Bank 164, 169–74
  exit consent 99–103
  foreign law 11–12, 31, 78–79
  internationalization of state contracts 25–30
  legal status of the creditor 77–80
  local courts as deferential to sovereign debtors 22–23
  local law advantage 22–23, 30–32
  pari passu clauses 80–97, 168
  preferred creditor status 63–74, 79–80, 170
  pricing effects 208

governing law (*cont.*)
   private international law 79
   private law subjects, states borrowing from 24–25, 77
   public international law 4–5, 11–12, 24–25, 57–76, 128–62, 163, 167–70
   secured creditors 61–63
   sovereign debt instruments, of 24–25
   sovereign immunity 78
   sovereign powers 3–4, 22–30, 186–87
   subordination 60–61, 79–80
   sustainable debt restructuring 23
   vulture fund legislation 120–27
Greece, 2012 debt restructuring in
   acts of State, exclusion of (*acte iure imperii*) 50–52
   amount of money 6
   austerity measures 16
   Bondholder Act 34, 36–37, 50, 51
   collective action clauses (CACs) 31, 36–37, 50–51, 101–2, 151–52
   commercial matters (*acta iure gestionis*) 35–37, 50–52
   court cases, number of 6
   discrimination, prohibition of 2, 157, 158, 201
   European Central Bank 2, 173
   European Financial Stability Mechanism (EFSM) 69–70
   expropriation, compensation for 50–51
   German law 50–52
   good faith standard 201
   holdout creditors 31, 34, 50
   legitimate expectations 150–51, 201
   litigation against Greece 21
   local law advantage 31–32
   majority voting procedure 34
   Mamatas decision 150–53, 156–59, 201
   minority creditors, retroactively binding 201
   non-professional retail investors 12
   Norwegian Sovereign Wealth Fund (NSWF) 2
   property, right to 36–37, 150–52
   Recast Brussels Regulation 34, 35–37
   retroactive interference with property rights 31–32, 34, 36–37
   Service Regulation 36, 37

Gulati, G Mitu 67, 84–85, 101, 107, 113–14, 166

haircuts 18–19, 105–6, 144–45
Hall, William Edward 131–32
holdout creditors 11, 100–2
   abuse of rights 192, 198, 201–2
   collective action clauses (CACs) 98, 100–2, 106, 108–10, 199, 204–5
   European Central Bank 174
   exit consent 98, 99
   free riders 20–21
   good faith standard 192, 199–200, 201–2
   illegitimate advantages 122, 126, 127
   injunctions 88–92, 96–97
   minority creditors 96, 100–1, 102, 178
   pari passu clauses 81–82, 88–92, 96–97
   vulture fund legislation 122, 124, 126–27, 178, 182–83
human rights law 3, *see also* **European Convention on Human Rights (ECHR), protection of property under ECHR**
   Charter of Fundamental Rights of the EU 17, 32, 158–59
   cultural rights 17–18
   International Covenant on Economic, Social and Cultural Rights 17
   property, rights of 38–39, 131–32
   social and economic rights 17–18
   sovereign immunity 44–45

IIAs *see* **international investment agreements (IIAs)**
ILC *see* **International Law Commission (ILC)**
immunity *see* **sovereign immunity**
insolvency proceedings
   domestic law 10, 195–96
     case law 109–10
     transferability of principles 192–94
   pari passu clauses 10, 165–66
   subordination 7, 60
   terminology 6
   transferability of domestic law principles 192–94, 195–96
institutional investors 2, 20
interconnected and conflicting rights 163, 175

de facto related rights 4–5, 163–64, 177
de jure related rights 4–5, 163–64, 177
domestic law 163–67, 169–70, 174
ECB's holdings of domestic law governed sovereign bonds, case study on 164, 169–74
intercreditor conflicts 20–21, 175
subjects of international law 163–64
International Court of Justice (ICJ)
general principles of international law 57–58, 176
Jurisdictional Immunities decision (ICJ) 44–45
Statute 57–58, 128, 189–91, 192–94
international investment agreements (IIAs) 128–29, 136–49, *see also* **fair and equitable treatment (FET)**; **most-favoured-nation (MFN) treatment standard**; **national treatment (NT) standard**
Abaclat v Argentina 136–37
arbitral tribunals 28–29, 104, 136–39, 140, 141–42, 144
BITs 28–29, 136–37, 138–40
causal links 149, 180
diplomatic protection 135
discrimination, prohibition against 179–82, 195
double reviews 137–38
expropriation clause 136, 143–46, 148–49, 181, 183–86, 200
good faith standard 200, 201
haircuts 139, 144–45
ICSID tribunals 137–40, 148
included protection 136–40
international investment tribunals 136, 137–40, 148–49
investment, definition of 136–38, 139–40, 143–44, 148
jurisdiction over sovereign debt claims 136–40
likeness of circumstances 140–42, 143, 148–49
nationality discrimination 140–41, 143, 148–49, 179–82, 183–86
objective approach 137–38, 140
preferred creditor status 136, 141, 143, 145
public international law 128–29, 136–49

same business or economic sector test 141–42, 148–49, 180
subjective approach 137–38
substantive approach 140–43
international law *see* **public international law**
International Law Commission (ILC)
Articles on the Responsibility of States for Internationally Wrongful Acts 76
Draft Articles on Diplomatic Protection 130, 133
Draft Articles on Jurisdictional Immunities of States and their Property 44–46
general principles of international law, formation of 191
international minimum standard 128–35
customary international law 130–32, 133–35
diplomatic protection, types of claims covered by 130–35
expropriation 132, 133–34
preferred creditor status 129, 130
substantive protection 129, 133–35
International Monetary Fund (IMF)
Articles of Agreement 68, 73
collective action clauses (CACs) 101–3
Covid-19 206–7
customary international law 65–67
international lenders of last resort 19–20, 64–65
Multilateral Debt Relief Initiative (MDRI) 124
negotiations 15–16
pari passu clauses 94, 95–96, 167–68
political will 207, 209
preferred creditor status 63, 64–67, 68, 69–71, 73, 118, 166–68
Sovereign Debt Restructuring Mechanism (SDRM) 68, 101–2, 207
special drawing rights (SDRs) 68
sustainable debt restructuring 13
vulture fund legislation 127
internationalization of state contracts, doctrines concerning 25–30
abandonment of doctrines 28–29
domestic law, decoupling from 26
general principles of domestic law 26, 29–30

internationalization of state contracts, doctrines concerning (*cont.*)
  international tribunals, decisions of 26, 28
  political risks of contracting with states, neutralizing 26–27, 28–29
  private law entities 25–28, 29–30
investment *see* international investment agreements (IIAs)
Isle of Man, vulture fund legislation in 125
Italy 52–53, 54, 55

Japan 100
Jennings, Robert Y 24
Jersey, vulture fund legislation in 125
jurisdiction *see also* choice of law; governing law; Recast Brussels Regulation, jurisdiction under; private international law
  English law 39–40, 41
  international investment agreements 136–40
  Recast Brussels Regulation 33–37, 40–41
  sovereign immunity 41, 44–46, 125

Keynes, John Maynard 16
Kolb, Robert 194, 196
Kupelyants, Hayk 104, 111–12

ladder of priority, definition of 8
Latvia, unconstitutionality of pension cuts in 17
Lauterpacht, Hersch 199
legal status of the creditor 77–80
legitimate expectations
  expropriation clause 144, 149, 200
  fair and equitable treatment 146–47, 149
  good faith standard 194, 200–2
  property, right to 150–51
local law advantage 22–23, 28–29, 30–32, 187, 188
  constitutions 32
  European Convention on Human Rights (ECHR) 32
  foreign law 187–88
  governing law 22–23, 30–32
  political will 207
  private parties, contracts with 30–31
  retroactive interference with property rights 31–32
  sustainable debt restructuring 187

McNair, Arnold 193
majority creditors *see also* collective action clauses (CACs); exit consent; majority voting provisions, abuse of minority rights in
  discriminatory decisions 110–12, 179
  good faith standard 111–18, 119, 179, 195–200
  judicial scrutiny of decisions 98–99, 110–12
  majority action clauses 99
majority voting provisions, abuse of minority rights in *see also* collective action clauses (CACs); exit consent
  discrimination, prohibition of 104, 157
  expropriation 116
  good faith standard 115, 195–96
  holdout creditors 174
  local law advantage 31, 32
  pari passu clauses 104, 178
  preferred creditor status 157
  reform 204
  retroactivity 32, 34
  uniform applicability provisions 103, 178
Mann, FA 30–31
Martha, Rutsel Silvestre J 63, 67, 75, 76, 166
Mexico C4P94
minority creditors *see also* majority voting provisions, abuse of minority rights in; vulture fund legislation
  binding 99–103, 110, 204–5
  collective action clauses (CACs) 99, 101, 105–20
  discrimination, prohibition of 117–18, 156–57, 179, 195–96
  exit consent 98
  G20 Operational Guidelines for Sustainable Financing 198
  good faith standard 111–18, 119, 179, 195–96, 199–200
  holdout creditors 96
  threshold 109, 119–20
  vulture funds legislation 178

most-favoured-nation (MFN) treatment
  standard 136, 139-43
  customary international law 140
  expropriation 145
  nationality discrimination 140, 143,
    148-49, 179-82, 183-86
Multilateral Debt Relief Initiative
  (MDRI) 124
multilateral financial institutions 61,
  63, 64-65

national treatment (NT) standard 136,
    139-43, 148-49
  customary international law 140
  expropriation 145
  nationality discrimination 140-41, 143,
    148-49, 179-82, 183-86
  same business or economic sector
    test 141-42, 148-49, 179-80
nationality discrimination 154, 159-60,
    161-62, 180-81
  expropriation clause 145-46, 149,
    181-82, 183-86
  fair and equitable treatment 146-48, 149,
    181-82, 183-86
  Gaygusuz v Austria 159
  international investment
    agreements 140-41, 143, 148-49,
    179-82, 183-86
  Lithgow v UK 159, 160
  most-favoured-nation (MFN) treatment
    standard 140-41, 143, 148-49,
    179-82, 183-86
  national treatment standard 140-41, 143,
    148-49, 179-82, 183-86
New York law 5-6
  collective action clauses (CACs) 98,
    100-1, 111-12, 119
  exit consent 98
  good faith standard 195-96, 199
  governing law 78, 79
  holdout creditors 88-92
  injunctions 88-92
  NML v Argentina decision 87, 88-97
  number of sovereign bonds
    issued 5-6
  pari passu clauses 83-84, 87-97, 167
  preferred creditor status 166-67
  pricing effects 208
  sovereign immunity 167-68

non-discrimination *see* discrimination,
  prohibition of
Norwegian Sovereign Wealth Fund
  (NSWF) 2

Olivares-Caminal, Rodrigo 84
Oppenheim, Lassa 190-91
Outright Monetary Transactions (OMT)
  programme 72-73, 171

Pac Man strategy 106-7, 108-9
pacta sunt servanda 24, 26, 58-59, 63, 194
pacta tertiis rule 58-59
Pam, Jeremiah S 81-83, 84
pari passu clauses 80-97
  Ajdler v Province of Mendoza 92-94, 96
  broad reading 81-82, 85-87
  case law 86-94
  collective action clauses (CACs) 94, 97,
    104-5, 178
  declarations 89-94
  *Elliott Associates v Banco de la Nacion and
    Peru* decision 86-87
  forms 80-81
  governing law 80-97, 165-67
  holdout creditors 81-82, 88-92,
    96-97
  injunctions 88-95, 96-97
  insolvency proceedings 10, 165-66
  interpretation 80-97, 165-66, 167,
    177, 194-95
  Knighthead v BNYM 89-92
  knowing receipt and acceptance of non-
    rateable payments 82
  legal ranking 81-82
  like circumstances 104
  majority voting provisions 104, 178
  narrow reading 85
  negative pledge clauses 82-83
  NML v Argentina decision 87,
    88-92, 93-97
  origin of the clause 82-86, 97
  payment, use of word 80-81, 96-97,
    167
  penalties 82
  priorities 81, 82-83, 92-94
  pro rata payments/rateable
    payments 81-82, 84, 86-97
  public international law 167-68
  rank, use of word 80-81, 96-97

pari passu clauses (*cont.*)
   restructured bonds, prevention of payment to holders of 81–82
   revisions 85
   secured creditors 82–83, 86
   specific performance 81–82
   subordination 81, 82–83, 84–85, 96
   sustainable debt restructuring 96–97
   trust indentures or trust deeds 83–84, 89–94
   unsecured creditors 80–81, 82–83, 86, 92–94, 96, 165–67
   variations of clause 95–96, 97
Paris Club 61, 66–67, 205–7
party autonomy 24–25, 33, 77, 79, 128, 178
Permanent Court of International Justice (PCIJ), list of cases of 167
political will 11–12, 207–9
   internationalization of state contracts 26–27, 28–29
   neutralizing risks 26–27, 28–29
   pricing effects 207–8
   reform 207–9
   sustainable debt restructuring 15
Portugal 17
preferred creditor status 2, 63–74, 129, 176
   acts of will, establishment through 68, 73, 75, 170, 178
   agreements conferring status 68, 73
   customary international law 63, 64, 65–68, 69, 170
   de facto status 67, 69–70, 165–66, 173–74
   de jure status 67, 69–70, 76, 165, 166
   diplomatic protection 130
   discrimination, prohibition of 98–99, 154, 156–59, 160–61, 162
   equality rule, compatibility with 63, 74–76
   EU multilateral financial institutions 69–74
   European Central Bank (ECB) 2, 69, 72–74
   European Financial Stability Mechanism (EFSM) 69–71
   European Stability Mechanism (ESM) 64, 69–72, 74
   exempted from restructuring, right to be 64
   expropriation clause 145
   governing law 79–80, 165–67
   IMF 63, 64–67, 68, 69–71, 73
   intergovernmental organizations 64–65
   international investment agreements 136, 141, 143, 145
   means of acquiring the status 68–74
   monetary and financial stability 64, 65
   multilateral financial institutions 63, 64–65, 69–74
   preferred creditor, definition of 7–8
   public international law 63–74, 165–69, 170
   ranking/priority rules 7–8, 64–66, 67–68, 74, 177, 178
   regional development banks 64
   unilateral acts, establishment by 68, 73
priorities *see* ranking/priority rules
private international law
   governing law 25, 79
   jurisdiction 3–4, 22–23, 32–40, 186–87
   public international law 24
private law entities
   contracts 24–30, 77
   Covid-19 206–7
   differential treatment 12
   domestic law 128
   governing law 24–25, 77
   internationalization of state contracts 25–28, 29–30
   legal status of creditors 77–78
   local law advantage 30–31
   public international law 25–28, 29–30, 128
   Serbian Loans Case 24
   sovereign immunity 46–47
   treaty-based rights 164
privatized economic crisis resolution measures 186–88
property, right to *see* protection of property under ECHR
proportionality
   discrimination, prohibition against 123–24, 154, 155–56, 158–59, 160, 161–62, 179–81, 183–86
   expropriation clause 144
   fair and equitable treatment 146–47
   property, right to 32, 151, 152
   Public Securities Purchase Programme (PSPP) 171–72
   vulture fund legislation 123–24

protection of property under
    ECHR 151–53, 179
  coercive measures 149, 151–52, 156
  collective action clauses (CACs), retroactive
    implementation of 151–52
  covered protection 150–51
  diplomatic protection 131–32
  discrimination, prohibition against 149,
    150, 154, 156, 159–61
  domestic law 149–62
  ECtHR, case law of 32, 150–51, 153
  existing claims to money or performance
    with a financial value 150–51
  existing property rights 150–51
  expropriation 149, 153, 159
  global financial crisis 2008 153
  good faith standard 200, 201
  legitimate aim, interference for a 151, 152
  legitimate expectations 150–51
  local law advantage 32
  margin of appreciation 153
  possession, definition of 150–51
  proportionality 32, 151, 152
  public interest 159–60
  retroactive interference 31–32
  vulture fund legislation 123–24, 126
public international law *see also* **general
    principles of public international
    law**
  diplomatic protection 130
  discrimination, prohibition of 128,
    149–62
  domestic law 3–5, 57–58, 128–62,
    163, 164–69
  equality rule 57, 58–59, 74–76
  good faith standard 190–92, 194
  governing law 4–5, 11–12, 24–25, 57–76,
    128–62, 163, 167–70
  interconnected and conflicting rights 4–5,
    163–64, 167–70, 174
  preferred creditor status 63–74, 170
  private international law 24
  private law, intersection with 3–4,
    187–88
  ranking/priority rules 177–78
  secured creditors 61–63
  sovereign immunity 44
  subordination 60–61
public policy 3, 5, 100–1, 175, 183–86,
    203–4

Public Securities Purchase Programme
    (PSPP) 73, 171–72
public spending, cuts in 14–15, 16–18

quantitative easing 73

ranking/priority rules 177–78, 182–83, *see
    also* **equality rule**
  equality rule 58–59, 74, 178
  good faith standard 189, 194–95
  ladder of priority, definition of 8
  legal ranking 7, 81–82
  preferred creditor status 7–8, 64–66,
    67–68, 71–72, 74, 177, 178
  priority, definition of 7
  public international law 177–78
  secured creditors 62–63
  subordinated debt, definition of 7
  unsecured creditors 10
Recast Brussels Regulation 33–37, 40–41
  acts of State, exclusion of (*acta iure
    imperii*) 34, 35–37, 40
  categorization of the restructuring act 34,
    35–37, 40
  CJEU, case law of 34, 35–37
  collective action clauses (CACs) 36–37
  commercial matters (*acta iure
    gestionis*) 33–37, 40
  consumer contracts 34
  contract, matters relating to a 34–35
  domicile 34–35
  employment contracts 34
  exclusive jurisdiction 34
  grounds of jurisdiction 34–35
  jurisdiction 33–37, 40–41
  place of performance 35
  residual jurisdiction of domestic
    courts 33–34
  special jurisdiction, establishing 34–35
  tort, delict or quasi-delict, matters relating
    to 34–35
  vulture fund legislation 123, 124
reform *see* **systemic reform**
regional finance-related institutions 15–16
Reinisch, August 145
**Romania, unconstitutionality of pension
    cuts in** 17
Russia 11–12

Schreuer, Christoph 131–32

Secondary Market Support Facility (SMSF) 71
secured creditors 61–63
  collateralized public international debt 61–62, 63
  equality rule 62–63
  pari passu clauses 82–83, 86
  public international law 61–63
  ranking/priority rules 62–63
  unsecured creditors 62–63
  Venezuelan Preferential decision 62–63
Securities Market Programme (SME) 72–73
service outside the jurisdiction 39–40
social and economic rights 17–18
social costs 16–18, 123
social security as a human right 17
Sovereign Debt Restructuring Mechanism (SDRM) 68, 101–2, 207
sovereign immunity 3–4, 22–23, 37–38, 41–56, 175, 186–87, *see also* United States, sovereign immunity in
  absolute immunity 42, 43, 46–47, 134–35
  acts of State, exclusion of (*acte iure imperii*) 42–43, 45–46, 53–56, 187
    commercial matters (*acta iure gestionis*) 42–43, 44–45, 53–54, 55–56, 187
    categorization of the restructuring act 42–43, 44–45, 53–54, 55–56, 187–88
  commercial matters (*acta iure gestionis*) 41, 42–46, 187–88
    acts of State, exclusion of (*acte iure imperii*) 42–43, 44–45, 53–54, 55–56, 187–88
    categorization of the restructuring act 42–43, 44–45, 53–54, 55–56, 187–88
    restrictive/relative immunity, doctrine of 41, 42, 44–46
  customary international law 53–54
  debt restructuring 45–53
  deemed consent to local jurisdiction 43
  definition 41
  diplomatic protection 134–35
  domestic law 43–44, 45–46, 167–68

  enforcement/execution, immunity from 15, 22–23, 41, 42, 43–44, 45–46, 53, 121
  European Convention on State Immunity 1972 44
  governing law 78, 165
  holdout creditors 167–68
  issuing sovereign bonds as decisive factor 53–54
  jurisdiction/adjudication, immunity from 41, 45–46
  mixed activities/continuous transactions 45–53, 54, 55
  multilateral instrument, lack of a 44–45
  private law nature of transactions 43, 46–47
  public international law 44, 167–68
  restrictive/relative immunity, doctrine of 41, 42, 44–46, 134–35
  sources of law 44–45
  sustainable debt restructuring 23
  UN Convention on Jurisdictional Immunities of States and their Property 1991 44–45, 125
  vulture fund legislation 121
  waiver 43, 45–46, 47, 54
sovereign powers in crisis resolution 3–4, 5, 22–56, 186–88
specific performance 81–82
standard terms 79, 101, 102–3, 104–9
state immunity *see* sovereign immunity
state sovereignty 41–42, 58–59
subordination 60–61
  collective action clauses (CACs) 60
  de facto subordination 60–61
  de jure subordination 60–61, 178
  definition 60
  domestic law 60, 79–80
  governing law 60–61, 79–80
  insolvency proceedings 7, 60
  multilateral financial institutions, exclusion of debt owed to 61
  pari passu clauses 81, 82–83, 84–85, 96
  priority, yielding 60–61
  subordinated debt, definition of 7
sustainable debt restructurings 9, 13–21, 176–77, 183, 186–87
  ad hoc arrangements 13
  aims and objectives 13

alternative crisis management tools 14–15
assessments 15–18
collective action clauses (CACs) 98,
  176–77, 204–5
conflicts between debtors-creditors 18–20
enforcement of judgments 15
excessive and/or confiscatory
  restructuring 19–20
fiscal policies, implementation of
  expansive 14–15, 18
governing law 23
information, availability of 15–16,
  19–20
intercreditor conflicts 20–21
jurisdiction 23
local law advantage 187
obstacles 13
pari passu clauses 96–97
politicization 15
privatized economic crisis resolution
  measures 188
public policy 175, 203–4
public spending, cuts in 14–15, 16–18
ranking/priority rules 182
sovereign immunity 23, 44, 46–47
structural reforms 14–16
systemic challenges 5, 176, 183
taxes, raising 14–15
threshold for restructuring, lack of 20
vulture fund legislation 182–86
systemic challenges 175, 176–88
  debtor states' room for
    manoeuvre 183–87, 188, 204–5
  diverging objectives 176–83
  flexibility 183, 186, 188–86
  fragmentation 176–83
  public policy 5, 175, 183–86
  sovereign powers and privatized
    economic crisis resolution
    measures 186–88
  sustainable debt restructuring 5, 176,
    183
systemic reform 5, 103, 203–9
  assessment of effects 17–18
  broader systemic reform, case study
    on 203–5
  conflicts between debtors-creditors 19–20
  Covid-19 205–7
  exogenous shocks 205–7
  fiscal policy 17–18

market-based reforms 204
political will 207–9
public spending, cuts in 17
sustainable debt restructuring 14–16

tax
  policies, implementation of
    expansive 14–15, 18
  public spending cuts 17–18
  raising taxes 14–15, 19–20
  tax havens 122
terminology 6–9
territorial sovereignty 59
tort, delict or quasi-delict, matters relating
  to 34–35
trust indentures or trust deeds 83–84,
  89–94, 113–14

UNCTAD Principles 196–97
uniform applicability clauses
  collective action clauses (CACs) 103,
    104–5, 108–9, 118–19, 178
  majority voting provisions 103, 178,
    179, 182–83
  minority creditor protection 179
  ranking/priority rules 177
unilateral modification of creditors'
  rights *see* local law
  advantage
United Kingdom *see also* English law;
  vulture fund legislation in United
  Kingdom
United Nations (UN)
  Convention on Jurisdictional Immunities
    of States and their Property
    1991 44–45, 125
  Independent Expert on foreign debt and
    human rights 17
  Independent Experts and Special
    Rapporteurs 17
  Principles on sovereign debt
    restructuring 198–99, 201–2, 207
United States *see also* New York law; United
  States, sovereign immunity in
  choice of forum clauses 37–38, 40
  collective action clauses
    (CACs) 101–2, 110–11
  expropriation, restructuring as
    an 38–39
  good faith standard 112–14

238 INDEX

United States (cont.)
  jurisdiction 37–39, 40, 41
  Katz v Oak Industries 112–14
  Sovereign Debt Restructuring Mechanism (SDRM) 207
United States, sovereign immunity in
  absolute immunity 46–47
  acts of State, exclusion of (acte iure imperii) 46–47
  Argentina, restructurings in
    Argentina v Weltover 46–47
    Foreign Sovereign Immunities Act of 1976 (FSIA) 165
  commercial matters (acta iure gestionis) 46–47, 54, 55–56
  commerciality exception in FSIA 37–39
  enforcement/adjudication immunity 54
  expropriation 38–39
  Foreign Sovereign Immunities Act of 1976 (FSIA) 37–38, 44, 46–47, 165
  mixed activities/continuous transactions 46–47
  nexus requirement 38
  restrictive/relative immunity, doctrine of 44
  state consent to exceptions 37–38
  waiver 37–38, 47, 51–52, 54
unsecured creditors
  arbitral tribunals, practice of 132
  discrimination, prohibition against 117
  equality rule 62–63
  pari passu clauses 80–81, 82–83, 86, 92–94, 96, 165–67
  ranking/priority rules 10
Uruguay 101, 102

Vázquez-Bermúdez, Marcelo 191
Vienna Convention on the Law of Treaties (VLCT) 58–59, 194
voluntary acceptance of restructuring agreements 1–2, 8–9, 10, 203–4
  equal (pro rata) treatment 10–11
  good faith standard 194–95
  intercreditor conflicts 20–21
  sustainable debt restructuring 13
  vulture fund legislation 120–21, 127
voluntary negotiations 98
voting see majority voting provisions, abuse of minority rights in
vulture fund legislation 120–27, see also vulture fund legislation in Belgium; vulture fund legislation in France; vulture fund legislation in United Kingdom business strategy, as 121
  discrimination, prohibition on 127, 178, 182–83, 195
  distressed debt funds 121
  free-riders 178
  good faith standard 196–97, 198
  holdout creditors 126–27, 178, 182–83
  illegitimate advantage 178, 182–83, 195
  ranking/priority rules 182–83
  sovereign immunity 121
  sustainable debt restructuring 182–86
  threats to sue or suing for full amount 120, 121–22
  triggering cause 121
vulture fund legislation in Belgium 122–24
  annulment proceedings 123–24
  arbitral awards, enforcement of foreign 123
  conditions 122–23
  Constitution 123–24
  developing assistance programmes 122
  discrimination 123–24, 127
  foreign countries and institutions, loans to 122
  holdout creditors, avoidance of illegitimate advantages to 122, 126, 127
  illegitimate advantage, definition of 122
  property, right to 123–24
  proportionality 123–24
  Recast Brussels Regulation 123, 124
  tax havens, creditors established in 122
vulture fund legislation in France 125–26
  Code of Civil Procedure of Enforcement 125
  conditions 125–26
  Constitution, compliance with 126
  developing countries 126
  foreign states, protection of 125–26
  holdout creditors 126
  time limits 126
vulture fund legislation in United Kingdom 124–25
  Debt Relief (Developing Countries) Act 2010 124–25
  heavily indebted poor countries (HIPCs), debt relief for 124–25, 126
  HIPC Initiative 124–25
  Isle of Man 125

Jersey 125
Multilateral Debt Relief Initiative
 (MDRI) 124
sunset clause 125

Waibel, Michael 132, 138, 139, 143, 147
Wautelet, Patrick 26–27

Webb, Philippa 43
Weidemaier, W Mark C 85, 95
Wood, Philip R 111–12
World Trade Organization (WTO) 104, 141–42

Zandstra, Deborah 104–5